Shi'i Jurisprudence and Constitution

Palgrave Series in Islamic Theology, Law, and History

This ground-breaking series, edited by one of the most influential scholars of Islamic law, presents a cumulative and progressive set of original studies that substantially raise the bar for rigorous scholarship in the field of Islamic Studies. By relying on original sources and challenging common scholarly stereotypes and inherited wisdoms, the volumes of the series attest to the exacting and demanding methodological and pedagogical standards necessary for contemporary studies of Islam. These volumes are chosen not only for their disciplined methodology, exhaustive research, or academic authoritativeness, but for their ability to make critical interventions in the process of understanding the world of Islam as it was, is, and is likely to become. They make central and even pivotal contributions to understanding the experience of the lived and living Islam, and the ways that this rich and creative Islamic tradition has been created and uncreated, or constructed, deconstructed, and reconstructed. In short, the volumes of this series are chosen for their great relevance to the many realities that shaped the ways that Muslims understand, represent, and practice their religion, and ultimately, to understanding the worlds that Muslims helped to shape, and in turn, the worlds that helped shaped Muslims.

Series Editor:
Khaled Abou El Fadl is the Omar and Azmeralda Alfi Distinguished Professor in Islamic Law at the UCLA School of Law, and Chair of the Islamic Studies Program at UCLA. Dr. Abou El Fadl received the University of Oslo Human Rights Award, the Leo and Lisl Eitinger Prize in 2007, and was named a Carnegie Scholar in Islamic Law in 2005. He is one of the world's leading authorities on Islamic law and Islam, and a prominent scholar in the field of human rights.

Titles:

Custom in Islamic Law and Legal Theory: The Development of the Concepts of 'Urf and 'Adah in the Islamic Legal Tradition
Ayman Shabana

The Islamic Law of War: Justifications and Regulations
Ahmed Al-Dawoody

Shi'i Jurisprudence and Constitution: Revolution in Iran
Amirhassan Boozari

Shi'i Jurisprudence and Constitution

Revolution in Iran

Amirhassan Boozari

palgrave
macmillan

SHI'I JURISPRUDENCE AND CONSTITUTION

First published in 2011 by
PALGRAVE MACMILLAN®
in the United States—a division of St. Martin's Press LLC,
175 Fifth Avenue, New York, NY 10010.

Where this book is distributed in the UK, Europe and the rest of the world, this is by Palgrave Macmillan, a division of Macmillan Publishers Limited, registered in England, company number 785998, of Houndmills, Basingstoke, Hampshire RG21 6XS.

Palgrave Macmillan is the global academic imprint of the above companies and has companies and representatives throughout the world.

Palgrave® and Macmillan® are registered trademarks in the United States, the United Kingdom, Europe and other countries.

ISBN: 978–0–230–11073–1

Library of Congress Cataloging-in-Publication Data

Boozari, Amirhassan, 1964–
Shi'i jurisprudence and constitution : revolution in Iran / Amirhassan Boozari.
p. cm.—(Palgrave series in Islamic theology, law)
Includes bibliographical references.
ISBN-13: 978–0–230–11073–1
ISBN-10: 0–230–11073–8
1. Constitutional history—Iran. 2. Iran—Politics and government—20th century. 3. Constitutional law (Islamic law) 4. Shi'ah—Doctrines. I. Title.

KMH2101.B66 2011
342.55—dc22 2010040762

A catalogue record of the book is available from the British Library.

Design by Newgen Imaging Systems (P) Ltd., Chennai, India.

First edition: March 2011

10 9 8 7 6 5 4 3 2 1

Printed and bound in Great Britain by
CPI Antony Rowe , Chippenham and Eastbourne

Contents

Foreword

This is the third book in the Palgrave Series on Islamic Law and Theology, and it is a book that I take special pride in introducing. The source of my pride is not only the friendship and intellectual bond that I share with its author, but more significantly, it is an awe-inspiring volume from which I learned a great deal about the challenge of constitutionalist governance and the largely unknown efforts by prominent Muslim jurists to wrestle with the role and function of Islamic law in the wake of modernity. In my view, this book needs to be carefully studied, analyzed, and pondered by every reader interested in the fields of political theology, constitutionalism, and democracy. But especially for those interested in the dynamics and possibilities of Islamic reform, this book is nothing short of indispensable and compulsory reading.

Islam, secularism, and democracy are among the most widely debated issues in the contemporary world. Nevertheless, despite the numerous commentaries and studies dealing with Islam, democracy, and constitutionalism, there has been surprisingly precious little scholarship on the substantive arguments, or what I prefer to call the micro-discourses, made by Muslim theologians and jurists wrestling with these issues. Effectively, this has meant that there is a serious ongoing failure to understand, leave alone to fairly and analytically engage, how Muslims have constructed and reconstructed their tradition in an effort to negotiate the relationship between the sacred and the profane as well as the nature of religious authority within the contingencies of time and space in the postcolonial age. Even more troubling is the fact that this failure to study or engage the micro-discourses of Islamic theology and law on the challenges of democracy and constitutionalism is a problem plaguing not just the academia of the non-Muslim world, but also the Western-styled academia of the Muslim world. This has led to an unmistakable and inescapable essentialism and reductionism in comprehending and analyzing the arguments of the Islamist discourse. Most poignantly, whether at the level of public discourses or public policy, writers with only cursory knowledge and perfunctory attitudes toward the micro-discourses and details of Islamic theology and law have been responsible for the propagation of the most detrimental generalizations about a claimed essential nature, or purported fundamental characteristics of Islamic thought, law, or culture.

This is where Amir Boozari's book fills a serious void. By virtue of its very subject, Boozari's book is timely and attractive, but it is the exactingly meticulous and commanding breadth of the scholarship that makes this volume a defining contribution in the field. Although treating a pressing and often contentious subject, Boozari skillfully avoids resigning himself to any essentialist paradigm or to a simplistic framework in unpacking and analyzing the debates of Muslim jurists for and against a constitutionalist system of government during a critically transformative period in the history of Iran and also Iraq. Having analyzed an exhaustively prodigious amount of primary and original sources, Amir Boozari presents a breathtaking study of the theological and jurisprudential arguments of Shi'i jurists who in the early twentieth century were on the brink of achieving a revolutionary constitutional movement. Boozari gives his readers access to a transformative doctrinal reformation within Shi'i Islam that to date has been insufficiently studied and poorly understood. As importantly, Boozari also explains why this revolutionary theological and jurisprudential movement ultimately failed.

By deliberately probing the theological and legal arguments made by pro-constitutionalist Shi'i jurists and their opponents, the author makes his book very relevant to the ongoing intellectual struggles not just in Iran or Iraq but (as those who read the book will discover) in the whole Muslim world. The reason is simple: the theological and legal arguments made by the Shi'i jurists in favor of constitutionalism are equally applicable to Sunni Islam. In my view, this is one of the most remarkable and attractive aspects of this study. Whether the readers are academics, scholars, policy-makers, teachers, students, or part of the interested public, be they Muslim or non-Muslim, I dare say that they will not only be edified but surprised at the flexibility and creativity of Shi'i jurists who fervently believed in a system of governance where the state is limited by the rule of law and individual rights are guaranteed. Readers will be able to assess first hand how Shi'i jurists conceived of and negotiated critical issues such as the nature of sacred and temporal authority, the divine will and its relationship to the popular or majoritarian will, the relationship between religious conviction and social and political identity and commitment, and the normative relationship between moral and ethical principles and Islamic law. Many of the debates and disagreements centered around foundational philosophical questions such as the nature and normative roles of reason and revelation. Readers will be able to reflect upon the extent to which these arguments as well as the rebuttals offered by jurists opposed to the constitutionalist movement are rooted in the Islamic tradition or are artificially grafted upon this tradition—whether the doctrines are natural outgrowths and authentic extensions from the evolving dynamics of the Islamic legacy as opposed to being apologetic constructs adopted in response to external political and cultural pressures or forced artificial transplants from the West. Readers will be able to evaluate the extent to which the constitutionalists failed because of internal and domestic pressures or external political pressures artificially imposed upon Muslim cultures. By exploring the trajectories of Muslim thought, and the contextual realities and limitations within which these trajectories unfold, Boozari empowers his readers to evaluate possible directions and potentials for the development of ideas, values, culture, and institutions in countries with a concentration of Shi'i Muslims such as Iran, Iraq, and Lebanon. But any reform-minded Sunni Muslim jurist will find that many of the arguments of the pro-constitutionalism Shi'i jurists are easily adaptable to the Sunni context, and that many of the challenges and hardships confronted by the Shi'i reformers are nearly identical to those confronted by their Sunni counterparts.

This book should become the standard reference source for researchers working on Iran, Shi'i theology and law, and Islam and democracy, among other topics. But beyond being an authoritative reference source, it helps us to make sense of the present and analyze the possibilities of the future. It is a book that clearly raises the bar and the scholastic and intellectual standards that must be met by any person who seeks to make a contribution to the discourses on Islamic law and theology, Islamic reform, and Islamic politics, leave alone Iran and its rich intellectual and political history.

KHALED ABOU EL FADL
Los Angeles, California
October 2010

Acknowledgments

Writing on Shīʿī origins of constitutionalism was my secondary premise of discussions about the 1997–2005 Reform Movement in Iran, but easily replaced it. This, for the most part, was because of my primary dealings with the jurisprudential dynamics of Shari'ah and reason in Shīʿī Law, which required heavy engagement with original sources. I was fascinated with the degree of precision that Muslim jurists had employed in their efforts.

I owe this intellectual journey to Professor Khaled Abou El Fadl who introduced, represented, and embodied the legacy of Islamic civilization to me. His impressive personal example of juristic precision is internationally renowned. I have always been fascinated with his deep, resourceful, and detailed discussions on a variety of subjects, from philosophy and theology to history and ethics, and law and politics to literature. His personal impact, through mastery, exactitude, rigorous scrutiny, and vast knowledge of his subject, combined with moral nobility, has never blunted his warmth, kindness, and passionate, unsparing support directed toward me during my years at UCLA. I am privileged to have been an assistant and a friend of his. But I will always take pride and feel honored to find myself, first and foremost, his student. He has taught me all that I desperately needed to know.

I am deeply grateful to Professor Hossein Modarressi for his invaluable comments on the early version of this book. With an incredible encyclopedic mastery of all the sources that I had just put my first steps in, he has educated me with his many points and comments. He has always responded to my questions with warmth and kindness, and provided me with his great support in many of my requests for help.

Professor Abou El Fadl also read the early version of the book, and made another set of invaluable points and comments. Without their comments, I would have made irreparable mistakes. However, I am responsible for possible inaccuracies or wrong conclusions.

This book is in part an attempt to appreciate an authoritative scholarship of Islamic law that is presented in the writings of Professors Modarressi and Abou El Fadl, most notably in their *Kharāj in Islamic Law* and *Rebellion in Islamic Law*, where Muslim jurists' *ma'rakat al-'ārā'* (marketplace of ideas) is in full display and motion. They have set the academic standards for analytical engagement with Islamic law and jurisprudence. If this book has met those standards, or contributed, to the slightest extent, to such scholarship, then my goals of writing it will have been fulfilled.

At the UCLA School of Law I have cherished great scholarship of a group of prominent scholars whose comments and thoughts have always been invaluable to me. Professor Stephen Gardbaum is an inspiring scholar whose vast knowledge of comparative constitutional law and highly technical scholarship, well displayed in his writings in the field of comparative constitutionalism, has always been a source of inspiration and learning for me. He has combined his remarkable expertise as a comparatist with a methodology and deep-seated intellectual belief that finds no barrier to universality of constitutionalism and its goals. His support of my early steps triggered my interest and encouraged me to choose to write about constitutionalism in Iran. I am grateful to his direct advice and continued support. Professor Kenneth Karst has always inspired me with his true example of academic prominence, moral stature, and keen support. Ken is a master at conveying his sophisticated and unmatchable scholarship of constitutional law with sympathy, great knowledge of history, and awareness of the importance of humanity's experiences in the establishment of constitutional democracy—all of which make him one of the most admirable intellectuals in my life. I am especially grateful to both Professors Karst and Gardbaum for providing me with their scholarly comments and insights on the first version of this book. I have utmost respect for both as long as I perform an academic duty.

This book could not be written without the constant love, encouragement, and support that my wife, Mandana, provided. Her sense of responsibility and sacrifice has often been greater than what a caring wife and mother is willing to offer. Unhesitant and forthright, she has always put my needs and those of our kids above her own on a daily basis. She is a true companion who has stood shoulder-to-shoulder in the ebbs and flows of life during the long years of my studentship.

AMIR BOOZARI
August 3, 2010

Introduction

Although "constitutionalism" is an essentially contestable concept, scholars agree that it has three major requirements: limitation of political power, rule of law, and protection of individual rights.[1] Substantial elements of constitutionalism, such as *garantisme*[2] and supremacy of constitution, establish yet another set of characteristics that do not necessarily oppose its relational requirements—such as separation of powers and checks and balances.[3] Furthermore, a "generally observed disposition to exercise of public power pursuant to publicly known rules, adherence to which actually provides a substantial motivation for acting or refraining from acting;...and a reasonably independent judiciary; and reasonably free and open elections with a reasonably widespread franchise"[4] provide both political and judicial processes in which constitutionalism can be achieved.

The political process belongs to the realm of political culture, which can tentatively be defined as "some kind of commonly shared political norms and values" reflected in a "consensual theory of justice and reliance on procedural solutions for the settlement of disputes in a constitutional state" colored with "tolerance and trust."[5] Consensus on these norms, when conceived as higher elements at the constitutional level, establish a "constitutional culture [that] is a web of interpretive norms, canons, and practices which most members of a particular community accept and employ (at least implicitly) to identify and maintain a two-level [i.e., constitutional and ordinary] system of the appropriate sort."[6]

As is well known, Thomas Paine has said: "A constitution is not the act of a government, but of people...*antecedent* to a government."[7] A serious engagement with the key term "antecedent"[8] requires a novel—or probably a renewed—treatment of concepts like precommitment, metaconstitutional, or preconstitutional norms that precede the adoption of a constitution.[9] From a legal perspective, in the event of inevitable, difficult, and divisive interpretive questions, a normal society invokes, returns to, and preserves these norms—embedded in the legal theory and precedent.[10] Historical examples suggest that conflicts between constitutional culture's norms and constitutional forms amount to a perplexing paradox between the constituent power of the people and the constituted power of the ruler, and thus to an unsuccessful experience of constitutionalism.[11] More complex problems arise from the practice of constitutional borrowing.[12]

The idea of constitutionalism entails those underpinning concepts, theories, and elements upon which the constitutional culture is structured.[13] The dialectical relations between the rule of law and supremacy of constitution, on the one hand, and between maintenance of social order and protection of individual rights, on the other, are delineated in yet broader contexts of common interests of society and legitimacy of the restricted government.[14] This is where concepts of liberty, equality, prohibition of arbitrary rule, condemnation of oppression, sanctity of individual rights, and public duties of government in each legal tradition step in.[15] The extent to which one can detach all these concepts from religious teachings is a moral, philosophical, historical, and legal question.[16]

A theoretical analysis of the idea of constitutionalism in Islamic legal tradition requires intertradition, analytical jurisprudence, and a legal approach to constitutionalism.[17] It is equally necessary to specify and trace juristic foundations of the ideas—be it in the form of fatwas or treatises or constitutional texts—that have supported Muslim societies' pursuit of constitutionalism in the past one hundred years. Any other approach will easily lead to a faulty depiction of the achievements and discontents of those experiences, and instead of a multilayered engagement with philosophical, historical, and juridical elements,[18] weakly performed and poorly developed analyses will emerge.

Modern historical facts and experiences provide fertile grounds upon which one can develop the aforementioned theoretical analysis. Because of their prescriptive nature, constitutionalist attempts can also be used as the building blocks of a model of constitutionalism that fits the need among Muslim societies for indigenous forms of constitutional government. The 1905–1911 Constitutional Revolution in Iran, undoubtedly, provided a Shīʿī version of popular sovereignty in the service of reconciling constitutionalism with the requirement of compliance to Shari'ah. "The Constantinople Majlis-e Mabʿūthān (Parliament of the emissaries) featured between 1908 and the First World War the first elected proto-federal Parliament in the Middle East, which included Ottoman subjects from present-day Turkey, Syria, Iraq, Israel-Palestine, and Saudi Arabia."[19] Before it was practically thwarted by the executive power, Egypt's Constitutional Court issued important verdicts in support of individual rights and provided a manifestation of Islamic human rights in a Muslim nation's constitution where Shari'ah was inscribed in full force as the source of law.[20] Ayatullah Khomeini's juristic arguments in favor of the idea of *wilāyat al-faqīh* was originally intended to reinstate the constitutional role of the learned jurists in legislation, which was incorporated in the constitution of the 1905 Revolution. The 1997–2005 Reform Movement in Iran reflected the tensions between pseudo-constitutional politics of an absolutist "constitutional" theory and democratic politics of Iranian constitutionalism, which revolved around protection of constitutional rights of the individuals, namely, their right to political participation.

This book is an attempt to engage in analytical jurisprudence of the Islamic idea of constitutionalism, as was played out in the 1905–1911 Revolution. In order to contextualize Islamic constitutionalism, one should read into the thematic arguments on components of constitutionalism that derive from mutually supporting and congenial realms developed by rationalist jurists, famously known as *Uṣūlīs*. For the most part, chapter 1 of this book deals with these issues and introduces the *Uṣūlī* doctrine of reason, the importance of rational arguments, and the place of rational proofs and indicators in the grand concept of *ijtihād*: the juristic effort of discovering the rule of Shari'ah. This effort is a de novo review of the previous rulings by considering the new facts, which usually emanate from the impacts of time and space on the legal reasoning. Far from its simplistic definition as independent opinion, *ijtihād* in *Uṣūlī* theory provides a dialectical analysis of the relation between man-made law and Divine Law.

In a Muslim society, religion is the most important component of constitutional culture, and Islamic legal tradition is the major source and fountainhead of searching for constitutional norms. Perhaps more than in any other society, law plays a central role in a Muslim one. If one is to single out the most important aspect of the Islamic civilization, one is left with law. For centuries, Muslim intellectuals have strived to articulate the presuppositions of law—as a system of norms that govern the relationship among individuals—and present them to a faith-based community of believers who had not only found a parallel between religion and law, but had also developed a deep perception of obligation, in the form of *taklīf* (legal-moral duty), before their God in every aspect of life. This two-sided perception, emanating from "presuppositions of law" and "*taklīf*," was by itself an expression of Muslims' will, which included both secular and sacred expectations: an expression that prior to the introduction of Islamic faith to the community had found manifestations in social customs, but after the introduction of faith was combined with religion. Therefore, *taklīf* became—and still is—the most focal concept and orbit of legal arguments in the Islamic legal tradition. Dynamisms between popular expressions—social customs—and the process of encircling the concept of *taklīf* amounted to a dialectical and mutual postulation of law through which jurists and judges introduced faith-based rules and laws and Muslims adopted them in order to form and repeatedly practice as new or revised social customs. In return, jurists and judges took thusly established customs as refined components of their fatwas and legal opinions. This process has provided the ground for accumulation of legal expectations and presuppositions. Many of the legal maxims in Islamic law reflect these dynamisms, especially in its larger part of nondevotional acts and rules. This process was in motion until the first decades of the twentieth century. One such maxim that exemplifies the endogenesis of law, introduced in chapter 3, was then a newly coined one that prohibited an individual's guardianship over another, except for the ones who were legally in need to be guarded. *Uṣūlī* jurists had created and then utilized it to make rebuttal arguments against the guardianship of jurists in social matters. In addition to this is the prevailing *Uṣūlī* doctrine of determination of compatibility with Shari'ah, introduced in chapter 4, where *Uṣūlī* jurists concluded that any contractual obligation that was not in apparent conflict with textually prohibited acts was in compliance with Shari'ah. This doctrine established the legitimacy of parliament's enactments in a legal tradition whose traditionist defenders had long held legislation as heresy. Dynamisms do not merely add to the number of maxims and rules. It is in such indefinite, all-ever-moving sets of actions that an *Uṣūlī* jurist emerges, moves further, and becomes a constitutionalist.

The 1905 Constitutional Revolution was, in part, the natural outcome of the long-standing legal crisis of legitimacy in the premodern Shīʿī political theory of just sultanate. This theory itself was the by-product of a two-sided prerequisite of legitimacy. On the one hand, based on the Shīʿī doctrine of Imāmah, legitimate leadership solely belonged to the person of the last Infallible Imam, known as the Hidden Imam. Any other form of domination over the temporal and spiritual affairs of the Shiite community that did not derive from this Occulted Infallible Imam was considered illegitimate. In the absence of the Imam, on the other hand, suspending the administration of those affairs until the unknown time of the advent of the Imam to power, especially in a long-awaited but then newly established Shīʿī state, was, to say the least, imprudent. In other words, it was impossible to abandon all the mundane and otherworldly affairs of the Shiite community and refrain from solving their day-to-day legal issues. Insofar as those issues emerged from the private laws of Shiite individuals, it was possible to employ the theory of jurist's agency of Imam. Brilliant jurists such as al-Karakī and Shahid Awwal who argued for such deputyship were aware that it would not only facilitate the flow and establishment of the legal system, but also help the individual perform his moral-legal obligations—to his coreligionist, neighbor, business partner, family, and compatriot—and live an enriched faithful life, as was the order of his religion.

Put another way, these jurists were cognizant of those social necessities that are part and parcel of a larger necessity, which in every society is called "legal order." For *Uṣūlī* jurists, however, the concept of legal order had yet another trajectory. They were fully cognizant of the fact that in the Shīʿa law and faith, a full-fledged legal order of society will materialize only when the Hidden Imam holds the power and leads. According to many Shīʿī jurists, in the absence of its Imam, the Shiite community is on the verge of dissention and partisan contentions. The delicate balance between the implications of the absence of Imam and the necessity of an orderly society will be struck only when the legal agent takes full responsibility in meticulous reduction of such implications. Wisdom of the process prescribes edification, erudition, and affinity with the arguments. It also does proscribe inertia, inadvertence, fancifulness, and ludicrous vignettes. Al-Karakī, as the reader will see in chapter 2, fully takes this responsibility and with prudence and deep adherence to the law strikes the balance in his juristic treatment of the Friday Prayer.

The theory of Just Sultanate was successful in providing the Shiite king with a well-designed system of rule of law. If in premodern England the law was what the king found just to his people—doing justice to his people was the king's royal duty to which he had been sworn by his coronation oath, and finding and implementing justice was part of his discretion[21]—in Safavid kingship, the Shiite sultan was entrusted with the task of executing the juristic findings of Shari'ah, which at the time functioned as the statutory laws of the realm. It was the leading jurist who was charged with finding the legal solutions for justice and defying injustice. Such jurist's discretion was also restricted to adherence to a law that other jurists prior to him had worked out, in detail, its vectors, rendered opinions, and even established consensus on numerous issues. In holding the religious authority, the leading jurist was to pledge his loyalty to the law and observe his status as one among many of the Imam's agents, and not as the principal person. The Shiite king, as the holder of political authority, was also missioned to uphold the rulings of such loyal and observant agent. His oath to establish and enforce justice and use his power as a just sultan was to be signed off by the leading jurist. Though ideal and seemingly practical at the same time, to keep the process's balance was as difficult as walking on a loose rope. World history is a good witness: the holder of religious authority did not maintain loyalty and observance, nor did the sultan stop at the border of pious execution, but easily and extensively overstepped the duties and abused the process. The relation between law and power was blurred.

Such a blurred relation was dominant at the dawn of the 1905 Revolution. It was not clear where the lines were in the relations between the monarch and the people, between religion and politics, between the monarch and the chancellor, and between the state and foreign diplomats. The fatwa issued by a religious leader in condemnation of a devastating royalty bargained the tobacco trade to a British businessman, and the large-scale following of people that culminated in its humiliating revocation by the king draws probably the only clear line in the then Iranian society. The just sultanate theory was breathing its last. What transformed, borrowing from Nā'īnī, an abject slavery to revived humanity was the people's revolt against the arbitrary rule of an unbridled kingship. *Uṣūlī* jurists led the crusade in two directions: against the despot king and against the anti-constitutionalist jurists. Two big names, among others, light up the path: Ākhūnd Khurāsānī and Nā'īnī. This book is about their jurisprudence of a constitution that was the most important achievement of the people's social movement. There are two other results. First, *Uṣūlī* jurists' detailed juridical theorization of legitimacy of a constitutionalist state in the absence of the Imam, which revolved around a key factor—popular sovereignty. Second, despite their historical rivalry and conflict of interests, Great Britain and Russia allied to abort the Constitutional Revolution's accomplishments.

This second result, however, needs more explanation. Alan Cromartie argues that the English Reformation was not based on the vestiges of Catholic modes of worship as the survival of a medieval institutional structure. He writes:

> Richard Hooker (1554–1600), succeeded in fusing defense of the church with regard for legal values, but later high churchmen adopted a more risky strategy. As their claims for the church became bolder, their politics became more absolutist. They regarded themselves and the crown as equally menaced by the aggression of the common lawyers, and looked to a powerful monarch to defend them. Though James was sympathetic, he rejected their political assistance; Charles by contrast went into alliance with an anti-erastian church, and in so doing, helped to doom both church and monarchy.[22]

In the 1905–1911 Revolution, the alliance between the king and the clergy was on the side of a non-*Uṣūlī* and semi-*Akhbārī* orientation of legal theory of Imāmah and just rulership. Both found themselves subject to strong attacks by *Uṣūlī*s who would not compromise the law and the Iranian constitutional culture with royal policies and prerogatives. Muẓaffar al-Dīn, the first monarch in the period, dodged the fight and died at the early stages of the movement. The second monarch, Muhammad Ali, allied with anti-constitutionalist jurists, however, and was about to "doom" both monarchy and anti-constitutionalist clergies. The only reason that prevented such "doom" was the external factor, the military and political intervention of the British empire and the aggressive expansionism of the Russian empire: an evil alliance of two major powers who had planned to divide Iran through an illegal treaty, in the midst of the floor discussions of First Majlis on transforming a legal instrument that wished for a kingly parliament to a constitution that was set to establish a parliamentary king.

Chapter 1

Uṣūlī Jurisprudence and Reason

Dynamisms of the Text

In Islamic jurisprudence, what God has addressed to human being is technically called *khiṭābāt* (plural form of *khiṭāb*) or Divine Pronouncements. Some of these pronouncements ordain a *ḥukm* (a specific ruling) to which a *taklīf* (legal obligation) is incumbent upon the individual. These pronouncements have been made in the Qur'an and the Sunnah, and are called *Naṣṣ* (Text), as the embodiment of binding guidelines found in the divine addresses. Dynamisms between the Text and its content are prevalent in Islamic legal tradition. For the most part, they operate in the processes in which the human agent has a role in the apprehension, articulation, and reformation of the legal rulings derived from the Text: not a dichotomy, but a dual dialectical interrelation that exists between law as an ideal and law as a process, on the one hand, and between method and substance, on the other. In order to contextualize these dynamisms, one should delve into the thematic arguments that emerge from mutually supportive and congenial realms developed in the rationalist school of Islamic legal tradition. Famously known as *Uṣūlī*s—as opposed to traditionists, that is, *ahl al-ḥadīth* and *Akhbarī*s—rationalist jurists start with the juristic tradition of engaging those endemic, trenchant, and didactic questions, raised in the Islamic Philosophy and *Kalām* (theology), that revolve around the Law of the divine and the human potential for acquiring knowledge about it. To treat it properly, a jurist ought to think about the essence of Divine Law; the ideal methods and means of acquiring knowledge; the nature and probative value of the available evidence; man's potentialities of and categorical limits in acquiring the knowledge, that is, the possibility of *kashf wāqi'* (matching the reality of the subject matter of such acquired knowledge with the axiomatic truth about the subject inherent in the Law of divine); and comparing and contrasting such ideal truth of the Law with the real—moral and legal—value of the practically acquired knowledge. Imbued with the panoply of rational reasoning, *Uṣūlī* jurists have established a rich legal doctrine on these dynamisms, where a significant role for human intellect has been assigned in discovering the Text's legal rules[1]; a logic of legislation has been offered that provides substantial authority for the nontextual findings of *'aql mustaqil* (the independent reason); and *'uqalā'* (rational people) have been found capable of, and designated for, discovering the inherent necessity of mandatory acts or dispositive deficit of prohibited ones. For the most part, this chapter will introduce some aspects of the *Uṣūlī* doctrine of reason, the importance of rational arguments, and the place of rational proofs and indicators in the grand concept of *ijtihād*: the juristic effort of discovering the rules of Shari'ah. Such effort is a de novo review of the previous opinions with, inter alia, consideration of new facts and the impacts of time and space on legal reasoning.

The first of such dynamisms in the relation between the Text and presuppositions of Law is in the conception of Shari'ah, the threshold concept deep-seated in any legal argument. Muslim jurists view Shari'ah as omnicompetent. When defined as God's Law, the self-fulfilling potential of Shari'ah becomes an attribute of nothing less than that of the All Knowing whose pronouncements were mediated through revelation to His Messengers, and through them to human beings. For *Uṣūlī*s, not only does the omnicompetence of Shari'ah spring from the divine revelations, but it is also intertwined with objectives embedded in them, which lay out the Law's philosophical and methodological components:[2] justice as the core of Divine Commands,[3] and reason, which man is instructed to employ in its establishment.[4] Thus, Shari'ah as an ideal embodies Laws that have been derived from the most just and the highest reason,[5] and sets the rationale for the concomitant derivative rules. This perception of ideal omnicompetence views Laws not only as general rules, maxims, eruditions, and positive statements, but also as flexible with the capacity of addressing new social problems.

The process of articulation of the law's presuppositions and presenting it to a faith-based community that has found a parallel between religion and law is the direct outcome of the Text in Islamic legal tradition. From early on Muslim jurists took it upon themselves to establish a methodology that would confirm and fully develop those rationales in human mind. What emerged from this process was a conception of legal maxims that was manifested in a relatively determinate body of procedures, dominated by technicality and micro-level reasoning on detailed application of

Law that would redefine the notion of exceptionless rules. It was true that legal rules and maxims derived originally from the Text, but they were not its unmediated or uncorroborated outcomes. If legal maxims were to connote the grounds or principles of the axiomatic bases of law—and for that matter, the legal reasoning—then, the possibility of change of the fixed rules was a direct dependent of the same authority that would find them immutable. In other words, while the authenticity of the Qur'an and its verses remains indisputable, there was—and still defies ceasing—an indefinite disagreement about a great number of the traditions attributed to the Prophet.[6] Alternatively, if there was doubt as to authenticity of the prophetic traditions, then the resulting rule/maxim could not be rigid and eternally true for—and applicable—in all cases and issues.

Ikhtilāf (disagreement) among Muslim jurists was manifested in two different categories: First, *ikhtilāf al-ḥadīth*, that is, disagreement on the content, methods of authentication, and categorization of *aḥādīth* (plural form of *ḥadīth*, Prophetic traditions), second, *ikhtilāf al-fuqahā'*, that is, disagreement among the jurists on deducing the Law from sources and its application to relevant legal issues.[7] Legal history of *ikhtilāf* demonstrates the fact that disagreement among the jurists, at least by the middle of the second/eighth century, was not intended to devaluate the inherent importance of the traditions but to critically analyze their content.[8] In other words, when Muslim jurists encountered a conflict between two different traditions, they chose one without denying the validity of the other. In both of its manifestations, disagreement was perceived not as a cause for sectarian prejudice, but as one for more freedom for a *mukallaf* (from similar root of *taklīf*, meaning duty-bound Muslim) in adopting one over another opinion.[9] Hence, depending on the plurality of opinions, there was more latitude in discharge or even absence of *taklīf* (legal obligation). The importance of the field of *ikhtilāf al-ḥadīth* in the establishment of normative status of the text in the processes of juristic determination is undeniable. There are reports about the Prophet's dissatisfaction with wrongful attributions of what had been quoted from him. Other probative evidence shows that the Prophet himself was weary of the negative effects of such faulty transmissions on the Muslim community at large.[10] By recognizing the conclusive authority of the Prophet's sayings and deeds in resolving the legal and political conflicts in Muslims' minds, there was a tendency among some of the jurists to refer more to the traditions in lieu of the Qur'an itself.[11] In many cases, therefore, confusing Shari'ah as "the right way to follow" with what *Muḥadiththūn* (compilers of the traditions)—who were essentially ineligible to render juristic opinions—had compiled in their books of *ḥadīth* was the unintended but practical outcome of the processes of compilation. There are also historical reports that, at least during the Rightly Guided Caliphate, the idea of over-reliance on traditions was not supported.[12]

From a purely technical perspective, however, reliance on books of compiled traditions was originally based on the belief in comprehensiveness of Shari'ah in the sense of providing answers to all questions.[13] An internal dynamism between belief and reliance was at place. The issue was not whether the Text was capable of providing authoritative bases from which jurists could deduce legal solutions. Voluminous compendia of Muslim jurists' books on jurisprudence are replete with such belief and defy any doubts. This belief, however, was not antithetical to similarly valid fact that the Text did not always furnish a positive rule for every detail of the legal issue.[14] The issue was whether the compiled books of the traditions presented a true narrative of the Prophet's Sunnah in a way that jurists could rely on.

Based on the technical arguments of *ḥujjiyat al-dalīl* (the probative value of the evidence), the *Uṣūlīs*' reaction to the problem was formal and substantial examination of the traditions in the form of a mutually supportive process of authentication and approbation. In general, an ideal proof is the one that is attested by the Text, and it is always preferable to furnish a sufficient number of *dalīl naqlī* (Text-based indicator/proof/evidence) for the validity of a juristic opinion. However, because of faulty transmissions or wrong attributions of the Prophetic remarks, the number of traditions that meet the conclusive presumption of reliability is very limited. In order to preserve the sacred truth transferred through revelation and to purge the Text from wrong attributions, it was of utmost importance to verify the authenticity of the traditions. It was after the second/eighth century that the relevant standards of such inquiries emerged. These new branches of knowledge were *'Ilm al-Rijāl* (the knowledge of requirements for evaluating the credibility of *ḥadīth* transmitters),[15] and concomitant to it, *'Ilm al-Jarḥ wa al-Ta'dīl* (the knowledge of balancing and preferring the content of *ḥadīth*).[16] In general, the traditions are divided into two main categories: (1) *akhbār mutawātir*, that is, reports that are transmitted by a reliable chain of transmitters whose veracity and trustworthiness are admitted and approved by the jurists, and the unbroken chain is verifiably traceable to its origin of utterance. The source of utterance is the Prophet, with the addition of the infallible Imams in Shī'ī Law. According to the majority of *Uṣūlī* jurists, only *mutawātir* traditions provide incontrovertible and conclusive knowledge of the Law. (2) *Akhbār āḥād*, that is, reports that lack one of the following requirements: (a) verifiable order in chain of transmission, (b) sufficient number of transmitters that is required for reliability of the traditions/reports, and (c) trustworthiness and veracity of their transmitters.[17]

Due to lack of sufficient valid traditions, the process of derivation of the rules in part revolves around such less-than-reliable reports or *akhbār āḥād*. It is this category of reports, however, that a traditionist jurist invokes to establish the validity of his opinion, whereas a great majority of the *Uṣūlī* jurists finds it merely ancillary for that matter.[18] This is also where the notion of sufficient knowledge, capable of proving a valid opinion, steps in. In other words, there is a conflict between traditionist and rationalist jurists on the concept of validity. Shīʿī *Akhbārī*s (traditionists) believed in the sufficiency of knowledge that emerged from reliance on *akhbār āḥād*. The main premises of this discourse are:

1. There is a Divine Pronouncement, mostly in the form of a tradition attributed to the Prophet (or the Imam).[19]
2. Subcategorization of the traditions to merely valid or invalid is wrong.[20]
3. All the traditions compiled in the canonical books are valid.[21]
4. The required knowledge to access the truth is far beyond man's capacity to acquire.[22]
5. Man's acquired knowledge is insufficient to establish a valid counterargument against a *dalīl naqlī* (Text-based evidence).[23]

In contrast, a rationalist jurist would seek other legitimate sources of knowledge that would establish validity. One of those legitimate sources is *dalīl ʿaqlī* (rational proof). The characteristics of the rationalist Shīʿī School of legal thought are:

1. General rejection of *akhbār āḥād* (traditions reported by less-than-reliable number of transmitters).[24]
2. Invoking such traditions, only if their content could be verified by external indicators.[25]
3. Acceptance of *akhbār mujmaʿun ʿalayh* (those traditions that the Shiite community had consented on their applicability).[26]
4. Acceptance of the Shiite community as an independent source of jurisprudence,[27] to the extent that al-Murtaḍā believed most of the Shari'ah rules are deducible from the established consensus in the Shiite community.[28]

What follow are some *Uṣūlī* Shīʿī jurists' arguments on these sources that continued to dominate the Shīʿī jurisprudence and the *Uṣūlī* doctrine of *ʿaql* (reason).

Legitimacy of *'Aql* as a Source

There are authenticated reports attributed to the Prophet and Imams in which reason has been described as the basis of the religion,[29] the messenger of the truth,[30] and God's internal proof along with His external proof, that is, the Prophet and Imams.[31] One of the earliest references to application of reason, as a method of discovering the Law, was made by Mufīd:

> Main origins of the Shari'ah rules are: God's Book, Tradition of the Prophet, and what has been stated by the Imams. Paths to recognition of a legitimate *ḥukm* (legal rule) from these sources are reason, language, and reports... An *āḥād* report that can assure the jurist of the absence of excuse [in his endeavor for finding the *ḥukm*] is the one that is supported by contextual proofs that establish knowledge to its authenticity. Such contextual evidence can be an argument developed by reason.[32]

Furthermore, Mufīd divided the *akhbār āḥād* into two major categories: (1) a tradition that is corroborated by *dalā'il mujib al-'ilm* (external indicators that establish knowledge), that is, reason, consensus, or custom; and (2) a tradition that is incapable of securing any of them. Mufīd believed that the second category traditions would not furnish a probative ground, and the jurist can utilize traditions of the first to take remedial measures for the Text's lack of incontrovertible evidence (*khabarun qāṭi'i 'udhr*) and render a valid opinion.[33] In addition to treatment of reason as a path to discovering the Law, Mufīd criticized his mentor Shaykh al-Ṣadūq,[34] one of the three main *Muḥadiththūn* (compilers) of traditions in Shī'ī history. Mufīd was especially concerned about al-Ṣadūq's mere adherence to the prima facie appearance of the traditions and applying them in legal issues, without critically distinguishing the right and wrong ones, and thus, following the transmitters and failing to render an opinion based on the probative value of the transmitted traditions.[35] Mufīd, therefore, designated *'aql* as a measure for evaluation of the content of *ḥadīth* and wrote: "When a tradition conflicts with the rules of reason, its *fasād* (incorrectness) should be rationally disproved. Such tradition cannot be the basis upon which a *ḥukm* (rule) would be discovered or gain validity."[36]

The nature of rejecting admissibility of *āḥād* traditions was mainly founded on methodological concerns. As a matter of principle, it was against the then standards of evaluation of traditions to render a less-than-reliable tradition admissible. According to al-Murtaḍā, those traditions did not meet the required qualifications for "lifting the falsehood from the content of a tradition."[37] On the invalidity of the *āḥād* traditions, al-Murtaḍā claimed that all the Shī'ī jurists have by *ijmā'* (consensus) rejected the idea of validity of non-corroborated traditions.[38] In his arguments on *ijmāʿ* and its rational basis of validity, al-Murtaḍā made yet another argument in favor of practical reason in Shīʿī law. By a rationalist account, support for the idea of "external indicators," which could remedy the lack of validity of the *āḥād* traditions, would also be found in analyzing whether or not it was possible to apply an invalid specific rule that the Shīʿī community had perceived acceptable. Practical reason had its origins in the concept of *luṭf*[39] (inherent grace of the divine guidance). A common belief exists on the importance and applicability of *luṭf* among Shiites and Mu'tazilites for the proof of rationality of Shari'ah. Summarily, this concept is employed to prove that God will and does only that which is good, so it brings the human beings close to His obedience and keeps them far from disobedience. In addition, Shiites employ this concept to prove the righteousness of Imāmah. In his discussion on the "beauty of the appointment of messengers" by God, al-Murtaḍā argued: "It would not be impossible [to assume] that [the rationale of] appointing the messengers by God was to emphasize the rules of reason, even if the appointed messenger brought no Law with himself."[40]

According to al-Murṭaḍā, it is not impossible to assume that God knows when *mukallafūn* (duty-bound individuals) perform acts, they do so because such performance accords to what they believe to be a rational duty and in conflict with rational prohibitions. Obviously, there are other acts that when carried out amount to performing prohibited acts and violating a mandatory obligation (*'amr wājib*). If it is acceptable that God is aware of all these varieties, then one should also accept the fact that God would inform the duty-bound individuals and let them know of His awareness, because informing people of this kind of matters is an established characteristic of God's inherent grace. Finally, in his arguments about the relation between *al-samʿ* (revelation) and *'aql* (reason), al-Murtaḍā wrote:

> When revelation is invoked for the claim of prohibition of a prohibited act, our knowledge acquired by reason will [also] prohibit it. Similarly, when revelation dismisses [the claim of] prohibition, our knowledge will find it obligatory. Then, if something is disclosed by our reason, and not by the revelation, it is what would be discovered from revelation, though explored by our reason and what we know of revelation. Thus, there is not conflict between rational finding and our acquired knowledge from the divine revelation. There is no circumstance in which the proven [rational] principles would establish opposition to or rejection of revelation. And the discovery of (the rule revealed in) revelation on the details of the matters is not possible but by discovering the [social] customs and experiences and what has been reported about them.[41]

These significant points of concurrence and convergence between reason and revelation, as introduced by al-Murtaḍā, were not limited to sole function of establishing *ijmāʿ* (consensus). In the process of evaluating the traditions, compiled in the books by famous Shiite compilers such as Kulaynī,[42] al-Murtaḍā advocated a critical review of such traditions by requiring "their submission to reason." If after being examined by valid indicators like the Qur'an and what is conceived therein, traditions were found correct, then, he held, "it would be permissible to render them 'right' and approve their veracity."[43] However, he cautioned that if the traditions narrated by unreliable transmitters were so found to be "permissible," such permissibility would establish neither conclusive correctness, nor veracity of their transmitters.[44] This was equal to rendering these traditions inconclusive. In this context, al-Murtaḍā is famously known to have established a long-standing rational principle that provided: "Doubt as to possibility of furnishing proof is equal to assured absence of probativity."[45]

The tension between the text and its content amounted to the next manifestation of disagreement among jurists. While the Qur'an and Sunnah were imperatively considered as primary authority sources of Law, in the factual instances of absence or silence of the Text, or at least where the jurists thought so, the necessity of resolving the legal issues required them to search for an ascertainable indicator of Law. In other words, when in doubt about existence, clarity, applicability, or silence of the Text as to a specific issue, the jurists still had to determine the status of *taklīf* (legal obligation). Far beyond a legal solution, this was a philosophical question. If legal obligation was the direct outcome of an existing, applicable, and ascertainable indicator of Law in the Text, then in the case of a legitimate doubt, absence of obligation or non-liability could or should be presumed. Heavily relying on the Qur'anic prohibitions against undeclared individual liability for duties and punishments,[46] this was the fundamental rationale for one of the four main procedural rules in the Islamic legal tradition that has been extensively discussed by *Uṣūlī* jurists under the general topic of *aṣālat al-barā'ah* (presumption of absence of obligation) and specific arguments on a famous legal maxim: *qāʿidat qubḥ al-ʿiqāb bi lā bayān wāṣil min al-Shāriʿ*.[47] Literally meaning "the inherent ugliness of any punishment for which a statement from The Legislator has not reached us," this jurisprudential principle, to a large extent, corresponds to universal prohibition of *ex post facto* punishments. According to a great majority of *Uṣūlī* jurists, these arguments are among *mustaqillāt al-ʿaqliyya* (rules of the independent reason), which enjoy the status of independent legal validity, even though Divine Pronouncements testify to their truth.

Ijtihād: Juristic De Novo Effort

In addition to classic sources of law, that is, Qur'an, Sunnah, and consensus, al-Muḥaqqiq expanded them by including *dalīl al-'aql* (rational proof) and *istiṣḥāb* (presumption of continuity of previously discovered rule). He divided the rational proofs into two subgroups: (1) *laḥn al-khiṭāb* (the literal construction of the Divine pronouncement),[48] *faḥwā al-khiṭāb* (the substance of Divine pronouncement),[49] and *dalīl al-khiṭāb* (the reason for the Divine pronouncement)[50]; and (2) *mustaqillāt al-'aqlīyya* (independent rational findings).[51] Putting the issue in a new perspective, Shahid al-Awwal made yet another categorization of rational proofs by dividing them into those that are based on Divine Pronouncements and those that are independent of such articulations.[52] Furthermore, 'Allāma built the juristic structure of unavoidable reliance on *ẓann* (supposition/probability) and its application in *ijtihād* as the main path toward discovering the rules, and wrote:

> Since the Qur'an has unmistakably prohibited whimsical utterances,[53] *Ijtihād* means the utmost effort that a jurist can apply to reflect on the uncertain [jurisprudential] matters, to the extent that no further effort could possibly be made... Such effort will amount to *ẓann* (supposition). Only the Prophet and the Imams are able to acquire conclusive knowledge: the Prophet with the means of revelation, and the Imams by [complete] reception of the Prophet's teachings or by inspiration from God. There are many instances in which the jurist's effort comes to a halt, even where a direct revelation has been introduced.[54] Although permissible to review them by *ijtihād*, for most of which [the effort] a reward is awaited, the door of *al-jazm* (assertion of finality) to the Shari'ah—as was conveyed from God The Exalted to the Prophet—is closed... The learned are allowed to strive on deriving the rules from *al-'umūmāt* (the general sources), that is, the Qur'an and Sunnah, and by weighing in the conflicting indicators, but not by analogy or discretionary opinions.[55]

'Allāma's delineation of the ways and methods by which a jurist is able to discover the rule revolves around two major concepts of *ẓann* (probability and supposition) and *al-jazm* (authoritative assertion). For him, and a great number of future jurists, the dialectical relationship between the two is the foundational characteristic of the greater relation between *ḥukm* (rule) and *taklīf* (duty), where the notion of finality would only materialize if conclusive proof—the Qur'an and or incontrovertible tradition—is in the jurist's reach. In other circumstances, the jurists' endeavor will only establish probability as to the derived rule of Shari'ah. Thus, the jurist should not assert authoritative discovery of law: all he can do is to examine the general sources and resolve conflicts among the available evidence, which is impossible without employment of reason and rational arguments.[56]

Like many other jurists, ʿAllāma provided that the act of *ijtihād* would be unfounded unless specifically required knowledge is obtained or the preconditions met. On the one hand, rational and jurisprudential arguments on the rules of Shari'ah require lexical and linguistic mastery and a high level of scholarship on letters and spirit of the Text, which are found either in the prima facie appearance of terms and phrases or in their metaphorical conjunctions. Therefore, a jurist should be well versed in the technical mandates of *al-takhṣīṣ wa al-naskh* (specification and abrogation) and causes of preference (*jihāt al-tarjīḥ*) in the case of conflict. He also required specialized knowledge of *asbāb al-nuzūl* (the occasions of revelation), *āyāt al-aḥkām* (Qur'anic verses of rules), the pertinent traditions about the rules, *al-ḥadd wa al-burhān*,[57] and *ijmāʿ* (consensus). Furthermore, a jurist is to have had developed extensive knowledge on *al-barā'a al-aṣlīyya* (presumption of non-liability). Only by meeting these qualifications is a jurist allowed to perform *ijtihād* while knowing that his efforts will not reach the status of discovery except with a *dalīl qaṭʿī* (decisive evidence).[58]

The jurists of Ḥilla, that is, al-Muḥaqqiq, Shahid al-Awwal, and ʿAllāma, bridged the gap between the theological origins of early rationalist jurists such as Mufīd and al-Murtaḍā, on the one hand, and the legal orientations of Shaykh al-Ṭā'ifa toward the presumptive validity of juristic finding, on the other.[59] Therefore, they contributed to a significant development of rationalism in Shīʿī law. Revival of the concept of *ijtihād*, which at the time was still burdened with early refutation,[60] was combined with de novo analysis of *akhbār āḥād* on the basis of formal methods of critical evaluation of transmitters,[61] substantial treatment of *uṣūl ʿaqlīyya* (rational principles), and their application in discovering the Law. Such de novo approach was heavily founded on the philosophical and theological conditions of acquiring knowledge and the role of human intellect, in which ʿAllāma was also deeply involved. In his many books in different fields of Shīʿī law and theology,[62] ʿAllāma followed philosophical origins of Shīʿī doctrine, which was developed at the time by Naṣīr al-Dīn Ṭūsī,[63] on the vectors of validity of the human acquisition of knowledge.[64] He also strongly rebutted the Ashʿarī discourse on predestination and rejection of human will.[65] Having such background, ʿAllāma established the validity of *al-ṭarīq ẓannīyya* (suppositional method) as congruent to the knowledge about Shari'ah, and defined *fiqh* (jurisprudence) thus:

> First: *fiqh* literally means comprehension, and technically means the knowledge of detailed rules of Shari'ah. [Only] people of distinction argue

about *fiqh*, because ordinary individuals are not charged to obtain such knowledge as a necessity of their faith. Thus, *fiqh* derives from the [learned] notables, rules of reason, following the precedent and the Divine and His angels' Knowledge, and the principles of Shari'ah. Someone who knows some of this knowledge should not be considered *faqīh* (jurist), and [such] incomplete knowledge is not *fiqh*. Knowledge requires a comprehensive ability, which is founded upon known principles. Suppositional method is not in conflict with the knowledge of *ḥukm* (the rule of Shari'ah).

Second: *wujūb* (mandate) of *taklīf* (duty) is proven by theology. If sufficient knowledge has not been furnished as to those Shari'ah rules that have been discovered through *fiqh*, *imtithāl* (compliance) would be incomplete. Therefore, it is mandatory to acquire the knowledge. Considering the Qur'anic verse,[66] fulfillment of such duty will be possible by the practice of sufficient number of individuals.

Fiqh is in order after theology, classical Arabic and grammar, *taṣrīf* (morphology of words), and *uṣūl* (principles of logic and jurisprudence). It benefits the laity in reaching happiness in the hereafter and educating them on how to manage their life through temporal interests. Subject matter of *fiqh* is the actions that the duty-bound individuals take out of necessity or by their choice. *Fiqh* emanates from theology, *uṣūl*, classical Arabic, *naḥw* (syntax), and the Qur'an and Sunnah.[67]

Reason and Presumption of Non-Liability

As discussed before, it is an established juristic principle that without a previously stated rule, no punishment is permitted. The other aspect of this principle is the inexistence of *taklīf* (duty of obedience) where the Text is silent or there is doubt about the existing rule's binding effect or applicability. According to ʿAllāma and many other Muslim jurists, the notion of non-liability is founded upon theological arguments about *imtināʿ taklīf mā lāyuṭāq* (invalidity of unbearable duties), which finds it against sound reason for God to exhaust the individual's burden with a duty that he is incapable of fulfilling. Among such unbearable duties are those that one is unaware of, or, after sufficient investigation, is unable to find an ascertainable indicator for its mandatory charge. Theological origins of the argument revolve around the issue of the pristine nature of human acts prior to the introduction of Divine Revelation.[68] Primarily, the argument was that, independent of the divine textual prescriptions, there is a *maṣlaḥa* (benefit) or *mafsada* (detriment) in every human act the determination of which is subject to either rational finding or divine textual prescription.[69] This proposition raised the question of the inherent characteristic of the act: Is the act inherently permitted or prohibited? Rationalist jurist-theologians believed that the rule for acts (prior to revelation) is either *ibāḥa* (permittedness)[70]or *tawaqquf* (suspension) because we do not exactly know what the rule is.[71] However, they opined that when the revealed Text was silent or devoid of explicit *ḥaẓr* (forbiddance), reason would rule for permissibility of the act.[72] The legal implication of this argument includes the occasions of doubt as to forbiddance or obligatoriness of an act for which no rule in the Text is available.[73]

The majority of rationalist jurists have adopted presumption of non-liability, and divided it to two major categories:[74]

First, *al-barā'at al-shar'iyya* (jurisprudential exemptions) according to which in occasions of doubt as to existence of an applicable *ḥukm shar'ī* (Text-based rule), the individual is not liable for performance of the subject matter *taklīf* (the duty). This position is supported by the Qur'an,[75]and an incontrovertible tradition from the Prophet attests to its correctness.[76] The thrust of the Text is directed at the absence of duty or potential punishment because of absence of access to the rule of Shari'ah.[77]

Second, *al-barā'at al-'aqliyya* (non-liability derived from rational finding) by which the jurist's holding of non-liability is supported by the fact that every nation or culture at all times and places has recognized the capacity of reason to examine and exhaust all the arguments relevant to the absence of punishment without previous constructive notice. In Islamic methodology of law, an opening argument would be whether or not the legal liability of a rule should be imposed equally on those who know the rule and those who do not. This issue is usually discussed under the topic of *ishtirāk al-aḥkām bayn al-'ālim wa al-jāhil* (common applicability of rules to knowledgeable and ignorant individuals) in books of *uṣūl al-fiqh*.[78] Primarily, *Uṣūlī* jurists argue that God's rule is self-proven and our knowledge does not impact its proof and general applicability. Our knowledge, however, does affect the rule's *tanajjuz* (realization and effectuation). If an individual is unaware of the rule, such unawareness strips the rule's effectiveness and bars the individual's liability. Legality of the rule is not necessitated by knowledge. The issue is the extent of charge and conditions of punishment, not the extent of knowledge of the rule. Thus, it does not matter if one has *al-'ilm ijmāli* (general/specific knowledge) or *al-'ilm tafṣīlī* (extensive knowledge).[79] On the one hand, since it is unreasonable to punish without prior statement of the rule, if one makes sufficient effort to investigate and is unable to establish a knowledge that would satisfy his conscience as to existence of textual indicators,[80] then his opposition to incumbency of the act in question will not result in liability. On the other hand, it is not reasonable to conclude the rule's general inclusion by the rule itself. More simply put, the rule does not attest for itself. For proving such generality, we need another reason that can be furnished by the *mutammim al-ja'l* (complementary assignment) of a supplement capable of helping us conclude its *natījat al-iṭlāq* (unexceptional application). A supplement of this nature would be our *qaṣd al-imtithāl bi amr al-wājib al-'ibādī* (intention to comply with mandatory rules in devotional acts), *ijmā'* (consensus), or the rule of reason in nondevotional mandatory acts for which general inclusion is not as commonly presumed as in devotional ones. We should notice that "intention of compliance," as a supplementary element, is not one of the classical sources of law. Thus, a legitimate argument that is approved by rational measures and collective reason can furnish proof for general inclusion of the rule.

Probative Value of Ẓann (Probability, Supposition)

In contrast to the traditionists' simplified and idealistic definition of *'ilm* (knowledge),[81] *Uṣūlīs* believe that reaching the status of certitude, with all its desirability, is an inherently difficult task that cannot be achieved by mere invocation of traditions except in rare occasions.[82] Bihbahānī made a compelling argument on the multifaceted layers of incertitude and barriers to conclusive knowledge in discovering the rules, and advocated a "right to investigate"[83] for the learned, reasonable individuals and inevitable resort to probability.[84] In this context, Bihbahānī and other *Uṣūlīs* argued for theoretical premises that later came to be known as "*muqaddimāt dalīl insidād bāb al-'ilm*" (prerequisites of the closure of the gate to conclusive knowledge), which relate to derivative consequences of the impossibility of certitude after the age of revelation.[85] These prerequisites are as follow:

1. We are certain, by *'ilm ijmālī* (brief knowledge), of the existence of duty in Shari'ah,[86] for exemption of which a certainty of inexistence of such duty is necessary.[87] The premise of this prerequisite is that *'ilm qaṭ'ī* (certain knowledge) derives only from revelation, but our access to it has been foreclosed with the start of the last Imam's *ghayba* (occultation). Thus, we do not have certain knowledge as to conclusive existence or inexistence of duty.
2. Except for the limited number of issues for which we have incontrovertible evidence, the gate to conclusive knowledge about the majority of those duties is closed.[88]
3. Impermissibility of negligence about *al-takālīf al-mushtabaha* (the suspicious duties) and general prohibition of seeking incompliance with them in one way or the other.[89] In other words, a cautionary

approach to the issue of existence or inexistence of duty is required, which is the outcome of having to rely on probability.

4. Inadmissibility of resolving the dilemma by referring them to *uṣūl al-ʿamalīyya* (procedural principles).[90] These principles are: *aṣālat al-barā'a* (presumption of non-liability), *aṣālat al-istiṣḥāb* (presumption of continuity),[91] *aṣālat al-iḥtīyāṭ* (presumption of precaution) in permissible acts, or *aṣālat al-ishtighāl* (presumption of engagement),[92] and *aṣālat al-takhyīr* (presumption of optional choice).[93] It is also impermissible to resolve the issue of existence or inexistence of duty by issuing fatwas.[94]
5. Impossibility of preferring the inferior (*marjūḥ*) over the superior (*rājiḥ*). In other words, it is rationally impermissible to prefer something that is less probable or even invalid over what is more probable or supported by evidence.[95]

Based on these prerequisites, the *Uṣūlī* jurists discuss whether or not a suppositional method of discovering the rule is valid. There is argument on whether it is possible to resort to a type of suppositional method whose validity is approved by Shari'ah, since obtaining conclusive knowledge about the existence or inexistence of a rule is impractical. When there are certainly known duties, exemption of duty has to also be ruled by certainty of knowledge, that is, by the means of ascertainable indicators of Law. Thus, because of closure of the door to conclusive knowledge, we are left with the rational presumption of sufficiency of probable knowledge, and considering it as valid. Otherwise we have to believe in either absolute inexistence of the duty—something that is *qaṭʿī al-fasād* (certainly detrimental)—or imposition of the unbearable duty of attainment of conclusive knowledge, and commit ourselves to perform the duty where it is not possible to establish such commitment. While none of the options is acceptable, we are also unable to resort to the precautionary rule of performing anything that we think is our duty because it will amount to *ʿusr wa ḥaraj* (hardship and harm) or a defective system of rules for a distressed community of individuals. Thus, if we do not approve the validity of suppositional knowledge, we have to employ alternative types of attaining "knowledge" that we know are invalid and void.

Although the aforementioned prerequisites were sufficiently strong to prove the validity of purely suppositional knowledge (*ẓann muṭlaq*), Bihbahānī and later *Uṣūlī* jurists were not willing to render all types of thusly attained knowledge admissible.[96] In doing so, they made a de novo review of the previous rationalist jurists' arguments about *akhbār āḥād* (the less than reliable traditions)[97]; they also revived the early rationalist jurists' opinions on the validity of any type of reports that would comply with the

Qur'an, valid Sunnah of the Prophet, and valid reports of the infallible Imams that meet the criteria and findings of *'ilm al-rijāl wa al-dirāya*.[98] They, however, assigned inconclusive determinacy to the less-than-reliable traditions' role in discovery of the rules.[99] To this end, Bihbahānī made the following arguments.[100]

1. When available and accessible, acquisition of a conclusive knowledge, as the preferred goal of the jurist to any other method, is superior to the suppositional method.[101]
2. Qur'anic condemnation of *shakk* (illusion) is an original truth.[102] However, with the passage of time and our deprivation of access to the Messenger of Revelation (Prophet Muhammad) and the infallible Imams, the existing sources of law do not provide more than suppositional knowledge. Therefore, the concept of illusion in its Qur'anic setting is very different from the concept of supposition that inevitably incurs in the jurists' utmost effort for discovering the rules at this time and age.[103]
3. Suppositional knowledge is restricted to the established standards of validity, that is, compatibility with the Qur'an and valid traditions.[104]
4. Similar to their customary and literal definitions, concepts of *ẓann* (supposition) and *'ilm* (conclusive knowledge) are qualified by where they are posited in the religious rules and by what is derivable from such positioning.[105]
5. The difference between *ẓann* (probability) and *wahm* (mere suspicion or fantasy) to which the *Akhbārī*s accused the Uṣūlī jurists of adhering.[106]
6. *Akhbārī*s held that their conception of conclusive knowledge was based on *'ilm al-'āddī* (ordinary knowledge), acquired by simple belief in the truth found in what is attributed to the infallible Imams, and verified by the individual's unrestrained faith in the Imams.[107] This new notion—*'ilm al-'āddī*—was antithetical to what they had advocated as requirement of conclusiveness. For *Uṣūlī*s, however, ordinary knowledge is rational knowledge accompanied by conscientious assurance as to the absence of contradictory elements. Such knowledge complies with the facts and is free from doubts.[108]
7. *Uṣūlī*s argued that except in rare occasions it is impossible to prove all the details and conditions of mandatory duties from within the Text.[109]

For Bihbahānī and other *Uṣūlī*s only *ẓann khāṣṣ* (a specified supposition), which can be substantiated by specific conclusive evidence, derived from rational or textual indicators, is a valid suppositional knowledge.[110] Thus, he concluded:

> Except in rare occasions, the door to conclusive knowledge is closed and, therefore, the exclusive path to knowledge, in the majority of occasions, is through supposition. In order to facilitate the path, we need to presume that the dispersed findings found in the suppositional outcomes of rules of logic and jurisprudence, or what could be achieved from linguistic, philological and grammatical treatment of religious rules, are a unified structure of knowledge, and assume its religious validity.[111]

Uṣūlī Doctrine of Reason

Uṣūlī jurists perceived rational approach to the religious rules, methodologically and substantively, as a fundamentally valid path in the discovery of the rule that was supported by the religion itself.[112] In one of his arguments on the power and capacity of rational arguments, Qummī, also famous as Ṣāḥib al-Qawānīn,[113] has said:

> Those who refuse to believe in the strength of rational findings must know that reason can achieve much deeper than they imagine. It is inferred from the reports of Imams on *'aql* that there is reward or punishment awaited, in the hereafter, for rational findings. According to one of those reports, "Reason is the closest companion to God, and can earn you the heaven." Getting to paradise by the means of reason is the prize for those who carry out the [type of] deeds that are rationally praised.[114]

The preliminary arguments on the definition and methodological tenets of the role of reason revolve around the following premises:

1. Absolute independence: whether or not reason is an independent source of law. In other words, does reason have the same status, as the Qur'an or the Sunnah? And if one fails to act in accordance with the rule of reason, has he refused to perform the rule of Law?
2. Hierarchy of the sources: should reason come after the exhaustion of the primary sources? Or can it be applied before them?
3. Scope of application: at issue is whether or not reason is only a path toward recognizing the validity of the Text-based religious rule. In other words, is it religion's rule that reason should lead us to? It is so held that the proper scope of application of reason is where there is no valid rule in the Text.

At the early stages of the formation of rationalist discourse in Shīʿī law, as discussed by Mufīd, reason was perceived as a method and path for reaching the rule of religion, that is, rules known by the Text. Later, reason could be viewed as one of the sources of law if other sources had not introduced the rule. Al-Muḥaqqiq divided the indicators of rule into two major categories: the rules that are premised by a *khiṭāb* and the ones that are independent and devoid of the need to the Divine pronouncements, that is, *mustaqillāt al-ʿaqlīyya*. By the requirements of the presumption of absence of obligation—as held by jurists such as ʿAllāma—it became apparent that in the absence of a Text-based rule, the issue of non-liability or incumbency of the duty is left to determination of reason. Where the rule has not reached the duty-bound individual, based on the prohibition of punishment for unstated laws, reason should also release the individual's burden of the charge of duty. To summarize, the rationalist jurists believed in instances of the sole application of reason, as in the equity-oriented issues and occasions of absence or silence or vagueness or inapplicability of the rule. In this case, the relevant rules found in the Text were considered ancillary to reason, not constitutive. It was necessary for the rationalist jurists to develop a substantive conceptual theory that would build the foundations for congruency and compliance between the Divine law and the law of reason. With this introduction, the following three layers of the *Uṣūlīs*' doctrine of *ʿaql* can be analyzed: (1) *maṣlaḥa* and *mafsada*, (2) *ḥusn* and *qubḥ*, and (3) *qāʿidat al-mulāzama*.

Dialectics of Rule, *Maṣlaḥa* (Benefit), and *Mafsada* (Detriment)

Primarily, Shīʿī rationalist jurists believe in the absence of imprecise and disproportionate elements in both the divine rules and consequent duties emanating from them. In other words, the divine rules are devoid of *jazāf* (arbitrary manner of haphazard or random determinations).[115] These jurists also believe in the existence of an imperative characteristic, as a rationally independent requirement, which manifests the necessarily prescriptive or dispositive-proscriptive nature of acts. A careful analysis of these characteristics, the *Uṣūlī* jurists argue, sets the standards of the logic of legislation of rules. Notwithstanding the divine rules, that analysis is based on exertion of the rational benefit or detriment that derives from the nature of mandated or prohibited act and the way that it affects man's well-being in this world or in the Hereafter. To rationalist jurists, this approach amounts to subordination of any rule, either Divine or man-made, to such inherent characteristic, that is, *maṣlaḥa* (benefit) or *mafsada* (detriment). Depending on the nature of the benefit or detriment in the act, the relevant rule is reflected in one of the five forms, famously known as *al-aḥkām al-khamsa al-taklīfiyya*:

1. When there is *maṣlaḥat mulzima* (an inherently necessary benefit) in performing the act, it is a *taklīf wājib* (mandatory duty).
2. When there is *mafsada mulzima* (a necessary detriment) in the act, its performance is *ḥarām* (prohibited).
3. If there is *maṣlaḥat ghhayr mulzima*, that is, a benefit in the act that does not inherently necessitate its performance, the rule for the act is *istiḥbāb* (encouragement).
4. When there is *mafsada ghayr mulzima*, that is, the act is detrimental, but not because of its inherently dispositive nature, the rule for the act is *kirāha* (discouragement).
5. And finally, the rule for an act that is indifferent as to a benefit or detriment is *ibāḥa* (permittedness).

Since there is no arbitrariness in devising the rules, there must exist rational grounds, in a textually valid rule, by which one can discern why a mandated act is beneficial and whose performance is inherently necessary, or why a prohibited one is detrimental, performance of which should definitively be rejected. The underpinning presumption is that the clarity in certainly known valid rules, especially the indisputable mandatory and prohibited ones, can assist the jurist to establish conclusive rational inferences as to both the existence and nature of benefit or detriment in their subject matter acts. Alternatively, if by independent rational analyses, one recognizes the benefit or detriment of an act, then one can independently conclude the mandatory or prohibitive nature of its rule. *Uṣūlī* jurists usually employ logical rules to make those inferences: by an inductive method, technically called *kashf innī*, they attempt to determine the nature of the act from a valid rule. By a deductive method, technically called *kashf limmī*, they draw conclusions about the nature of the rule from rationally independent analysis of the characteristics of acts.[116]

Contrary to this, the *Ash'arī* jurists argue on the absence of inherent benefit or detriment in an act. The nature of an act depends on the rule that has been ordained by the Divine, and it is possible for God to change the rule and require performance of an act that is detrimental. This will amount to transformation of the nature of the act from being *dhu al-mafsada* (detrimental) to a *dhu al-maṣlaḥa* (beneficial), or vice versa. Rationalist jurists rejected this proposition, originally on theological grounds. 'Allāma found this and similar propositions defective because they require a circular reasoning. In pertinent arguments against *Ash'arī* rejection of reason's capability to determine mandatory duty of knowing God, 'Allāma wrote:

> Ash'arites hold that the mandate of knowing God derives from the revelation, not from reason. Such proposition requires a circular reasoning that is necessarily void, because it makes us stop the knowledge of the obligation (*ījāb*) at the knowledge of obligating (*mujib*). Certainly, no knowledge is acquired from mere *al-i'tibārāt* (the notional capacities). We will know about the necessity, [but] we will not know that it is mandatory. Therefore, knowledge from what is obligating will not lead us to what the obligation is, and that requires a circular reasoning.[117]

To elaborate on what is meant by circular reasoning, an *Uṣūlī* jurist may argue that there is a duty to acquire knowledge about God. When found mandatory by God's rule, it will amount to the interference of God's will on its enforcement. Differentiating between the nature of an act and duty, 'Allāma makes further argument that a Divine Interference transforms the duty of knowing God into something that prerequisites compliance. Such transformed duty would be unbearable for someone who has not yet acquired knowledge about God. Not only will it make the individual comply with a mandatory duty, but it will also restrict the ways in which one may acquire knowledge about what should be in compliance with the mandated duty.[118] Furthermore, notional assumptions only provide grounds for more legal arguments. They do not necessarily establish a valid reasoning. Knowledge about an obligation is different from knowing what the obligating factors are. If one is obligated to undertake the charge of performing an act, it is because there is a rationally recognizable congruence between the benefit or detriment embedded in the act with its mandate or prohibition, not because we can argue whether or not God will possibly take the unusual step of transforming a rationally verifiable rule, stemming from the inherent characteristic of the nature of its subject matter act, to an unverifiable rule that is in conflict with such natural characteristic, recognized by rational minds. Similar reasoning can be employed in responding to Ash'arites' rejection of reason's capability to determine the nature of an act. For Shī'ī *Uṣūlīs*, the aforementioned *Ash'arī* proposition constitutes an incomplete truth because it fails to provide a cause for the act of legislation and an effect for its outcome. It also ignores the critically important absence of *jazāf* (arbitrariness and disproportional factor) in the Divine rulings. Performance of an act is ruled to be mandatory or prohibited because the Legislator, prior to His Ruling, has determined its inherent benefit or detriment. Furthermore, the revelation is God's Gifts (*luṭf*) to the realm of human intellect. While the Messengers of God are His external source for the individual's access to the Truth, the human intellect is the other equally reliable, though internal, source for that matter.[119] In its pristine condition, man's *fiṭrah* (natural disposition) functions in complete harmony with God and there is no conflict between Divine Rules and rational articulations. *Fiṭrah* is man's rational articulation of the truth and correctness by which he concludes obedience to God. The evil nature of oppression and goodness of justice and many other facts and rules, be it prior to or after their ordainment, are part and parcel of Divine Laws.[120] It is due to moral vices and blemishes as well as negative social influences—emanated from injustices created by the human being himself—that such pristine nature deviates from its "straight path."[121] If God had not sent His Messengers for the guidance of human beings, man himself would still be able to act—as God may have wanted him—by employing his endowed faculties of intellect and choice, and obtain well-being,[122] had he not been subject to the loss of his nature.[123] Rules of ethics in the revelation are intended to revive and purge the human nature from such blemishes. Thus, Divine Revelation is Divine's grace upon man's rational capability of articulating the benefits and detriments.

Rational Treatment of *Ḥusn* (Beauty) and *Qubḥ* (Ugliness)

Another equally important argument in support of independent rational proof is the *Uṣūlī* approach to the concepts of *ḥusn* and *qubḥ*. Although it is reasonably predictable to presume and conclude that, in its rationalist context, every benefit is beautiful and every detriment ugly,[124] these concepts have also been subject to theological debates by two powerful jurisprudential doctrines in the Islamic law, that is, *Uṣūlī* rationalism and *Ash'arīyya*.

Similar to their arguments on benefit and detriment, Ash'arites have held that there is no inherent reality or reference to the Truth in the form of beauty or ugliness of objects or acts.[125] Therefore, similar to benefit or detriment, reason is unable to render an act evil or good unless there is a Divine Rule to that effect.[126] According to their argument, there is no beauty or ugliness beyond what has been determined by God: whatever the Legislator has ruled to be mandatory, it is good and vice versa. It is also within the Divine's power to transform the nature and characteristic of the act from one to the other.[127] *Uṣūlīs* have made several counterarguments against the Ash'arites' claims. One of them is based on the rejection of predestinarianism in *Uṣūlī* theology. Relying on previous Shī'ī theologians' opinions, Anṣārī wrote: "The *Ash'arī* denial of beauty and ugliness is based on belief in the existence of predestination in the Divine actions. The *'Adliyya*'s response is that the way that Ash'arites deny ugliness will not change or refute the free will, nor will it affect the correlation between the rational and religious rules."[128] Notwithstanding the divine rule, *Uṣūlī*s argue that acts and objects possess inherent real values: what is *ḥasan* (good) should be good by its nature and what is *qabīḥ* (ugly) should be inherently evil. It is based on such inherent value and nature that the Legislator commands the mandate of good deeds, and prohibits the evil ones.[129] Furthermore, the concepts of beauty and ugliness have three different layers of definition. First, sometimes they connote what elevates and perfects *nafs* (the soul, the moral self) of the human being, which is a *ḥasan*. What causes its downfalls and imperfections is also a *qabīḥ*.[130] Second, what is in harmony with the moral self of the human being and provides his serenity is beautiful and good, and what causes its dissension and provides discord and conflict of the self and soul is ugly and evil.[131] Third, any act that the rational minds judge on its goodness and praise its doer is good, and what they judge to be forbidden and blame its doer is ugly and evil.[132] For *Uṣūlī*s, generally abstract concepts of beauty or ugliness were not separated from their concrete specified reality as was reflected in society. The path to determination of the inherent nature of acts and their values should also pass through the collectivity of the rational minds' judgment. In fact, they hold the final locus of reality of beauty or ugliness, and good or evil, to be the mind of rational individuals. It is by their judgment, in the majority of issues and cases, that performance of an act is to be commanded or prohibited. The latter measure was raised in the philosophical arguments of reason, developed by Muslim philosophers, in the relation between *'aql al-naẓarī* (speculative intelligence) and *'aql al-'amalī* (practical reason).

'Aql al-Naẓarī (Speculative Intelligence) and *'Aql al-'Amalī* (Practical Reason)

For *Uṣūlī*s, beauty or ugliness is a matter of recognition. Prior to mandating or prohibiting the performance of an act, it is required to determine whether or not the act elevates the soul or is in harmony with the moral self. In the process of rational engagement (*mudrak al-'aql*), rational people need to acquire the knowledge required for responding to questions such as what elevates the souls, and what causes its downfall? *Uṣūlī*s argue that human intellect is philosophically endowed, solely with the capacity of *idrāk* (perception), and thus, unable to command or prohibit. However, after articulation of answers, it is in the social acceptance of such perception—practiced by the rational people—that rational outcomes can be translated to legal rules. In fact, when they talk about *ḥukm al-'aql* (rule of reason), they mean that practical perception. Thus, the process of recognition of good or evil should be divided into two categories: First, whether the act in question conforms to harmony and advancement of moral self, including rules of religion, second, whether such conformity or nonconformity meets the social criteria of acceptability and is followed by rational people's praise or blame. Speculative reason deals with the first issue, where the rational perception of harmony and advancement is examined by *ārā' al-maḥmūda* (technically means maxims of wisdom that are shared between God and man).[133] The second issue is examined by *'aql al-'amalī*, which is the reflection of that shared wisdom in the practical application of reason in society, where a commonly upheld judgment on the mandatory or prohibitory nature of acts is rendered.

*Uṣūlī*s believe there is congruity between *sīra al-'uqalā'/binā' al-'uqalā'* (rational people's course of action or judgment) and what is ordained by God. They hold that the Ash'arites' "denial of the existence of beauty or ugliness, beyond what has been declared by God" lacks precision: if the issue is whether or not there is an external and physical manifestation of truth in what elevates the soul or what is in harmony with the moral self, the answer is in the negative. Except for rational apprehension of the concepts in its social context, there is no evidence of external truth of evil and good in the proposition: "Repression is evil, and justice is good." But if the issue is whether or not perception of beauty or ugliness exists, the answer is strongly positive. There is ample evidence of a recognized perception of good and evil in the mind and practice of rational individuals in every social setting. Therefore, the existence of beauty or ugliness is a reality that originates from the socially gained truth of those acts that are in harmony with the self or elevate the soul. When rational minds discover the good and evil, there is no reason to believe that God would reject the validity and credibility of their findings and ordain an antithetical rule.[134] Not only would an antithetical order amount to logical and rational contradictions in the general plan of man's creation, but it will also be against *irādat al-takwīnīyya* (the Divine's Will of creation) of *fiṭrah* (natural disposition to affinity to God) in human beings, which is supposed to be in harmony with God, and reach the final conclusion of His obedience by employment of reason. Otherwise, it would mean that God has created a device in human being that is essentially in conflict with its purpose. To hold such contradiction valid would be equal to coercion, which is incongruent with what has been rejected in the Qur'an, namely burdening the soul with unbearable duties.[135] An antithetical rule will also contradict *irādat al-tashrī'īyya* (Divine's Will of legislation) because, borrowing an *Uṣūlī* expression, God is *Ra'īs al-'uqalā'* (Epitome of reason/Ultimate Rational Mind). Therefore, it would be logically impossible for God to command what is contrary to rationality or to demand what is inconsistent with the findings of rational minds.[136]

Rule of Correlation between Rational and Religion's Rules

One of the main *Uṣūlī* methodological postulations of the relation between reason and revelation is reflected in Shīʿī *uṣūl al-fiqh* as: "whatever is ordered by reason is also ordered by religion, and whatever is ordered by religion is also ordered by reason."[137] Anṣārī has said: "The truth is that there is a real correlation between rational rule and rule of Shari'ah, and our predecessors have strongly supported it... What is meant from *mulāzama* (correlation) is that the Divine rule would be proven by rational rule, and the rational rule is a proof for the Divine rule."[138] This bipartite principle,[139] famously known as *qā'idat al-mulāzama* or rule of correlation, is normal conclusion of the arguments on benefit or detriment and beauty or ugliness.[140] When the commonly held maxims of wisdom are at issue, such as evilness of oppression and goodness of justice, there is no tension in congruity between the rational articulation of a rule and the Divine ordainment, because the Divine rule has not established or constituted a new rule. One measure of determination of congruity between the divine rules and rational rules, offered by *Uṣūlī* jurists, is dividing them into *aḥkām al-ta'sīsiyya* (constitutive rules) and *aḥkām al-imḍā'īyya* (ratified rules).[141] A constitutive rule is a rule that has established an unprecedented rule, such as prohibition of consuming wine or usury. A ratified rule is a rule that has signed off the existing applicable rule, such as fasting and prayers that were ruled by monotheist religions prior to Islam, though different in performance, or permissibility of many of the customary conventions in trade and contractual relations. It is held that the constitutive rules are to be followed because reasonable individuals can find essential benefits in them. Ratified rules are also held to be the signs of Legislator's agreement with what the rational persons have already established, either by obedience to previous religions or by their own findings.[142] The issue, however, is on the nature of authority exerted from Divine Commands.[143] More precisely laid out, it is believed that the authoritative nature of Divine Commands on the mandate or prohibition of acts is divided into two categories: some of them emanate from God's Sovereignty, technically known as *awāmir mawlawī*, and some are based on His Guidance, known as *awāmir irshādī*. A sovereignty-based command is usually defined by its nature as follows:

> A true representation and demand, which is derived from the existing benefit in its subject matter. A command whose obedience or denial is rationally

held to be rewarded or punished, like ordering prayers and fasting and whatever which is the result of obeying God. Sovereignty Command intends to acquire two objectives: (1) fulfilling the Divine intention of commanding, that is, the individual's reach to the existing benefits of prayers and fasting, and (2) abidance, based on the extent of the individual's rational finding on entitlement to reward or punishment.[144]

On the other hand,

a guiding command is a formal order [and not true demand and command as postulated in sovereignty-based commands], which when precisely analyzed will inform [the rational people] and guide them to the benefit of an act that every rational person and social custom would [independently and similarly] agree on its benefit and would not allow its dissolution.[145]

According to Mishkīnī, there are four measures for determining a guiding command:

1. When reason can independently recognize the subject of the command, that is, there is a rational argument that, in the absence of Divine's Utterance of command, provides similarity between the rule of reason and Divine Guidance.
2. When it can be established that the independent utterance of Legislator conforms to previous apprehension of reason. In other words, one can conclude by rational arguments that reason, prior to revelation, had already established what has been informed later by revelation.
3. When in the process of determination, one encounters a rational conflict, such as circular reasoning, the command at issue is a sovereignty one. Otherwise, it is a guiding one.
4. When a rational person would recommend the same conclusion that is imparted from the command in question.[146]

The methods of determination of sovereignty or guiding commands can also be approached by the concept of reward and punishment. Another scholar has offered the following:

If there is a required benefit or dispositive prohibition in a command, because of which an incumbency or refrain from its performance is ordered, and there is a reward or punishment for each of them, the command is a sovereignty order. Otherwise, the command is a guiding order. In other words, a guiding command is nothing more than encouraging the individual to comply with the required benefit [which is found in a reason-based prescription of the command] or dispositive detriment [which is found in a reason-based proscription of the command].[147]

In general, rationalist jurists hold that the rules for devotional duties are sovereignty commands, because such duties do not need to be bolstered by justified rational reasoning. Every other rule, however, is a guiding one.[148] The nature of authority in a sovereignty command requires faith-based obedience and is devoid of further need to rational articulation.[149] On the other hand, the nature of authority in a guiding rule is to remind the faithful of their need to perform acts that are more in tune with the purpose of their creation and final well-being.[150] One regularly discussed example is the Qur'anic verse that states, "O you, who believe, obey God and the Prophet and those in authority among you."[151] Grammatically, this verse is an imperative sentence. The question is whether or not the rule mentioned in the verse is also imperative. In other words, has the rule derived from Divine's Sovereignty or Divine's Guidance? If this command would not have been mentioned in the Qur'an, would derivation of its purpose be out of the reach of rational people? The majority of jurists have held that this verse is referring to a guiding command because rational persons would concur on the necessity of obedience to God and His Messenger and those who are their exemplary representatives.[152] The question is: Is there any difference between what God ordains and what the rational minds would find through their rational investigation of the rule? *Uṣūlī*s hold that there is none.[153] They argue that the Divine is the most rational being and will not issue a rule that is in conflict with other rational agents' findings.[154] They also believe that not only should rational persons not deviate from such Divine rules, but every rational rule is also a Divine rule. In other words, due to common grounds upon which rational persons found their rules and the Divine ordains His Rules, namely the requirement of benefit or detriment, there is no lack of harmony and congruence between the two.

Based on the *Uṣūlī* jurists' arguments, the following conclusions can be drawn: First, although reason is not able to uncover all the details of the Sacred and Truth, where the correlation of the rational rule and religion's rule is established, rational evidence is a powerful basis upon which a jurist can make a compelling case for the truth and correctness of his finding and discovery of Divine Law. Arguments for existence of such capability for reason are supported by the Qur'an, valid Prophetic Sunnah, and the infallible Imams' reports.

Second, rational people are generally prohibited from applying *qīyās* (analogy) except when there is a textual basis for their analogical reasoning or *qīyās manṣūṣ al-ʿilla*, and rendering of discretionary opinions (technically known as *istiḥsān*): an arbitrary finding that is not based on the beauty-ugliness and benefit-detriment precepts that amount to formation of rational praise-blame and reward-punishment results.

Third, for the following reasons the scope of applicability of the Prophetic Sunnah and traditions/reports attributed to the infallible Imams is restricted to limited occasions and issues: (1) they are *mashkūk al-sanad* (not corroborated by a reliable chain of transmitters), and (2) *ẓannī al-dalāla* (the scope of their applicability is unclear).

Therefore, our advanced rational arguments—that is, *ẓann khāṣṣ* (specified suppositional knowledge)—of the primary imparts of the valid texts in addition to our apprehension of *wāqiʿ amr* (the reality of rule), derived from the most reachable and closest rules to the core of Revelation,[155] are valid and can be considered as a source of law.[156]

Chapter 2

Authority: Theories, Models, Discords

Imāmah and Universal Authority of the Imam

The issue of political power and leadership has been one of the key concepts in Shīʿī theology and jurisprudence, which is mainly reflected in the doctrine of *Imāmah* (leadership).[1] The origins of Imāmah go back to the historical events during the life and immediate aftermath of the Prophet Muhammad's death. At the core of Shīʿī theological doctrine is that the right to succeed the Prophet in the leadership of Muslim community belonged to *Ahl al-Bayt* (the House of the Prophet), meaning the members of the Prophet's family.[2] Historically, only one member of the Prophet's house, that is, the first Shīʿī Imam Ali ibn Abī Ṭālib (d. 40/660–661), was able to take the reign as the fourth Rightly Guided caliph. Shiites also believe that deviation of Umayyad and Abbasid rulers by transforming the Islamic model of leadership (caliphate/Imamite) to kingship (*ṭawāghīyya/salṭana/mulūkīyya*) is largely responsible for the Shīʿī Imams' deprivation of their right to leadership.[3] Thus, according to the Shiites, the Muslim community continued to suffer from the lack of justice in the society that they deserved to live in—a society that was to be based heavily on Qur'anic teachings of just rule as had been perfectly practiced by the Prophet and Imam Ali.

Shīʿī rationalist jurists developed the underpinning theological arguments for the necessity of the existence of an *Imam* as the proof of God. According to Mufīd, "the twelve Shīʿī Imams were the vicegerents of the Prophet responsible for verification of the applicable Shari'ah rules governing the legal issues of Muslims; to put in operation of the Divine Rights (*Ḥudūd Allah*); defending the Rules of *Sharāyi'* (that is, every monotheistic Law); and guiding the human beings."[4] This theory is heavily founded on the concept of *taklīf* (duty), since the institution of the Imam is devised to provide the faithful with the right teachings about their *maṣāliḥ* (benefits, pl. of *maṣlaḥa*), and when the duties charged upon the individuals do exist, it is necessary for God to apply His Grace (*luṭf*)[5] by appointing their *Imams* (leaders).[6] *Imāmah* was characterized by "*rīyāsatun 'āmma fī umūr al-dunyā wa al-dīn li shakhṣin min al-ashkhāṣ nīyābatan 'an al-Nabī*"[7] or "universal authority in the things of religion and the world to some person and derives from the Prophet."[8] To this end, an Imam is not just an interpreter of the Qur'an or the Prophetic Sunnah, he is also the spiritual leader of the community of the faithful whose commands are binding; obedience to him is presumed.[9] According to the Shī'ī doctrine of Imāmah, the most important reasons for the legitimacy of the Imams' right to the spiritual leadership were their divinely devised capacities of *'iṣma*[10] (infallibility, impeccability, immunity from committing sin) and *'ilm*, that is, comprehensive knowledge of Law. The main instrument by which an Imam could be verified was the existence of a specific designation (*naṣṣ*) for their appointment in the form of the previous Imam's *waṣīyya* (testament).[11] It is so argued that the absence of immunity from making mistakes and the commission of sin would amount to an illogical necessity of circular reasoning in any of the following circumstances:

> (a) appointing an Imam is required because he is supposed to determine other individuals' faults, (b) that the Imam is the protector of Shari'ah, and there is no indicator in the Book or Sunnah or the consensus of Muslims that would allow the Imam to have less than comprehensive knowledge on all the detailed rules (*iḥāṭatihu bi jamī' al-aḥkām al-tafṣīlīyya*), (c) if he makes a mistake, it would be mandatory to reject his obedience, (d) if he commits a sin, it would be against the rationale of appointing an Imam, (e) if he commits a sin, then comes the requirement of rendering him *aqall darajat min al-'awām* (the least of the laity) whereas his faculty of reasoning and knowledge of God and what is rewarded and punished is so assumed to be the most extensive, and commission of sins is what the least of the laity do.[12]

According to Shiites' strongly held belief, the Imams have acquired their *'ilm* or comprehensive knowledge by full reception of the Prophet's teachings on the Qur'an.[13] They are "the treasurers of the knowledge."[14] So, the Divine, based on His Grace, has intended to educate them with what is necessary in leadership.[15] They are also "the most learned"; upon them "the Knowledge has been conferred."[16] They have inherited the knowledge from the Prophet,[17] and "possess the Books that have never been available to the lay people or other religious leaders."[18] This is why they are God's proof on Earth.[19] Such capacities by and large provided the Imams with intertwined authority for furthering the Muslim community's knowledge of the divine laws by skillful mastery in discovering the right solutions for legal issues of any kind, and thus, the religious leadership—in the sense of guiding human beings in their temporal and otherworldly affairs—of the Muslim community.[20] The threshold issue was whether the Imams' religious leadership amounted to their duty of taking the office of *amr* (political rule) or not. As mentioned before, Shiites believe that the right to rule was concomitant to the spiritual authority that belonged to the members of the House of Prophet, that is, the Shīʿī Imams. As Modarressi has extensively discussed, both historical events throughout the lives of the Imams and valid traditions correctly transmitted from them firmly establish the prevailing Shīʿī belief that the charge of political and religious rule after the occultation of the last Imam—that is, *Qā'im* (the Rising Imam, also known as the Awaited Imam and or the Hidden Imam)—is left to him whose time of reappearance is not known to the Shiites.[21] Therefore, not only is the theory of *Imāmah* in Shīʿī jurisprudence heavily founded upon religious authority, but also absolute legitimacy of the political rule exclusively and unequivocally belongs to the last Imam.[22]

Religious Authority vs Political Authority

Based on the highly respected status of the Imam and his exclusive authority to lead, Shīʿī jurists held an opinion that rendered every other ruler *jā'ir* (oppressor, usurper, unjust, illegitimate).[23] This should not suggest that the Shiites did not believe in the existential necessity of government in society. On the other hand, the idea of a non-Imam "just sultan" or "just ruler" who would practically assume political power in the time of the Hidden Imam's occultation—mainly in the form of a Shīʿī king—was not completely rejected. Modarressi argues that the concept of *al-sulṭān al-ʿādil* (just ruler) mentioned by some jurists meant "the Imam or his deputy" or "pious *faqīh*."[24] He does not hesitate to clarify the fact, and introduce the sources, that in the earlier sources where the term "just ruler" has been mentioned, the jurists had made Imam-based qualifications and restrictions such as "being appointed by God" or "infallible" or the requirement of the Imam's presence, for such just ruler's legitimacy.[25] In other words, the sense of oppression behind the term *jā'ir* should be perceived as an expression of the usurpation of the Hidden Imam's authority, whose practical hold on power could not be determined for a definite period of time but who at the same time enjoyed the unquestionable right to rule inherently.[26] In this context, given the historical fact of the Shiites' long subordination to non-Shīʿī rulers under the reign of either the Sunni caliphate or non-Muslims, by establishing a stable Shīʿī government, juristic justification of the Shīʿī sultan's rule was the natural outcome of the need for security and the physical survival of the polity. The degree to which such justifications could attach to or deviate from the ideal theory of Imāmah, and thus provide or not provide the so-called just sultan with one or another form of legitimacy, however, was subject to controversial debates. In general, as Modarressi reports, during the first Shīʿī government, that is, the Safavid dynasty (1502–1722), some jurists developed the theory of *dawlat al-ḥaqq* (true rule) by which obedience to such a government was found to be obligatory.[27] Later, with the rise of the Qājār kings to power (1794–1925), some other jurists defended the rule of kings by ascribing the Qur'anic concept of *ulu 'l-amr* (holder of the rule)[28] to them.[29] Whereas "traditionally . . . all Shīʿī scholars have restricted the title *ulu 'l-amr* to the Imams, (such) new interpretation appeared to be a breach of consensus and against the Shīʿī doctrine."[30]

Despite the genuine strength and clarity of the authoritative doctrine of Imāmah, Shīʿī jurists have always been concerned about the lawfulness of accepting and holding office under a non-Imam ruler. While it was obvious that any other ruler would never attain this state of legitimacy, the jurists found it permissible for a Shiite to work for a non-Imamite government only in an emergency, when one is threatened with harm or hardship. He could also accept the job as long as such cooperation enhanced other Shiites' ease of life under non-Shīʿī rule.[31] The issue, thus, was whether similar restrictions apply to working for a Shīʿī sultan or not. Power-oriented juristic discourses devised quasi-legitimacy for the Shīʿī sultan, coupled with an intermediary role for a competent mujtahid as a means of compensating for the sultan's lack of required knowledge of the Shari'ah and tendency to commit sins. To this effect, al-Karakī (d. 940/1534)[32] set a practical example. While never recognizing the Safavid king as a legitimate deputy of the Imam, al-Karakī was the official holder of "religious authority" in contrast to the "political power" of the king. Whether al-Karakī, at the time, believed that the legitimacy of his authority derived from the king is heavily disputable. Nevertheless, in practice, he applied his authority

> to prohibit debauchery and punish the offenders, abrogate the laws conflicting with the Shari'ah, purge (the society) from sins and all immoral conducts prohibited by religion (like drinking and sale of wine or gambling), execute the religious punishments, public safeguarding of mandatory religious rituals and Friday Prayers and fasting and teachings about the

> Imams' lives, punishment of criminals, and (finally) making arrangements for the laity's religious education.[33]

Although this excerpt contains some repetitious phrases, it is clear that for al-Karakī, religious authority included a wide range of issues from crimes to education. The important point, however, seems to be that he did not consider involvement in politics to be one of his duties. He also provided the king with the most sophisticated and authoritative juristic opinions about the daily affairs of the sultanate.[34] It seems that al-Karakī restricted the scope of the just king's rule to two major qualifications: (i) the division and sharing of the Hidden Imam's two-tiered authorities—that is, religious authority and political authority—wherein religious authority could be allocated to the jurists; and (ii) with regards to all layers of the political authority, only enforcement of the jurists' religious authority could be left to the kings.[35] By this design, it seems that *wilāyat al-amr* (the right to rule), or political authority, was preserved for the Hidden Imam. On the issue of whether a competent jurist could succeed the Imam in religious authority, al-Karakī's response was in the affirmative. In support of his opinion, al-Karakī invoked those Shīʿī reports in which it was attributed to the Imams to have ordered the Shiites to refer their legal disputes to a Shīʿī judge. By such invocation, he not only justified working with a non-Imam Shiite king, but also consolidated the jurist's authority, as the deputy of the Imam, on a wide range of important social matters.[36] On the other hand, the political impact of al-Karakī's discourse was not limited to juristic attempts at assisting in the stabilization of a newly established Shīʿī kingdom. It went on to renew and redefine the very subject of dividing power between authority to determine the law—which belonged to the Shīʿī jurists—and the requirement of abiding to it—which was the duty of the ruler/king and the people. In this context, al-Karakī's discourse would amount to an expansion of the concept of law, institutionalizing the superior authority of the jurist above the king, as well as the religious entrenchment of political authority. This authority so deeply relied on religious delineation—under the necessity of discovering Shari'ah rules—that it too could encompass political rule. The idea of the division of religious and political authority in the relationship between the jurists and the caliphs/kings was hardly new to the long history of other Muslim governments.[37] The novelty, however, was in theorizing it in a Shīʿī state and including political rule within the religious power of a non-Imam. To al-Karakī, not only could such division of authority not compromise the original and doctrinal lack of legitimacy of a non-Imam ruler,[38] but even the religious authority of the competent jurist—which in his language came to be known as the *Mujtahid al-Zamān* (mujtahid of the time)—was charged with limits in purely religious issues. In other words, he strictly preserved the Imam's religious rule in the areas of law that had already been established as immutable, mandatory, or prohibitory rules. This was evident in his treatment of the issue of Friday Prayer, which included a juristic-political dilemma and theoretical disagreement. To elaborate more, I need to explain that Friday Prayer is a type of congregational prayer that is supposed to be performed on "the day of assembly," or Friday, and differs from the regular five daily prayers in both its introductory rituals and its performance. It is also presumed that in a Friday Prayer, the leader of prayers should inform, educate, and discuss the most important issues related to all Muslims, including political and social ones. Thus, the leader of prayer should be either the Imam himself, or one of the most knowledgeable Muslims of each given time and place who has the Imam's prior *idhn* (permission) and *naṣb* (appointment). For Shīʿī jurists, the question has been whether the authority for granting permission to perform the Friday Prayer in the time of the occultation of the Imam should be reserved and restricted to the life and presence of the Imam, or whether it belongs to the transferable authorities of the Imam—like the adjudication of legal disputes—in which case it could be granted by the Imam's deputy. This issue, for the most part, was responsible for an extensive debate and disagreement among the Shīʿī jurists as to the nature of performing the Friday Prayer, and whether it was *wājib ʿaynī* (individually mandatory) or *wājib takhyīrī* (optionally mandatory) or *ḥurmat* (prohibition).[39] In this regard, al-Karakī, long before undertaking his state-sponsored official religious authority, had taken a sophisticated position and said:

> Our Imami jurists, generation by generation after the time of presence [of Imams] until now, have rejected (*intifāʾ*) the performance of the Friday Prayer in the time of occultation [of the last Imam] to be as every individual's mandatory duty (*wujūb al-ʿaynī*)[40] ... and its secret is that because formation of an assembly of sufficient individuals in one place for the performance of the Friday Prayer—as is necessary in all cities—depends on their *al-tanāzuʿ wa al-tajādhub* (contention and attraction), thus *with the absence of the presence of Imam and [the absence of] effectiveness of his rules*, such assembly is very likely to transform to an incentive for sedition and mischief. Thus it is not appropriate to rule its performance absolutely mandatory[41] ... to rule the Friday Prayer mandatory is qualified to the [presence of the] *al-sulṭān al-ʿādil* (just sultan),[42] that is the Imam, may peace be upon him, or his deputy in general[43] ... In the time of occultation, by consensus, its *al-wujūb al-ḥatmī* (conclusive necessity) is rejected [*emphasis mine*].[44]

The limits of jurist's deputyship in religious authority are manifested in three major points in this opinion:

1. The Shiite king—the so-called holder of the political authority—was not a "deputy in general" of the Imam; therefore, the discussion on the Friday Prayer (whether it is to be mandatory or not) is a purely religious issue.
2. To al-Karakī, the one who could either determine the existence or inexistence of the jurists' consensus or bear the title of *nā'ib 'āmm* (the general deputy of the Imam) is exclusively *al-faqīh al-'adl al-Imāmī al-jāmi' al-sharā'it* (the fully competent just Twelver Shī'ī jurist) who meets all the necessary qualifications of *ijtihād*.[45]
3. When there is not enough evidence to prove the mandate of the acts in question, the jurist has to render them recommendatory and not individually mandatory.[46]

Accordingly, it was necessary for the Shī'ī jurists—as "deputies in general" of the Imam—to have reached *ijmā'* (consensus: as an indicator of the proof of the mandated duty) on the details of the mandatory nature of rules and their subject matter acts in order to render the act conclusively mandatory. Otherwise, in the absence of such a mutual meeting of minds, the religious authority is limited to the sole determination of inconclusive mandatory rules of the deputy of the Imam. In other words, according to al-Karakī, such determination can remedy the absence of consensus only where there is doubt as to the existence of a conclusively mandated individual duty. The logical inference of the arguments is that the application of the deputy's authority is restricted to either of two occasions:

1. The absence of conclusive mandatory duty, that is, the deputy should not apply his authority when there is no doubt as to existence of a mandatory duty.
2. The absence of the jurists' consensus on the details of a mandatory rule, that is, the deputy should not apply his authority when there is such consensus.

In the case of Friday Prayer, there is consensus as to the requirement of the Imam's *idhn* (permission) as a prerequisite to the act's mandate so that the jurist is not allowed to argue against the rule to be nonmandatory. Thus, the question is whether the deputy has the authority to issue the permission on the Imam's behalf or not. Al-Karakī's response is a qualified yes. According to him, *li anna l'-faqīh manṣūb min qibalihim ḥākiman fī jamīʿ al-umūr al-sharʿīyya* (the deputy, generally, has authority to do so in all religious matters).[47] However, since there is also another consensus among the jurists in that the Shiite society, in the absence of their Imam, is *mathār al-sharr wa al-fasād* (vulnerable to sedition and mischief),[48] ruling the act individually mandatory *lazima al-taklīf bi mā lā yuṭāq* (requires burdening the individual with an unbearable duty),[49] which will further such vulnerability. Therefore, the deputy cannot fulfill the Imam's function on prevention of evil and mischief. Otherwise it would be like drawing an equation between the Imam's specific abilities—which is based on his trite characteristics of appointment by text, infallibility, and knowledge—and his deputy's, who does not have these characteristics.

Finally, (a) in the absence of the Imam and lack of access to his appointment of the leader of the Friday Prayer, and (b) the consensus of the Shīʿī jurists on the inconclusiveness of the mandatory nature of the duty of performing the Friday Prayer incumbent upon every individual Muslim in the time of Imam's occultation, al-Karakī, as the deputy of Imam, rendered his opinion on Friday Prayer to be *al-wujūb al-takhyīrī* (optionally mandatory).[50] One last point is that al-Karakī, as the precursor theoretician of *wilāyat al-faqīh*, did not find himself eligible to apply his potentially full jurisdiction and general capacity to act as the deputy of the Imam in order to render an opinion that conflicted with the other jurists' opinions.

While al-Karakī adopted a sophisticated approach to the issues of the Shīʿī sultan's legitimacy and the deputyship of the Imam, Majlisī, by designing an esoteric hierarchy of individuals, put the king in high rank and equal footing with the jurists.[51] In his theory, the kings' kingship was considered a Divine Intent reflected as a sign of expanded grace that primarily included the Imams' existence![52] To him, since the king provides for the "security" of the Islamic land and defends it against enemies, he deserves his people's full obedience if he gives them their dues by being just to them. In this context, Majlisī's discourse does not go further than regular sermons and admonishments to the kings by reminding him, and the people, of their awareness of moral duties. To Majlisī, if a king acts unjustly and oppressively, people should appeal to God for the king's change of heart while keeping their obedience to him.[53]

Although Majlisī shared views similar to al-Karakī's on the absence of the type of legitimacy that exclusively belongs to the Imam and avoided vesting it to any other non-Imam ruler, he did not hesitate to ensure a type of legitimacy for the king that was yet to meet juristic thresholds. Despite the prominent place of mutuality of rights between the people and the kings in the theory of *Imāmah*, which gave it a contractualist aspect, Majlisī's discourse was completely oblivious to the people's rights and heavily sided with the kings. The only explanation for the justification of Majlisī's derogative measure[54]—expanding the concept of Divine Benevolence to the Shiite king—can probably be the various political turbulences that finally plagued the Safavid dynasty, as well as the exigencies involved in preserving the Shiite polity. Similar to al-Karakī's discourse, Majlisī's also provides that the superiority of the religious authority of the jurist is above the king's political authority, and it is the jurist who delineates the scope and limits of the ruler's power. In other words, the state was theoretically subordinated to the law, that is, the rules of the Shari'ah. The type of law that Majlisī and other *Akhbārī* jurists would provide the 'just' king with was largely at variance with the one that the Shī'ī jurists had already defined.[55]

In conflict with the *Uṣūlī* methodology of discovering the rules of Shari'ah, for Majlisī the process of determining law was merely limited to finding the "right" applicable tradition or report. As mentioned before, obviously unreliable or invalid traditions (such as the ones that Majlisī invoked) could function as acceptable grounds for procuring legitimacy for the so-called just sultan. Furthermore, the people were to obey both such "legitimate" sultan's rule as well as such jurist's law.

Chapter 3

The 1905 Constitutional Revolution: Shi'i Jurisprudence and Constitutionalism

The Constitution: 1906 Fundamental Law and 1907 Supplementary Law

It is an established fact that the 1905 Constitutional Revolution, like every other constitutionalist revolution, was an anti-despotic revolution aimed at restricting the ruler's power. By all historical accounts,[1] Iranians' first major experience in constitutionalism in the modern sense was intended to restrict the unbridled tyranny of the Qājār dynasty's monarchs who had become even more corrupt by being praised as "the shadow of God" and "the possessor of the subjects."[2] Such anti-despotism, theoretically and practically, represented a renewed interpretation of the relationship between the state and society—which was advocated by some of the elites and many of the then famous *Uṣūlī* jurists—and resulted in the victory of the national movement, at least in its early stage, against the monarchy.

Under the heavy political pressure of the jurists and their lay supporters (who had taken refuge in the British Embassy, to protest against the government's oppression),[3] the then ailing Qājār king Muẓaffar al-Dīn Shah (d. 1285/1906) finally acquiesced to the people's and the jurists' demands for the establishment of a "House of Justice." In his *farmān* (Royal Proclamation), issued in August 1906, the king declared that

> an Assembly of delegates elected by the Princes, the "ulamā," the Qājār family, the nobles and notables, the land-owners, the merchants, and the

> guilds shall be formed and constituted, through elections by the classes mentioned above in the capital, Tehran; the Assembly shall carry out the *requisite deliberations and investigations* on all necessary subjects connected with the important affairs of the State and the Empire and the public interests, and shall *render the necessary help and assistance to our Cabinet of Ministers* in such reforms as are designed to promote the happiness and well-being of Persia, and shall, with complete confidence and security, through the instrumentality of the first Lord of the State, *submit their proposals to Us*, so that these, having been *duly ratified* by Us, may be carried into effect. (Emphasis mine)[4]

The king issued two other prerequisite proclamations: one on the Electoral Law (in September 1906), and the other on the Fundamental Laws (submitted to the Majlis in December 1906). The First Majlis was inaugurated in October 1906 and within two years, inter alia, enacted different laws on the abolition of fiefs and the ratification of tax reforms (March–April 1907), the establishment of provincial councils (May 1907), the mayoral law (May 1907), the press law (April 1908), the formation of provinces and the governors' duties (1908), along with two annual budgets, and the establishment of a national bank. However, most important of all, the First Majlis amended the Fundamental Laws and passed a Supplement that transformed it to a full scale Constitution (October 1907). The First Majlis also encountered the political impact of the Anglo-Russian Treaty[5] (signed in August 1907 by the British and Russian Empires) in which Iran's territory had been divided between the two powers; this occurred alongside an unsuccessful coup attempt by the new despot king Muhammad Ali Shah (December 1907). The king finally succeeded in bombarding and demolishing the building of the Majlis in June 1908 with the assistance of the Russian-trained Cossack Brigade. This was followed by the persecution and execution of progressive constitutionalist intellectuals, which practically put an end to the peaceful stage of the Constitutional Revolution. The Second Majlis convened in November 1909 only after a civil war broke out between the pro-constitution revolutionary forces and the Russian-backed government troops in July 1908 during which the despot king was defeated and deposed of in July 1909. He retreated to St. Petersburg in September 1909; shortly after, his twelve-year-old son was crowned. Suffocated by the sociopolitical implications of incompetent and unstable governments from November 1909 until December 1911, the Second Majlis had to deal with unduly issued British and Russian political ultimatums and military threats (October 1910–November 1911), to which the Majlis did not allow any concessions, as well as a failed coup attempt by former king that was also heavily supported by the Russian Empire (July–August 1911).[6] The then puppet prime minister, backed by Russian military might and the British Empire's political support, however, carried out a successful coup (December 1911) in consequence of which the most important northern cities of Iran were bombarded and occupied by Russian troops; moreover, many constitutionalist leaders as well as ordinary people were either massacred or highly persecuted.[7] After the coup, the Anglo-Russian alliance completed the militarized implementation of the so-called dividing 1907 Treaty via the British occupation of the southern cities of Iran (its assigned share in the Treaty). In the process, they succeeded in aborting the Constitutional Revolution.[8]

The Fundamental Laws (December 30, 1906) were the political product of deliberations and proposals made by the newly inaugurated members of the First Majlis who sought to establish a prominent role for the parliament in legislation in lieu of providing nonbinding consultations to the Qājār Kings.[9] The monarchy was very resistant to the Majlis's demands and pursued a policy of presenting nitpicking excuses in order to restore its absolute dominance in the person of the soon-to-be king Muhammad Ali Mīrzā.[10]

Through a 51-Article instrument, however, important constitutionalist achievements found constitutional manifestation in the Fundamental Laws. The people's right to vote and to participate politically (in the Preamble as well as in Articles 2, 5, 11, and 45) was complemented by the right to submit complaints against the government's violation of the fundamental rights of the citizens to the Majlis (Article 32). The Parliament attained the right to represent the nation (Article 2), to submit legislative measures to the king for his *tawshīḥ* (signature and ratification) (Articles 15 and 33), and to approve all laws related to the ministries (Articles 16 and 21). In addition to regular legislative function of drafting, modifying, and abrogating laws (Article 17), as well as the ability to propose and approve legislative measures (Articles 33 and 39), the Majlis held sole jurisdiction over taxes, revenues, and financial laws (Articles 18, 22, 23, 24, 25, and especially 46). It also had the power to subpoena, question, issue warnings, and request dismissal (from the King) of the ministers for their negligence or violation of enacted laws (Articles 27, 29, 40, 41, and 42). The Fundamental Laws portrayed the establishment of a bicameral legislature with the formation of a Senate (Articles 43, 45, and 46), and reserved the authority of enacting the Senate's Internal Regulations for the Majlis (Article 44).[11] In the context of legislation, the king's original power as sole legislator was limited to signing or ratifying the laws passed by both the Majlis and the Senate (Articles 15, 17, and 33). The right to simultaneously dissolve the Majlis in the case of an irresolvable dispute between the two chambers and to order the reelection of a new Majlis (Article 48) was also vested in the king but could only be carried out once during each parliamentary session (Article 49) whereby the reelection of the dissolved Majlis was retained for its members (Article 48).[12]

The Fundamental Laws, however, failed to introduce and put forward the people's constitutional rights, and popular sovereignty, not to mention the very word "constitution"! They also failed to make any explicit reference to the judicial branch. Ambiguities surrounding the separation of powers, and the nature of the King's right to sign or ratify enactments (despite clear references to the parliament's right to legislate or control and investigate the executive power) were left unresolved. Most important of all, popular dissatisfaction with the Law, which had been voiced by local representatives in the provincial councils, provided the grounds for amending the Fundamental Laws. During a turbulent period filled with terror and fear, the very same First Majlis passed the Supplementary Fundamental Laws of 1907 in less than ten months.[13]

In addition to the already established rights of political participation and voting, a whole chapter 2 was devoted to individuals' constitutional rights in the Supplementary Law (October 7, 1907). These rights were: equality before the state laws (Article 8), the right to a fair trial (Articles 9, 10, 11, 12, and 14), the security of sanctuaries (Article 13) and correspondence (Articles 22, and 23), prohibition against the confiscation of properties (Articles 15, 16, and 17), freedom of expression (Article 20), the right to form associations and peaceful assemblies (Article 21), the mandatory duty of the government to provide education (Article 19), and the legality and equality of all taxes levied against individuals (Articles 94, 95, 96, 97, and 99). These articles, as the embodiment of the "Rights of the Persian Nation," were organic laws intended to further pronounce the exceptional legal circumstances according to which the passage of a law was ordained.

The Supplementary Law also clearly ordained that all power derived from the people (Articles 2, 26, 35, and 39). The Legislative power would emerge from three sources—the Majlis, the Senate, and the king—as long as their legislative initiatives were not in conflict with the Shari'ah (Articles 2 and 27). The Majlis maintained its exclusive jurisdiction over financial laws (Articles 94–99), and attained the right to interpret the Constitution (Article 27). The king's right to ratify the enactments was restricted to the issuance of executive decrees effecting enforcement that under no circumstances could cause postponement or suspension of their implementation (Article 49). Both Chambers represented the whole nation (Article 30), and had the right to investigate and examine every affair of the state (Article 33). The executive had to inform chambers about the secret covenants and agreements after the passage of the exigent time (Article 52). Chambers also had the right to subpoena, question, interrogate (Articles 60 and 65), and impeach (Article 67) the ministers. These investigations, in instances of gross negligence or criminal charges, could result in application of the Chamber's power to refer the ministers' cases of nonimplementation or violation of laws to the Court of Cassation (Article 69).

The king had to take an oath to protect the Constitution and the people's rights (Article 39), and was vested with the rights to appoint or dismiss the ministers (Article 46) and directors of the administrative agencies (Article 48) from among the pool of candidates—a pool from which his first degree relatives (i.e., the princes) were constitutionally excluded (Article 59). He held the position of commander-in-chief (Article 50), and could declare war or peace (Article 51). He could also order the Chambers to convene under emergency circumstances (Article 54). The king's authority was limited to the rights enumerated in the Constitution (Article 57), and the royal court's expenses could not exceed the amount appropriated in annual budgets (Article 56). On the other hand, the ministers and the Cabinet were individually and collectively accountable to the Chambers (Article 61), and disavowed from invoking the king's oral or written orders for their misapplication or the violation of laws (Article 64). No minister was allowed to take more than one executive office (Article 68).

The judiciary was in charge of adjudicating legal disputes and public grievances. It was comprised of the Court of Cassation and lower "courts of justice" in which matters within the Shari'ah's jurisdiction were to be decided by the mujtahid judges (Article 71). According to Article 73, establishment of any court should have been by law, especially the military tribunals (Article 87). Proceedings for political and press crimes had to be followed in the courts of justice (Article 72) with the presence of a jury (Article 79). All proceedings were to be public except for those concerning sexual crimes, or when judges would determine that a public hearing could endanger the public order (Article 76); this stipulation did not apply to political or press crimes where a unanimous determination by all sitting judges was required (Article 77). Article 78 mandated the legality of judicial decisions that were supported by sound legal reasoning, and public pronouncements in public hearings. Judges were protected from undue removal, dismissal, or change of office unless by their consent or resignation (Articles 81 and 82), and banned from taking another office (Article 85). The king's appointment of the General Prosecutor was qualified by the highest jurist-judge's pre-approval (Article 83). Appellate Courts were to be established in each province's capital (Article 86). Finally, The Court of Cassation sat in Tehran without any primary jurisdiction over the cases, except in accusations against the Ministers (Article 75), and enjoyed the authority to resolve jurisdictional conflicts between administrative agencies (Article 88).

The most important addition to the Fundamental Laws was Article 2 according to which:

> At any time, any legal enactment of the Sacred National Consultative Assembly [the Majlis], [which is] established by the favor of and assistance of His Holiness the Imam of the Age [the Hidden Imam], the favor of his majesty the King of Islam [the Qājār King], the care of the jurists, and the whole people of the Persian nation, must be at variance with the sacred principles of Islam or the laws established by His Holiness the Best of Mankind [the Prophet Muhammad] (on whom and whose household be the Blessings of God and His Peace).
>
> It is hereby declared that it is for the learned doctors of theology [i.e., the highest competent jurists] to determine whether such laws, as may be proposed, are or are not conformable to the principles of Islam. It is, therefore, officially enacted that there shall at all times exist a Committee composed of not less than five mujtahids or other devout theologians, cognizant also of the requirements of the age. The committee shall be elected in the following manner: The *Marja' al-Taqlīd*s [the most knowledgeable jurists upon whom the individuals place their utmost religious reliance] shall present to the National Consultative Assembly the names of twenty of the jurists possessing the attributes mentioned above; and the members of the National Consultative Assembly shall, either by unanimous acclamation [consensus], or by taking lot, designate five or more of these, according to the exigencies of the time, and recognize these as members so that they may carefully discuss and consider all matters proposed in the Assembly, and reject and repudiate, wholly or in part, any such proposal which is at variance [in fact, in conflict] with the Sacred Laws of Islam, so that it shall not obtain the title of legality. In such matters, the decision of this Ecclesiastical Committee shall be followed and obeyed, and this Article shall continue unchanged until the appearance of His Holiness the Proof of the Age.[14]

The Key Role of *Uṣūlī* Religious Leaders

In the process of enacting the Fundamental Laws and its Supplement and throughout the turbulent aftermath of that period, many Shīʿī jurists were heavily involved, and the majority of them supported the legitimacy and implementation of the Laws as a reliable legal-juristic basis upon which the relation between the king and the people could be regulated.[15] Among them were the most prominent jurists of the Najaf Seminary—the most important Shīʿī intellectual center at the time—all of them Iranians and acknowledged as Shīʿī Religious Leaders (*Marājiʿ al-Taqlīd*).[16] Led by Ākhūnd Khurāsānī (d. 1329/1911),[17] they issued numerous fatwas, especially after the attacks against the Majlis and the Constitution, in which the protection of constitutionalism in Iran was repeatedly declared to be an individually mandatory duty.[18]

There is no doubt that the leadership and support of prominent jurists for all of the events prior to and after the 1905 Constitutional Revolution was a key factor in its victory.[19] In fact, within an Iranian sociopolitical context that had hardly experienced constitutional rule,[20] not only would it completely make sense, but it was also necessary for every new concept and institution introduced in the 1906–7 Constitution to be legitimized by the jurists' approval.[21] Therefore, one can easily assume that every aspect of the 1905 Revolution, as the manifestation of Iranians' will, including the Constitution with all its institutional and political achievements as the instrument of this will, was subject to juristic analysis by prominent *Uṣūlī* jurists such as Ākhūnd, Māzandarānī (d. 1330–1331/1912),[22] Khalīlī (d. 1326/1908),[23] Nā'īnī (d. 1355/1936),[24] and others.[25] Thus, had there not been theoretical grounds in Shīʿī jurisprudence, their approval of constitutionalism would not have been secured.[26] In other words, if sufficiently valid juridical reasoning for the legitimacy of will or instrument were not available, they would not conclude the imperativeness of constitutionalism. Such normative evaluation was based on certain proscriptions and prescriptions, the determination of which would not have been possible without a substantive and methodological juristic treatment of the duties and rights of the ruled and the ruler.

Therefore, the late-1905 peaceful national movement,[27] and subsequent events were a historical forum for analyzing the concept of popular sovereignty as a prerequisite of constitutionalism in Shīʿī jurisprudence.[28] In addition to a de novo review of the yet to be reexamined issue of a Shīʿī government in the absence of the Imam, it was also necessary for the Imāmah doctrine to articulate an interpretation of the concept of mutual rights and duties between the ruler and the ruled at the epicenter of its underpinning contractarian approach.[29] In order to achieve this goal, the then most brilliant *Uṣūlī* jurists utilized the legacy of anti-tyrannical discourse already developed in Islamic political and legal philosophy,[30] and reviewed it based on new vectors and concepts—such as the inherent freedom and equality of every individual. The new interpretation also extensively utilized the indisputable historical facts of the Prophet Muhammad and Imam Ali's practice of power. The main context within which the Shīʿī theory of constitutionalism could be constructed was, apparently, the recurrent issue of political rule in the absence of the infallible Imam. The predominant Imāmah theory, heavily revolving around the infallibility of the Imam as the eternal leader of spiritual and temporal affairs, had postulated the irrefutable correlation between the two concepts of infallibility and legitimacy while excluding the latter from any type of non-Imamite rule. It was, however, necessary to go well beyond general formulas and make a de novo analysis of the issue of the legitimacy of the Shīʿī government. In doing so, with undeniable theoretical and historical facts related to the indeterminacy of the time of Absent Imam's reappearance and advent to power still in force, jurists had to consider the new historical circumstances where the Iranians' popular will had manifested its demands in the form of a Majlis that had enacted a Constitution as a key fact.

The constitutionalist theory had to deeply engage the just sultanate discourse that, in its attempt to accommodate the Safavid dynasty's lack of legitimacy, had established two main theories: (1) vesting the religious authority upon jurists as the Imam's general deputies, which was developed in the theory of *wilāyat al-faqīh*. This was a crucial issue, especially when one noticed the prevalent just sultanate's orientation toward the proposition that the non-Imam's rule can obtain legitimacy by the general deputy's approval of such rule; and (2) restricting the people's entitlement and right to rebel to "praying for the softening of the oppressor king's heart," and "expressing their complaints to and seeking support from the jurists, as the general deputies of Imam." If popular sovereignty was a modern concept for proof of which the constitutionalist jurists had to undertake new juridical efforts, no renewed effort was necessary for proponents of the power-oriented just sultanate discourse, who had already tended to appropriate more lenience toward the king's side of the equation and emphasized concepts such as social order and the historical experiment of kingship.

In their renewed evaluation of issues, the constitutionalist jurists employed the then prevailing *Uṣūlī* theory of limited or prohibited legal-political guardianship of the general deputies of the Hidden Imam.[31] The implication of the *Uṣūlī* theory, on the one hand, was to revise the broader concept of legitimacy and discuss it in a new context: if the general deputy's scope of authority was limited or even prohibited, then what would fill the Shīʿī government's vacuum of legitimacy in the time of the Imam's occultation? On the other hand, as will be discussed, constitutionalist jurisprudence was based on a certain type of constitutional review of the parliament's enactments in which the Article Two Committee jurists' role was to review the legislative pieces that, in one way or the other, were to comply with the Shari'ah, namely judicial laws. It was within the context of this constructive constitutionalist jurisprudence that other prerequisites or concomitant themes of constitutionalism such as tyranny, equality, rule of law, popular control over power by entertaining the right to political participation, freedoms of expression and assembly, and, finally, legitimacy of the new constitutional order could emerge.

In the following subchapters, I will introduce and argue for the Shīʿī origins of constitutionalism. In chapter 4 I will argue that not only did the constitutionalist jurists apply the facts of the people's movement against despotism and establishment of parliament in their juristic scheme of the most legitimate and the closest system of political rule to the utopian Imamite model, but they also reassessed the concepts of legitimacy and infallibility with extensive consideration for the concept of popular sovereignty in the relationship between the ruler and the ruled.

Jurisprudence of Constitutionalism

The Rights-Based Doctrine of Shīʿī Constitutionalism

While many of the jurists committed themselves to playing leading roles in the social movement, a rift emerged between them over how to yoke the tyranny. At the apex of the disagreements was a substantive conflict on the very concept of constitutionalism that inherently bore the modern prerequisite of popular sovereignty as embodied in the legislative power. Due to historical reasons, a specific treatment of the concept of popular sovereignty was long left undiscussed by jurists.[32] The theory of Imāmah as perceived and interpreted in its classical and premodern context on the one hand, and the "just sultan" discourse on the other had been developed through the absence of a substantive approach to popular sovereignty that could claim standing in the theorization of a constitutional doctrine. Therefore, it is anachronistic to expect premodern jurists to have designated a definitive role for the people in the continuum linking one theory to the other[33]—as either a source of political sovereignty or constituent power. The Imāmah theory, however, when practiced during the reign of Imam Ali (35–40/655–660), did strongly recognize the people as the main party to a bi-party contract between the ruler and the ruled. In one of his sermons, Imam Ali said:

> God, by placing me over your affairs, has created my right over you, and you too have a right over me like mine over you. A right is very vast in description but very narrow in equitability of action. It does not accrue to any person unless it accrues against him also, and right does not accrue against a person unless it also accrues in his favor. If there is any right which is only in favor of a person with no corresponding right accruing

against him, it is solely for Allah, and not for His creatures, by virtue of His might over His creatures and by virtue of the justice permeating all His decrees... Then, from His rights, He mandated certain rights for certain people against others. *He equated [the beneficiaries and the obligators] with one another. Some of these rights establish other rights. Some rights are such that they do not accrue except with others. The greatest of the rights that Allah has made obligatory is the right of the ruler over the ruled and the right of the ruled over the ruler.* Allah has placed this obligation on each other. He has made it the basis of their mutual affection, and an honor for their religion. Thus, when the ruler fulfills his obligation to enforce the rights of the ruled and the ruled do the same for the ruler, the right will become precious to them, and the paths to the religion will become visible, and the signs of justice will appear, and the Prophet's teachings will duly be implemented. (Emphasis mine)[34]

In theory, for Shīʿī jurists, like every other Muslim jurist in the premodern era, the rulers were to fulfill the general duty of providing security and welfare for the people within the context of the Shari'ah; as long as the rulers fulfilled this duty, a duty of obedience was incumbent upon the people. In that very sermon, however, Imam Ali clearly qualified the duty of obedience by the rulers and the people alike to the one that should be fulfilled exclusively before God, and what He has ordained.[35] He also conditioned the relationship between the ruler and the ruled to the people's right to counsel and advise each other and the ruler by expressing their mind on issues related to justice and the rights of the ruler,[36] and the ruler's vulnerability to err:

You should therefore counsel each other [for the fulfillment of your obligations] and cooperate with each other. However extremely eager a person may be to secure the pleasure of Allah, and however fully he strives for it, he cannot discharge [his obligation for] obedience to Allah, as is really due to Him, and *it is an obligatory right of Allah over the people that they should advise each other to the best of their ability and cooperate with each other for the establishment of truth among them. No person, however great his position in the matter of truth, and however advanced his distinction in religion may be, is above cooperation in connection with the obligations placed on him by Allah. Again, no man, however small he may be regarded by others, and however humble he may appear before eyes, is too low to cooperate or to be afforded cooperation in this matter...* In the view of virtuous people, the worst position is that it may be thought about them that they love glory, and their affairs may be taken to be based on pride. I would really hate that it may occur to your mind that I love high praises or to hear eulogies. By the grace of Allah, I am not like this. Even if I had

> loved to be mentioned like this, I would have given it up in submissiveness before Allah, rather than accept greatness and sublimity to which He is more entitled. Generally, people feel pleased at praise after good performances. But do not mention for me handsome praise for the obligations that I have discharged towards Allah and towards you, because of my fear about those obligations which I have not discharged. Neither address me in the manner despots are addressed, nor isolate yourselves from me like when you do with the tyrants who are to be treated so. Do not meet me with flattery and do not think that I shall take it ill if truth is said to me, because the person, who feels disgusted when truth is said to him or a just matter is placed before him, would find it more difficult to act upon them. *Therefore, do not abstain from saying a truth or consulting me on a matter of justice because I neither regard myself above erring and nor am immune of erring in my actions* unless Allah would assist me in controlling my soul because He is more powerful than I am. (Emphasis mine)[37]

It was in such a rights-based context that the concepts of oppression and tyranny as well as the definitive nature and importance of the popular will in demanding constitutionalism, a constitution, a parliament, and the right to control and oversee political power were viewed.[38] The juristic discourse of just sultanate, on the other hand, did not go beyond delineating a division between the political authority of the kings and the jurists' deputyship of the Absent Imam—according to which the jurists would supposedly represent the people's rights. In other words, if the "constitutional" tendency in the theory of Imāmah was oriented toward the establishment of a "contractual equilibrium" and a balance between the rights of the ruled and the ruler, the just sultanate's was an attempt to define the state in terms of *aḥkām* (rules), or positive law,[39] and not law in terms of the state. In this context, the king was perceived to hold a dual status (1) as the executor of religious rules as determined or approved by the jurists, and (2) as one of the pillars of the "Islamic" sultanate, and the provider of peace and order.[40] In order to further elaborate on this aspect of the just sultanate discourse, the exemplary issue of the land-tax, which has always been one of the main sources of revenue for a Shīʿī state, would provide sufficient materials. In his treatment of the issue, Qummī mentioned general juridical rules about public ownership of *kharāj* lands (i.e., state lands), and the mandate of spending the revenue in the common interest of Muslims before he cautiously relied on the general discourse of the jurists' deputyship of the Imam.[41] Finally, he categorized unjust sultans into two groups: *sultan-i jā'ir-i Shīʿa* (the unjust Shīʿī sultan) and *sultan-i jā'ir-i mukhālif* (literally meaning the opposing unjust sultan, but intending non-Shīʿī sultans). On the issue of such sultan's discretion over the expenditure of the revenues, he wrote:

> There is *ishkāl-i 'aẓīm* (a huge problem) on the unjust Shiite sultan's *idhn* (permission) [on how to expend the revenue]"[42]...because our sultan, contrary to non-Shiite sultans who invoke genuine entitlement [to succeed the Prophet] in their power, knows that he is not entitled to take the office of Imām (*faqd istiḥqāq bi manṣab*), and also knows that it is not legitimate for him to receive the revenue [it is the Imam who has the inherent right to do so]. Therefore, *the most preferred and cautious measure* for him to adopt is to not receive it without the competent jurist's permission...although it is permissible for the non-Shiite unjust sultan to spend it on the common interests of Muslim society,[43] doing so is impermissible for the Shiite sultan, unless [determined and approved] by the jurist's prior permission. (Emphasis mine)[44]

According to this view, the issue revolves around following Shari'ah rules dictating the expenditure of the land tax revenue in the common interest of Muslims. As long as the rules were implemented, it is as if a just Imam holds power; to that effect, there is no difference between *Imam 'ādil* (an upright Imam) and *sultan-i jā'ir-i mukhālif-i musallaṭ* (a ruling non-Shī'a unjust sultan).[45] The reason behind this resemblance is that the legitimate ends, notwithstanding the means, are met.[46] In the case of a Shiite unjust sultan, however, this general rule is trajected toward observance of the prevailing Shī'ī doctrine of the sole and universal authority of the Hidden Imam to power. The jurist's role, as the deputy of the Imam and in the form of prior involvement in legitimizing any act by the Shī'ī unjust sultan, is intended to provide the grounds for reconciliation between the sultan's lack of any inherent entitlement to rule, and the Imam's absence. More specifically, the jurist is assigned to undertake one of two functions. The first involves (1) determining which manifestation of the public interest the revenue should be expended for, and (2) rendering vicarious permission on the Imam's behalf with an utmost consideration that would resemble the manner in which the Imam would vest discretions in his governor-appointees if he were present. The second involves legitimizing the unjust Shī'ī sultan's role in executing one or more acts, the performance of which is among the Imam's authorities, for example, the distribution of revenues among public agents such as judges and army soldiers. The issue is whether a combination of an arbiter-jurist and an executor-sultan would legitimize the unjust Shī'ī sultan's rule or not. The proponents of just sultanate theory would suggest that the answer is positive. However, any valid analysis of the role of the jurist as incorporated in their discourse has to be qualified by the prerequisite determination of the rule on the as-yet apparent issue of the original legitimacy of the said jurist's deputyship, and the juridical validity of his determination and control. In Shī'ī jurisprudence, issues of this nature are generally discussed under the topic of qualifications and differences between two main contrasting concepts: "*ḥaqq*" (a right, or authority) and "*ḥukm*" (a positive rule). Briefly, *ḥaqq* is distinguished by the proprietorship of the subject of the right as held against others, that is, there is a proprietary element in the right that establishes its holder's authority against others. By contrast, the authority devised in *ḥukm* is set to provide a solution for a non-adversarial legal issue based on the best interests of the parties. While there is an inherent and recognized temporal benefit for the holder of a right in entertaining his authority, a positive rule is intended to reward its holder in the hereafter. The prevailing classical view in *wilāyat al-faqīh* (the jurist's guardianship) is that the jurist does not have *ḥaqq* to undertake authority, and his stewardship is to be analyzed according to the conditions of *ḥukm*. Obviously, for a Shī'ī jurist, like any other kind of jurists, it is of utmost importance to analyze the textual and factual evidence that would establish the grounds for determining right or rule.[47] I will discuss later how, for the constitutionalist jurists who followed the prevailing *Uṣūlī* view, the text of juridical indicators—based on which the proponents of just sultanate could assume the jurists' total succession of the Imam—was insufficient to establish such comprehensive authority.

It is important to note that the notion of the people's rights in the just sultanate discourse was also included in the jurists' role. Accordingly, depending on a jurist's views regarding the extent and legitimacy of the notion, the people's entitlement and capability to apply their rights could range anywhere from "praying for the softening of the oppressor king's heart" to "expressing complaints to the jurists and seeking their sanctuary and support."[48] Thus, an independent right to actively rebel against a ruler who has abused the people's legitimate rights was completely absent in the just sultanate discourse. By contrast, the writings of Ākhūnd and his colleagues are replete with such references. In an important analysis of illegitimate rule, the Trite Religious Leaders declared that "rebellion against a ruler who is the embodiment of oppression and pretends to have pledged his rule on the basis of the Shari'ah" is mandatory for Muslims. So, they opined, the "people must take this *naṭ'-i khūn-'ālūd* [a bloody leather mat that in older times was used during executions, a very strong belletristic metaphor that identifies oppressive rule with the killing innocent individuals] away from their path [to legitimate right]."[49] It was obvious that despotic monarchism would not yield to the people's rights, especially when its legitimacy was justified and supported by seemingly valid premises and precepts.[50]

For constitutionalist jurists, religious statements similar to the aforementioned sermon as well as the historical precedents of the life and rule of the Prophet and Imam Ali provided valid religious and jurisprudential grounds for vesting human beings with inherent *ḥurriya* (liberty) and *musāwāt* (equality) in their relationship with the rulers. In expressing his views while addressing army commanders, Ākhūnd declared that "*'Iṣmat va nāmūs-i a'ẓam-i dīn va vaṭan* (the religion's and the homeland's grand purity and honor) are in adherence with and protection of religious-national human rights."[51] On yet another occasion, he asked the preachers and journalists to "introduce the truth of God-given liberty to the people, which is freedom from humiliatingly compulsive slavery to the arbitrary commands of the royal court's functionaries and agents, and not from obedience to God and *ilqā'-i quyūd-i shar'iyya* (meeting the instructions of Shari'ah)." He also asked them to "make it clear to everyone that the true definition of equality is equality between the powerful and the weak, and the rich and the poor, in their rights and before the law."[52] Maḥallātī, in explaining the concept of liberty as introduced by the Religious Leaders, wrote:

> To make it sound and clear, it should be said that *ḥuriyyat* (liberty) does not mean that the people are allowed to enjoy absolute freedom and act arbitrarily in whatever manner they wish against other's property and reputation and life.[53] Neither religious nor non-religious groups of human beings have suggested and supported this definition, because it would amount to nothing but absolute chaos and the complete destruction of order in the community. *In this context, liberty means people's freedom from any type of capricious rule, unaccountability, and coercion by any powerful individual, even the king. So no one could impose his dominance, because of power, on the weak, not even the weakest individual of all, except under the rule of law as has been enacted and implemented by those nations that mandate equal protection and abidance on all the people from the king to the pauper. To this end, liberty is one of mustaqillāt-i 'aqlīyya (independent reason's findings) and of the necessities of the religion of Islam, which, briefly, [includes] abolishing the power-holders' oppression against the people.* (Emphasis mine)[54]

In order to provide an elaborate and more nuanced treatment of the origins of liberty as a God-given right in Ākhūnd's opinions, Nā'īnī made an important argument on why the Prophet Muhammad's model of rule transformed into the despotism and tyranny of the Umayyad dynasty (40–132/661–750). This model, according to Nā'īnī, was founded on liberty, equality, and consultation, and followed by the first two Rightly Guided Caliphs and Imam Ali (himself the fourth and last one of them). After a lengthy analysis of the Qur'anic example of the children of Israel's intense affliction with the Pharaohs' oppression, Nā'īnī comes full-circle when he compares their suffering with Muslims' suffering under the rule of kings. In conclusion, Nā'īnī argued that "*maqhūriyyat-i bay'at va ṭawāghiyyat-i ummat* (the people's weakened and submissive bargaining power when pledging allegiance to the rulers, and the rulers' undue resemblance to God's absolute power), and the *'ubūdiyyat* (servitude or slave-like obedience) of the people to such rulers" had caused these calamities.[55] Nā'īnī also found that, in addition to oppressive rulers' coercion, another force that "legitimized" the nation's servitude was the disperse and derogatory interpretations of religious teachings presented by those "religious scholars" who served the despot kings, and justified despotism and tyranny as well as the *ummah*'s deprivation from participation and entertainment of their rights in political affairs.[56] Therefore, using very strong wording, he declared that there was an unsacred unity of dual evils, and correlative and complementing despotisms operating together to maintain the deprivation that had plagued Muslims with a state of vegetative passivism, and stripped their conscious knowledge of the purpose of creation. He finalized his thoughts as follows:

> In general, obedience to the autocratic orders of the rebellious tyrants of the *ummah* and the bandits of the nation is not only an injustice to *one's own life and liberty, which are among the greatest endowments granted by God, holy be His names, to human beings.* In addition, according to the explicit text of the worthy Qur'an and the traditions of the infallible ones, it is tantamount to idolatry, or taking associates with God, for God alone deserves the attributes of an ultimate possession of creation, and unquestionable authority in whatever He deems necessary. He alone can be free of responsibility in what He does. All of these are among His holy attributes. He who arrogates these attributes for himself and usurps this status is not only a tyrant and *ghāṣib-i maqām-i wilāyat* (a usurper of the station of stewardship), but also, according to the holy texts, a pretender to the divine mantle and a transgressor of His inviolate realm. Conversely, liberation from such abject servitude not only releases the soul from its vegetative state and animal status into the realm of noble humanity; it also is of the stages and statuses of monotheism and of the requirements of having faith in it, as is of the stages and names of *khāṣṣa* [the designated by God, i.e., the prophets]. *That is why rescuing the usurped liberty of the nations and releasing them from the yoke of slavery and abject servitude and enabling them to entertain their God-given rights and liberties has been among the most significant goals of the prophets, peace be upon them.* (Emphasis mine)[57]

By establishing the inherent character of liberty and equality in human beings as divinely bestowed rights, Nā'īnī continued to prove the fundamental importance of every ruler's—even the Infallible ones'—duty to practice the utmost care in preserving equality and prohibiting the abuse of religious or political authority. In doing so, he invoked historical precedents from Prophetic as well as Caliphate/Imamite practices and models, and categorized equality according to three main manifestations: *musāwāt dar ḥuqūq* (equality in rights), *musāwāt dar aḥkām* (equality before laws), and *musāwāt dar muqāṣṣa va mujāzāt* (equality in liability and punishment).[58] With regards to equality in rights, he referred to the example of the Prophet's precision, and his sensitivity in the preservation and equal implementation of Muslims' individual and collective rights, as previously established by tribal customary rules, even though this position conflicted with his daughter's interests when he was in a position to employ his dual religious and political authorities to act otherwise.[59] With regards to equality before the laws, Nā'īnī utilized another Prophetic example to prove his point. After the first war between Muslims and the Meccans, Muslims arrested seventy war prisoners—including the Prophet's uncle and cousins—and tied their arms with rope. The universal rule for freedom was to pay different amounts of money or gold, depending on the war prisoner's wealth. The Prophet neither allowed discrimination in exempting his relatives or loosening their physical restraints, nor offered any exemption or reduction in their payments.[60] With regards to the equality of liability and punishment, the prophetic examples were at use again. In the last days of his life, the Prophet availed himself to Muslims' right to equal retaliation of personal injuries, and also, on another occasion, declared that even if his beloved daughter (i.e., Fāṭimah) would commit theft, he (i.e., the Prophet) would make no excuse in her punishment.[61] Nā'īnī cited similar anecdotes from the second Rightly Guided Caliph as well as Imam Ali.[62]

For constitutionalist jurists, these examples interpreted the nature of political authority with the utmost duty of care, and not the ultra vires application of power. Given that the constitutionalist jurists' doctrine relied fundamentally and heavily on the *Uṣūlī* school of Shīʿī law, three important conclusions that are relevant to the concept of inherent liberty and equality can be drawn. First, the Prophet's practice of leadership was based on the divinely ordained inviolability of rights, rather than his guardianship of and authority over the lives and properties of the faithful. The constitutionalist jurists believed in the apparently valid principle that the *infallibility* of the Prophet Muhammad and the Imams was the key element to the ultimate validity of their determination of Shari'ah laws and to their unmatchable eminence in holding power and leading the faithful. They, however, did not believe that such infallibility should translate into entitlement to or establishment of a superior status above the law for them.[63] *Uṣūlī* jurists certainly recognize the infallibles' legislative jurisdiction of authority in determining Shari'ah rules for new legal issues. The crucial point, however, is that once the law is discovered, even the infallible is under the duty of obedience. Thus, there are fundamental legal limits or thresholds that should be observed and could not be overstepped; among those limits are the preservation and protection of the established rights.[64]

Second, in Nā'īnī's arguments, the examples of individual and collective rights were of the kind whose validity and binding effect had already been recognized as established rights by tribal customs and conventions, or *sharāyi' al-sābiqah* (the rules of previous religious laws, more specifically here the law of retaliation), and not necessarily by Islamic Shari'ah in the specific sense of a definition. The Prophet's *iltizām 'amalī* (practical pledge) to honor established rights, for the most part, had stemmed from his adherence and original pledge to observe the inherent characteristic of equality. To this end, as long as the established rights in question did not conflict with the main characteristics of Shari'ah laws, that is, fairness and rationality, it would not matter if they had not emerged or specifically originated from the particular rules of the Islamic Shari'ah. The duty of preservation and consideration is the rule and is incumbent upon the ruler, even if he is as highly esteemed and just as the Prophet. This duty extends to the point in time when a new law is ordained. Until then, the social manifestation of rights enjoys the status of the acquired rights of the citizens, and functions as a legal measure in individual and/or collective relations. Finally, such established rights should not fall into the category of the ruler's jurisdiction until a new rule replaces them.[65] The important point is that this new rule should have also been ordained with an absolute observance of justice, to which the human reason would substantially lend its compliance. As has been recorded in his *wathā'iq* (letters of appointment),[66] when the Prophet appointed governors to the Islamic government in newly annexed territories, he clearly ordered them to preserve the inhabitants' proprietary rights (i.e., the right to their property and land), to respect their choice of religion and faith, to pay dues when they fulfill what has been assigned as their duties, and to educate them with the teachings of Islam. He also prohibited the governors from requiring the people to undertake unbearable acts. For newly converted Muslims, an additional careful assessment of their payments to the government (*zakāt*) as well as blood money (*dīya*) for bodily harm offenses was also mentioned.[67] The Prophet was aware that substantially new rules should be introduced with complete regard for society's capacity to absorb and observe the incremental nature of legal developments. In principle, there was no exception to the specific constitutive rules of Islamic Shari'ah in this context; they were thus introduced in different stages as well as in socially, culturally, and historically contingent circumstances. Rules such as the abolition of usury; the abolition of the inhumane treatment of women and arbitrary divorce by men; women's individual rights to the independent ownership of economic wealth and the management of financial affairs; the prohibition of alcohol consumption; equality between Arabs and non-Arabs; and the emancipation of slaves; all were only enforced after their social and legal foundations had been established through a sufficient level of social practice.[68]

Third, the nature of political power changed after the so-called successors to the Prophet, that is, the Umayyad caliphs, began to restore the inequalities and discriminations that had been practiced before the Prophetic rule, and ignored the precedent set by the Prophet. This historical transition-restoration was coupled with a fundamentally abusive approach to the Shari'ah in theoretical observation and practical implementation as well as a misinterpretation of its mandates in favor of the new political establishment's interests. Caliphs and jurists—who provided the juridical justifications of such transition—were to be held responsible. Based on this analysis, Nā'īnī took a very harsh stance against those jurists who, despite the Prophet's firm prohibition against companionship between the kings and the learned religious scholars, had sought from the despot rulers mundane rewards—the kind that would provide them with high legal positions and economic grants in return for their self-justificatory abuse of the Shari'ah.[69] In his opinion, the restitution of damages—to the individuals who had been deprived of their rights—caused by such abuse was even more difficult to achieve than toppling the despot kings and establishing a constitutionalist system.[70]

It is impossible to explain why and how prominent *Uṣūlī* jurists such as Ākhūnd and his colleagues chose to support constitutionalism and insisted strongly on its juridical authenticity and validity without an analytical treatment of the underpinning jurisprudential theories that supported the logical outcome of the inviolability of rights. Despite the mainstream approach, one that limits the origins of constitutionalism in Shīʿī jurisprudence to the constitutionalist jurists' total rejection of oppression and despotism,[71] there are indisputable facts that strongly suggest, well beyond the concepts of oppression and tyranny, that those jurists found complete harmony between the Shari'ah and constitutionalism. Moreover, I contend, they founded this harmony on a crucial prerequisite: popular sovereignty.

The Shīʿī Origins of Popular Sovereignty

In order to set up the argument, I begin with a revealing but at the same time highly discursive piece of key evidence. Directly addressing the despot king, Ākhūnd, also writing for the opinions of other constitutionalist Religious Leaders, declared:

> Based on the religious duty incumbent upon us and the responsibility that we find ourselves charged with before the Divine's Justice, we will not halt our efforts to eliminate the ignorant traitors' oppression, and to establish the foundation of the holy Shari'ah and the restitution of the Muslims' usurped rights. We will, therefore, apply our utmost strife to materialize the necessities of religion,[72] *that the sovereignty of the political rule belongs to jumhūr-i Muslimīn (the general public of Muslims) during the absence of Hidden Imam, may God Hasten his return.* We have informed, and will continue to let the Muslim community know about this duty [i.e., materialization of the public's sovereignty]... In order to protect the Divine Laws and the necessities of religion from the intrigue and indignation of *mughriḍīn* (those who have a grudge, the malevolent) and *mubdiʿīn* (the innovators of illegitimate religious rules, heretics),[73] we declare in a plain and commonly understandable language that *mashrūṭiyyat-i dawlat* (the constitutionalism of the government) is conditioned by the imposition of the highest level of limitation, to the possible extent, on the dominance and oppressive free disposal of the illegitimate authority of the king's functionaries and their capricious treatment of the people. Diligent labor for constraining such dominance and shortening such free disposal to whatever possible degree and by any potential means [to such end], is *az aẓhar-i ḍarūriyyāt-i dīn-i Eslām* (of the clearest necessities of Islam). Whoever rejects the jurisprudential foundations of its *wujūb* (mandatoriness) in any of the forms should be perceived as one who rejects the other necessities of religion. *Moreover, anyone who believes that the idea of vesting the right to plenipotentiary acts and absolute authority to the non-infallible*[74] *is one of the religion's rules is to be presumed, at least, a heretic.* (Emphasis mine)[75]

As can be seen, the foundational basis of this opinion is the notion of usurping the office of the Imam's political power during his absence. In order to deconstruct the position of Ākhūnd and others on this issue, however, it is necessary to introduce and analyze the underpinning theories upon which such an unprecedented and multifaceted reference to popular sovereignty in Shīʿī law could be made.

The Prohibition of Oppression and Tyranny

As a universally agreed principle, despotism is based on oppression, and an absolute disregard for and deprivation of the people from their legitimate rights, in the interest of the despot's personal advantages. Not only did the constitutionalist jurists have no objection to the validity of such rational definitions, but they also believed that many of the theoretical and legal premises of constitutionalism, including the discourse against despotism, originally emanated from religious teachings.[76] Prior to the enactment of the 1907 Constitution, in a stark rejection of tyranny, Ākhūnd declared it a mandatory duty for every Muslim to resist oppression and close the gates against despotic aggressions.[77] This fatwa was primarily based on the rationally apparent and eternal truth of the evilness of oppression[78] as heavily supported by a wide array of Qur'anic evidence.[79] On the other hand, given the limitless border of the Qājār kings' despotism, Ākhūnd and his colleagues found a direct relationship between jurisprudential rejection of despotism and the imperative of constitutionalism in their various edicts and letters by enumerating the corruption of oppressive rule. To Iranians as well as their Religious Leaders, in addition to the loss of large parts of Iran's territory,[80] the despotic Qājār dynasty's acquiescence to Russian and British Empires' financial and economic penetrations had amounted to *istīlā'-i khārijī* (foreigners' dominance) and *taslīm-i mamlakat* (surrendering the country). The despotic rule had led to the plundering of all the national wealth and power, and destruction of its domestic business and industry.[81]

To the constitutionalist jurists, "uprooting despotism and the arbitrary application of oppression by tyrants, was not only a mandatory prerequisite for protecting *bayḍah-i Islam* (literally meaning the territory of Islam where the community of Muslims takes root[82] or has been formed),[83] but also was *az aẓhar-i ḍarūrīyyāt-i dīn-i mubīn*, that is, of the clearest necessities of the true religion." Without meeting those prerequisites, "commanding right and prohibiting wrong was impossible."[84] The guaranteed measure of protecting the Islamic state, in the Trite Jurist Leaders' mind, was in making all the necessary efforts to acquire this *mashrū'-i muqaddas* (sacred legitimate matter), which was the establishment of *Dār al-Shūrāyi Millī* (National House of Consultation, or the Majlis) and *ijrāyi qānūn-i musāwāt-i Qur'ānī* (the implementation of the Qur'anic law of equality).[85] Further elaboration is in order here. *Bayḍat al-Islam* (the Persian version is *Bayḍah-e Islam*) is a technical term that, in juristic sources, has been used as the equivalent to homeland in arguments concerning the second main category of jihad, that is, *al-jihad al-difā'ī* (defensive holy war), and delineating the qualifications of defensive jihad for protecting the territorial borders of a Muslim country.[86] The constitutionalist jurists' prevalent reference to the term, as a characteristic of the Majlis,[87] was based on their juristic finding of correlative existence of and direct relation between domestic despotic rule and the colonialist states' dominance over the Muslim societies. In other words, they believed that a colonial state's undue political influence over a Muslim state should be considered, if not necessarily as a ground for its intention for conducting military strikes against Muslims' homeland, then, as a similarly threatening danger to the identity of Muslim community; any of these conditions required Muslims' awareness and precaution,[88] hence was subject to being perceived as an issue related to defensive jihad.[89] To them, such undue influence could only be gained when a despotic political establishment had usurped power. This is because a despot would only care for his own interests and not the nation's, and therefore would easily concede and acquiesce to the colonialist states' demands and pressures; as such, he would provide the means for colonial dominance over Muslim countries. In this context, uprooting despotism was tantamount to defending the religion and the nation by undercutting the undue influence of colonialist states. It would not be surprising therefore to notice that, in many of their edicts, constitutionalist jurists equated the establishment of the Majlis (as the symbol of constitutionalism) with the protection of *Bayḍah-e Islam*; the Majlis was seen to be the means to its accomplishment. This alone proves that constitutionalism was heavily perceived to be if not equal to Shari'ah, then at least one of its key elements.

Furthermore, despotism was based on a "shortsightedness of opinions oriented toward personal interests and ignoring the common interests"[90] and a "usurpation of the nation's naturally-given and divinely ordained liberty."[91] Therefore, since "the despotic monarchy had usurped the state and endangered the existence of the people,[92] destroyed the required unity of the state and the nation and caused bloody confrontations between them,[93] sustained the chaos and absence of order,[94] and employed an unbridled and unlimited oppression throughout its rule,[95] there was no Shari'ah-based ground for its legitimacy."[96]

The Dialectic between Just Rule and the Qualified Agency of an Unjust Ruler

Although the general prohibition of oppression was a fertile ground for rejecting despotism, there were many more juristic arguments at stake to conclude the imperative of constitutionalism. The general presumption of the illegitimacy of any non-Imamite rule still posed the formidable issue of a vacuum of legitimacy for a constitutionalist political regime. In other words, if to proponents of just sultanate discourse the vacuum could be filled with the widespread role of a jurist as the deputy of the Imam, the question as to how the *Uṣūlī* School should approach and resolve the issue was yet to be answered. In my opinion, in addition to rejecting tyranny, the origins of the answer are to be found in a jurisprudential analysis of the recurrent issue of working with an unjust ruler, which itself represented yet another aspect of general prohibition of oppression in Shīʿī law. It is my contention that the *Uṣūlī* treatment of the issue, coupled with the constitutionalist jurists' views on the imperative of constitutionalism, provides juridical grounds for making a reliable connection between the people's rights and legitimacy.

Theoretically, Shīʿī *Uṣūlī* jurists have consensually agreed on *manʿ al-wilāya min qibal al-jā'ir* (the general impermissibility of the agency of an oppressive ruler).[97] The main reason behind such impermissibility is the rational and juridical set of arguments revolving around *ḥurmat al-iʿānat ʿalā al-ithm wa ḥurmat iʿānat ʿalā al-ẓālim fī ẓulmihi* (the prohibition against assisting in the realization of the ruler's injustice)[98] and the inseparability of this agency from the commission of sin.[99] Jurists have adopted both objective and subjective approaches to the issue. By an objective approach, they have agreed on the permissibility of an individual's work for an unjust ruler where *ikrāh* (duress) or *iḍṭirār* (compulsory necessity) has been imposed against the individual's life, property, or reputation for accepting the office.[100] However, beyond legally mitigating factors, there is disagreement on the subject matter of impermissibility among the jurists. Based on the traditions—by whose tone and content (i.e., the infallible Imams' statements), the agency of an unjust ruler is absolutely prohibited—some jurists found that the address of impermissibility was directed at the inherent prohibitory character of any act that such a ruler does.[101] Some others held that impermissibility was limited to the ruler's inhibited acts or those that include an inhibited act, and thus excluded the permitted acts.[102] However, beside compulsion, Anṣārī believed the main theory that justified the state of permissibility was *al-qiyām bi maṣāliḥ al-ʿibād* (rising up for the common cause of Muslims' best interests).[103] Anṣārī quoted an opinion[104] rendered originally by reliance on a sixth-century/twelfth-century text that read, "Acceptance of an unjust ruler's agency is permitted in [exclusive] occasions where the so called agent would be able to restore an entitled individual's violated right." He then claimed both the consensus of the jurists and the support of the correct traditions on the validity of such qualification,[105] and argued:

> Prior to invoking such consensus, rational injunctions and reasoning indicate that if the agency of an unjust ruler is prohibited because of its *muḥarramat li dhātihā* (innate essence), accepting it is [to be] permitted. *Because there are occasions in which the importance of meeting the best interests and repulsion of detriments outweigh the [subjective status of] being outwardly included among the agents of such ruler.* Moreover, if it is impermissible because *wa in kānat li istilzāmihā al-ẓulm ʿalā al-ghayr* (some external factors have caused the agency to require an oppression), then [according to this viewpoint], no oppression would take place by accepting the agency [because the origin of injustice is to be directed at the external factor, not at the agency]. (Emphasis mine)[106]

Primarily, it is necessary to note that Anṣārī, in his sophisticated opinion, believed that in the process of materializing the best interests of Muslims there are duties whose undertaking requires no agency from the ruler. In other words, Anṣārī put common interests before and above any type of potential act by the ruler[107] and distinguished them from the issue of agency. This process, I contend, amounts to a premodern conception of individuals' scope of self-determination in Anṣārī's mind. He argues that the incumbency of certain duties in the realm of the best interest of society is both free from the complexities of juristic debates,[108] and independent from the specifically conceptualized perception of legitimacy.[109] On purely technical grounds, the following precepts provide that the act of undertaking this duty is independent from the requirement of working for a ruler:

(1) The general impermissibility of agency in prohibited acts,
(2) The general exclusion of the best interests of the Muslim community from prohibited acts,
(3) Acts concomitant to rising for the best interest of community are superior to *dalīl mukhaṣṣiṣ* (a particularizing evidence or proof). It is so analyzed that those acts, by their external accord, do in fact particularize other general rules.[110]

By referring to the particularizing characteristic of the acts, Anṣārī intended to distinguish acts that relate to those social duties that are directed toward meeting and establishing the best interests of society. This, in Anṣārī's mind, is the measure by which a jurist should analyze and balance duty-bound Muslims' legal reaction to the notion of agency from an unjust ruler, and, to that extent, any other issue that relates to such an agency—the most important of which is the issue of legitimacy. A premodern approach could enumerate examples of such duties as "building public bridges and roads or channeling water from rivers to lands or putting lights in the streets and roads,"[111] but to the constitutionalist jurists, as will be discussed later, the scope of the notion of the best interests of Muslim society could extend well beyond the premodern context.

Another aspect of Anṣārī's discourse is the mandatory character of such an agency in the process of balancing the mandates of commanding right and forbidding wrong when these mandates are in conflict with the prohibition of agency from an unjust ruler. In order to prove his case, Anṣārī made lengthy arguments; I will introduce them briefly here. On the exceptional permissibility of *wilāyat* (agency, representation) he cited and quoted different traditions/reports from the infallible Imams and concluded that the prima facie impart of such textual evidence refers to the necessity of *al-muwāsāt wa al-iḥsān bi al-ikhwān* (comforting and benefiting the coreligionists).[112] By analyzing the relevant traditions/reports, he then categorized the permissible agency into the following types:

1. *Al-wilāyat al-marjūḥa* (literally meaning swinging agency, but intending the reprehensible agency) where, because of the necessities of life, the agent agrees to take office from the unjust ruler, and at the same time has the intention to ease Muslims' lives and limit the detriments of the oppressive rule upon them.[113]
2. *Al-wilāyat al-mustaḥabba* (recommended agency) where the sole purpose of agency is the agent's intention to comfort the faithful.[114]
3. *Al-wilāyat al-wājiba* (mandatory agency) where the performance of the mandatory duty of commanding right and forbidding wrong exclusively depends on acceptance of such agency.

To prove his case, Anṣārī based his argument on an important *Uṣūlī* rational principle according to which "the prerequisite acts necessary for performing a mandatory act are also mandatory."[115] He then concluded that if the performance of the duty of commanding right and forbidding wrong becomes mandatory, it would also be mandatory for the individual to perform all the necessary acts prerequisite to this principal mandate—including taking office from an unjust ruler.[116]

It is the third type of permissible agency that distinguishes Anṣārī from other jurists. Concisely, a juristic analysis of Anṣārī provides the following results:[117]

1. The permissibility of agency is based on *tamakkun li amr bi 'l-ma'rūf* (the possibility of performing the duty of commanding right).[118] In other words, the permissibility only emerges from the circumstances in which it is possible for the duty-bound Muslim (*mukallaf*) to perform his duty of commanding right and forbidding wrong. Otherwise, there is no permissibility or mandate for the duty-bound Muslim's act of agency.
2. Permissibility is general in character (*jawāz bi l-ma'nī al-a'am*)[119] and includes both *umūr mubāḥ* (permissible acts) and *umūr wājib* (mandatory acts).
3. Anṣārī mentioned, "those jurists, who utilized the connotation of *istiḥbāb* (recommendation) in their juristic treatment of agency, had meant *istiḥbāb 'aynī*[120] (individually recommendatory) which is not substantially different from *wujūb kifāyī* (the mandatoriness of those duties the performance of which would be religiously fulfilled by sufficient individuals' undertaking them)."[121] For example, when jurists say that undertaking the charge of adjudication is a recommended

duty for anyone who is capable and confident of doing such, they are in fact referring to a mandatory act (i.e., adjudication) the fulfillment of which would be achieved if a sufficient number of capable individuals would undertake its performance. In other words, it is not mandatory for every individual to perform the duty.

This important argument has to be analyzed in further details. The authority to determine the incumbency of the duty (i.e., whether an individual must undertake its performance or not) is vested upon the duty-bound individual.[122] In order to make such a determination, the only requirement is the individual's *qudrat al-'aqlīyya* (rational faculty) in apprehension of his *qudrat al-ḥāiyya al-'urfiyya*[123] (a potentiality that is commonly held as normal strength) in undertaking the duty. Therefore, as long as the individual has not come to conclude that an individual duty is incumbent upon him, he is not required to take charge of its performance.

4. If it is obvious that performing a mandatory right has been left unattended, or that a forbidden wrong is being committed (which would mean that the mandate of the duty of forbidding it has been realized), the duty of commanding right or forbidding wrong is incumbent upon the individual.[124] Therefore, it becomes mandatory for the duty-bound Muslim to accept the agency as a prerequisite for his duty.[125]

The underpinning presumption of Anṣārī's arguments in favor of the individual's right to determine his duty is, with regards to legally superior independent social acts, inherently based on the belief that there is an original and individual right to self-determination for the Muslims upon which they can participate in their political destiny. By further analysis of Anṣārī's arguments, it can also be concluded that the independent acts necessary for the realization of the common interests of the Muslim community share the same characteristics of the duty of commanding right and forbidding wrong.[126] Put another way, given the superior status of those independent acts and the importance of the duty of commanding right and forbidding wrong in the Shī'ī contractualist theory of rights, the duty of commanding right transmits to the superior independent acts that are capable of defining the nature of a just government. Such transmission evolves into a quintessential congruity between the two concepts without the existence of which the dilemma of validity—and even of the mandate—of taking office and agency from an unjust ruler will not be resolved. On the one hand, there is congruity between "the duty of rising up for the common interests of the Muslim community through comforting and benefiting coreligionists," and "the duty of commanding right and forbidding wrong." On the other, there is yet another congruity between the "existence of superior independent acts" and "the individual's authority in determining 'the nature of duty' that emanates from recognition of the qualifications of the act."

The juridical-political inference of such combined congruity is that there is a correlation between the "possibility of commanding right and forbidding wrong," and the "just or unjust characteristic of the government" that can be translated into the semi- or even real legitimacy of political rule.[127] Despite the fact that Anṣārī cited and quoted some of the Shīʿī jurists' arguments that refer to "just sultan,"[128] he never attempted to prove that such a sultan—with the exception of quintessential faith in reappearance of the Imam—could ever come to the fore and hold political power.[129] At the same time, he did not approve of "just sultanate discourse" either. Moreover, he rejected the jurists' deputyship of the Imam in political power and their intermediary role in filling the non-Imam rule's vacuum of legitimacy.[130] The reason was simply that if it were possible to establish a legitimate just sultanate with the intermediacy of jurists, there would have been no need to discuss the necessity of the pristine qualification of infallibility of the Imam as the sole authorized individual capable of holding political power. By *Uṣūlī* accounts, the intermediary role of the jurist, in the form of the deputyship of the Imam as employed in legitimizing unjust rule, would be equal to leveling the infallibility of the Imam to the jurist, and considering such an exclusive characteristic to be a transferable subject—an idea that no jurist would support. My point here is not to rebut such an impossible equation. It is, however, to argue that the whole discourse embodies an emphasis on the duty of commanding right and forbidding wrong. In other words, if the principal conditions for the establishment of a just political rule are similar to those based on which the prohibitory nature of agency from an unjust ruler could be transmitted to a mandatory duty, then the key issue is not the type of government. Rather, it is the possibility of performing the duty of rising up for the best common interests of the Muslim community, which includes commanding right and forbidding wrong. In addition, the yardstick of justness of political sovereignty is the possibility of fulfillment in performing such mandatory duties wherever possible even in an unjust rule.[131] The final point is that by vesting the authority of determination to the individual, Anṣārī rejects any special discretionary role for the jurist, and therefore opens the argument for declaring that any political agent who violates such individual authority has, in fact, committed an injustice by infringing upon the individual rights of Muslims.[132]

This analysis leads us to the complementary discussion of the next main issues, that is, the conditions for performing the duty in the absence of the Imam, and the dialectic between these conditions and *ḥisba* matters,[133] on the one hand, and the absence of authority for the jurist of guardianship of the Shiites' political life, on the other.

"Commanding Right and Forbidding Wrong" and Ḥisba Issues

Again, in order to present the discussion, I find it necessary to begin with the constitutionalist jurists' opinions. After the cruel dissolution of the Majlis, the Trite Jurist Leaders, in stark support of the Majlis and constitutionalism, wrote:

> Usurpation of the Shīʿī government is [one] of the necessities of the *Jaʿfarī Madhhab* (the Twelver Shīʿī School)... With regards to hidden exigencies and the time's expediency, we have to conceal our intentions [of unfolding the technicalities of juristic debates]. We should, however, briefly state the present time duty of all Muslims [i.e., the Shiites of Iran] that *in the time of absence [of the infallible Imam], ʿuqalā'-i Muslimīn va thiqāt-i mu'minīn (the rational and discerning individuals of Muslims and the trustworthy of the faithful people) are authorized to take the charge of administering the ʿurfī*[134] *and ḥisbiyya (representation-guardianship) duties. The embodiment of such [authority] was the very Consultative Assembly [i.e., the Majlis] that has been coerced to dissolve by the tyrants' and the disobedient sinners' oppression. Today, it is individually mandatory to all Muslims to employ their utmost strife for the cause of re-establishment and reinstatement of the Assembly.* Being lazy and recalcitrant in doing so is tantamount to retreating from [battle fields of] the holy war and, therefore, a major sin. (Emphasis mine)[135]

As can be clearly inferred, the constitutionalist jurists advocated such a broad base of authority for this specific group of individuals that, in any social categorization, they would share characteristics similar to those of the elected legislators and executive authorities. It is, however, necessary to discuss the technical terms (*ḥisbiyya* duties and *ʿurfī* issues) that they used in their theory. It is my contention that the constitutionalist jurists' utilization of the terms for theorizing their views on constitutionalism emanates from the concept of independent duties for the achievement of the common good and the interests of the Muslim community that Anṣārī had previously developed. In other words, the customary and *ḥisbiyya* duties share the identity of the duties that are related to *al-qiyām bi maṣāliḥ al-ʿibād* (rising up for the best interests of the Muslim community).

Ḥisbiyya discourse is generally perceived as the founding juristic theory of, but not limited to, Islamic administrative law.[136] In Sunni sources, the issue has been studied in close relation to the general duty of commanding right and forbidding wrong.[137] Sunni jurists have also employed the concept as a term of art for the specific duties of the market inspector in an Islamic government.[138] By technical definition, *ḥisba* in Sunni Law is "any *munkar* (illegal act) which: (1) is being committed in the present time, (2) *Muḥtasib* (the public administrator who has the authority to perform the duty of prohibiting illegal acts) can discover without investigation [i.e., only an illicit flagrant offence], and (3) can be verified as illegal without recourse to *ijtihād*."[139] In this context, the discussion of *ḥisba* has been developed in two general categories of conditions attached to the *ḥisba* and the qualifications of the *muḥtasib*.[140] Based on the distinctions made by Māwardī, it has been so argued that "the jurisdiction of *ḥisba* lies midway between that of *qaḍā* (the decisions made in the law courts) and that of the *maẓālim* (the decisions made in the courts of wrongs)."[141] An *ḥisba* duty, in general, has to be analyzed and enforced in three subcategories. First, *ḥuqūq Allah* (the rights of God, mostly categorized in *'ibādāt* or acts of worshipping, as a relative equivalent to public rights). Second, *ḥuqūq al-ādamiyīn* (the rights of individuals, mostly categorized in *mu'āmilāt* or relations between individuals such as transactions and established social customs, or an equivalent of private rights). Third, *ḥuqūq al-mukhtaliṭa* (the combined rights of God and individuals where both are commonly concerned).[142] The illegal acts are also categorized in yet another three subgroups: those that affect worshipping God (cases such as an individual's attempt to contravene devotional rules or to change established forms), those that involve reprehensible conducts (i.e., dubious situations that incur the suspicion of committing illegal acts), and those where an individual's divinely devised right is being infringed (e.g., when the prohibited act of an undue searching of homes is done by someone who hides in a place from where he can spy inside another's house without knowledge of the owner of the house).[143] Given the sophisticated jurisprudential analysis of the concept of *ḥaqq* (right) in Islamic law, and its inherent relation to the notion of duty, any categorization of rights was also nuanced by philosophical trajectories in which relevant issues such as adjudication and the discovery of rules found prominent place in the arguments of *ḥisba*.[144] It was in this context that *muḥtasib*s (the administrators of *ḥisba* duties), based on the jurists' findings in the three aforementioned categories of rights, were assigned to regulate the practical manifestations of such rights and implement the jurists' findings. This was where the religious concepts of *ma'rūf* (right) and *munkar* (wrong) would take the forms of "legal" and "illegal," respectively. Throughout the history of Muslim societies, the classical institution of *ḥisba* and the office of *muḥtasib* transmuted into the duty of inspecting the market. Such a transition should be viewed in a direct relation between the state's degree of adherence to the implementation of the universal duty of commanding right and prohibiting wrong, on the one hand, and the adoption of policies tolerant toward prevalent practice of the duty by individuals, on the other. In other words, from the rich[145] and broad base embedded in the juristic discourse of commanding right and prohibiting wrong (which was transmitted in the "enforcement of the law and the prevention of illegality"),[146] the importance and value of the institution diminished and plummeted to measuring the weights and setting the market price of goods.[147]

In Shīʿī Law, while the duty of commanding right and forbidding wrong as the core of the concept was upheld,[148] it has been viewed in a different scope,[149] which also included non-litigious matters.[150] According to a Shīʿī scholar, a *ḥisba* duty has four major qualifications:

> (1) There should be an expedience for the establishment of the legitimacy of the duty in private matters or in public matters. As a private issue, the example could be the protection and administration of an absent third party's proprietary rights in emergency circumstances when the property is unattended and obtaining a judicial permission is practically impossible. For example, when the neighbor is absent and his house needs repair and maintenance. In the public sphere, however, the administration of any unattended public duty is at issue. (2) The intended matter should not be among the intending individual's personal interests, (3) It should be performed with the intention of accomplishing the best interest and expediency of the third party or the public, and (4) Such expedience, according to the Shari'ah, should not be left unattended.[151]

Given the fluid characteristics of the acts and the complicated nature of the difficult concept of *ḥisba* embedded in jurists' definition of the term,[152] two important issues are at stake: (i) the question of fact or the issue of clarification (i.e., what exactly the manifestations of *ḥisba* are). This issue becomes substantially controversial when we notice that the legal presumption of prerequisite authority, by its nature, may linger between "representation" and the "guardianship" of the third party or the public's interest. (ii) The right person to carry out the duty and the qualifications he should have. It is an indisputable fact that Shīʿī jurists have serious disagreements on both issues.

The Issue of the Clarification of Ḥisba in Shīʿī Jurisprudence. In general, Shīʿī jurists agree that the protective custodial duties of two groups of individuals are among the indisputable manifestations of *ḥisba* duties: (1) the *ghuyyab* (those who are absent) and the protection of their proprietary rights, and (2) the life and properties of the *quṣṣar* (those who lack sufficient capacity for the administration of their rights and are prohibited from intervention in their rights, like insane and minor individuals whose legal guardians are not available).[153] In its classical and traditional approach to the issue, the main measure by which the Shīʿī jurists have deciphered and categorized *ḥisba* matters/duties is the existence or inexistence of a valid text in which a person in charge of performing the duty has been designated. While it takes a very powerful legal imagination to determine and enumerate all the matters that could fit within such a broad context,[154] the Shīʿī jurists have applied an ad hoc analysis of a variety of judicial and litigious issues in order to clarify the scope of *ḥisba*. Some of those issues are:

> paying an abstaining party's debts from his properties where a judicial verdict has been issued to that effect, stopping the sale of an endowed property in the absence of legitimate cause, stopping the sale of a mortgaged property when it accrues an unrecoverable damage for the owner, designating a trustee [an escrow-like agent, even without the owner's consent] charged with protecting the property until the legal disputes are resolved, designating a guardian for a minor or an insane person when presumptive guardians [i.e., father and paternal grandfather] are dead or unavailable, requiring the abstaining husband to pay alimony to or divorce his wife, adding an aide to a testator who is unable to perform his duties, deposing a testator who has violated the duty of care and refrains from resignation after his miscarriage of duty is established by the testimony of witnesses.[155]

In a much more technical analysis, other concepts are also added to the argument. A classic Shīʿī conception of the term provides the following definition:

> *Ḥisba* means *qurba* (proximity) which connotes seeking proximity to God. A *ḥisba* matter is any good deed, the realization of which we know is at the bequest of religion in the world, while a specific person is not appointed to take the charge of its performance.[156] Among those deeds is performance of the important duty of commanding right, when its omission has appeared, and forbidding wrong—when it is being committed.[157]

In this technical setting, *ḥisba* issues relate to those legitimate duties the undertaking of which, we have certain jurisprudential knowledge, will satisfy God.[158] In other words, we know by certitude that God will be dissatisfied if those duties are left unlooked after. The argument becomes more complicated when jurists take the intertwined notion of proximity to God into consideration. Ṣadr mentions: "What is meant by 'act for proximity' is any act for whose legitimate realization in the world, a will exists that our knowledge about it [the will], does not [merely] emanate from the divine ordainments."[159]

Put differently, while we do not have certain specific text-based knowledge about the act or its rule, we know, by our own apprehension of the broader context of legitimate necessity, that there is a legitimate cause for undertaking the act and for the necessity in realizing (i.e., coming to existence) its consequent results. In order to clarify those acts and their consequent results, Shīʿī jurists have taken a case-by-case approach in their jurisprudential treatment of the concept of *ḥisba*. In the following, I will introduce some examples of such ad hoc designations in jurists' arguments:[160]

1. In a legal action when the assignee of a bill of exchange denies receiving the assigned money, he is allowed to introduce less than the legally required number of witnesses. Such testimony, as evidence, is called *bayyina ḥisba*.[161] The objectives are to preserve social order, to prevent undue enrichment, and to protect the sanctity of legitimate property. The rule clearly is to loosen the strictness of the evidentiary rule on the required number of witnesses to be produced in a financial dispute and to allow for the circumstantial evidence to stand. This solution provides the *right to raise a legitimate defense* for the assignee.
2. Based on a *ḥisba* right, a nonparty individual has the permission to remove belongings that are combined with a usurped property.[162] The objectives are to preserve social order, to prevent an undue enrichment, and to protect the sanctity of legitimate property. The rule is the separation of legitimate properties and their protection from illegitimate disposition. The solution is to honor and uphold the *right to possession of legitimate property in urgent circumstances.*
3. If (i) someone has access to a deceased person's estate, (ii) is aware that the deceased has allocated a fee for hiring an agent to perform his/her failed duty of pilgrimage to Mecca, and (iii) knows that the deceased's heirs will not honor the deceased's decision of such allocation, then, based on a *ḥisba*-oriented rule, he is allowed to put aside an equal amount of the fee for performing the pilgrimage from the deceased's assets.[163] The objectives revolve around (i) commanding right, which involves (a) honoring *the deceased's continued proprietary right*, (b) honoring *the legitimate right of the deceased to the vicarious performance of his religious duty*, and (ii) prohibiting wrong through the prevention of the undue disposition of the heirs over the legitimate rights of the deceased person. The rule is devising authority for the quasi-testator over the deceased's assets. The solution is to support the *legitimacy of the quasi-testator's duty-authority* in dividing the asset for a legitimate cause.

4. In a case when the appointed executor of the testament has been *fāsiq* (a person who does not meet the legal requirement of righteousness), and we were not aware of his status, the issue is whether the executor's implemented decisions prior to our knowledge are legally binding or not. ʿAllāma and Shahīd al-Awwal held negative opinions. Fāḍil, however, based on the logic of *ḥisba*, held that the executor's decisions are *nāfiḍ* (legally effectual) because of the mere requirement of necessity.[164] The objectives here are the preservation of social order, and prevention of probable damages incurred by *restitutio in integrum,* including irreparable damage to the properties. The rule is the legal effectuation of a nonqualified testator's decisions. The solution is the presumption of the *exceptional validity of the testator's decisions* in exigent circumstances.
5. It is mandatory for the minor heirs of a deceased father or paternal grandfather to uphold their legal guardians' appointment of an executor who is entrusted with control over the minors' proprietary rights. Even when such guardians have not appointed an executor, the minors still have to uphold the decisions made by any duty-bound Muslim who, based on a *ḥisba*-oriented duty to assist in the coming into existence of the deceased individual's legal right as reflected in his/her testament, has stepped in to protect their rights.[165] The objectives here are to preserve social order, and to prevent minors from interfering with their properties. The rule is the derivative duty of obedience incumbent upon the minors to honor their presumptive guardians' decisions. The solution involves devising an *authority for a non-appointed testator to intervene with legitimate cause* in the protection of the minors' proprietary rights.
6. If the spouses, when in *shiqāq* (marital dispute and physical severance prior to divorce), refrain from assigning their arbitrators, it is the *ḥisba* duty of the judge to assign the arbitrators on their behalf.[166] The objectives here are the preservation of social order, commanding the right of abiding by the Qur'anic rule requiring the intervention of the assigned arbitrators, and forbidding the wrong of omitting the Qur'anic rule on the duty of disputant spouses to assign their arbitrators. The rule here is the judicial authority of the judge to act on behalf of the refraining parties. The solution is to devise an *exceptional judicial authority for the judge* to act on behalf of refraining spouses in marital dispute.
7. When analyzing whether a defendant accused of committing a *ḥudūd* crime[167] has the right to appoint an agent to defend on his behalf or not, Karakī held that every duty-bound Muslim who has sufficient knowledge to prove or disprove the crimes can

represent the defendant. He argued that the *ḥisba* theory of the presumption of *istiwā' al-mukallafīn* (the equality of all the duty-bound Muslims) governs over the case.[168] The objectives here are the preservation of social order, and the purging of judicial proceeding from undue injustice against the accused. The rule here is the presumption of equality in qualified individuals' right-duty-authority to interfere in the judicial processes of proving a predetermined crime. The solution here is the *legitimacy of providing the accused with the right to legal assistance* in questionable occasions.

8. If someone, without prior knowledge that a property had previously been put in trust, possesses the property, and then realizes its trusted status, and when there is a fear that the property will be destroyed, the possessor has a *ḥisba* authority to sell the property with the intention of protecting the absent trustee's proprietary rights. Such intention should be based on a *niyyat ḥisba al-Sharʿīyya* (an intention that is binding by Shari'ah rules). If the possessor takes necessary care of the property but is not able to save it, the possessor is *muḥsin* (beneficent) and, therefore, not liable.[169] Such possession is based on fiduciary and trust.[170] The nature of the act is revealed by the intention of doing a charitable act with the objective of preventing a halt or disorder that may incur the order of society; it is founded on *ḥisba*, and commanding right and prohibiting wrong that is recognizable for the Legislator through *shahāda ḥisbī* (*ḥisba* testimony).[171] The objectives here are the preservation of social order, and honoring *the absent owner's proprietary rights*. The rule is a bona fide possessor's fiduciary duty to take the utmost care of an unowned property in preservation of the owner's right under exigent circumstances. The solution is the *legitimacy of the exceptional authority of a bona fide possessor* of an unowned property to sell it on behalf of its owner.
9. According to a *ḥisba* rule, an individual who has revived an uncultivated land is vested with legal priority in possession over everyone else.[172] The objective is the maintenance of social order. The rule involves honoring the legitimate labor of the individual. The solution is the *legitimacy of the right to priority* of the laborer over possession.
10. If a husband refrains from paying his wife's *mahr*[173] (dowry), the judge has a *ḥisba* right-authority to confiscate the refraining husband's assets at the amount of his debt to the wife.[174] The same is true if the executor refrains from paying the *nafaqa* (alimony)[175] of the deceased's wife.[176] The objective here is the preservation of social order, the preservation of *the individual rights of women*

during and after marriage, and the prevention of wrong by depriving women of their legitimate marital monetary rights. The rule here is that the husband, or his appointed testator, is required to pay the spousal dues and benefits of his wife. The solution in this case is to devise an *exceptional judicial authority for the judge* over the refraining husband's assets or a legal testator's miscarriage in the management of assets by depriving the wife of her financial rights.

11. On the legal occasions when a woman has a right to divorce and her husband refrains from doing so, the judge has a *ḥisba* right-authority to divorce her on behalf of the refraining husband. If the judge fails to render the verdict of divorce, the authority is vested in the most just individuals among the faithful.[177] The objectives here are preservation of social order, and honoring *the individual rights of women*. The rule is that the husband must honor his wife's right to divorce. The solution is to devise an *exceptional judicial authority for the judge* to act on behalf of the refraining spouse in the performance of marital duties, and devise a substitute *exceptional authority for specified and qualified individuals* to act on behalf of both the failing judge and the refraining husband in the protection or performance of marital duties.

As can be perceived, in the context of balancing individual rights and preserving social order while reviewing the general rules governing the facts of each case, Shīʿī jurists have suggested different solutions that—according to their views on justice and fairness—best served the parties' legitimate interests. The issue is not whether they could come up with better solutions. It is the element of justness and fairness in the juristic process—as epitomized in the duty of commanding right and forbidding wrong in the context of the combined objectives of honoring rights and preserving social order—that matters. Through the medium of new rules, then, another right, duty, or authority emerges from that process. The judicial nature of the argument and the manifestation of the process in exclusively diverse judicial atmospheres correspond with yet another obvious fact: it is only in the context of judicial cases that new rules and opinions, and to that effect, new theories, come into existence. One should also note that the underpinning presumption of the jurists in rendering opinions was their general observation of the exclusive authority of the Imam in having the final word in all legal and religious issues,[178] as well as the specific provision of whether his authority is transferable to the jurists or not.[179] The prevailing view in Shīʿī law on validity of juristic finding considers these discoveries to be fallible, and subject to final approval on Resurrection Day. Therefore, Shīʿī jurists have always been heavily inclined to declare their opinions as the most achievable, rather than the most authoritative.[180]

In having further analyzed the jurists' opinions, it is now necessary to discuss the underpinning concept of proximity—that is, a legal analysis of "the legitimate cause for the realization of the act and its consequent results," which is considered to be based on both Shari'ah rules and our rational perception.[181] In his long and sophisticated debate on the permissibility and legitimacy of hiring an agent and paying for the vicarious performance of acts of proximity—and whether or not such gain and receipt of payment is legal—Anṣārī argued in favor of the general permissibility of acting on behalf of others and receiving payment for it.[182] He excluded, however, receiving payment in two major categories. First, he excluded *wājibāt aw mustaḥabbāt 'aynī*[183] (mandated or recommended individual duties), where due to the requirement of personal incumbency and the performance of mandatory or recommended acts, vicarious proximity is held to be impossible. In other words, purity in proximity to God should necessarily be experienced—and fulfilled—by the individual through the personal incumbency of the act, and does not come into existence by another's agency. Second, he excluded *wājibāt kifāyī* (mandatory public/social duties)[184]; these are those unspecified mandatory duties that if performed by a sufficient number of duty-bound Muslims, the others' burden would be released. By contextualizing the argument within three premises, Anṣārī contrasted the notion of acts of proximity with the important issue of public or individual interests. The three precepts were:

1. Maintaining the order of society is a mandatory duty.
2. Specialized public duties transform into the mandatory individual duties of the specialists. Since no one else is capable of completely protecting the interests embedded in these duties, they practically and specifically transform into the individually mandatory duty of those who have the prerequisite knowledge of performing them. For example, the adjudication and medical treatment of patients are, in general, mandatorily incumbent on those who have the required knowledge of law and medicine. It transforms into their individual mandatory duty when a public or individual interest is left unattended and there is a need to perform the duty for the protection of said interest.
3. Those public duties, upon which the order of society has been founded, are among the mandatory public duties.

The technical question is that, given the theoretical impermissibility of receiving payment on mandatory public duties, how can one justify compensation for performing those public duties?[185] In response to this question, Anṣārī introduced seven competing juristic arguments.[186] While arguments regarding the issue of compensation do not directly relate to my discussion, Anṣārī's seventh argument does provide invaluable and authoritative insight into the relationship between the *ḥisba* and public interests on the one hand, and the issue of the fundamental rights of the individual in Shīʿī Law on the other. According to that argument:

> *The mode of mandatoriness of the act of performing public duties is not essentially embedded in the act itself. They are mandatory because accomplishing the higher objective and mandate of a sustained order in the society is due upon their subject matter acts. Public duties also become mandatory on the basis of what is necessary for the preservation of [the right to] life.* Maintenance of the social order cannot solely be achieved by *al-'amal tabarru'an* (voluntary charitable acts), it is also based on *al-'amal bi al-'ujrat* (compensable acts). In the case of medical services, what is mandatory in the preservation of the right to life and maintenance of the social order is that the physician avail himself and his knowledge to the patient, not to do it without compensation. He can opt for undertaking it as either a charitable or a compensable act. Thus, if the patient pays him, it becomes his mandatory duty to cure the patient. If the patient does not pay, however, considering the necessity of curing the patient in preserving his life [which makes it, yet again, mandatory for the physician to cure the patient], the judge, based on the logic of *ḥisba*, will order the patient to pay the physician's fees. In either of the circumstances, it is permissible for the physician to undertake the duty with the intention of receiving compensation. Even if the patient does not have any money to pay the physician, he bears the burden of paying a debt that can be made at a later time in life or even after his death. If he is found unable to pay, the debt should be paid from collected alms or other sources. (Emphasis mine)[187]

The prevailing theory of accomplishing the "higher objective of sustained order in the society" is heavily based on[188] the duty of commanding right and forbidding wrong.[189] Such duty in turn corresponds to a well-established precept in Islamic law, which calls for any act that "*ḥāfiẓat li 'l-maqāṣid al-khamsah allatī taqtaḍī bi wujūb ḥifẓuhā al-'aql ka al-sharʿ*" (protects the five objectives whose preservation is required by the rule of reason as well as the Shari'ah).[190] These five objectives are preservation of human life, property, reason, honor, and progeny.[191] Therefore, the legitimate cause for the realization of a *ḥisba* is any premise that is instrumental for and intermediates in the coming into existence of social order, which in turn is based on the preservation of the five fundamental rights. In the aforementioned case of the physician, the judge's verdict on payment to the physician is an instrument that not only regulates the relationship between the patient and the physician by accommodating the physician's legitimate right and intention to be paid (if he has such intention), it also provides for the greater good of society, that is, the social order that is to be maintained, and the implementation of its underpinning duty of preservation. The context in which all of these dynamics play out is the broader concept of commanding right and forbidding wrong.

The notion of proximity to God is not a stranger to this context. It is present in the intention of every individual who undertakes the duty of commanding right and forbidding wrong, and for that matter a *ḥisba*. Proximity to God is manifested in acting in observance of the effort to honor the universally applicable rights of individuals—for which God has ordained His Shari'ah—and undertaking the fiduciary duty of utmost care for the preservation of other's interest—be it an individual or the public—when the preservation of this right or interest is unattended. Whatever it is, proximity exists in the deeper layers of those dynamics; this proximity belongs to the realm of individual moral experience and spiritual bargains made between God and the individual, which are mostly approached through the devotional and worshipping nature of the act.

Anṣārī then went on to discuss the legitimacy of the rule of compensating for the services of two other mandatory individual duties: that of an appointed testator's fees,[192] which is a *ḥukm taklīfī* (an injunctive ruling),[193] and that of a mother's right to be compensated for breast-feeding her newborn baby,[194] which is a *ḥukm waḍ'ī* (a declaratory ruling).[195] He finally concluded:

> If an act is one of mandatory public duties [upon which the social order is founded], it is permissible to hire someone [to perform the act on behalf of others]. By the employee's performance, the mandatoriness of the duty is fulfilled, and therefore, no one else is in charge even if the objective of *imtithāl* [i.e., similarity between the two intentions of the employer and the employee] is not achieved.
>
> Receiving payment for a physician upon whom performance of the [general] duty [of treating patients] is specifically incumbent, and who has made his services available to the patient, is of this nature. Although the act of treatment has been specified, providing the necessary co-presence of physician and patient—which is the threshold step toward treatment—includes an unspecified [joint] mandatory duty. The physician's duty [i.e., every physician has to provide medical services to patients], and the duty of the patient's relatives [i.e., the duty of providing a physician] is incumbent upon every member of the patient's family. The physician's presence is tantamount to performing a mandatory public duty, just as providing for his presence is the unspecified duty of the patient's relatives for realization of which paying the physician is permissible. [*So we have three different duties: (1) the individual mandatory duty incumbent*

upon the specified physician, (2) the public duty of the physician to render his medical services to patients, and (3) the general duty of a patient's relatives to provide the patient with the presence of a physician. The permissibility of making and receiving payment emanates from the benefit that the patient receives from physician's presence, not the physician's act in rendering medical service.]

Any act from whose evidence we discover an individual right which is to be honored by any duty-bound Muslim is [also] excluded from those compensable acts, because by performing the act, it is the mandated duty [of honoring the right] that has been fulfilled, and it is not permissible to receive payment for performing mandatory duties. It is so held from the prima facie evidence of the mandatory duty of burying a deceased person, that the deceased person has the right to burial. Anyone who participates in undertaking the duty, in fact, honors the deceased's right, and it is impermissible for individuals to receive payment for honoring such right. It is similarly true for teaching the rules of mandatory worshipping acts to those who do not have the required knowledge and are in need of knowing them... *A lutfun qarīḥat (an ingenious précised [legal] mind) is needed to determine what is an individual right and what is not.* (Emphasis mine)[196]

Based on Anṣārī's debates and the jurists' employment of the concept of *ḥisba* in their opinions, one can draw the following conclusions:

1. *Ḥisba* as a *ḥukm* (rule) is a legal permission that is rendered when there is a legitimate cause for the protection of social order and individual rights.
2. *Ḥisba* as a *ḥaqq* (right) is an entitlement that represents the individual's right or the public's interest in dubious, suspicious, or necessary circumstances.
3. *Ḥisba* as a *taklīf* (an obligation, a duty) is, by nature, a mandatory public duty that should be honored when it is discovered after balancing rights and rules.
4. *Ḥisba* as *wilāyat* (authority on representation) is an exceptional authority devised for a judge or a qualified individual where the principal in charge of the duty, in which a legitimate right or interest of a beneficiary exists, is refraining from taking the proper action, or is absent or unable to protect the legitimate right or interest. It should not be confused with *Ḥisba* as a *ḥaqq*.
5. *Ḥisba* matters need to be discovered by legal minds and judges, and performed by those who have sufficient legal capacity to interfere with the order of society and the protection of individual rights.
6. In *ḥisba* discourse, both the order of society and individual rights are to be strictly scrutinized. In fact, while it is very difficult to theorize

which outweighs the other, it is of utmost importance to balance them in each specific case.

The Issue of Authority in Charge of Ḥisba in Shīʿī Jurisprudence. With regard to the earlier conclusions, I will now discuss the second main issue of *ḥisba* discourse, the authority in charge of *ḥisba* matters. As mentioned before, next to the question of fact, the other fundamental element of any *ḥisba* issue was that a specific person is not appointed by God to undertake the charge of implementation of the duties that emerge from a *ḥisba*.[197] The notion of the absence of a specific, appointed person in charge can be viewed as seemingly conflictive with the broader concept of God's satisfaction with the realization of *ḥisba*. In other words, it can amount to an antithetical proposition where it remains unclear as to how God could be satisfied with the performance of a duty without informing the legal agents and the duty-bound Muslims as to which one of them is in charge of its undertaking. In theory, this would be a misguidance that may contradict God's widespread *luṭf* (benevolence) in the human beings' path toward knowing His Laws. A more thorough juristic view, however, leads us to conclude that the logical postulate of an absence of appointment is equal to assuming generality in the existence of the duty for all. In other words, if no one is specified, it means that everybody is in charge. This idea is based on two intertwined juristic arguments: first, with an absence of appointment, the subject matter act is a public duty. As discussed before, mandatory duties are divided into two categories: mandatory individual duties and mandatory public duties. The main element in an individual duty is the specificity of its incumbent charge. By contrast, a mandatory public duty is general. The logic of a public duty is that if anyone undertakes its performance, the burden of the rest will be released because the objective of the charge was achieved by one such performance. Second, as described earlier, the concept of *ḥisba* is another equivalent to the duty of commanding right and forbidding wrong. It is obvious that such duty is a public charge, and not an individual one.[198] In fact, one can conclude that it is the performance of the duty of commanding right and forbidding wrong that, if left unattended, would leave God dissatisfied. The main context for the duty, as mentioned before, is the preservation of the five higher objectives of the Shari'ah, meaning the protection of every human being's life, property, honor, reason, and progeny. This rich and comprehensive context, as can be imagined,[199] allows the issue of authority in *ḥisba* to provide for thorough arguments on the modern subjects of individual rights and freedoms as well as the breadth or limitation of political power. Given the key element of "legitimate cause" in the form of an individual interest, or public expediency in the process of realizing a *ḥisba*, and the importance of observing this cause and expedience by the person in charge, Shīʿī jurists have proposed two main responses to the issue: (i) The premodern theory in Shīʿī jurisprudence that is based on a sequel in performance of the duty by the jurists, in the first place, and the most reliable and just of the faithful, after them; and (ii) the modern theory that the constitutionalist jurists proposed and designated the most reliable and just individuals to be the sole authority in charge. Two important consequential factors heavily count for the difference between these two responses. The first of these concerns the absence or existence of a social order in which realization of *ḥisba* is institutionally organized. The premodern response had developed in a sociopolitical order that had historically been characterized by despotism, and a widespread disregard for rights and the best interest of the community. Whereas the modern response gleaned a new order in which the Majlis and a structured judiciary, as social institutions responsible for the regulation and organization of the processes of realizing a *ḥisba*, were on the scene, these two important institutions were virtually absent in nineteenth-century Iran.[200] The second factor is the longstanding traditional role of jurists as adjudicators. In the absence of a structured judiciary, the jurists usually took the office of judge and adjudicated legal disputes. Consequently, the state's obligation was to honor and enforce their verdicts. Moreover, the jurists played a prominent role in supporting individuals through the socioculturally supported practice of *bast-nishīnī*,[201] by which those who were under the state's persecution could seek a respected jurist's support by taking refuge in his house.[202] Although there were a whole host of juristic reasons made by the proponents of the first theory in support of the jurists' priority in undertaking the *ḥisba* duties, such social roles also fed into the reinforcement of their opinion. One last point is that through the formation of legislative and judicial institutions, and the diminishing role of the jurists as judges and rule-makers, the issue of authority over *ḥisba* duties had practically been reduced to theoretical discussions about the guardianship of incapacitated individuals.

Most of the juristic literature and discourse prior to the 1905 Revolution can be found in the scattered arguments for or against the broader issue of the scope of a jurist's deputyship for the infallible Imam.[203] Those who adhered to the jurisprudential validity of the jurists' widespread agency found the authority to determine and implement *ḥisba* matters to be congruent with this agency. On the other hand, the main counterarguments were made in rejection of the widespread authority for the jurist, and not specifically on the authority over *ḥisba*. I must mention, however, that some of the proponents of the jurist's guardianship of political power believe that authority theoretically derived from the *ḥisba* discourse. In other words, they took the issue of governance to be one of the main *ḥisba* duties.[204] In order to conclude these arguments, the rest of this chapter will discuss two main issues: the concept of *wilāyah* (authority), especially when the person of the Imam is absent, and the broader issue of *wilāyat al-faqīh*—the heart of controversy.

Wilāyah: The Authority of Guardianship or Representation? The underpinning essence of my argument is the concept of *wilāyah* (a specific authority generally conceived as guardianship). The nature of this authority is technically analyzed as *ḥukm* (a positive rule). A positive rule is defined as "something that is devised for the prohibition or permission or effectuation of an act, which relates to one's duty or a circumstance that requires any of such to be devised."[205] In the context of *wilāyah*, the concept of positive rule has to be contrasted with *ḥaqq* (a right), which provides its holder with absolute powers of possession, transfer (by contracts or inheritance), and forfeiture (by voluntary acts) against others.[206] While

> *ḥaqq* is a *shayʿ al-thābit* (static object or phenomenon, can be loosely translated as a legal notion) that causes an authority to be established and employed by its holder against an adversary, *wilāyah* is the essence of authority that the holder of the right has devised in favor of another. Devising such authority should be examined in two contexts: (1) from the viewpoint of the [scope of] effectuation—in this context, *wilāyah*, only and for the most part, includes authority over *mā huwa lah wa li maṣliḥatihi* (what is in the benefit and expedience of the principal right-holder)—and (2) from the viewpoint of exercise, which only includes the occasions in which there is *naqṣ fi al-muwallā ʿalayh* (a legal impediment on the individual who is placed under guardianship) and the necessity of referring his interest, in unity, to that of the society in the broader context of the social order.[207]

Therefore, *wilāyah* is a circumstantial rule supported by reason and the Shari'ah, which provides a non-right-based authority for its holder over the principal's life and property.[208] It does not provide the holder of *wilāyah* with absolute authority over the transferability or forfeiture of the guarded right and expedience. In other words, the holder of *wilāyah* cannot transfer his authority to others or cause the principal right's forfeiture. According to prevailing opinion in Shīʿī law, what can be deduced from the concept of *wilāyah* is that the authority derives from the duty to protect the expediency and the best interests of the person who needs to be guarded and lacks the capacity of recognition.[209] To this extent—and as part of the broader notion of proximity—the holder of authority, in fact, protects the right-holder's interests by acting and assuming how the right-holder would act in normal circumstances. It is also important to notice that with the authority to protect the interests of the right-holder comes the fiduciary duty of utmost care and avoidance of conflict between the holder of authority's and the right-holder's respective interests. That is why the jurists believe the authority derives from the *sha'n* (status) of the person in need of guardianship, and not the qualifications of the holder of authority.[210] A broad and unmatched *wilāyah* to command and demand obedience over the lives and properties of the people, according to Shīʿī law, is reserved exclusively for the infallibles (i.e., the Prophet and Imams), which in turn has been devised by God.[211] From this rule, one can infer that the infallibles' authority derives from God's right to command and demand obedience. The issue, however, is whether the infallible persons have absolute authority over individuals or not. In other words, what is the infallible persons' duty-authority with regards to individuals' lives and properties? By analyzing the infallible persons' authority on this issue, jurists have argued that there are two possible definitions for such authority.

> (1) The Infallible persons' valid authority together with the duty of abiding by them, and (2) any discretionary authority over people's lives and belongings depending on what the infallible person wills, similar to that of an [ordinary] individual's, where no sin has been committed to invalidate such [individual] authority. For example, allowing the infallible person to marry a mentally mature adult woman without her permission [and consent], or purchase one's property without the owner's permission because the infallible persons have authority over their bodies and belongings. The first type of authority is permissible because obedience to the infallible person is tantamount to obedience to God. [The author has intended to inform that the infallible persons' determination of the rules of Shari'ah derives from Divine's Will]. The second type, however, is subject to further reflection. From all the exegetic interpretations of the Qur'anic verse on the Prophet's superiority over the faithful people's lives,[212] such [an arbitrary] authority has not emerged. What has been found in the relevant traditions, on the mandate of obedience, refutes opposition to the first definition and is devoid of the second one. [On the issue of will], the base upon which the superiority is placed—as the apparent impart of the verse may suggest—is that the will of Infallible Person is superior to the faithful people's lives. [The base], however, does not establish proof for [arbitrary] authority. Nor does it confer ownership of the Muslims' lives or belongings as objects. There is, however, a possibility to establish superiority in the infallible persons' favor, that is, in the [exceptional] case of conflict between their [individual] expediency and the society's interests. In this case, if after balancing between the two, the infallible person has determined that his expediency is above the community's interest, then one can establish such priority. *Otherwise, an analysis would require a rather erratic*

> *presumption of legal impediment [against the faithful individuals] similar to that of the persons in need of guardianship, considering them as objects, and putting them in an inherently unequal footing as human beings.* Such evaluation of the verse and the indicators found in the traditions will take us to the first definition and is devoid of any impart to the second one. *If there is no evidence to prove the second definition, then, it should be measured by al-aṣl 'adam (presumption of inexistence) [an Uṣūlī principle]. Such subjection to the presumption of inexistence is supported by the infallible persons' course of conduct with the people, and the relation of some of them with some of the individuals [i.e., the faithful people].* They always sought a mentally mature adult woman's permission for marriage, and an owner's permission for sale, and refrained from possessing a minor's property when his presumptive guardian [i.e., father or paternal grandfather] was there. So they put their hand on an individual's belonging after the owener's permission was granted, *and any other action [of this kind]that makes man certain about the equality in their [i.e., infallible persons'] transactions among the people* by [the fact of] the transactions that some of them engaged with some of the people. *Altogether, there is no domination over the people for the Infallible Persons, similar to that of a slave-owner's, therefrom would allow the authority of disposition [of their belongings and lives] to be drawn by desire of what is not [found] in any of other [respectful] prominent individuals.* [Emphasis mine][213]

As can be seen, the fundamental bases upon which a *wilāyah* relation between the Imam and the people is established are original equality in their being as humans in the form of an absence of presumption of legal impediments for individuals, and the prohibition of arbitrariness in the application of authority in the form of an absence of undue domination over the people. Thus, not surprisingly, in addition to the aforementioned delineation of *wilāyah*, the prevailing juristic rule on guardianship in Shīʿī law is based on *al-aṣl 'adami wilāyat aḥadin 'alā aḥad* (the principle of the inexistence of guardianship for one individual over another).[214] This principle is a reflection of yet another very important and universally agreed upon legal rule in Islamic law in the form of *qā'idat al-fiqhī* (a general jurisprudential rule, or a legal maxim) that provides "*inn al-nāsa musallaṭūna 'alā amwālihim wa anfusihim*"[215] (people have [complete] domination over their belongings and lives), which is famously known as *qā'idat al-taslīṭ.*[216] Based on these two jurisprudential sources, jurists have rendered a whole host of legal rules and opinions that all support the individual's rights to property and life. In retrospect, all of these opinions establish the inherent exceptionality of *wilāyah*. Apparently, by an objective legal measure, Shīʿī jurists follow the logical rule of universally agreed circumstances in which the guardianship is presumed, like that of interdicted individuals or those for whom a consensus has already been established.[217] The disagreement stems from other legal occasions, mainly in judicial cases, where the legitimate necessity of fulfilling the right action on behalf of an individual's interest or the public expediency remains unattended. The general rule that has been invoked by jurists in their arguments reads: "*Al-sulṭānu waliyyun man lā waliyyu lah*" (the ruler is the guardian of all for whom no guardian has been appointed).[218] Although jurists have registered the rule in three different versions,[219] the underpinning precept is that the duty of guardianship is incumbent on the Imam who has the original authority on both.[220] Thus, the authority derived from the latter general rule is itself a derivative of the infallible persons' original authority whose possible deputyship is subject to textual or rational proof.[221] For the most part, as mentioned before, the notion of deputyship was strongly limited to custodial duties.

The Premises of the Jurist's Authority. For some of the jurists, the earlier conclusions regarding nature of authority did not resolve all the disputes over determination and the clarification of *ḥisba*. One of the major issues was whether the duty of political governance, as the most important element in maintaining the social order and protecting rights, was itself a *ḥisba* matter or not. With the utmost importance of Imāmah doctrine in Shīʿī law, it seems counterintuitive to imagine that a Shīʿī jurist may have reached the point of arguing in favor of the jurists' authority-right to governance as a *ḥisba,* or in any other type of discussion to that effect. This legitimate doubt can be resolved by facts. In a historical continuum where the kings incompetently ruled over Iranians' *umūr al-dunyā* (the social affairs of the Muslim community), the Shīʿī jurists were heavily concerned about taking the correct approach to the best interest of the community, and found it necessary to reevaluate the authority-duty of governance within its proper jurisprudential context, that is, *ḥisba*.[222] In a complex context of correlation between historical crises, an engagement in the political affairs of the ruling kings, the introduction of new or even modern political institutions, and the force of social and political necessities, it is not surprising to see an attempt to rearticulate the Imāmah doctrine. One can trace the Shīʿī approach to the institution of government to al-Karakī (d. 940/1534) during the early Safavid dynasty, when he based the jurists' exclusive role of undertaking the duty of juridical control over governmental activities on the concept of jurists' *niyābat ʿāmma aw niyābat khāṣṣa* (the general or specific deputyship of the Hidden Imam).[223] From the middle of Safavid rule until the present time, not the notion of deputyship from Imam, but the scope of such vice-regency has always been a hotly debated and contested issue by some of the most prominent Shīʿī jurists. Before a quick survey of the jurists' opinions, however, some important points are in order:

1. In general, the jurists' main duty is to promote the cause of the religion by educating the laity and providing them with the required knowledge about the correct performance of their religious devotional obligations. Jurists also have the duty of educating the common people in the permissible course of conduct to be observed and implemented in mundane affairs, which involve legitimate businesses and contracts, wills and testaments, and marriage or divorce. It has been customary throughout the long-standing social traditions for people to refer their religious questions to the jurists in whose knowledge and piety they trust. To this extent, the jurists have been perceived to be the deputies of the Hidden Imam. This is where the concept of *taqlīd* (literally, emulation) comes to the fore.
2. For the most part, the title of "infallible" is a general reference to the Prophet or the Imams. By virtue of a technical stretch, it can also be an exclusive reference to the last Imam, that is, the Hidden Imam. In juristic discussions, the infallible could refer to any one of the three.
3. In general, a large part of the jurist's authority emanates from his knowledge of the law, and from his juridical skills and mastery. In all of the jurists' books, the very technical and sometime controversial terms of "*ḥākim*" (ruler) or "*ḥākim al-sharʿ*" (ruler of the Shari'ah), are used to refer to this type of jurist. As juristic terms of art in Shīʿī literature with complete observance of the infallible persons' pristine and inherent authority in judgment, these words unquestionably define the jurist as a judge, and not a king, caliph, or any other political authority.[224]
4. The authority to make judicial decisions in either *ḥisba* or non-*ḥisba* disputes heavily depends on determination, by juristic standards, of whether it is possible to represent the infallible person or not.[225] In other words, *aḥkām ikhtiṣāṣī li Imām* (issues the ruling on which is exclusively reserved for Infallible Imam, or the last Imam)[226] are excluded from the jurist's authority.
5. Given the detailed and meticulously developed technicalities and standards for Shari'ah rules on adjudication in *kutub al-qaḍā'* (books of judgment), only someone who is "*al-faqīh al-jāmiʿ li sharā'iṭ al-fatwā*" (a jurist who has all the required qualifications to issue a fatwa)[227] can hold the office of judgeship.
6. Under a whole host of circumstances, including the technically termed *shuʾūn al-qaḍā'* (approximately, judicial discretionary

> authorities)[228] and especially *ḥisba* cases, the jurist's authority to make judicial decisions is heavily qualified by his ability to determine the legitimate cause (i.e., *maṣlaḥa*)[229] that is embedded in the best interest and expedience of the parties. It also may take the form of determining the best method for introducing and implementing the rules of the Shari'ah so that judgments do not turn out to be an aberration to the Shari'ah. At least one jurist has held that the faculty used to determine the best interests of the community is reserved for the infallible Imam alone, and that the ordinary jurist is incapable of acquiring it.[230]

With these introductory caveats in mind, a survey of the opinions on the points of agreement or disagreement over the course of the mid-nineteenth century among the Shīʿī jurists is necessary. As will be shown, so long as juristic ethics and standards of discovering new rules were observed, rendering opinions that either partially or entirely went against the prevailing or unanimous ones was completely accepted, well-developed, and prevalent. A general survey of the jurists' opinions on the most important issues prior to the introduction of the theory of all-inclusive authority of jurists reveals that they agreed on the jurists' authority in *qaḍā'* (adjudication),[231] *iftā'* (issuing fatwa),[232] and *wilāyah ḥisbī* (guardianship over some of *ḥisba* duties).[233] They heavily disagreed, however, on the jurisdiction of the jurist's authority in a whole host of other issues like *khums* (a one-fifth, religious tax levied against certain amounts of income),[234] *zakāt* (another religious tax levied against certain commodities),[235] Friday Prayer,[236] the possibility of executing *ḥudūd* (predetermined punishments) in the time of the Imam's absence,[237] and *anfāl* (public properties).[238]

Social Affairs and *Wilāyat al-Faqīh* (Jurists' Guardianship)

An all-inclusive theory of *wilāyat al-faqīh* was introduced by Ahmad Narāqī (d. 1245/1829) in the early-to-middle period of Qājār rule; Narāqī took the argument to a sharply new height.[239] In a premodern context, jurists' perception of social affairs and governing authority was limited to legal issues related to personal status. In those issues, Narāqī was no exception and did not go beyond what had already been argued for the jurist's guardianship in Shīʿī jurisprudence. After some introductory remarks on why he defended all-inclusive authority for jurists, however, Narāqī cited seventeen traditions/reports attributed to the Prophet and the

Imams. In those sources, jurists are praised as the heirs to the Prophet,[240] the trustees,[241] the successors of the Prophet,[242] the strongholds of Islam for the faithful,[243] the trustees of the Prophet (as long as they do not tend toward the mundane),[244] similar to previous Prophets,[245] having similar status as that of the Prophets of the children of Israel,[246] the best people if pious,[247] enjoying superiority over the laity similar to that of the Prophet's over the least worthy individuals,[248] rulers over the kings,[249] source of reference in future events,[250] the guardian of the orphans of the Prophet's House,[251] the point of reference to which the disputes should be referred,[252] the judge of permitted and prohibited acts,[253] and the holders of the rules and the correct flow of affairs.[254] According to a report cited by Narāqī, the people were obliged to obey the judgments made by such a jurist.[255] Finally, by citing a long report, Narāqī intended to present the jurists as *ulu 'l-amr* (the holder of the rule, ruler).[256] Interestingly, Narāqī admitted that some of the traditions/reports do not meet the juristic criteria of validity and, in an effort to compensate for their lack of validity, invoked previous jurists' citation of them as evidence of the reports' probative value.[257] Based on these reports/traditions, Narāqī examined the ten following issues as samples of the jurist's *wilāyah*: (1) Issuing fatwas, (2) adjudication, (3) the execution of predetermined punishments, (4) safeguarding orphans' belongings, (5) safeguarding interdicted individuals' belongings, (6) protecting absentees' properties, (7) interference in interdicted individuals' marriage, (8) interference in interdicted individuals' occupation and wages, (9) interference in the taxes payable to the Imam, and (10) all the tasks that the Imams used to undertake during their lives.[258] Before discussing these issues, Narāqī laid down two major jurisdictions of authority in favor of the jurist:

> (A) On all of the affairs over which the Prophet and the Imams had *wilāyah*, the jurist also has authority, except where it is excluded by *ijmā'* (consensus among jurists), *naṣṣ* (textual evidence found in the Qur'an or Sunnah), or other Shari'ah-based probative evidence to that effect, and
>
> (B) On all the acts that belong to the people's religious and social affairs that are, inescapably, to be performed. Be it "rationally" or "habitually," or "ordained by Shari'ah" or "consensus," or by the "prohibition of harm and causing damage," or by "hardship and necessity," or "corruption upon Muslims," [such religious and social affairs are] perceived as that of those that the individual's or the community's religious or mundane life depends on, and the order of the religion and this-world is due upon them. In addition, those acts that God has allowed the performance of but has not appointed a specific person or group to be in charge of are among them. [In this case], although we are aware of the mandatory duty of the performance, we do not know what exactly they are or on what issues permission

has been granted [i.e., *ḥisba* matters]. On all of these, it is for the jurist to undertake the duty of their performance, and [to apply] his authority of *taṣarruf* (disposition) over them.[259]

He then made two supplementary arguments as to why he rendered jurists to be the successors of the infallible persons. First, in addition to the unanimously held opinion on the jurists' main duty (i.e., promoting the religion's cause), Narāqī invoked the aforementioned words of praise as evidence that the infallible Imam had indeed intended to bestow all of his authority on the jurists. In support of this argument, he insisted that if a ruler, with the intention of appointing an interim successor, would have stated those words about any individual, it would have been sufficient to prove by common sense that the appointed individual has obtained all of the ruler's authority. According to him, by referring to the jurists as heirs, successors, or trustees, common sense would lead us to conclude that the infallible person has complete trust in the jurist to entertain all of the authority and power that belongs to him (i.e., the infallible person) on his behalf.[260] In order to reinforce his second argument, Narāqī relied heavily on the concept of *ḥisba*:

First, there is no doubt that in all affairs of such importance, the Wise Compassionate Legislator must have appointed a guardian or a custodian or an entrusted individual. *The presumption of non-appointment of a specified individual or group applies to non-jurists. Jurists have been praised with these nice qualifications and high privileges, and it suffices to assume their appointment.* Second, after proving the necessity of appointment and the inexistence of any possibility in which these affairs may be left unguarded—something that nobody has yet alleged—then we will say, that the individuals who may perform the duties of non-appointed issues must be from among the just and reliable Muslims. Therefore the jurist is present amongst all of the individuals upon whom the appointment of responsibility and the entertainment of the authority [of guardianship] may be assigned. [Jurist has all such qualifications]. A contrary proposition would not hold. As is with every group of people for whom *wilāyah* would be permissible, jurists are also included. Arguing for the proof of jurists' *wilāyah* does not support the proof of other groups' authority, especially when we notice that the jurist has been recognized as the best of people after the prophets as well as the most knowledgeable, the trustee, the successor, the source, and the holder of rules.[261] Therefore, the jurist's ability to undertake the charge and prove his *wilāyah* is incontrovertible... *If someone would say that the authority of the jurist is vested in those issues where there is already permission for the jurist, but only in mandatory public duties, and the presumption is that jurists are not mandated to undertake them, then I will say, [that] mandatory public duty certainly does include jurists. What we may doubt is whether or not this duty is*

> *mandatory for other individuals.* Finally, when in doubt [about the inclusion of others in undertaking the duty], we should apply the principle of inexistence and conclude that there is no duty for them. [He also rejects the idea of the inapplicability of the jurist's characteristics as a key factor in undertaking the charge of performing mandatory public duties]. (Emphasis mine)[262]

In the normal course of argument—and as far as the typical issues that Narāqī took it upon himself to somehow render new opinions about (i.e., the ten areas mentioned earlier) are concerned—his arguments would not have aroused any major controversy. In fact, as shown before, *ikhtilāf* (juristic disagreement) on the scope of jurist's *wilāyah* was not a new phenomenon for the jurists. What distinguished Narāqī from other jurists was his methodology of reasoning. The main critique of his reasoning revolves around the confusion between inclusion and all-inclusion. By relying on invalid or irrelevant and noninclusive traditions/reports, he attempted to transform the jurists' exclusive authority over adjudication and fatwa into an overall inclusion of them in the performance of public mandatory duties; he also attempted to establish a theoretical foundation that could suit his conclusion regarding the all-inclusive authority of the jurist. While it was true that the notion of *wilāyah*—if discovered—could include jurists, and that they would fit in any group upon whom the authority may have been assigned, there was no independent specific evidence that could support the jurist's exclusive authority over all the potential dimensions of authority. In addition to the fact that there was a serious disagreement among the jurists on each area of authority for jurists, as opinions rendered by previous jurists made clear, there was the certain fact that any consensus on the scope of the jurist's authority except for adjudication and the issuance of fatwas could not be achieved. Narāqī correctly limited *wilāyat al-faqīh* to the existence of juristically valid proofs that would provide permissibility; he even confessed that he himself was not convinced as to whether or not there was *wilāyah* for jurists on some legal issues that had been raised contemporarily in the course of the people's demand for the intermediary role of the jurist.[263] What he failed to do, however, was to introduce sufficiently valid juristic evidence beyond his dual lines of reasoning[264] to claim the jurist's authority in all other contexts. It was precisely because there were too many details, technicalities, and unknowns in the process of discovering and establishing *wilāyah* and its application in *ḥisba* that Shīʿī jurists prior to Narāqī hesitated to approach the concept of authority so widely and freely.

It is possible to explain that, because of the then static sociopolitical condition, what Narāqī claimed to be "social and religious affairs" were in fact the very ten issues that he examined in order to prove his case. There were certainly more known issues to discuss. Narāqī was engaged in good relations with the then Qājār king's court[265] and was completely aware, even on a personal level,[266] of the injustice and tyranny that had plagued the very same sociopolitical scene. As a highly sophisticated figure,[267] his awareness of other issues, however, makes it even more difficult to analyze his nuanced discourse. On the one hand, by choosing to be silent about the relationship between the ruler and the ruled, it is possible to infer that Narāqī understood the then existing nature of this relationship to be acceptable, and therefore, beyond the scope of the jurist's all-inclusive authority.

Analyzing Narāqī's practical and theoretical position on the complicated issue of the legitimacy of Shīʿī political rule in the time of the Imam's absence is very difficult. In this context, Narāqī bore a strong resemblance to Majlisī from the Safavid period. Just like Majlisī, he was very generous in extolling the sultans and praising the Qājār king as the "high shadow of God on earth and a warrior of His Path" as well as the "founder and reviver of the religion…and the legislator of just laws and rules" whose "justice and fairness…would burn the oppression and…whose sun-like light lightens the face of the Shari'ah."[268] By virtue of his methods and measures, this Shīʿī sultan's rule would certainly meet the criteria of legitimacy and thus be compatible with just sultanate discourse. Once again, in delineating the people's rights against the ruler, Narāqī, like Majlisī, quoted and cited those questionable traditions/reports that would not support the people's right to rebel.[269]

On the other hand, he developed a theory that, by every standard, is an attempt to replicate a Shīʿī political order in which the Imam's rights would probably be best safeguarded by his deputies' all-inclusive authority. Despite the fact that he only analyzed limited issues, the way in which the subject matter of "social and religious affairs" was so extensively defined and categorized makes it difficult to assume the exclusion of political relations from the picture. Thus, one may conclude with heightened good faith that "Narāqī pragmatically used his good relations with the king to develop a quasi-political-juridical theory that had long been in Shīʿī jurists' minds."[270]

The Juristic Critique of the Jurist's Guardianship

As was explicitly clear in previous opinions, Shīʿī jurists had not specified an exclusive place for the "jurist" in *ḥisba* issues. Nor had they attempted to distinguish jurists from other trustworthy faithful individuals that could establish a similar specified status. The jurists' exclusive authority over adjudication was also significantly qualified by their mastery of religious knowledge, and limited to such jurisprudential technicalities and precepts that no individual jurist would ever be able to disregard them. In the absence of the appointment of a designated individual in charge of *ḥisba*, the presumption of the general inclusion of the jurist amongst the potential candidates was a simplified rule that ignored all of the previous jurists' efforts to discover and prove, piece by piece, a right or rule by introducing valid evidence in every little detail. Furthermore, the infallible Imam's highly regarded position was heavily based on theological grounds, the most important of them being the Imams' *'ismah* (infallibility) and *ṭahāra* (purity from sins), by which their exclusive authority to lead temporal and spiritual affairs, as developed in the doctrine of Imāmah, could be established. The whole idea behind the exclusive authority of the Imam is that the legitimate leadership of social affairs is such a meticulously precise duty that only individuals with adequately high caliber characteristics are able to undertake it. If another individual, for example, a jurist, could represent all of the Imam's authority in social affairs, then such personal characteristics would have been futile in the first place. The whole argument, then, should be divided into two distinctive subjects: whether the leadership of social and religious affairs is devisable or not, and if so, whether or not the Imam has vested the jurist with such permission.

Responding to these questions heavily depended on the capacity and sufficiency of the available proofs. In a technical setting, jurists such as Anṣārī, Ākhūnd, Nā'īnī, and others found that traditions/reports, as introduced by Narāqī to prove *wilāyat al-faqīh*, lack the quintessential standards of validity and juristic possibility required to devise the all-inclusive authority of the jurist.[271] My arguments on clarifying *ḥisba* and *wilāyah* have intended to prove the point that the majority of Shī'ī jurists have developed a consensus on the exclusive authority of the jurist in adjudication, the issuance of fatwas, and ordering the ranks according to the custodial duties of the guardianship of the interdicted. In other words, they do not hold a strong consensus on other issues. In this context, I will briefly introduce the opinions of Anṣārī and Ākhūnd[272] and leave further detailed discussions for the next chapter where I introduce the constitutionalist jurists' opinions on constitutionalism per se.

Anṣārī first enumerated three subjects. He discussed these subjects in the context of the jurist's authority: issuing fatwas, adjudication, and *wilāyah* over others' belongings and selves. He then classified the issue of *wilāyah* and contextualized it according to two logical circumstances:

1. The holder of *wilāyah*'s *independent authority of disposition* where his disposition does not depend on another's permission in a way that such permission could be a *cause* for the permissibility of disposition.

2. The absence of independence in the disposition of authority, and the dependence of that authority on another's permission in a way that such permission would be a *condition* for permissibility of disposition.

Permission in the latter scenario could take one of three forms of agency (like representing the judge or the ruler), authorization (like authorizing the executor of an endowed property), and consent (like the judge's permission to perform the required prayer for a deceased who has no heirs).[273] Emphasizing the paramount "principle of the inexistence of guardianship for one individual over another individual," he found that the first category *wilāyah* can only stand for the Prophet and the Imams, and that it excluded everyone else from being capable of even entertaining the principle.[274] On the second type, that is, the conditionality of dispositive authority to grant permission, Anṣārī made it clear that such authority is against the principle unless there is evidence as to its permissibility. In this context, he distinguished between the issues whose desirable interest is devised by the Divine Legislator for all (and not a specific individual, for whom punishments, the protection of the incapacitated, and the popular rise for their rights are reserved), and the ones whose interest is devised for specified individuals. Anṣārī argued that permission for the first category of issues is to be referred to the leader of society, that is, *ulu al-amr* (the holder of rule), or the Imam and his agents.[275] In analyzing the second category, however, he held that all the valid traditions/reports in praise of the jurist can only be utilized to prove the jurist's responsibility in declaring the rule of the Shari'ah, not his authority as the holder of a *wilāyah* similar to that of the Imam's.[276] On the other hand, regarding the original categorization of duties as public and individual, he doubly subcategorized the duties, that is, the good acts in the sense of commanding right, to those the performance of which requires the Imam's permission and the ones that are devoid of such a requirement. Thus, on the topic of whether or not the jurist in the time of absence of Imam had the authority to permit others to act upon issues that are subject to the Imam's permission, Anṣārī said,

> In every *ma'rūf* (good in the sense of commanding right, that is *ḥisba*), the realization of which entails God's satisfaction: if (a) it is not clear that the performance of the duty is incumbent upon a specific group of people, or (b) the public is capable of fulfilling it, and (c) there is a probability that the jurist's opinion as to its coming into existence or mandatoriness would be necessary, then, it is mandatory to seek a jurist's opinion. If after examining the evidence, the jurist found that the issue does not require the Imam's or his specified agent's permission, it is permissible for the jurist to undertake the duty and employ the direct or indirect practice of authority. Otherwise,

> he is not allowed to undertake the charge and ought to refrain from the employment of any practice of authority.[277]

Therefore, there are some good acts that we may not be able to achieve, or that would be exempted from performance as our duties. If, under any circumstances, God has demanded our charge of the duty, then we should disregard the issue of the Imam's presence and settle on the jurist's authority. Otherwise, if there are duties whose realization is subject to the Imam's presence, then the jurist's authority is obviously limited. Given that there is disagreement on many issues of this nature, like the execution of predetermined punishments, the performance of Friday Prayer, and the permissibility of receiving religious taxes, it is not possible for the jurist to rely on his authority to adjudicate or to issue fatwas. The jurists' arguments evidently prove that numerous pieces of conclusive evidence must be available to resolve the conflict—something to which we do not have access. As to other issues, where we know that their realization does not require the Imam's presence, the question is whether the jurist has the authority to take them under his control or is limited to allow others to know of his opinion? Again, Anṣārī held that although there is a preference in the order of holding authority for a jurist, he only has the duty to issue fatwas and to render an opinion. In other words, it is up to the jurist to either hold authority, or to leave it up to others to undertake its control. Nevertheless, he must determine the subject matter act's legitimacy and inform the society of such, especially when he is questioned by his followers. In the case of conflict between two or more jurists, following the general rule in the Shī'ī theory of *marja'īyya* (the leadership of Shiites in religious affairs), it is only the opinion of *faqīh a'lam* (the most knowledgeable jurist) that counts; others' opinions are not conclusive.[278]

Ākhūnd shared similar conclusions, but differed in his reasoning. First, he distinguished his opinions from Anṣārī's with regard to the preliminary typology of *wilāyah*, and refused to recognize the possibility of establishing *wilāyah* by authorization or consent; instead, he limited its manifestations to agency.[279] On the issue of an independent *wilāyah,* he held that the Imam does not have absolute authority—as discussed before—over individuals' personal rights, and opined that the impart exclusively emanating from the Imam's authority is the individuals' duty of obedience to his determinations in leading the Muslim society, and not his right to impose his will against the individuals' rights.[280] Therefore, with the absence of the original authority of the Imam, there is no room for the jurist's secondary authority either.[281] With regards to the outcome of the valid traditions, he, like Anṣārī, held that they do not provide authority for the jurist except in the duty of declaring the rules of Shari'ah. Neither in the prima facie impart of the rules in those traditions that held the jurists to be the source of reference for all the upcoming events, nor in the one according to which "the knowledgeable are [declared to be] the proofs of the Imam"[282] did Ākhūnd find conclusive evidence for the jurist's all-inclusive authority. His final opinion is a clear reference to the place and importance of rational arguments, as delineated and maintained by *Uṣūlī* jurists. He held that "in the absence of a rational or customary correlation between proving the Imam's authority and *wilāyah*, as Anṣārī discussed, these traditions do not hold to prove the jurist's authority in every religious issue."[283] Furthermore, he found no specific distinction between a jurist and any other individual regarding the necessity of undertaking public charges and duties. He also believed that after the mandatoriness of the act is discovered, there is no difference between the jurist and any other duty-bound individual—except the ones that require specialized knowledge like medicine or jurisprudence.[284] Like Anṣārī, Ākhūnd concluded that

> on the mandatoriness of the duties for which we have doubt in knowledge, the jurist should resolve the doubt and determine whether the desirability of the duty is due to the Imam's presence or mandated in an absolute fashion. If the performance of the duty is considered mandatory in the time of the Imam's presence, or if we have doubt as to whether or not the address of the duty is directed at a specific person, then, based on the presumption of non-obligation,[285] we should hold that the subject matter act is not mandatory, and we rely on the jurist's determination. Therefore, despite the fact that there is a problem in the evidence of the jurist's independent or un-independent *wilāyah*, they establish the jurist's permission in undertaking the charge in the form of *qadr al-mutayaqqin* (the least amount of certainty).[286] This form does not prove the jurist's *wilāyah* from among those whose personal undertaking or opinions are probable, like the most just of the faithful individuals, when there is no jurist to take charge of the custodial duties of the insane or minors.[287]

In conclusion, I have to mention that both jurists believed in the priority of the jurists' ability to undertake the custodial duties of incapacitated individuals, along with their exclusive authority in issuing fatwa and adjudication. Although they did not agree with the jurist's all-inclusive authority and limited his authority to the aforementioned issues, Anṣārī and Ākhūnd did agree on the judicial nature of unknown issues and found jurists to be the most competent ones for resolving them. In the next chapter, I will discuss how the authority of determination in the constitutionalist jurists' theory was heavily limited to judicial issues, and did not include political ones.

Chapter 4

Constitutionalist Jurisprudence

Fundamental Issues and Conflicts

Based on the jurisprudential foundations explained in chapter 3, I contend, the constitutionalist jurists developed their theory of the legitimacy of constitutionalism. They developed a juristically valid theory of constitutionalism in which the role of the constitution, and what was inscribed in it, was well defined. In addition, they also articulated the Shīʿī approach to the inherent dilemma of legitimacy of non-Imam rule. In a comparative analysis of constitutionalism, Ākhūnd and Māzandarānī wrote:

> Constitutionalism in every nation is conditionality and restriction of the rulers and all governmental agencies to absence of any violation of the laws and regulations which are enacted in compliance with the nation's official religion. The other side of constitutionalism is tyranny and despotism of the state, which allows the rulers and agencies to rule arbitrarily, omnipotent, unaccountably, coercive and cruelly over their people and nation.
>
> Freedom of every nation, on which the state's constitutionalism relies, is founded on the absence of subjugation to the authoritarian rule of the ruler, and of the barrier in realization of their legitimate rights and entitlements. Retrospectively, servitude is also being subjugated and dispossessed of anything before the government's will and power.
>
> Since the official religion of Iran is this upright Islam and the righteous Twelver Imamite faith, therefore, the truth of constitutionalism in Iran and its freedom is based on the absence of the state's and the nation's violation of general and specific rules derived from the religion. This principle, which should be implemented, shall be founded upon protection of the

> nation's religious and national sacred honors and rights; prohibition of religious wrongs, expansion of justice and eradication of oppression and closing the gates of authoritarian acts, protection of *bayḍah-i Islam wa ḥawzah-i Muslimīn* (homeland and Muslims' society), and expending the taxes paid by people on their universal interests that include social order and safeguarding the borders.
>
> The nation's elected members of Majlis will also be those trusted individuals whose complete trustworthiness, reliability, and knowledge should be recognized and known to people by comprehensive acquaintance. People have elected them to oversee the aforementioned matters.[1]

This general platform, laid down in later period of Revolution and after the victory of the constitutionalist fighters in the civil war, was yet another manifestation of what the constitutionalist jurists meant by constitutionalism. Given the generality of terms and references, one should bear in mind that constitutionalist jurists were among the best intellectuals that Shīʿī jurisprudence had produced in its history. The core of their scholarship and knowledge was based on the most advanced developments of *Uṣūlī* doctrine at the time. Therefore, in this chapter, I will rely mostly on their writings to explain constitutionalism in Iran.

In order to build the foundations, constitutionalist jurists raised the following four main questions:

1. What is the essence of political rule in Islam? Moreover, how can despotic rule be limited?
2. What is the Shiites' duty in the time of absence of the Imam? Is it mandatory to limit the ruler's authority in the time of such absence?
3. Is constitutionalism, as introduced and incorporated in the 1906–7 Constitution, a legitimate and efficient means to limit such rule?
4. What are the conditions of legitimacy for the elected representatives' role in legislation and their enactments?

Before describing the constitutionalist jurists' responses, it is necessary to introduce the counterarguments in opposition to constitutionalism as raised by proponents of *mashrūṭah-i mashrū'a* (Shari'ah-based constitutionalism) or anti-constitutionalist jurists.[2] In addition to these questions, the constitutionalist jurists attempted to respond to their opponents' semi-juristic critiques against the constitution and the Majlis, and in a polemical fashion devoted important parts of their arguments to them. Not surprisingly, the anti-constitutionalist jurists developed their discourse on the general assumption of illegitimacy of any non-Imamite rule. They, however, adopted three different major approaches to the juristic origins and practical issues of the 1905 Revolution that can be summarized as follows:

1. Underpinning approach to the individual's entitlements and rights: As discussed before, the constitutionalist jurists founded their theory on the concepts of liberty, equality, and the concomitant right to political participation as the "purpose and goal of all the Prophets." The anti-constitutionalists, however, put emphasis on the notions of the "fear of God," the "hope to His Grace," and the encouragement of "the children of Adam to focus on the hereafter and seclude from the mundane" as such[3] as the key determinants of the individuals' duties and rights.[4] In other words, the constitutionalist jurists opined that the path toward social justice and welfare passed through individual entitlement to political and social equality and that "God given liberty" from servitude to the political rule. Anti-constitutionalist jurists, by contrast, believed that a fair and balanced society could only be established by the individual's practical adherence to the type of religious outlook and faith that they advocated.[5] The latter group heavily rendered the idea of liberty and equality among the individuals as un-Islamic and claimed that there is no equality in Islam![6] According to them, there is no doubt that invidious propensities prevail in the human beings' souls and they are unable to achieve moral virtues, build peace, and cooperate with each other except by the education of religious knowledge. Until the maturity of such knowledge is achieved, a powerful ruler who punishes their mischief and oppression should rule. Therefore, it is necessary to support and uphold his rule so peace and order could be sustained in society.[7]
2. Approach to the Shari'ah and Legislation: There is no doubt that all Muslim jurists believe in God's absolute sovereignty and the finality of His Laws in governing man's life. As mentioned before, such faith-based belief has manifested in two major approaches to the concept of derivation and the discovery of those Laws, namely the *Uṣūlī* and *Akhbārī* schools. To anti-constitutionalist jurists with strong textualist tendencies, the all-encompassing, all-inclusive, and superior characteristics of such Laws were perceived to be elements of a religious-legal system whose texts were capable of providing all answers to all questions at all times.[8] Muslim society, therefore, would have no need to adopt legal solutions suggested in non-Muslim nations.[9] In their mind, not only is man viewed as inherently incapable of legislation, but also any attempt to enact laws would be interfering with what the Divine as Legislator and Lawgiver has

already devised, and thus, would constitute an heretical act of putting oneself on equal standing with the Divine.[10] For many of the textualist jurists, this general presumption had no other meaning than referring to the text, that is, the Qur'an and the Sunnah, and finding the answers therein.[11] Therefore, they repeatedly opined on the illegitimacy of constitutionalism and condemned the notion of majority rule in the Majlis's decision-making process.[12] As argued in chapter 1, while *Uṣūlī* jurists are faithful adherents to the perfectness of Divine Law and heavily represented by the constitutionalists, they believe in correlation and harmony between the core of any of such Laws and human reason's perception and apprehension of those Laws' inherent impart. Such belief, in turn, establishes an active role for the rational individual to not only derive the core, but also act and create rules that do not conflict with the Shari'ah. In other words, *Uṣūlī*s perceive the Shari'ah as a legal system that, rather than being an inflexible and static collection of rules, consists of both objectives and guidelines, on the one hand, and cause for the establishment of a dynamic realm where human beings as subjects of those goals and guidelines can participate in the formation of new rules, on the other. It was based on their *Uṣūlī* perspective that the constitutionalist jurists welcomed the idea of the Majlis as the institutionalized participation of rational individuals in law-making. To the contrary, the anti-constitutionalists not only were unwilling to recognize a meaningful place for reason in the process of discovering the law, but also heavily and explicitly denied viewing the Majlis as an instrument of such dynamism.[13] Not surprisingly, the claim to rational proof for their opinions was tainted with an evasive and abusive treatment of rational findings[14] that raised serious doubts about their *Akhbārī* tendencies.[15]

3. Approach to the nature of rule and the treatment of laws: In order to achieve justice, anti-constitutionalist jurists argued, one should obey and implement the rules of the Shari'ah. "The nature and essence of an Islamic rule was based on two major factors and operators: (a) the deputyship of the jurist in *umūr-i nubuwwatī-ye 'āmma* (those public affairs that the Prophet was in charge of) and his decisive role in the determination of Shari'ah rules, and (b) the monarch's *salṭanat* (monarchical dominance, kingship) by which thusly determined rules would be executed." They claimed that

> in Islam, Rules are based on *indhār* (warning) and *wa'd wa wa'īd* (promise and threat). One can even say that the warning side is more important than the other, and requires fear of God and admitting to *Mabda' wa Ma'ād* (the Origin and Return) which, in turn, amounts

> to *khawf wa rajā'* (fear and hope). *The latter two spiritual experiences [i.e., fear and hope] are more effective than rising to do the right and avoid the wrong in establishment of the core of justice.* The stronger the conviction is in 'the Origin and Return' and 'fear of God and hope to His Grace,' the more expanded justice will be in life and society, and vice versa. In the earlier periods of Islam, because of closeness to the time of the Prophet and the presence of the infallible persons, the scope of justice was wider and more prevalent in society. After the Imam's Occultation, when the command fell upon the specific or general deputies, due to events, the faith gradually began to demise and, depending on the degree of the jurists' and sultans' strife in different times, injustice pervaded. Following this introduction, it is clear that if there is an intention of expanding justice, it must be intended (and achieved) through the reinforcement of those two groups: *ḥamalat al-aḥkām wa ulu al-shawka min ahl al-Islam* (those who are charged with determining the rules, [i.e., the jurists,] and the holders of power and might among Muslims, [i.e., the kings.]) This is the [exclusive] way of accomplishing valid and fruitful justice. (Emphasis mine)[16]

In different instances, the anti-constitutionalist jurists supported the then despot king and his orders to demolish the "*dār al-fisq*" (house of debauchery) and "*kufr khānah*" (house of infidelity)—demeaning words for the Majlis—and the persecution of constitutionalists. Furthermore, they demanded the people's appreciation and prayed for the king's "solemn" action in protecting the religion.[17]

Beyond historical facts, however, the anti-constitutionalists clung to the just sultanate discourse and asked for the jurists' exclusive authority in the determination of rules as the cornerstone of their theory of political rule and as an alternative to constitutionalism. One of their main objections to the constitutionalist order was the "incompetency" of those members of the Majlis who were elected through class distribution of representation,[18] and to that effect, the anti-constitutionalists did not hesitate to bash the idea that the power of legislation would be vested in such elected members of the Majlis.[19] Although they clearly rejected the formation and institutionalization of the Majlis as something foreign to their perception of the Shari'ah, an assembly whose membership was exclusively limited to jurists who would determine the compatibility of the king's proclamations[20] and executive authority with Shari'ah could be a conceivable outcome of their discourse.

Other detailed points of disagreement and conflict are to be found in either the very *Uṣūlī*-Imamite concepts that the constitutionalist jurists strived to reintroduce to the field or new issues that were in need of juristic reactions. To anti-constitutionalist jurists, the valid assumption of illegitimacy of any non-Imam rule was the basis for disregarding the people's role and rights in political affairs to the extent that—it was so argued—there was no place for the people in the formation or evaluation of the ruling monarchy's legitimacy. The constitutionalist jurists, however, believed that the general illegitimacy of non-Imam rule, once viewed in the context of the reality of Hidden Imam's occultation and the absence of true knowledge as to the time of his reappearance, would be balanced in a constitutionalist rule that represented some aspects of the broader concept of legitimacy in an Infallible Imam's rule. Those aspects included the duty of observance of the inherent rights ordained for human beings—even by the Prophet—and the rational people's capacity in comprehension of the best interests of the society and practice of a controlling power that limits the tyrannical propensities of the rulers. It was exactly such a conception of rights, and the concomitant potential for substituting an Infallible Imam's characteristics of rationality and piety that the anti-constitutionalist jurists would not relent and relinquish to non-jurists.

The Essence of Rule in an Islamic State

Heavily relying on the *Uṣūlī* articulation of the concept of *wilāyah*, Nā'īnī made a preliminary argument about the distinctions between *salṭanat tamallukīyya va istibdādiyya* (possessive and despotic rule)[21] and a form of rule that is *mashrūṭa va maḥdūda* (constitutionalist and limited).[22] According to Nā'īnī, in a possessive system, the nature of rule is founded upon the ruler's authority to own his subjects; the ruler enjoys absolute power, and treats his people like slaves as if they were created to serve his desires and whims. The people under oppressive rule could appropriately be called debilitated and lynched slaves. To the contrary, in a limited system, "the notion of ownership of any kind is completely out of the picture. It, also, is solely based on accomplishing the individuals' universal rights and interests." These individuals "enjoy equality and partnership with the ruler in all sources of power and wealth, and the right to hold accountable the executive officers." In this system, power is to be abided by the legal conditions—that is, the constitution—that govern the legitimate causes, the realization of which is required for the people's rights and interests.[23] By the "universal rights of people," to be upheld by any government, Nā'īnī had already meant two groups of internal and external protections:

1. The protection of domestic order, the education of the citizenry, ensuring that rights are allotted to the rightful individuals, and deterring people from invading others' rights—these are among the internal duties of

> government. 2. The protection of the nation from foreign invasion, neutralizing the typical maneuvers in such cases, providing for a defensive force, and so on—these are what the experts in terminology call the "protection of the essential constitution of Islam."[24] . . . Individuals' entitlements are: a right to welfare, the rule of law, the protection of honor and dignity, education, justice and restitution, and also the protection of their motherland.[25]

It was by contrasting possessive rule with the limited one that Nā'īnī, based on previous jurists' arguments on the nature of *wilāyah*, introduced the constitutionalists' theory of constitutionalism:

> *The nature and essence of the latter form of government [i.e., limited rule] is wilāyah on maintaining social order and protection of the nation, and not ownership. It is [characterized by] amānat naw'īyya (typical trust, fiduciary duty) on all sources of the nation's powers and using them for the people's interests, and not for personal desires.* From this point of view, the sultan's power is limited to the extent to which wilāyah could be [applied] over the above mentioned duties, and his authority, be it legitimate or usurped,[26] is conditioned to restriction by such limit. *Citizens are partners with the government in the ownership of the nation's powers and resources. Everyone has equal rights, and the administrators are all trustees—not owners and masters—who like other members and elements of the political rule are responsible for discharge of their fiduciary duties to the nation, and will be held accountable for the slightest violations. Derived from their participation in power and equality in (enjoyment and) practice of rights, all citizens are entitled and secured to ask question and demand answers from the authorities.*[27] *They are free in raising their objections, without bearing the yoke of servitude of the sovereign sultan or his courtiers* . . . The people under such system are called *muḥtasibīn (protectors of the duty of commanding right and forbidding wrong,) free, and alive.*
>
> Since the essence of this type of rule, as is now known to you, derives from [the concepts of] *wilāyah* and *amāna* (trust) and like any other type of representational care and trust is conditioned by the absence of infringements [of the trusted duty or interest], thus undoubtedly, it bears resemblance to other types of fiduciary duties and trusts. In order to safeguard this essence and prevent its transmutation to a system of absolute possession and violations and infringements, its protection should exclusively be subject to similarly comprehensive accountability and control, and complete responsibility that are imposed on [and expected from] the trustees and holders of *wilāyah* [in any other legal circumstance similar to it].
>
> The best imaginable means for protection [of the absence] and avoidance of transmutation and correct performance of trust, as well as prevention from the slightest whimsical desire or despotic behavior or slavery that may be carried out, is the very *'iṣmat* (infallibility) upon which the

> principles of our [i.e., the Shiites] faith is founded... We are neither able to access such an exalted presence, nor is there a meaningful possibility of having a sultan like Anūshīravān (an ancient Iranian legendary King). He possessed all the virtues, and at the same time, was accompanied by individuals like Būzarjomehr (his Chancellor) from whom he was able to obtain *quwwa-yi 'ilmiyya* (power of knowledge) and choose a *hay'at-i musaddida* (literally meaning prohibiting bureau, but intending a controlling assembly). It was because of the combination of such personal virtues and companionship that he established a [well functioning] system of control, accountability, and responsibility. Notwithstanding other facts, participation in power and equality between the ruled and the ruler, and clogging the gates of monopolizing the financial resources and other issues, and people's freedom of protest and rights of that nature are all inaccessible because their coming to existence emerges from God's blessings, not from our being deserved.[28] Therefore, the official realization and continued existence of such a system is an impossible event to happen. *The solution that human beings' power of intellect has been able to envision and materialize is in two things: the Constitution and the Parliament. So it substitutes the infallibility, be it as shadow and face, or as a metaphor of truth, which encompasses all of the rights, knowledge, and prohibiting organs in a continued official existence. Furthermore, it presumably substitutes the faculty of the infallible individuals' impeccability, even by usurpation of their status.* (Emphasis mine)[29]

It was in this context that Nā'īnī developed his theory about the essence of power in Islamic law and wrote:

> The essence of an Islamic rule is *wilāyah* over the political affairs of the Muslim nation. Found in all religions and laws, such essence, undoubtedly, is based on the rules governing the fiduciary duties of the holder of *wilāyah*, and not the arbitrary rule and coercion and possession of others' lives and properties. *In fact, the ruler's duty is similar to that of the executor of an endowed property who should observe the beneficiaries' rights in orderly maintenance of the property and equal distribution of its dividends and benefits.* In a Divine setting, such *wilāyah* is bestowed upon the Prophet and Imams—arguments about which should be made in the Imāmah doctrine. (Emphasis mine)[30]

By further elaborating on the nature of governance, Nā'īnī explained that the main characteristic of the alternative rule to an Islamic rule, which has been advocated by *jamī'-i sharāyi' va adyān* (all religions and laws), is "coercion and yoking the people under the arbitrary implementation of power. Not only does such alternative belong to the gravest forms of oppression, but it also is tantamount to the usurpation of God's rules by treating the people in explicit conflict with objectives that the prophets had intended to achieve."[31] Such coercive rule has been condemned strongly by all religions. Therefore:

> The reference made in Islamic law; even in all religions and laws, to the concepts of *wilāyah* and *amāna* (trust, fiduciary duty) of anyone who shares and benefits from *ḥuqūq mushtaraka naw'īyya* (universal rights of the human beings), relates to the restrictions of such *wilāyah*, so it would not transmute to a despotic arbitrary and coercive rule. These are of the clearest necessities of Islam, perhaps of all the religions and laws.[32]

Nā'īnī found the essence to be commonly upheld by both Shiites and Sunnis. According to his analysis, although Sunni Muslims did not support the notion of the Infallible Imam and his exclusive authority to rule, they did emphasize the formation of a limited *wilāyah*. In the Sunni scheme, the members of *ahl al-ḥall wa al-'aqd* (the people who have the power of contract and choose) pledge their *bay'a* (allegiance) to the ruler under the condition of his obedience to the laws found in the Qur'an and the Prophet's Sunnah, provided that any violation of those laws would amount to deposing the ruler from power.[33] According to Nā'īnī,

> Notwithstanding the stage of the holder of power's legal capacity and what is necessary for the state of infallibility—which is a specific issue in Shī'ī law—the limitation of the Islamic state in the prohibition of such arbitrariness in rule is the confirmed common ground between the two groups. It is also a certainly agreed upon opinion, as a necessity of religion. Since, it is impossible to preserve such a certain and confirmed level of limit... therefore, [when established] no Muslim would deny the necessity of its protection with every possible means, even by the rule of a usurper sultan.[34]

Methods of Protection of Limitations

Based on the opinions of constitutionalist jurists that were supported by religious precepts it was the duty of Muslims to strive to transmute despotic possessive rule to limited rule. Such strife was in complete accordance with Islamic faith by which Muslims were not only entitled to be treated as free and alive individuals, but were also capable of performing their duty of commanding right and forbidding wrong as a *muḥtasib*. According to Nā'īnī—notwithstanding the social circumstances in which they were or were not able to perform such duty—it was, theoretically, a mandatory duty to change despotic rule. Such change was directed against a political rule that had usurped the sovereignty of God through the indignant treatment of individuals, and directed toward another political rule in which the pristine duty of preserving individuals' rights would be honored, where all the sources and means would be utilized to achieve the society's best interests.[35] It was necessary to analyze this change in the context of the Shī'ī doctrine of Imāmah. In doing so, Nā'īnī employed the *ḥisba* discourse:

> According to our Imamite faith, in the age of the absence of the Hidden Imam, *ḥisba* duties are those *wilāyāt naw'īyya* (typical *wilāyahs*), that if left unattended, would dissatisfy God. In these duties, by applying the measure of *qadr al-mutayaqqin* (the least amount of certainty),[36] the general deputyship of the jurists is (considered to be) proven. Even if we refuse (to agree with) the proof of such deputyship in all positions (for jurists), it is an obvious fact that the duty of safeguarding the order of Muslim society is superior to other duties. It is also clear that God will be dissatisfied if the duty of restoring order to society and protecting the homeland—all being among the *ḥisba* duties—were to be left unattended. Therefore, the jurists' deputyship in undertaking such duties is one of the certainties of religion.[37]

The third argument, made by Nā'īnī, was on the issue of oversight. According to him, in all cases in which *wilāyah* is at issue—for example, in the properties endowed for public or private beneficiaries—jurists hold by consensus that it is possible to control and oversee actions. If a *mutawallī* (the executor) violates the laws of rights and the duties of *wilāyah*-holders—for example, by seizing and holding the rights of the endowed property's beneficiaries in a continued fashion—then the beneficiaries can entertain their right to constitute a controlling body. Such a body limits the violator's acts as well as protecting the endowed property from abuse and the waste of profits that are at the free disposal of the executor's personal interests.[38] Orthodox jurists as well as rational atheist individuals have universally approved the logic and wisdom behind such controlling actions.[39] By considering these three lines of reasoning, Nā'īnī concluded that

> there is no doubt that it is mandatory to change *salṭanat-i jā'irah-i ghāsiba* (the oppressive and usurping rule, that is, any non-Imam rule) from the primary form [i.e., possessive] to the secondary form [i.e., limited rule], even when it is impossible to change the ruler. As you understood, the primary form usurps the Divine scope of authority and is an oppressor against God's exalted uniqueness, *and* usurps the exclusive authority of the Imam and is an oppressor to his sacred scope, *and* yokes the individuals and cities [under his authoritarian arbitrary rule] and is an oppressor against the people. To the contrary, the secondary form does not usurp the Divine's scope of authority and is not an oppressor against God's uniqueness and people, but it does usurp the exclusive authority to rule of the Imam and oppress against him. Thus, ... implementation of the second form of rule is limited to providing for social order and protection of the homeland... In

other words, the authority employed in the secondary form is tantamount to *taṣarrufāt-i wilāyatiyya* (*wilāyah*-based authorities) in which *wilāyah* is authorized for those who deserve holding it. *The incompetence of such ruler [on holding the rule] is like the interference of an illegitimate executor of endowed property in the property's affairs, which can be resolved by constituting a controlling body whose authority to control is vested by the principal holder of authority.* In this [new circumstance], the secondary form will not usurp the status of Imam anymore[40]... *The transmutation of this form of rule is exactly similar to that of electing overseers charged with the protection of the usurped endowed property and imposing restrictions on the usurping executor's disposition [of authority], in favor of its beneficiaries' rights*... In general, imposition of a certain level of restrictions, which is commonly upheld by all members of Islamic ummah, is among the necessities of religion. In addition, it is, inherently, one of the most important duties of Muslims, of all creeds, and among the highest honors of the religion... It is included under the duty of commanding right and prohibiting wrong in the context of the preservation of the right to life, property and the honor of Muslims and the prevention of the oppression of oppressors. (Emphasis mine)[41]

These arguments by Nā'īnī and other constitutionalist jurists could not be made in a vacuum. At the end of this section, Nā'īnī argued that beyond pure juristic discussions, historical facts prove that the speed of progress that the Muslim state enjoyed at its inception—and spread across the world in less than fifty years—had emanated from its characteristics. A system of just consultative rule—in which the equality of rights and rules between the people and the caliphs (i.e., the Rightly Guided Caliphs) and their officers—was dominant. In Nā'īnī's mind, this represented not only the best system for domestic rule from which Muslims must take their model, but also the best defense against international aggression: it was through a system of limited rule that Muslims could defend their homeland against colonialist aggressions, assert their equality with the ruler, and participate in power.[42]

The Legitimacy of Constitutionalism

The next question was whether *mashrūṭah-i rasmiyya* (official constitutionalism), as incorporated in the text of the constitution, met the juristic criteria of legitimacy or not. In responding to this issue, Nā'īnī analyzed three concepts: *shūrā* (consultation), *quwwah-i musaddada yā quwwah-i rādi'a* (controlling or prohibiting power), and *dastūr* (constitution). It was within these analyses that Nā'īnī articulated a solution for the dilemma of legitimacy of a non-Imam rule in the time of the absence of the Imam.

Shūrā (Consultation)

As mentioned before, Nā'īnī held that the essence of Islamic rule is limited to *wilāyah* over social and political affairs, which itself was founded upon the nation's participation in all matters. Such participation, according to constitutionalist jurists, was manifested in the very institution of the Majlis. The main origin of the right to political participation was in theoretical juristic treatments of the concept of consultation with rational individuals among the people. Nā'īnī's references to consultation as an inseparable element of the early Islamic state were based on valid juristic arguments. In delineation of the Text-based imperative of consultation, Nā'īnī drew a very strong conclusion from the Qur'anic verses on consultation,[43] to the effect that consultation was a Divine Ordinance that should be carried out on "all matters with all members of the society."[44] In making his conclusion, Nā'īnī not only relied on an exegetical analysis of the verse—which called for "consulting them on all affairs"[45]—but also applied rational reasoning in support of his definition of the term *al-amr* (matter) to all political affairs and the address of "them" to all individuals.[46] There was only one exception, that of Text-based Shari'ah rules.[47] With regard to this exception, however, he wrote: "the exclusion of Divine Rules from the generality of consultation derives from *takhaṣṣuṣ* (specialty) and not from *takhṣīṣ* (particularization.)"[48] The juristic import of this opinion was that, except for the discovery of Shari'ah rules, which needs highly specialized knowledge, all other affairs are subject to deliberation—even for Infallible Persons. By particularization, he meant that the exclusion of such Rules from the generality of the Qur'anic order on consultation does not permit the exclusion of other affairs from rule and the possibility of their particularization.

In support of his arguments, Nā'īnī cited two crucial facts: the Prophet's recurrent practice of consultation during his rule,[49] and Imam Ali's invitation to the people to express their minds and consult rulers.[50] For Nā'īnī, the imperative of consultation was binding for all rulers, including even the Prophet with all his undisputable moral and rational superiority. In addition, in a pertinent part of his sermon, Imam Ali declared: "Therefore, do not abstain from saying a truth or consulting me on a matter of justice because I neither regard myself above erring nor am I immune of erring in my actions."[51] By referring to these facts, Nā'īnī intended to prove the importance of individual rights. To constitutionalist jurists, the Prophet's practice of consultation and consequent agreement with the majority's opinion, or the Imam's mention of his subjection to err—despite their attributes of infallibility and immunity from sin—was a clear manifestation of the Prophet's or Imam's obligation to honor the people's right to participation and decision-making in the best interests of society.[52] In other words, not only was the right to participation an indispensable element of Islamic rule, but also the characteristic of infallibility could not substitute or replace the people's right in deciding on Muslim society's political affairs. This was in complete accord with what the *Uṣūlī* jurists had already argued for, that is, a limited *wilāyah* that signaled the absence of ownership over individual rights.[53]

Controlling Power and the Substitution of Infallibility

The next issue was raised in the context of the recurrent but most critical question of legitimacy. While as a principle every known non-Imam rule was perceived to suffer from an inherent lack of legitimacy, the main issue was where and how a constitutionalist state would stand in the continuum. The answer was to be found in the broader context of the best model of Imamite rule. Invoking a famous juristic rational maxim,[54] Nā'īnī and other constitutionalist jurists held that when the infallible Imam's comprehensive rule is not attainable, the whole idea of establishing a model that stands closest to it should not be left out. This approach was not new to Shī'ī jurists and had been applied by premodern jurists who attempted to legitimize the Shī'ī Safavid state. As mentioned before, many of them adhered to the just sultanate discourse in one way or the other to the extent that it dominated the field for a long time until the 1905 Revolution. The just sultanate discourse—with all of its reception in juristic circles and the legitimate emphasis that it put on the idea of a state ruled by law—had become the cornerstone of many jurists' justification of the then existing rule of the Qājār kings. For that very reason, however, it was unable to explain the people's role in the formation and preservation of the Revolution.

The anti-constitutionalist jurists had also relied on the just sultanate discourse to dent the legitimacy of the Majlis. They had raised "juristic" doubts about the constitutionalist state to the effect that the general Imāmah (as leadership over religious and social affairs) in the form of *salṭanat* (rule) of the Hidden Imam is a purely Divine Rule in the process of realization within which no role for the people was assumed.

This was the most problematic issue on which the constitutionalist jurists developed their critique of the anti-constitutionalists and introduced a new approach to the old issue of the closest model to Imamite rule. In one of his important opinions, while inviting Muslims to rise for what he called "*īn mashrū'-i muqaddas*" (this sacred legitimate cause, i.e., the restoration of the Majlis and the implementation of the Qur'anic imperative of equality), Ākhūnd heavily criticized the anti-constitutionalist jurists' adherence to the just sultanate discourse on the legitimacy of despotic rule.[55] He wrote:

> If we make the wrong assumption that our (political-territorial) independence, with the divine approvals and the Hidden Imam's blessings, will

> still be preserved while the despotic oppressive establishment has the rule, nevertheless, *the constitutionalist rule and justice and equality in all ḥisba matters is much closer to Shari'ah than tyranny. It is obvious that numerous reasonable individuals will better comprehend the latent and concealed dimensions of the objects than a single one, and oppression and tyranny and abuse will be reduced, to many degrees, by the rule of those who are elected by the people.* (Emphasis mine)[56]

He then summarized the threshold argument upon which both adherents to premodern discourse and constitutionalist jurists could agree but from which drew very different conclusions:

> It is surprising how Muslims, especially the *'ulamā'* (religious scholars) of Iran, have forgotten the necessity of religion. That provides that the legitimate rule is established when the office of authority, over people's public affairs and administration of the Muslims' general matters and resolution of all important issues, is held by the person of the Infallible. The Infallible is supported and appointed and commissioned by the divine text, like the prophets and the chosen—God's greetings be upon them—and like Imam Ali's caliphate, and the time when the Hidden Imam reappears and rises to power. Thus, if the absolute ruler is fallible, his rule is illegitimate. This rule applies during the occultation. *The illegitimate rule is divided into two categories: just, like the constitutionalist state in which the reasonable and pious individuals administer public affairs, and unjust-oppressor, where absolute sovereignty is vested in an omnipotent ruler.* By the clear rule of reason and the apparent text of the Shari'ah, an illegitimate just rule is certainly superior to an illegitimate unjust one. It is obvious, by the experience and accurate precision and careful investigations, that nine-tenths of the despotic rule's abuse of power will be reduced in a constitutionalist system. It is also mandatory to repudiate the most legally defective and evil in favor of the lesser one. Now, how would a Muslim adhere to the legitimacy of an illegitimate unjust rule, when one of the necessities of the *Ja'farī* School (i.e. Twelver Shī'īsm) is the usurpation of Shī'ī rule? *And if the statue of cruelty and oppression (i.e. the despot king) would claim that his abusive power complies with Shari'ah rules, then the book should be closed, written again, and this bloody mat be removed from the Muslims' path.* (Emphasis mine)[57]

Therefore, for constitutionalist jurists, the source of legitimacy of a just but "illegitimate" state was the participation of rational individuals in the collective process of comprehending of social problems and the administration of solutions that would extensively reduce the amount and degree of power abused. To them, the group of rational individuals could only assemble in a parliament, and an Islamic rule—with all its requirements that were foundational to their theorization of it—would find its best embodiment in a constitutionalist system. Such resemblance would not necessarily resolve the problem of legitimacy, but it was the best that could be offered.[58] In yet another articulation of the constitutionalist theory, it was only in a constitutionalist state—to borrow from Nā'īnī's terminology—that measures preventing transmutation to possessive rule could be implemented. The main perceivable measure was the point to which Nā'īnī returned when he argued that the Majlis is the very organ that can limit the possibility of a reverse transmutation. Although in a very complicated fashion, he wrote:

> In the time that we do not have access to the infallible Imam, and face the type of administrators who lack piety, justness, and knowledge, and, even worse, represent the true embodiment of the exact opposite of such characteristics, and while it is also necessarily known that the commonly held degree of restriction of the Islamic state is one of the necessities of the religion, *it is not possible to preserve the Islamic state, whose consultative nature is proven by the text of the Qur'an and the Sunnah, unless a musaddid va rādi'-i khārijī (an external controlling and preventing organ) is commissioned to substitute quwwah-i 'āṣimah ilāhiyya (the divinely devised protective power of the infallible Imam). A substitution of that nature is limited to the extent that human reason can bear the charge, at least in representing the rational power and the faculties of justness and piety [of the Infallibles].* Otherwise, it would be like leaving the charge of safeguarding the sheep to wolves! Therefore, (the necessary and important) establishment of such a controlling organ is clearly undeniable. It is inherently obvious that the external controlling and preventive power will be useful and effective, and able to act on behalf of those human characteristics [i.e., justness and piety] only if it would follow the logic of formation of such characteristics. In other words, just as when the human determination, in forming such characteristics, stems from his rational faculties and apprehensions, the administrators authorized to act as an executive power should only be those whose authority stems from what the controlling organ, by its rational faculty, determines to be in the best interests of society. (Emphasis mine)[59]

By "commonly held degree of restriction," Nā'īnī was referring to the common grounds upon which both Shiites and Sunnis share an approach to the Islamic state. The most important issue was the idea of substituting the Imam's infallibility through the institution of the Majlis—as a controlling and preventative organ—by rational individuals who have been recognized as just and pious. By calling "external" the qualification of this organ, Nā'īnī was making reference to the imperative of a separation of powers and bearing in mind the historical fact of the Qājār kings' recurrent proclamations on assigning quasi-controlling charges to the same oligarchy of corrupt administrators who were the source of the problems. It can also be inferred that the "external" has been used to reject the idea of a division of authority between the religious and the political as the main underpinning categorization of duties in the just sultanate discourse, a discourse that assigned the former to jurists and the latter to rulers (sultans). To Nā'īnī, genuine control could only be carried out by rational individuals outside of both the king's prerogative authorities and the possessive system, and in the form of an officially and legally established institution, that is, a constitutional organ. Furthermore, the ruler and his administrators should only undertake the duty of fulfilling what the legislative power finds to be within the best interest of society, and not more.

Nevertheless, well beyond historical facts, it was the theoretical implications of substituting infallibility that shaped the core of Nā'īnī's theory of legitimacy in non-Imamite rule. For Nā'īnī and the constitutionalist jurists, on the one hand, the absence of the Imam's presence and his actual hold on power could not be equated with the Shiites' consent to and approval of the possessive rule whose undue legitimacy had been justified by the religious branch of despotism.[60] Nor did it justify their inaction, and surrender them to the kings' rule by ignoring religious teachings and disregarding the cruel reality of an incompetent despotic rule that had acquiesced to colonial greed and expansionism. To the contrary, such an absence should have motivated them to strive for liberty, equality, and the eradication of possessive rule through enlightenment, awareness, education, active participation, and protest against abject slavery and lack of determination.[61] For Nā'īnī, the main objective in the Qur'anic imperative of consultation and the Prophet's submission to the majority's opinions was protection of the pristine and essential existence of human beings' inviolable right to self-determination. This objective emanated from two sets of facts: first, the Prophet's practice of rule by promoting equality and liberty for all Muslims, and second, the people's contractual share of power and right to participate in social affairs, commanding right and forbidding wrong, and rebellion against oppressive treatment. Any other interpretation would be antithetical to devising rational faculties in the Divine's act of creating human beings and their right to make choices between what would be best for them and what would not. If there were no such right, the religious faith in divine punishments and rewards on Resurrection Day would have been deeply undermined by a whole host of legitimate questions. Given the undeniable place of reason in the realm of discovering the rules of the Shari'ah (as perceived and articulated by *Uṣūlī* jurists in their arguments) such original right could only take root in the human rational faculty. Furthermore, they had already rejected the typical positivist approach that corrupt mainstream jurists had used to justify their determinations of the rules that governed the relation between the ruler and the ruled.[62] Thus, the possibility of substituting the qualification of infallibility in political rule and the social destiny of Shiites over and above anything else was based on *Uṣūlī* arguments about reason.[63] In the context of constitutionalism, those arguments provided a new approach to the infallible Imams' limited *wilāyah* on the issue of guardianship or authority over human beings' lives and properties; this would amount to limiting applicable scope of their qualification of infallibility, namely with regards to the determination of rights as they are recognized in the Divine Law.[64] The source of limitation of such authority was directed at humans' right to self-determination,[65] particularly where possessive rule had unduly seized power and political dominance. By rejecting possessive rule's all-inclusive authority over subjects, the concept of substitution could emerge in the common ground between the Imam's theoretical limitation of power and the human beings' area of authority—what the constitutionalist jurists called the "God given rights of the people."[66] Given the similarities between the substitution of the infallible Imam's protective power and the notion of the deputyship of the Imam (which was at the center of just sultanate discourse's point of strength), I will later explain how Ākhūnd, Nā'īnī, and the other constitutionalist jurists drew fine lines over substitution in the practice of legislation. This was what the Majlis and the Balancing Committee were assigned to carry out.

The Constitution

As mentioned earlier, Nā'īnī believed that the implementation of the last solution that human reason has been able to envision for limiting the paths of transmutation of an Islamic state to a possessive one was in the substitution of the Imam's infallibility by constitution and parliament.[67] The concept of the constitution was under heavy attack by the anti-constitutionalist jurists. Through quasi-valid treatises, they had disseminated the idea that a Muslim society does not need a legally binding document like a constitution because the laws and rules for all issues can be found in the Qur'an and the Sunnah. For them, the installment of a new binding legal instrument in Muslims' social and political affairs was tantamount to *tashrīʿ* (legislation) and triple *bidʿa* (heresy), conclusions that would suggest the existence of a failure in the Divine Law. In addition, they believed that in such legal instruments, duties were devised that did not meet the requirements of validity and the juristic mandate of obedience; thus, it was illegitimate to hold someone accountable who had violated illegitimately mandated constitutional duties. Given the seriousness of the charge of heresy and the religious capacity for provoking the people against the Constitution, a response was necessary. While resembling anti-constitutionalist jurists and their edicts to *Khawārij* (a group of extremist Muslims)[68] and *Akhbārīs*,[69] Nā'īnī made two juristic counterarguments:

> First, it is one of clear facts in Islamic law, to which all the jurists have agreed, that opposing the mechanisms [and precepts] of the Divine Appointment of Messengers by attempting to legislate laws and rendering rules that are contrary to what the Sacred Legislator has ordained, is called *bid'a* (heresy) and, in juristic technical language, *tashrī'* (legislation). Heresy takes place when a *ghayr maj'ūl shar'ī* (something that has not been approved by Shari'ah), be it a rule on a petty personal issue or a general public issue or a book of general instructions or something else, is offered as *maj'ūl shar'ī* (something approved by the Shari'ah) and as a Divine Rule, and is asked to be mandatorily abided by the duty-bound Muslims. Otherwise, in the absence of the intention to establish a conjunction to the title [i.e., being a Divine Rule], other types of requirements and obligations [as to the performance of duty of this unconnected-to-Divine rule] will not be *bid'a* and *tashrī'*...Second, similar to those legal circumstances in which the legal inclusion of a non-mandatory act to a mandatory contract transmits the nature of the non-mandatory act to a mandatory one, if performing a mandatory duty is due to prerequisite performance of a non-mandatory act, it is rational to rule that such prerequisite non-mandatory act will also change to a mandatory duty. Therefore, it is clear that the act of laying down a constitution, in which the legitimate limitations on the illegitimate oppressive dominance in compliance with the necessities of religion will be completely and comprehensively imposed, is mandatory. It is also mandatory because the establishment and preservation of social order, and the fundamental necessity of limiting and holding accountable a usurping rule is an obvious fact. In the absence of any claim that the constitution has derived from the Divine, the charge of *bid'a* and *tashrī'* is completely irrelevant. It emanates, by reasoning on similar faulty slips, precisely from the foolish *Akhbārīs*' grudge, deception and vulgarity which, due to their inability to apprehend the truth of heresy and legislation, claimed that the jurists' writing of practical treatises is heretical and legislative. (Emphasis mine)[70]

According to Nā'īnī, in theory, a constitution was the written document of a binding contract between the ruler and the ruled. The most important part of such a contract was the inclusion of all the limitations that should be imposed on the ruler's dominance over the nation's sources of power. To that effect, a constitution was the prerequisite instrument for the higher objective of limitation (as a mandatory goal), which had to be realized so that an Islamic state could be established. Although Nā'īnī employed an *Uṣūlī* argument to prove the mandatoriness of the Constitution, the more important outcome of such technical reasoning is to be viewed in the context of its external manifestations. In other words, by concluding the validity of the Constitution, not only would an officially formal document of law represent substantive juristic arguments on limitation, but also the text of the Constitution would have had to represent the culmination of arguments that at times seemed to be continuing indefinitely. For someone like Nā'īnī, as one of the most prominent *Uṣūlī* jurists of his time, an individual who was completely aware of all the juristic discussions on *naṣṣ* (text,) *alfāẓ* (words and utterances), and their close ties to the substance of Shari'ah rules, the ascription of characteristics such as representation to the Constitution as a formal text was not an unknown legal phenomenon. The assumption of the validity of a Constitution that reflected the juristic arguments was, undoubtedly, innovative and unprecedented. In other words, considering all the legal implications embedded in any conception of validity, a juristically valid constitution represented nothing but a new approach to the notion of mandatory acts, source of validity, and the coming into existence of a legitimate cause that would contribute to and meet the underpinning legal-juristic requirements of constitutionalism.[71] The introduction and conclusion of such developments in Shī'ī jurisprudence—being even more instrumental in the regular enactments of the Majlis—could not find recognition in juristic circles without the acceptance of those jurists who possessed prominence in standing and presented credible arguments. Ākhūnd and the religious leadership of the Constitutional Revolution provided this type of prominence and credibility; they supported and approved all of the arguments made by Nā'īnī and Maḥallātī.[72]

In order to make it more accessible and show the importance of a *dastūr-i asāsī* (constitution)[73] for an Islamic state, Nā'īnī used the familiar concept of *risālah 'amaliyya* (a practical treatise written by high rank jurists) for conveying his message. In general, every non-jurist Shiite Muslim is supposed to follow the legal rules discovered by a *mujtahid* (a jurist capable of *ijtihād*) of his choice; these are usually collected in practical treatises and include the required religious black letters of law necessary for daily devotional and transactional duties as a guideline. Nā'īnī emphasized that absence of such a legally binding document, as a source of reference in which the rules of control, and the limitation of rulers and administrators as well as their duties are presumed officially enforceable, is tantamount to disorder and futility.[74] According to him:

> Clearly, *the essence of contracting a constitution is exclusively based on controlling the administrators' behavior and limiting their dominance by determining (the executive power's) typically necessary tasks and distinguishing them from unnecessary ones.* Detailed laws are either customary policies that are enacted to protect the order of society or the Shari'ah rules that are commonly applicable to the public, not the ones for specified groups. Such detailed laws have no relevance to those duties that every Muslim

> undertakes because of his faith—like devotional duties or non-devotional ones in marriage, transactions, religious punishments, wills and inheritance, and other similar issues that are mentioned in the jurists' practical treatises or fatwas. Dealing with these issues is out of the legislature's scope of authority. (Emphasis mine)[75]

Therefore, the Constitution should be interpreted in the following theoretical context:

1. The limitation of the possibilities of transmutation from an Islamic state to possessive rule.
2. The consultative nature of the Islamic state.
3. The foundation of the state upon the principles of liberty and equality, where the "sacred institution of equality" is manifested in "*'anāwīn-i awwaliyyah-i mushtaraka* (universal primary titles). This includes the security of life, honor, property, and home, the absence of undue invasion and the investigation of *khafāyā* (privacy, or hidden acts that are not in the public's plain view), the prohibition of arrest or physical separation from hometown or sanctuary without legal cause, and the absence of any undue deprivation of the right to legitimate assembly among other rights. All of these rights do not belong to any specific (religious or social) group."[76]
4. The institution of a controlling and prohibiting organ that undertakes the duty of substitution.
5. The rule of law, or in other words the enactment of those laws and regulations that related to the issues that, in one way or another, deal with social order and should be published, for the public as well as state administrators' awareness in the form of books of law.[77]
6. The adoption and incorporation of all these general principles and rules from the Shari'ah.[78]

With regards to the aforementioned context, a constitution is a comprehensive text in which the following prescriptive and proscriptive rules and limits are incorporated:

1. Limitations to power:[79] the guaranteed limits of the king's power; the guaranteed rights of people from different social classes; all the required policies that would prevent the king and other administrators from betraying their fiduciary duties and undermining people's rights; the assignment of no more than the sole duty of implementation of the controlling organ's enactments to the executive power; the people's right to oversee the decisions made and the laws enacted

by the controlling organ (i.e., the Majlis) as well as their right to hold it accountable.[80]

2. Inviolable public interests and goals:[81] the taxation and management of public finances and expenditure; the formation of a national military armed with necessary and updated knowledge and artillery; the development of public roads and provision of security from bandits and other criminals; the adjudication of legal disputes and the provision of a court system that efficiently accommodates public grievances, public affairs, and benefits such as education, the publication of educational journals, individual freedoms, the protection of endowed properties, security, the protection of the public interest in business and trade, the defense of national borders against foreign invasion and aggression, and the protection of rights of Iranians who have immigrated to foreign countries.

Legislative Authority and Compliance to the Shari'ah

The scope of the Majlis' legislative authority (as the controlling organ of illegitimate rule) was one of the most controversial issues in the Constitution and subject to many disputes. As mentioned earlier, the constitutionalist jurists believed that the Majlis, as a legislator, should adopt and incorporate the rules of the Shari'ah in its work-product, specifically in the arena of social order and public interest. Two important questions were explicitly at issue: what were the rules of the Shari'ah that had been invoked? Moreover, how could one define "adoption and incorporation"? Given the utmost importance of "judicial philosophies," and the "juristic orientations" of the constitutionalist and anti-constitutionalist jurists toward defining the contents of the Shari'ah, every response to these questions was crucial to an interpretation of the legislative power's constitutional authority. Concomitant with such a response was the scope of authority of the selected jurists who, according to Article Two of the 1907 Supplement, were assigned to implement the constitutional duty of balancing the legislature's enactments with the Shari'ah. At first, I will discuss the anti-constitutionalist jurists' reaction to this issue.

The anti-constitutionalist discourse on the nature of legislative enactments was put forward in the context of their rejection of equality before law. Article eight of the 1907 Supplement provided that "the people of the Persian Empire are to enjoy equal rights before the (State's) Law."[82] The anti-constitutionalists argued that the doctrine behind constitutional equality disregarded the applicable rules of the Shari'ah on the discriminatory legal treatment of specific social groups. In their mind, the interdicted religious minorities, and women were to be treated by relevant laws that formed an inseparable part of the Shari'ah and required discrimination, not equality. The anti-constitutionalists argued that it was impossible to disregard such rules and then claim compliance to the Shari'ah in any conceivable way. They concluded that the combination of including the principle of equality, generally conceived, while disregarding Shari'ah rules was a clandestine attempt to abrogate the Shari'ah in the name of justice, equality, and constitutionalism. It was in this context that they analyzed the concept of legislation through five overlapping hypotheses.[83]

1. If the enactments of the Majlis were to comply with the Shari'ah, disregarding legal discrimination against those specific groups would not be acceptable.
2. If the phrase "state laws," in Article eight was intended to suggest that new rules on issues of this nature would be allowed to pass, this article was in direct conflict with the already established "valid and explicit" rules of the Shari'ah.
3. More broadly, if the Majlis was being institutionalized in order to enact new laws, as connoted in the title of *quwwah-i muqanninah* (legislative power), such enactments were absolutely forbidden by the Shari'ah,
4. If the Majlis had been assigned to enact laws that were compatible with the Shari'ah, the then members of the Majlis did not have the required competence or specialized knowledge required to make appropriate determinations, and thus, were not allowed to employ the authority of enactment. Such competence and authority exclusively belonged to the Imam's general deputies, that is, the jurists.
5. Finally, if the Majlis was supposed to enact laws regarding the detailed duties of administrators, these enactments fell within the scope of the king's authority and not the Majlis's.

The anti-constitutionalists' approach to the concept of rule of the Shari'ah, as law, appeared to be a static one. In their reading of Shī'ī jurisprudence, *istiḥsān 'aqlī* (discretionary rational preference) was prohibited. As a result, the jurist was not permitted to go beyond what had been collected in the books of the traditions and the reports,[84] nor could he draw rational conclusions based on the influence of time and space. Using language similar to the *Akhbārī*s, Nūrī wrote:

> Not only does Divine Law consist of devotional rules; it also includes sufficient rules for all the political issues in the best and most complete fashion, even for *arsh al-khadsh* (the amount of blood-money received for the slightest physical wounds)...If someone thinks that necessities of time

> would be capable of changing some of those Divine Laws or would complement them, such an individual has abandoned the Islamic faith... Devising law of any type is in conflict with Islam. This is the job of the Messengers of God and the Law that the Prophet Muhammad has delivered is the perfect one. It is devoid of any defect and applicable to all people at all times. Such Law has been mediated by revelation to the Prophet, not by *istiḥsānāt shakhṣiyya* (personal discretionary preferences)... In conclusion, Muslims have no right to enact law... I have no belief in someone who would enact law and prefer something other than Divine Law, someone who would believe that the necessities of the age can change Divine Law, and at the same time would claim to have faith in the religion of the Prophet.[85]

In addition, they argued that in a Shari'ah-oriented form of constitutionalism, the most knowledgeable jurist or group of jurists should determine the rules of the Shari'ah *'alā naḥw al-muqarrar al-masṭūr fi al-kutub al-fiqhiyya* (based on the established ways that are written in the juristic books).[86] It was obvious that the anti-constitutionalists did not employ a meaningful apprehension of the concept of equality; they intentionally or unwittingly confused this concept with traditional rules[87] that were not under any form of legal or constitutional dispute at the time.

In response, the constitutionalist jurists made the following arguments:

1. In general, the special treatment of social groups in their entitlements to rights, duties, and protections (or prohibitions) is subject to judicial decision.
2. Because of their rational and legal clarity, similarly traditional rules about the differential treatment of the interdicted can be found in every other legal system.
3. Therefore, such traditional rules do not represent the true meaning of equality.

Nā'īnī and Maḥallātī did not reject the validity of traditional rules in the Shari'ah; they believed, however, that because of the generally inclusive and consultative nature of the constitutionalist state as well as the payment of taxes, every citizen had an equal right to control the government and participate in the process of political decision-making. Consequently, every citizen also had the right to be treated equally before the laws the Majlis enacted and to enjoy the rule of law.[88]

The problem with conclusions like those made by the anti-constitutionalists was their palpable ignorance of two important issues. The first involved the concept of consultation that had been recognized in the Qur'an and the practice of the infallibles persons, and operated as the birthplace of the individual right to political participation. The second involved the process of determining and discovering law, a process that had already been developed by the *Uṣūlīs*.

The Legislative Authority of the Majlis

It was in this context that the constitutionalist jurists determined the issues that were subject to the legislative authority of the Majlis and those that were not. Nā'īnī enumerated the required qualifications of the elected members of the Majlis. He wrote:

> The valid conditions of correctness and legitimacy—prerequisite to the elected members of the Majlis's involvement in public and *ḥisba* duties—are the "permission of the *mujtahid nāfidh al-ḥukūma* (a jurist who has dispositive authority in determining the rules of the Shari'ah),"[89] and the "inclusion of a certain number of jurists, who are versed in politics in the Majlis for [the purpose of] correcting and ratifying enactments" as has been required by Article Two of the Constitution. The important part is the combination of these conditions and the possession of the virtuous qualifications of perfect moral characteristics. The main such characteristics of the members of Majlis are:
>
> (1) Perfect knowledge of politics, international law and an awareness of the details and secrets there employed, as well as awareness of their duties and of the proclivities of the age and time;
>
> (2) Dispassionateness and disinterestedness in the collection of mundane riches and the plundering of national wealth, impartiality, a resistance to the influence of (political) power, and [a state of being] purged from greed, fear and acquisitiveness;
>
> (3) Passion for and benevolence to the religion, the Muslim nation, and the motherland in a fashion that would prioritize the borders of the homeland over personal sanctuary and belongings while considering the lives, honor, and property of different layers of people above personal life, honor and property.
>
> Even non-Muslims, because of their partnership [with Muslims] in national wealth and because of the all-inclusive nature of consultation, are allowed to participate in deliberations on all matters, and to elect their members to the Majlis. While it is not expected from them to protect the Islamic faith, their benevolence and good faith in the protection of the motherland and the people would suffice in their being qualified for membership (in the Majlis.)[90]

He then categorized the laws into "general" and "detailed" ones. Nā'īnī wrote:

> In general, the National Consultative Assembly is established in order to control the administrators and the implementation of duties related to the

> social order, to protect the nation, to manage the people's social affairs, to preserve their rights, and not to employ religious authority and to issue fatwas or to perform group prayer[91] ... Detailed laws are either customary policies that are devised to protect the order of society or *Shari'ah rules that are commonly applicable to the public*, not specified groups. Such detailed laws have no relevance to those duties that every Muslim undertakes because of his faith, such as devotional duties or non-devotional ones in marriage, transactions, religious punishments, wills and inheritance, and other similar issues that are mentioned in the jurists' practical treatises or fatwas. *Dealing with these issues is out of the legislature's scope of authority.* (Emphasis mine)[92]

Through this categorization, Nā'īnī clearly emphasized the supervisory duty of the legislative power in the general duties of the government, the protection of the social order and people's rights, and the management of social affairs. He recognized two groups of rules related to these issues: the commonly applicable rules of the Shari'ah, and customary policies. It is important to note that, though commonly applicable, Nā'īnī primarily made a reference to the rules in which the prohibition of the people's servitude and the rulers' absolute dominance were at issue. In addition, the general rules like prohibiting usury and drinking wine, or the duty to pay one-fifth (a special tax) were at stake. Nā'īnī then made the following important and technical categorization, that is, immutable and variable rule:

> All the duties related to social order, the protection of the nation, and the management of the people's affairs and rights, be they primary rules that deal with the instructions of typical duties or the ones that particularize and limit the applicability of such general instructions, are necessarily categorized in either of the two following groups: The first [category involves] *Manṣūṣ* (written, text-based) instructions whose practical duty is specified and where there is a specifically devised rule in the Shari'ah for the duty. The second [category involves] *ghayr-i manṣūṣ* (unwritten, non-text-based) instructions whose practical duty is unspecified because a particular measure and person in charge of their performance is not specified, and therefore they are left to the determination and preference of the typical holder of *wilāyah* (i.e. the infallible Imam).
>
> It is obvious that the validity of the first category of rules (and their relevant duties) cannot be changed or disputed during the times, and, until Resurrection Day, no other duty except obedience, as expected in reaction to a religious text, is imaginable. Similarly, the second category of rules, depending on the interests and necessities of the time, are to different degrees subject to change and dispute. Similar to the time of the presence of a divinely appointed holder of *wilāyah* (that is, the Infallible) who has *basṭ-i yad* (open-handedness), even in other geographical regions,[93] for the determination of such rules [and duties] depends on the preferences made

> by his appointees' decisions (that is, his governors'). In the time of occultation [also] such determination is left to the preferences made by either general deputies, or those who have obtained permission to do so (i.e. to make such preferences) from *'amman lahu wilāyat al-idhn* (those who have the required authority to vest such permissions).[94]

Before I discuss the text-based instructions, I will explain the second categorization:

1. By non-text-based duties, Nā'īnī referred to a whole host of issues. First, he made it clear that the Shari'ah is not a collection of static rules that are applicable to all issues at all times. In fact, his reference to the contingency of rules in a diversity of circumstances was a clear response to the anti-constitutionalists' discourse. He declared that the concepts of law and legislation are not limited to archaic and superficial analyses of the text of the rules of the Shari'ah, in the sense of being eternally valid because the previous jurists had discovered them in their books. To the contrary, he reclaimed the heavily supported idea in Shī'ī jurisprudence—rather, the Islamic legal tradition—that every jurist attempts to rediscover the rules of the Shari'ah within the contingencies of his time and age. In so doing, the jurist depends on his best understanding of the rules and examines them in the context of the best interest of the society in which he lives. Thus, it is completely possible to believe in the validity of previous jurists' opinions on a variety of issues in the current context, but it is not imperative to follow them blindly just because they once rendered a valid opinion. Similar issues were hotly debated at the time between the *Uṣūlī* jurists and the *Akhbārī*s, specifically with regards to the permissibility or impermissibility of following the opinions of a deceased *mujtahid*. The *Akhbārī*s argued that it is permissible to follow the valid opinions of a deceased jurist because validity is beyond time and place. In other words, they opined that any opinion that, by *Akhbārī* standards, has been directly derived from *aḥādīth* (the traditions) is unchangeable because all such traditions are eternally valid and unchangeable. In contrast, the *Uṣūlī*s believed that validity was subject to the possibility of a jurist's ability to defend against the scrutiny and critique of other jurists, or a curious follower's demand for the disclosure of the evidence upon which the jurist had adopted his specific opinion. For *Uṣūlī*s, if a jurist did not avail himself to his opponent's dispute, inter alia, it may very well mean that he is not able to make persuasive or authoritative arguments about the validity of his opinions; the death of said

jurist did not constitute an exception to this rule. Given the prevailing standard in Shī'ī jurisprudence as to the nonfinality of jurists' discoveries,[95] a presumably valid opinion is the one that is capable of resolving all the disputes against its validity. Therefore, it is impermissible to follow a deceased jurist's opinions.[96] This argument alone suggested that validity was a contestable concept for which factual contingencies and changes in time and space played a crucial role.

2. Second, a simple examination of the characteristics of non-text-based rules makes it clear that Nā'īnī has made a substantial reference to *ḥisba* issues. As discussed before, Anṣārī argued that "the mode of mandatoriness of the act of performing *wājibāt kifāyī* (public duties) is not essentially embedded in the act itself; they are mandatory because accomplishing the higher objective and mandate of a sustained order in society is contingent upon their subject matter acts. Public duties also become mandatory on the basis of what is necessary for preservation of (the right to) life."[97] Such a broad base for determining the mandatoriness of a public duty, and its measurement against the higher objectives of a sustained social order and the right to life required the jurist to engage in factors that, according to a modern rendition, would equate to political rule and individual rights. By *Uṣūlī* standards, in cases of absence, vagueness, silence, or the inapplicability of the textual rules of the Shari'ah, it is the duty of reason, with all its underpinning juristic arguments, to discover and recognize the best form of rule to meet the criteria of mandatoriness. The constitutionalist jurists had already made their case about the dual Anṣārīan factors; it was now necessary to deal with the issue of making a juridical balance between them, and thus, discussing the applicable rules in the Majlis as the institutionalized place of practice for rational individuals. By putting the issue of public duty in its original context, that is, *ḥisba*, with further explicit categorizations of public duty in non-text-based duties, Nā'īnī not only revisited the discussion of the changeability of *ḥisba* rules, but also contextualized it in the application of the *Uṣūlī* theory of reason. The theoretical implications and outcomes of Nā'īnī's approach were virtually unlimited. They included, inter alia, the validity and applicability of those "new" rules that were established by rational individuals about the kind of state or individual rights that they deemed most commensurate and fitting at any given time (e.g., constitutionalism in the age of the 1905–11 Revolution) as well as the rules inscribed in the Constitution.

3. In his analysis of non-textual duties, Nā'īnī raised two distinguishable subjects: (a) the theoretical authority of determining the particular

measures applicable to such unspecified duties, and (b) the possibility of practical application or vesting of the authority of determination. While there is no doubt, in Nā'īnī's opinion, that the Infallible Imam has the authority to hold *wilāyah* on determinations of preference to the best interests of Muslim society, by referring to the infallible Imam's *basṭ al-yad* (open-handedness), he demanded a renewed assessment of the issue. The question was whether it had always been practically possible for the Imam to apply his authority or vest such authority to others, and/or implement such determinations in favor of the Muslim community's preferences and interests. A longstanding element in jurists' analyses of the Imam's or his deputy's practical authority, Shīʿī jurists have generally defined *mabsūṭ al-yad* (someone who is open-handed) as *mutamakkinan min al-taṣarrruf* (someone who has the power of administration).[98] There is no doubt that the concept has played an enormously important role in jurists' determination of the mode of specific or general duties. It has generally been argued that if an Infallible Imam does not have the power to administer his decisions and practically implement them, he may choose to refrain from employing his inherent theoretical authority of ruling over Muslims' social and religious affairs and opt for *taqīyya* (dissimulation).[99] When the presumption of the general deputyship of the jurists from the Imam was at issue, Shīʿī jurists have generally been cautious about the expansion of such vicegerent authority[100] in the time of occultation; they redefined the concept of *wilāyah* with the less authoritative measure of *jawāz al-taṣarruf* (permission to administer). As discussed before, they included jurists among the individuals who were permitted to engage in the *ḥisba* issues.

4. The fourth and final point concerns the constitutionalist jurists' approach to the concept of the power of administration during the 1905–11 Revolution. Putting together the dual Anṣārīan higher objectives, that is, maintaining social order and protecting the right to life, measures that in Nā'īnī's book were coined as "particular measures of preference," Nā'īnī, in the context of the "determination of the non-textual rules" of the Shari'ah, constituted the foundations of the authority of "legislation" by rational individuals in the Majlis. Regarding the "power of administration," Nā'īnī believed that the people's movement toward establishing a constitutionalist order and entertaining their newly achieved right to vote as the manifestation of their political participation were the sources of the power of administration vested in members of the Majlis. Not only could the representatives enact laws necessary for the maintenance of social order and the protection of the people's rights, but also control the

> executive power and limit it to implementing the very same laws that they had enacted. In other words, with the phrase "those who have the authority to vest the permission of making particular measures of preference," Nā'īnī distinguished "jurists" from "those who have obtained permission to do so." The latter group is the very people who vest the authority over the protection of their rights and the maintenance of social order in the members of the Majlis, that is, those who have the capacity to undertake an *ḥisba* duty as the rational and reliable ones among the faithful. It is obvious that by electing members of the Majlis, Nā'īnī believed that it was the people who had the original authority to vest such permission.[101] In some instances, the constitutionalist jurists interpreted the people's movement as another source of their religious authority and engagement with political affairs.[102]

In his further explanations, Nā'īnī clarified that political issues are largely included in the category of non-text-based rules,[103] and therefore, under the *wilāyah* of the Imam (or his general or specific deputies), and subject to consultation.[104] Those rules are only qualified by the careful and sufficient considerations of the members of the Majlis with regards to the maintenance of social order, the restriction of undue usurpation of individual rights by administrators, and prohibitions against administrative aggressions against the Majlis's legislative authority.[105]

Compliance to the Shari'ah

As demonstrated earlier, Article Two of the 1907 Constitution provided that the most learned jurists of the time present to the Majlis names of the twenty jurists capable of undertaking the constitutional duty of balancing enactments with the rules of the Shari'ah, so that the members of the Majlis could choose at least five of them. Such a special committee of jurists was authorized to "determine whether the proposed laws are or are not conformable to the principles of Islam...they may carefully discuss and consider all matters proposed in the Assembly, and reject and repudiate, wholly or in part, any such proposal which is *at variance with the Sacred Laws of Islam*, so that it shall not obtain the title of legality." The jurists were supposed to be included as members of the Majlis, and therefore, part of the legislature. It is obvious that the essence and nature of this authority, as well as the methods by which it could be employed, are the most formidable issues in any theoretical or practical treatment of constitutionalism in Islamic Law. Moreover, I hope my arguments, from the beginning of this book until now, have explained the problems and solutions found therein.

In this section, I will introduce the constitutionalist jurists' specific arguments on the issue. It is also important to analyze some historical facts about the formation and practical functions of the said committee before I conclude this chapter.

In his writings, Nā'īnī referred to authority as "*imḍā' wa idhn man lahu al-imḍā' wa al-idhn*" (the signature and permission of those who have the authority to sign and permit). He also mentioned that the meaning of "legislative power" and its technical equivalent, *quwwa 'ilmīyya* (the knowledge-based power) of the Majlis, was manifest in the combination of the signature and permission, and the careful and sufficient considerations of the members of the Majlis as the source of the official legality of the enactments of the Majlis.[106] In Nā'īnī's theory, the signature and permission in the time of occultation was to be issued by the "Imam's general or specific deputies" when they make determinations on "particular measures of preference" in specific issues proposed by the Majlis as an enactment.[107] Relying on the categorization of rules, when the text-based rule of the Shari'ah was at issue, all authority was allotted to the jurists. In fact, Nā'īnī made it clear that "*Laws and orders whose compliance with the Shari'ah shall plausibly be controlled and scrutinized, are limited to the first category (that is, text-based rules of Shari'ah), and any control or scrutiny as to the second category (i.e. non-text-based rules) is originally unwarranted and unnecessary.*"[108] This involved an extremely important exclusion of the *ḥisba* or non-text-based rules, including political issues, from the jurisdiction of the special committee. Therefore, the whole concept of control over the enactments was limited to balancing them with the text-based rules of the Shari'ah, or what is technically called *dalā'il naqlī*. As extensively argued before, the whole notion of text-based rules, in its traditionist context being an all-encompassing and all-responsive set of readily available rules, was heavily contested by *Uṣūlī* jurists.[109] Therefore, it is imperative to notice that the underpinning theory of text-based rules was founded upon the *Uṣūlī* approach to law. In this context, however, the question was to what extent the jurists of the said committee were allowed to apply their authority. The answer is to be analyzed according to the following premises.

1. By text-based instructions, Nā'īnī referred to those rules that are found in the Qur'an and valid traditions. As a sacred text, Qur'anic verses on rules include instructions and laws that, for the most part, are intended to guide human beings in their lives. Since the details are not usually dealt with in the Scriptures, it is commonly held that these rules are general, immutable, and as such the mother of all other laws.[110] The generality of rules should not suggest that there are no temporal or specific rules in the Qur'an that cannot be viewed in their historical contexts.[111] In fact, some of the Qur'anic rules refer to specific problems that,

at the time of revelation, were to be strongly prohibited or changed,[112] while some others refer to problems whose subject matter is no longer relevant in the present.[113] There are also some rules that refer to the specific circumstances that duty-bound individuals may encounter, and can be interpreted in their generality and their specificity.[114] In yet another context, some of the Qur'anic verses qualify the implementation of any laws to the absence of hardship,[115] human beings' limitations,[116] justice, and rationality.[117] Depending on the occasion of the revelation, some rules seem to be referring to a specific issue whose general treatment is subject to the mastery of historical and juristic knowledge.[118] One must have acquired the required knowledge to figure out how such qualifiers or contingencies can be evaluated and approached, and whether the Qur'anic rules can be particularized or abrogated by the Sunnah. Resolving substantial or methodological sophistications has always been the subject of high level juristic technical debates, which in turn puts the issue of the determination of text-based rules of the Shari'ah in the sole jurisdiction of the learned who possess specialized knowledge, and not in the realm of consultation.[119] While it was obvious that no jurist, constitutionalist or non-constitutionalist, would ever believe in the variability of the Qur'anic verses and the established, incontrovertible rules of the Shari'ah in the Sunnah, the technical definition of *naṣṣ* (text) was also crucial in the degree to which the special committee engaged with enactments. Accordingly, a *naṣṣ* (text) is one of the manifestations of *khiṭāb* (Divine Pronouncements exclusively mediated by revelation), which is a "*lafẓ mubayyan* (apparent utterance) whose signification of meaning is clear and unequivocal; its knowledge is imparted by prima facie expression, and does not bear *ta'wīl* (hermeneutical interpretation)."[120] This type of utterance is usually contrasted with *mujmal* (indeterminate) utterance that is ambivalent and imparts a nonspecific knowledge. Such an indeterminate utterance is unclear because of a whole host of causes such as *ishtirāk lafẓī* (commonality in expression), *ishtirāk maʿnawī* (commonality in definition), and summation in the imparted knowledge.[121] Not only is it necessary to distinguish an apparent utterance from an indeterminate one, it is also imperative to examine the text in other interpretive contexts, for example, generality or particularity, capacity of abrogation, ambiguity and clarity, and the absoluteness or conditionality of the utterances. Distinguishing between these contexts, resolving their conflicts, and preferring the prevailing one require a deep and thorough knowledge in different areas—that I referred to in chapter 1. Therefore, a textual rule is every rule that, after required evaluations, can unequivocally be imparted from the Qur'an and the Sunnah.[122]

The important point, therefore, is the juristic approach that the committee should adopt. According to *Uṣūlī* doctrine, as discussed before, the rules of Qur'anic verses or valid traditions have been finally subcategorized into two groups that take their roots either from God's Sovereignty or His Guidance.[123] If by the rational apprehension of the required necessity of a rule one would conclude that the rule has imparted an unprecedented command that had not previously been recognized or verified by independent reason, such a command is perceived to have stemmed from God's Sovereignty. Thus, it is an *amr mawlawī* (sovereign command) to which the duty of obedience is incumbent upon individuals. Some jurists argued that sovereign commands are mostly devotional, and thus, generally recognizable by the subjection of their relevant duty to reward or punishment. On the other hand, text-based rules may impart yet another type of command that is not unprecedented, that is *amr irshādī* (guiding command), because the reason has either previously rendered a similar injunction or is independently able to verify its correctness at any given time; the necessity of its application and embedded duty is to be undertaken accordingly.[124] As a result, it is not unusual to render them immutable. Nā'īnī's mention of obedience, as is to be expected in a religious text,[125] is general and does not distinguish between the two types of orders.

On the other hand, the basis of validity of any law, whether text-based or not, in the constitutionalists' mind was the *Uṣūlī* principle of *qubḥ-i ẓulm wa ḥusn-i 'adl* (the ugliness of oppression and the beauty of justice).[126] As discussed before, any conception of law in the constitutionalist jurists' general theory of laws, and constitutionalism in particular, was heavily based on the *Uṣūlī* doctrine of reason in which the role of reason in discovering the rules of the Shari'ah was perceived to be a widespread one. It was generally argued that in occasions of absence or silence or vagueness or the inapplicability of the text-based rules, it is the duty of reason to introduce a legal solution and rule. In this case, other relevant—but not specific—rules that are available and can be found in the text will be considered ancillary to reason, not constitutive of it. The underpinning approach to reason was founded upon the principle of correlation between the rational findings and the rules of the Shari'ah. According to this principle, because of the independence of reason in the comprehension of the roots and causes of a law, it is credited with recognizing the nature of required necessity embedded in a mandatory or prohibitory rule of the Shari'ah, or to that effect, any other rule that may or may not have been devised by the Divine in an apparent form. Therefore, not only do rational finding by rational individuals in social praxis amount to prescribing acceptance or denial to an already recognized or soon to-be-established rule—which is considered a valid source of law—but it is also inherently compatible with and verifiable by the religion, and to that effect, by the rules of the Shari'ah. It was based on such a profound adherence to the congruent and harmonious nature between the rules of the Shari'ah and rational findings that the constitutionalist jurists had already found the Majlis to be the place where rational individuals, whose enactments inherently enjoy legal and juridical validity, could congregate. Such validity was qualified, however, by the absence of conflict with the methodological requirements (and not necessarily the precedents) of the legal system in which the laws were devised, that is, Shīʿī jurisprudence. Briefly, those requirements are: (1) the verification of the rational formulation of a rule's compliance with the Qur'an and the valid Prophetic Sunnah as well as reports attributed to the Imams,[127] and (2) the verification of whether or not rational finding had been formed by juristically prohibited methods. Those methods are *qīyās mustanbiṭ al-ʿilla* (inferential analogy, which stands in contrast to *qīyās manṣūṣ al-ʿilla* or text-based analogy, the latter being permissible) and *istiḥsān* (arbitrary or discretionary opinions).

2. As discussed before, Shīʿī jurists believe that due to a variety of factors, it is not possible to derive the exact and unquestionable impart of the Shari'ah rules.[128] This issue deals with yet another important point about the absence of finality in the jurists' findings. In its technical setting, the question of finality has divided Muslim jurists into two groups: *Mukhaṭṭiʿah* and *Muṣawwibah*.[129] Shīʿī jurists strongly adhere to *Mukhaṭṭiʿah* and reject the ideas of the other group. Revolving around a Prophetic tradition in which the Prophet declared that jurists will be rewarded for their strife as well as for discovering the rules of the Shari'ah, both groups believed in the jurists' entitlement to a reward. They heavily disagreed, however, on whether or not a jurist is capable of discovering a right and correct opinion that is in complete accord with the truth embedded in the Shari'ah's rules and their exact imparts and injunctions. *Muṣawwibah* claimed that every opinion held by a jurist is practically right and subject to the reward, whereas *Mukhaṭṭiʿah* argued that there is always potential for a jurist to make a mistake and hold incorrect opinions. Some jurists from both groups held that there is at least one certainly correct opinion in the pool of the jurists' numerous opinions. They based their argument on *luṭf* (Divine Grace)—which is utilized to prove that God will and does only that which is good—so as to bring human beings close to His obedience and keeps them far from disobedience. Nā'īnī, in his lectures on *Uṣūl al-Fiqh*, held that the majority of *Uṣūlī* jurists do not agree with this argument; instead he asserted that the principle of *luṭf* does not require the Imam to reveal the truth through jurists' opinions in the time of occultation. To the contrary, it requires him to inform the people of the good and the evil, or the necessary benefits and detriments embedded in rules, by normal means. Therefore, if due to unusual circumstances

the truth still rests beyond the people's reach, it is not up to the Imam to employ unusual means in order to show them the real and true rules.[130] Excluding the incontrovertible rules of the Shari'ah (like mandatoriness of prayer[131] and other similar principles) from the discussion, Shīʿī *Uṣūlī*s hold that if a duty-bound Muslim is able to reach certainty through evidences that provide certitude,[132] such certain knowledge is *ḥujja* (proof). When it complies with *wāqiʿ* (actuality or reality) it can prove the actual rule in the Shari'ah. However, when it does not comply with *wāqiʿ*, there is *ʿudhr muwajjah* (a legitimate excuse) for the duty-bound individual to be held accountable. If, however, he is unable to establish certainty by those means, he must consult *ʾamārāt* (the plural of *ʾamāra*, meaning indicators); *amāra* refers to every legal circumstance that can provide probable cause for the proof of a rule. Examples of such indicators are *akhbār āḥād* (less than reliable reports), *ijmāʿ* (jurists' consensus), and prima facie utterances of the Qur'anic verses and traditions.[133] In the absence of indicators, *Uṣūl al-ʿamalīyya* (procedural principles) come into play.[134] According to Shīʿī *Uṣūlī* jurists, indicators and procedural principles do not establish the interests or new rules by themselves. They are valid because the Legislator has intended them to show the path. If they match reality, then the actual rule is proven. Otherwise, indicators will provide another legitimate excuse. The point is that a proof, based on indicators or procedural principles, does not represent the actual Divine rule; there is always the possibility of fault. As such, analyzing certain or probable evidences and finding a rule of Shari'ah will not be equal to the *Muṣawwibah* kind of conclusive rules. Nevertheless, the question remains as to how a jurist can allow adherence to indicators or procedural principles that do not provide access to the actual rules of the Shari'ah, especially when he knows that they fail in this regard and that Shīʿī theory requires the existence of the perpetual possibility of precisely such a failure. Put more technically, if it is true that there is the possibility of fault, then concomitant to that there are also *tafwīt maṣlaḥa* (distance from or alienation or even elimination of the Shari'ah rule's inherent benefit) and *ilqāʾ mafsada* (possible realization of detriment). Under these conditions, how does the jurist find an outcome of adherence to indicators and procedural principles that can substitute for such potential failures in the duty-bound Muslim's performance and his subjection to responsibility before God including subsequent punishments?

In order to resolve this dilemma, Shīʿī *Uṣūlī* jurists have offered two theories. Anṣārī based his solution on the definition of *maṣlaḥa* (benefit) and suggested that:

> If we assume that there is a benefit [i.e., legitimate cause] in the adoption of indicators, and match them [i.e., the indicators] with the performance of

the subject matter act of the true rule, then, in the case of an existence of fault in the indicators, the potentially alienated benefit of the true rule will be compensated with such performance. Therefore, not only are the indicators capable of showing the path to the actual rules of the Shari'ah (or what he called *ṭarīqiyyat al-'amārāt*), but also they are the causes of realization of them [or what he called *sababīyyat al-'amārāt*].[135]

He called such presumptive benefits *Maṣlaḥat Sulūkī* (a harmonizing benefit). As he put it, the

presumption of this harmonizing benefit is based on the existence of an interest for the duty-bound individual that has been established by relying on the indicators and invoking them in acting upon what they produce as the presumed act embedded in the actual rule. This adoption of indicators will compensate for the potentially eliminated interests of the actual rules—that may be realized in the case of a reliance on faulty indicators—without presuming an exact and real interest in the concluded act. This harmonizing presumption would not constitute a *Muṣawwibah* type of rule, which the Shiites do not approve of.[136]

Furthermore, Ākhūnd argued that

the absence of validity in a reliance on indicators would be tantamount to the Legislator's insistence on conclusiveness and the certitude of our knowledge of true rules without providing us sufficient means to acquire such knowledge. This, in turn would be equal to putting duty-bound individuals in hardship, especially in those daily and mundane acts that they are accustomed to perform in their already established fashions and have been approved by rational individuals in society.[137]

Therefore, "there is strong evidence to hold that the Legislator has allowed us to follow the indicators, because, due to His refrain from hardship, He has wished for an easing of the path to true rules so they could be available to the people." He held that

maṣlaḥat tasḥīl (facilitating benefits, particularly in making duties easy for the people) is one of *al-maṣāliḥ al-naw'īyya* (the collective interests), and that the Legislator prioritizes such collective interests over individual interests (that is, Divine interest), which may be eliminated by faulty indicators. This is what we learn from the method of Islamic Shari'ah: a Law which is founded upon ease and making things easy for people.[138]

Both of the solutions' underpinning theory rest at the intersection between Shari'ah rules and human reason. Anṣārī and Ākhūnd found that, one the one hand, there is a common area between collective reason's perception of the correctness of performing concluding acts, which are the outcome of a reliance on the indicators' capability of showing the path to actual rules, and presumptive acts, which are what the Shari'ah rules have intended to require duty-bound individuals to perform. On the other hand, they believed in human reason's ability to discover—though without absolute certainty—what the Divine has intended and demanded in His Laws—though not clearly and unequivocally. Therefore, there is an indefinite dynamism between human being's strife in discovering the rules of the Shari'ah and the indeterminacy of Shari'ah rules. This dynamism in Shīʿī jurisprudence can only be understood as the perpetual possibility of making faults in discovering the rules, which in turn requires both the presence of constant utmost strife, and the closure of what ʿAllāma called *al-jazm* (the assertion of finality) except for the Prophet and the Infallible Imams.[139]

For the jurists on the special committee, the practical implications of these arguments would have been caution and diligence. In particular, it should have been an immense moral responsibility for such jurists to render an opinion on laws that would bind the nation. Undertaking such a responsibility not only required sufficient knowledge and mastery of the religious teachings, but also a moral bravery in the religious realm that could shield the jurist from being held accountable in the hereafter and on Resurrection Day before God. This was an important obstacle for the jurists who were later invited by Ākhūnd to sit in the special committee, especially when we consider the then existing religious culture that accommodated religious moral latitude only for those who had been chosen by Muslims as *marjaʿ al-taqlīd* (leader of the followers).

3. Nā'īnī strongly rejected the anti-constitutionalists' general allegations of invalidity and the illegitimacy of constitutionalism where they claimed that any involvement by the Majlis in decision-making about public affairs was an intrusion in the Imam's inherent *wilāyah*. Relying on the just individuals' authority in *ḥisba* matters and the generality of the concept of consultation, he wrote:

> There are two other issues in performing the *ḥisba* duties: first, it is not necessary for the jurist to practically hold the authority of determination. His permission would suffice to render the act valid and legitimate…second, performance of *ḥisba* duties is not limited to the occasions in which the jurists are able to undertake the duty of performance. In case of the jurists' inability to do so, the *wilāyah* of performance of the duty passes to the just individuals among the faithful. It is also held that in the case of the just individuals' inability, such *wilāyah* can even pass to the morally imperfect

individuals to undertake the duty... *Therefore, the means of performing the necessary duties, and imposing limitation to the ruler's power by the measures adopted in officially and internationally recognized constitutionalism, along with upholding the people's chosen way of such, is limited to the adoption of the general requirements of constitutionalism. Without this adoption, neither will it be possible to assign jurists the charge of determination, nor would it be possible to officially recognize constitutionalism in Iran being one of the constitutionalist nations.... It is also impossible to preserve jahat wilāyatiyya (the characteristic of the wilāyah aspect) of ḥisba duties [without constitutionalism]. Considering all the required precautionary measures, the least that can be achieved [occurs through two paths], first, the realization of the principle of election and the participation of the elected individuals by permission of mujtahid nāfidh al-ḥukūma (a jurist who has dispositive authority in determining the rules of the Shari'ah), and second, the qualification of the validity of the elected individuals' enactments to the correction and ratification of a certain number of jurists as devised in Article Two.* (Emphasis mine)[140]

There are two important points to deal with here: (a) it was the "jurist's permission" that mattered and not his individual engagement in performance of the duty, and (b) the nature of "signature and permission" was the legal determination of compliance between legislative activities and Shari'ah rules, which had found their constitutional embodiment in the special committee's "correction and ratification." According to Nā'īnī, a legal determination of this kind could be made by the Majlis through the prior authorization of a jurist with dispositive authority, or by the special committee's involvement in the act of balancing. Given that a limited number of the members in the Majlis were jurists, authorizing the Majlis to make such legal determinations was of utmost importance to revealing the constitutionalist jurists' emphasis on the competence of collective reason to substitute for religious rulings. As argued before, Nā'īnī was of the opinion that the collective reason of the Majlis was capable of substituting for the infallibility of the Imam. At this juncture, Nā'īnī found it impossible to preserve the Shī'ī doctrine of *wilāyah* without the establishment of a universally acclaimed theory of constitutionalism.

It is not possible to discover the extent to which Nā'īnī was aware of the methods of constitutional review that were adopted and employed in other constitutionalist states at the time. It is, however, possible to draw comparable theoretical similarities between judicial review, as the primary method employed in constitutionalist states, and the juristic review of parliamentary enactments as incorporated in the Iranian model. We know that Nā'īnī found the "determination of compliance" to be the fundamental measure upon which the Iranian legal system had been established. In addition to Ākhūnd,[141] he also on different occasions considered constitutionalism to be a human achievement that had derived from practical *ḥikma* (wisdom),[142] itself a source of knowledge for *Uṣūlī* jurists. Moreover, Nā'īnī praised the knowledge of the first learned individual who articulated the idea of constitutionalism.[143] Insofar as the 1906–1907 Constitution was concerned, the incorporation of fundamental rights with equality, citizens' entitlement to a variety of individual rights, the separation of powers, the origination of power from the people, judicial structure, and the exclusive jurisdiction of the parliament in financial matters were either completely in accordance with Shī'ī law or, at the very least, not in conflict with it. Theoretically, the notion of the special committee's supervision was considered to be part of the general approval of constitutionalism.[144] Although constitutional review, as defined and adopted in constitutionalist states, was heavily based on the supremacy of the constitution over statutory laws, in the Iranian Shī'ī form of review, it was theoretically both co-opted by and expanded through the jurisprudential review of statutory laws. Nā'īnī made it clear that the scope of this review was limited to text-based rules, and did not include the larger part of political affairs. This, by itself suggested that the special committee had no standing in deciding on the normal political process of legislation, and only had to deal with the purely juristic technicalities of compliance. As discussed before, the *Uṣūlī* jurists' approach in their theory of "juristic review" was strongly based on Anṣārīan dual factors (i.e., maintaining social order and preservation of individual rights) in determining the mandatoriness of duties. The juristic implications of such factors would also provide the grounds for the argument that the important issue involved meeting the requirements of what Anṣārī called *luṭfun qarīḥat* (an ingenious and precise legal mind). It was in accordance with the determinations of such a legal mind that, on the one hand, the manifestations of individual rights would be checked, and, on the other, the required balance between the constitutional rules on rights and the social order could be achieved. Nā'īnī's clear reference to the immateriality of the jurists' individual undertaking of public duties, and his rejection of the jurist's all-inclusive authority, inter alia, strongly suggest that the members of the special committee were assigned to undertake such important charges, rather than employing a power-based, vague, and arbitrary authority. In other words, the nature of the most learned jurist's signature and permission—as one of the methods of legitimizing the Majlis—was to validate legal arguments, including all the juristic technical details about the issue at hand. This did not include the imposition of undue influence and personally—or corporate—sought after interests against the enactments of the Majlis.

4. Maḥallātī's technical arguments provide additional grounds for the legitimacy of the Majlis and constitutionalism, on the one hand, and

the scope of the Special Committee's authority, on the other. The anti-constitutionalists argued that, in the time of occultation, *wilāyah* on political affairs rests exclusively with the *ḥukkām al-sharʿ* (jurists), and there is no place for or legitimacy in the interference of the non-jurist members in the Majlis. While emphasizing the imperative of consultation, Maḥallātī made a counterargument when he said:

> In case *ḥākim al-sharʿ* (the jurist, or the holder of authority in judicial decision making) happens to hold political power, he has to act in accordance with what rational individuals have recognized as the best interest of society, balance his policies with their approbations, and implement them. He has no more authority than a trustee or guardian of Muslims' rights wherein the rights of all Muslims and non-Muslims would be immune from aggression and violation. This is because there is no exclusive proprietary right over Muslims' affairs for a jurist, especially when there is an absence of authority for others to entertain the right to reject or approve (his determinations).[145]

He then made a compelling case against the juristic claim to exclusive authority:

> In safeguarding the rights and delivering them to their owners, *wilayah* restricts the jurist to hold the authority of determining rights, which in turn is applicable in practice, and the implementation of all the required actions that relate to each of the determined rights. Only in this context should people follow his instructions, not the authority in determining rights nor the distinction between wrong and right or the establishment of one against the other. This is because there are only two determinative capacities in proving or disproving rights, (a) In *ḥuqūq kubrawiyya* (rights in general) the purpose of which is to determine the rights in general. This capacity does not hold for the jurist in the context of *wilāyah*; it relates to the issue of a fatwa where a jurist extracts an opinion and relays it to the people through the medium of a fatwa, and the people subsequently follow such an opinion. (b) *Where the determinative capacity is in ṣughrā-yi ḥuqūq (details of rights), it is imperative that such a capacity belongs to those rational individuals who are among the beneficiaries of the right in question, and that their determination should be the measure by which the issue should be evaluated. They have the authority to determine shakhṣīyyāt-i maṣāliḥ-i nawʿīyyah-i Muslimīn (the specifications of the Muslims' general interests), distinguish the benefits and detriments therein, and clarify in which to protect the public's rights. Public policies should be adopted accordingly.* Expansion of the *wilāyah* of *ḥākim al-sharʿ*, who holds rule over everything from the execution of rights to the determination of the ways in which to protect those rights, would be equal to the presumption of the nullification and invalidity of the rational individuals' determinations. Furthermore, it would amount to the

> assumption of their insanity and their minority status and the subsequent implications that ensue to the degree that they should be required to follow obediently whatever the jurist rules. This would be tantamount to denying rational individuals their right to rejection or approval. Consequently, the kind of rights that are established for the nation in an Islamic state will not be proven by their generalities. They will be qualified by what the jurist has limited them to in his opinion, and shortened by the criteria that his opinion implicates. Such a rule is against the historical precedent set in the earlier ages of Islam. (Emphasis mine)[146]

Although at the time a hypothetical argument, the merits of Maḥallātī's argument lie in his references to rational individuals' rights to: (1) determine the specifications of the public interests, (2) distinguish detriments and benefits, all together, (3) clarify the ways in which to protect rights, and (4) reject or approve of jurists' determinations. In this regard, the merits of Maḥallātī's arguments go well beyond a hypothetical analysis. Building on these suppositions, the following conclusions can be made:

(a) The notion of the jurists' deputyship of the Imam in political affairs is limited to safeguarding individual rights. It does not extend to the determination of benefits, or the detriments of the interests that the Majlis—as the designated institution of rational individuals' involvement in political affairs—has already made. This is in complete agreement with Nā'īnī's exclusion of political issues from the scope of the special committee's jurisdiction.

(b) The jurists' main duty is the protection of rights, and so it should be the special committee's priority to determine compliance. In other words, following the earlier discussion and Anṣārī's theory of dual factors, the jurists on the special committee have the sole duty of analyzing the enactments' compliance from the perspective of protecting individual rights.

(c) The special committee's jurisdiction is limited to the legal-juristic determination of rights in general, and not the means of protection. Put differently, given rational individuals' authority in determining such means, the jurists on the special committee are left to determine rights with generality. If the Majlis's enactment conflicts with the rights in the governing principles and theories, then the committee has the authority to make necessary corrections or even to reject it.

(d) Maḥallātī is clear in his assertion that the faulty presumption depriving rational individuals' from the right to make determinations—a presumption that would qualify them as insane or a minor—is invalid because such a right ought to be honored in every imaginable situation. Therefore, despite being theoretically and practically exceptional, it can be deduced that the members of the Majlis also had the right to reject or approve determinations. It is not possible then to find out whether the members of the Majlis reached similar conclusions or not, and, if they did, how they employed their right. It is, however, possible to suggest that the Majlis could enact a new law in the scope of political affairs that would reduce or even eliminate the impact of special committee determinations, which the Majlis would not approve of. This was similar to the way in which other constitutionalist states accommodated their parliaments.

The Standard of Determination and the Practice of Authority

Reflecting on the text of Article Two, religious leaders made an equation between the "absence of conflict" and "compliance" on different occasions.[147] This equation was a clear and important methodological measure according to which the enactments should have been considered "Islamic"[148] as long as they were not in conflict with Shari'ah rules. This very important standard had its roots in the *Uṣūlī* Shīʿī theory of determination.

The Uṣūlī Shīʿī Theory of Determination

As has been extensively discussed, the concept of determination is an indispensable part of the broader concept of *ijtihād*. Despite the fact that the term "*tashkhīṣ*" or determination is generally held to be the equivalent of a juristic opinion in Iranian Constitutions,[149] it is not the technical term that Shīʿī jurists have used to discuss the by-products of juristic strife over the derivation of rules through the practice of *ijtihād*.[150] Notwithstanding the disparities, Shīʿī jurists in their analytical arguments have mainly discussed the act of conceptual inference involved in determination as discovering the "absence of inconsistency" or the absence of conflict with the Qur'an and the Sunnah under valid conditions of contracts. According to the Shīʿī law of contracts, the following four qualifications are required for a condition to be considered a valid element of both the construction of a contractual obligation and prevention of its corrosion: (1) Practicability, that is, a party to the contract should be capable of performing his/her obligation. (2) Permissibility, that is, the subject and performance of the condition should not be *ḥarām* (forbidden by the Qur'an or the Sunnah). (3) Rationality, that is, the subject and performance of the condition must be reasonable. (4) Congruity, that is, the subject and performance of the condition should not conflict with the Qur'an and the Sunnah. This fourth qualification relates to the concept of determination.[151] The other side of an "absence of conflict" is *muwafiqa* (agreement and conformity). While for obvious reasons conformity is desirable, Shīʿī jurists argued that it is the absence of conflict that will most probably create congruency between a contract and the text-based rules of the Shari'ah. In their opinion, "*any condition which does not particularly contradict the Text, and accords with general rules that have provided the individuals with the permissibility of every non-prohibited disposition of authority in their properties and lives, is in agreement with Text.*"[152] It remains to be seen what exactly stands in conflict with the Text. Jurists argued that, in general, such a conflict could follow from either the condition or the ensuing obligating act. Since acts are ruled to be either mandatory, encouraged, permissible, discouraged, or forbidden, given the nature of the rules it is fair to say that the question of congruity and compliance is raised when the act in question is a *mubāḥ* (permitted) act. In other words, permissibility of a *mubāḥ* act stems from equal value of its action or omission: it is the combined characteristics of indifference and permittedness—inherent in the act where permissibility is presumed—which makes it subject of potential congruence or conflict with the Text.

In his analysis of whether being obligated to a contractual condition that requires the omission of a permitted act would be in conflict with its permissibility or not, Anṣārī invoked two traditions or reports. In one of the reports, the conditioning party was prohibited from demanding the performance of a contractual condition that would render a forbidden act permissible, or vice versa.[153] The other report allowed conditions, on anything, that were not prevented by the Text.[154] By combining the two, Anṣārī concluded that the kind of obligation that will establish conflict is the underlying forbidden act, and not the permissible one. For Anṣārī, the act of demanding and conditioning something that was against what had previously been rendered forbidden was equally as prohibited as doing so with something that had previously been rendered permissible because it would limit both the scope of the permissibility of the acts as well as the permissible acts themselves. It was in this context that—in response to the question "What is meant by the rule of the Text (that is, the Qur'an and the Sunnah)?"—Anṣārī said: "The Rule of Text, for which the absence of conflict of the condition or the act of conditioning is demanded, is the very rule whose maintained stability and unchangeable validity is proven by [analysis of] such a condition that requires change in its underlying subject through the act of conditioning."[155]

In other words, the Text's rule is immutable and will not be conversely affected by modifications, or the contingency of the conditions imposed against the parties in contract. It is obvious that a contractual condition will generally qualify the legal result of its subject matter act by the corresponding satisfactory performance of its underlying obligation, and thus, will create a new legal subject and concomitantly a new legal rule. Logically, the next question is: "How do we prove that a rule has maintained its stability and unchanged validity?" In answering this question, Anṣārī analyzed two categories and ways by which the rules are recognized and proven for the subjects.[156] First, *Abstract Rules* are proven by *the essence and nature of their underlying subjects. They are free from the impacts of other titles that could be assigned to them, and require the absence of tanāfī (mutual incompatibility) between the proof of the first rule and the second one.* A difference in the two titles would be possible—like forbiddance and discouragement—but a congenial nature should exist in subject matter acts and their corresponding rules. This is also possible because the devised permission for action, or the omission of the act, has been exclusively founded upon considering the act in the abstract with complete disregard for anomalous rules. Eating meat is *mubāḥ* (a permitted act), but an individual can voluntarily ban it by, for example, taking a binding oath to that effect. Treating permitted acts in this manner is not in conflict with the Text because the abstract nature of the permissibility of the act (i.e., eating meat), and the equal value of its action or omission allows such a ban. In addition, as a prerequisite to mandatory duties or acts, for example, taking a binding oath, they may even change to mandatory acts. Second, there are *Non-Abstract Rules.* These rules are proven by the impact of other titles that inflict their underlying subject, and *require mutual incompatibility* between their proof and the proof of secondary titles like many of the forbidding and mandatory acts. In this category, the rules of forbiddance or omission are *muṭlaq* (absolute), that is, they are not limited to a nature that does not exist in the underlying subject except if they are established titles like *'usr wa ḥaraj* (difficulty and restraint).[157] Therefore, when the second rule applies, there inevitably exists a conflict between the evidence supporting each rule, be they primary and secondary. Under these circumstances, the jurist should examine the supporting evidence for each and determine the one that is inherently preferential—like interpreting valid traditions against less reliable ones. To conclude, if the condition is against the first type of rules, that is, abstract rules, undertaking the subsequent obligation is not in conflict with the Text, and we presume that there is no contradiction between the rule of Text and the reason behind its contractual obligation. By contrast, when it is in the context of the second type, the condition is in conflict with the Text. It does not matter if the condition itself is in conflict with the Text, or if the resultant cause of this condition is intended to create a conflict with the Text.

Anṣārī is agile enough to say that such categorizations will not resolve all the problems because it is very difficult to distinguish them from each other.[158] He excluded the occasions in which the prima facie utterance of the Text imparts an explicit and general inclusion of the subject matter act of the issue at hand.[159] Otherwise, it is the jurist's duty to employ his utmost efforts in *tamayyuz* (making distinction) in order to distinguish between the two rules through careful consideration of all the evidence, indicators, and facts as well as the applicable rules, be they primary or secondary.[160] If such a distinction cannot be established, the jurist ought to invoke *aṣālat al-ʿadam al-mukhālifat* (the presumption of the absence of inconsistency) between the condition and the rules of the Text, and apply the general principle of honoring contracts and obligations that emerge from the conditions therein.[161]

What establishes a conflict is *taḥrīm al-ḥalāl aw taḥlīl al-ḥarām* (forbidding a permitted act or permitting a forbidden act). According to Anṣārī:

> The transition of the nature—and subsequent rule—of the act takes place only when there is a conflict between the indicators that make a condition obligatory and the indicators that prove the primarily imparted injunctions, to the extent that makes it necessary to refuse the obligatoriness of the underlying act of the condition. However, if the indicator of the primary injunction would only be useful to prove the rule as to acts in their state of *lau khullīy al-mawḍūʿ wa ṭabʿahu* (emptied from subject matter and its character or nature), such conflict cannot be established[162]... The indicators of permitted acts often, or even under all circumstances, prove their rules in such an abstract state. Therefore, it would not be mutually incompatible to permit their forbiddance by conditions[163]... Finally, in the two forms of *iṭlāq* (general inclusion), conditions would be conflictive (1) if the evidence would prove permittedness in general so that no qualifier or condition would be included, and (2) when an external indicator would prove the general inclusion of the permitted act[164]... There is no such problem, however, on the "permitting the forbidden act" side [of the argument] because forbidden rules are generally inclusive and impart their prohibitory injunctions in a way that would not allow deviation.[165]

Although the abstract nature of these kinds of arguments is unfamiliar and hard to follow for nonspecialists, it was clear to Shīʿī jurists, at the, time that the scope of the conflict was limited to forbidding rules that are clear in their general inclusion and do not allow deviation. Given that a large majority of jurists, including Ākhūnd and Nāʾīnī, have concurred with Anṣārī and his categorization of rules to different degrees,[166] it is an indisputable fact that these standard-setting arguments built the foundations for the prevailing theory of determination in Shīʿī Law.[167] By applied resort to procedural and practical rules and principles, jurists were careful to avoid taking scrupulous, reactionary, and idiosyncratic approaches to the issues at hand and to adopt a careful method that was free from blind or extreme applications of questionable non-*Uṣūlī* or semi-juristic discourses on the Shari'ah.[168] Finally, they had to provide laxity and ease in the course of conduct that their followers pursued daily. There was no theoretical obstacle against extending the juristic outcome of the debate—even though it was made in the context of the law of contracts—to encompass the special committee's scope of authority. Similarly, not only did this model provide the Majlis latitude in adopting and enacting measures and laws, but it also required the special committee to deal with the limited scope of forbidden rules. In other words, the selected jurists had the exclusive duty of determining points of conflict with forbidden rules in the enactments of Majlis. In all other cases, it had to be so concluded, the scope of legislation was broad and devoid of a potentially theoretical conflict with Shari'ah rules. This latter point must be analyzed in the special committee's effort to practice its authority, a task to which I will return now.

The Special Committee in Practice

Not surprisingly, there was a variety of constitutional and practical issues regarding the formation and practice of the special committee.[169] In the early days of the Second Majlis, that is, the reinstated parliament after the civil war, Ākhūnd and Māzandarānī advised the Majlis to act urgently in the establishment of the Senate.[170] In addition, they asked the Majlis to appoint a number of commonly known jurists from Tehran as the special committee's interim members until their investigation and due diligence on the final candidates was underway.[171] After a hot debate, the Majlis found this recommendation unconstitutional and impractical because Article Two had required the religious leaders, and not the Majlis, to present the names.[172] After Religious Leaders proposed the names of twenty jurist-candidates,[173] the members of the Majlis disagreed on whether by "taking lot," as one of the constitutional methods suggested in the text of Article Two, the majority of votes was intended or not.[174] Due to the members' unfamiliarity with the proposed names, this issue had to be decided by interpretation. Thereby, the Majlis established an ad hoc commission to interpret the term.[175] The interpretation, however, made it even more ambiguous by rendering that "taking lot could also mean [a] majority of votes."[176] Finally, after four ballots, only one candidate was selected by consensus (itself being majority of the votes!); due to the absence of a majority, the Majlis selected the remaining four by drawing lots![177] In practice, only two of the five selected jurists attended the Majlis[178] and the committee never formally convened.[179] The Second Majlis did not last its constitutionally ordered tenure and was coerced to close down in 1329/ November 1911 by virtue of Russian military pressure and British political support. The Russo-Anglo backed government did not hold elections for almost three years. The Third Majlis was inaugurated in Muharram 1333/December 1914, but did not last more than one year and was forced to dissolve in Muharram 1334/November 1915 because of the impact of World War I and the invasion of Iran by Russian and British troops. It took yet another five years for the Fourth Majlis to convene (Shawwal 1339/June 1921-Dhul-Qadah 1341/July 1923); this occurred right after the British-backed coup that installed Reza Khan as prime minister, an act intended to further weaken the last Qājār King.[180] The inaugurations of the Fifth Majlis in Rajab 1342/February1924, and the Sixth Majlis in late1344/mid-1926, however, were more in order than the previous ones. After the inauguration of the Fifth Majlis, Nā'īnī and two other prominent Religious Leaders attempted to revive the special committee; they proposed the names of twenty candidates, but the new political order had no intention to accommodate their proposal.[181]

In their letter proposing the list of jurists-candidates for the special committee, Ākhūnd and Māzandarānī delineated the scope of their authority:

> The *waẓīfa maqāmiyya* (status-based duty) of the selected jurists is to observe the compliance of *sīyāsāt mamlakatī* (public policies), whatever it may be, with *aḥkām khāṣṣa wa 'āmma shar'īyya* (the particular or general rules of Shari'ah). The selected jurists have absolutely no jurisdiction over liquidation, balancing the budget, financial affairs, or the compliance between the nation's expenses and the Shari'ah.[182]
>
> With regards to the laws and regulations involved in the adjudication and resolution of the disputes, *qiṣāṣ* (retaliation, *lex talionis*), *ḥudūd* (predetermined punishments), and the other areas that the task of judgment is specifically assigned to *ḥukkām al-shar'* (mujtahid-judges), there is no authority for the cabinet of ministers to interfere [i.e., to propose any laws] except by (a) referring the cases to those mujtahids who are qualified to adjudicate, and (b) executing their judgments as they always have. Nor does the Majlis have the jurisdiction to enact laws and pass instructions for mujtahid-judges because such laws and instructions are *mubayyan wa ma'lūm* (clear and known in Shari'ah). The duty of the Majlis in this context will only be (a) to regulate the processes of referral [of such judicial cases to the mujtahid-judges], (b) the execution [of the verdicts], and (c) *tashkhīṣ miṣdāq* (determining the required qualifications) for the office of mujtahid-judges in a way that, with Exalted God's Assistance, the true ones would be appointed.[183]

By status-based duty, Religious Leaders intended to distinguish between the jurists' authority to issue fatwas and determine compliance.

They made it clear that the selected jurists were not allowed to issue fatwas. In other words, their job was to determine whether or not there was a conflict between public policies—as enacted by the Majlis—and text-based Shari'ah rules; they were not responsible for making general statements of law. Considering the constitutionalist jurists' theory of the essence of laws, that is, limiting the transmutation of the constitutionalist state to possessive rule, "public policies" meant any law that would contradict such limitations. Finally, given the duality of the court system recognized by Articles 27 and 71 of the 1907 Constitution—that is, the courts of justice and the Shari'ah courts—the Religious Leaders' emphasis on the exclusive authority of the jurists was directed at the Shari'ah courts and did not include regular courts.[184] Given the historical background of adjudication and the heavily un-institutionalized system of judicial courts and proceedings,[185] Religious Leaders' explicit support of Shari'ah courts with such a broad jurisdiction contained two different messages. The first involved the selected jurists' exclusive duty of supervising enactments on judicial issues; in other words, no other enactments passed by the Majlis were to be reviewed by them. This was in complete agreement with the views of Ākhūnd and Māzandarānī and all other constitutionalist jurists who rejected the jurist's all-inclusive *wilāyah* and limited it to the issuance of fatwas and adjudication. The second involved drawing a distinction between the *'urfī* disputes (which included political and non-Shari'ah-oriented cases) and Shari'ah-oriented disputes.[186] The references made about the appointment of qualified jurist-judges to Shari'ah courts—and practically other courts as well—were an important duty that Religious Leaders clearly left to the discretion of the constitutionalist Majlis; they did not even assign it to themselves, even though they were the main source of authority for devising the measured qualifications of the candidates for such a position.[187]

As mentioned before, the special committee did not take an institutionalized form. Further, the few selected jurists' opinions on different enactments were not documented in a systematic fashion. Based on the reports and minutes of the floor debates of the Majlis and some secondary sources, in the absence of a constitutionally defined procedure, it can be said that the enactments were sent to the selected jurists to review and sign.[188] On the other hand, it seems that a majority of the members of the Majlis, when in the process of enactment, usually chose to adopt their positions in debated arguments in accord with the side taken by the selected jurists in floor discussions.[189]

This conventional procedure was practiced as long as Sayyid Hassan Mudarris (d.1316sh/1927)[190] was in the Majlis. As one of three jurists originally selected, he had maintained his authority as a member of succeeding parliamentary sessions until the end of the Fifth Majlis. He employed his authority of supervision with extremely positive impact. Following the instructions of Religious Leaders, Mudarris was heavily involved in drafting and revising the bills proposed by the ministry of justice, especially the ones about the court system and governing procedural laws,[191] as major codes of law that were enacted for the first time in Iran's history. Due to a long-standing oppression imposed through a dysfunctional court and justice system, from the early days of Revolution the establishment of *'Adālat-Khāna* (the House of Justice) was the first in a long list of national demands.[192] Obviously, adjudication was an extremely important issue that had to be revisited from scratch. During the Safavid era, judicial system had taken an orderly institutionalized form where *Dīvān-Begīs* (the King's Courts) and regular courts (mostly Shari'ah courts) had relatively well-defined jurisdictions.[193] However, under an unbridled despotism as tyrannical as the Qājār kings', there was in fact no meaningful justice system at all. Apparently, not only did the despot kings not follow the Safavid model properly, but they also refused to support the newer models that were meant to establish a law-abiding and functional court system. These models had been offered by a few prudent and wise reformist prime ministers such as Amir Kabir (d.1268/1851) and Mīrzā Hossein Sipah-sālār (d. 1299sh/1920).[194] In this system, in order for the king's—and his long list of dependents', governors', and even the local leaders of villages'—whims to take a legitimized form, not a well-structured justice system, but rather a sham, chaotic, and abusive one was mostly and widely sought after. In a quixotic emulation of the legendary ancient Persian King Anūshīravān, the Qājār king Nāṣir al-Dīn Shah, in one of his semi-serious attempts to control the system, ordered the installment of boxes in cities so that the ordinary people's letter of grievance could be sent directly to him. The Shah then established an office for preliminary investigations called *Majlis-i Taḥqīq-i Maẓālim* (the bureau of investigation of grievances).[195] Although local authorities used to threaten grieving individuals or groups of people,[196] according to a valid report, more than 2016 letters were registered in the bureau's repertoire in a three-year period (1300–1303/1882–1885).[197] After preliminary investigations by the bureau, the Shah would handwrite his order in the margin of the letter and send it back to the local authorities of the original place—the very authorities about whom people had grieved to Shah.[198] Apparently, not only did many of the king's orders fail to be just or to follow a legal logic, but also the local authorities did not pay attention to the ones that were issued in support of the grieving individuals.[199] The more important point in my argument, however, concerns the grounds upon which the people laid their complaints; they believed that such grievances should fall under the jurisdiction of the king's authority. This is where the public's perception of non-Shari'ah issues and disputes could rest. Based on the briefs of some of the complaints, as reported by two prominent Iranian historians, a majority of the complaints were about taxation (i.e., over-taxation, and the coercive collection of taxes by fief owners),[200] local authorities' oppressions,[201] requesting tax exemptions or tax reductions,[202] local authorities' abuse of power,[203] requesting the construction of public bath-houses and schools,[204] objections against the British or Russian customs functionaries,[205] counterfeit bills and the insufficient flow of coins in the market,[206] objections against Russian citizens' illegal ownership of lands and the registration of their documents in the governmental offices,[207] and, finally, complaints about the presence of multiple organs with judicial or semi-judicial power.[208] Occasionally, some of these grievances would lead to the appointment of special investigators by the king; their reports reveal an even more vivid picture of the governors' poor administration of social affairs, corruption, and partnership with fief owners' oppressive tax policies.[209]

Thus, it was completely normal for the first judicial bill after the 1905 Revolution proposed by Mushīr al-Dawlah (d. 1314sh/1925), the minister of justice at the time, to be about the court system and structure. According to "The Law on the Principles of the Judicial Organization" (passed on Rajab 21, 1329/July 18, 1911), the courts were divided into three major categories:

1. Public Courts, which included Peace Courts, Courts of First Instance, and Appellate Courts.
2. Specialized Courts, which included Commercial Courts, Military Tribunals, Courts of Major Crimes, and Disciplinary Court for Judges.
3. Shari'ah Courts.

A Court of Cassation, as the court of last resort, also sat above all of the non-Shari'ah courts. Despite initial disagreements between Mudarris and Mushīr al-Dawlah on the jurisdiction of the Shari'ah Courts,[210] their cooperation later led to a series of well-developed enactments such as the law of civil procedure (Dhul-Qa'dah 19, 1329/November 11, 1911), the law of criminal procedure (Ramadan 9, 1330/August 22, 1912),[211] and the law of commercial courts (July 1915). Every one of these and similar laws deserve detailed analysis so that the in-depth and innovative nature of legal-juristic solutions found in the context of the aforementioned cooperation could be revealed. In this part, however, I will limit my analysis to a short review of the following two issues: (1) the issue of distinction between Shari'ah and non-Shari'ah or customary judicial cases, and

(2) the harmony between the selected jurists' practice of supervision and the majority of Majlis.

First: For an extended period of time, the issue of distinctions between Shari'ah and customary/non-Shari'ah cases has been subject to dispute.[212] The concept of adjudication and judicial issues had received extensive treatment in Shīʿī law as the prevailing legal tradition.[213] It was, however, difficult to distinguish what jurists had already developed in their books as the rules of the Shari'ah in judicial cases, from what now was the outcome of the new social order, which in turn could also be new to the legal tradition. On the one hand, the jurists had usually been judges, and obviously issued verdicts on a majority of cases. On the other hand, the problem with such verdicts in the mid-end of Qājār rule involved the not-so-exceptional cases of whimsical judgments, the absence of systematic control, and the absence of precedent or legal standards in these types of verdicts when they were issued in cities or other localities in one region.[214] In addition, juristic adjudication suffered from a lack of codification and a more centralized structure of hierarchy.[215] However, not only was it necessary to reorganize the judicial system, but also to resolve the long-standing duality of Shari'ah-based and non-Shari'ah-based disputes. The first steps were taken in the aforementioned law of judicial organization when the Courts for Major Crimes, being mainly a Shari'ah Court itself, enjoyed the original jurisdiction over the crimes for which a Shari'ah punishment was assigned.[216] The law of criminal procedure, however, provided further clarification. In it the court was allowed to decide on the crimes for which the punishment is limited to *ḥadd* (predetermined) or *taʿzīr* (a type of punishment that is left to be assessed by a jurist-judge and must be lower than *ḥadd*) in the Shari'ah, or where the punishment according to Islamic law is *qiṣāṣ* (retaliation) or execution.[217] Although the law did not clarify the exact crimes that should fall in the court's jurisdiction, potential cases could, inter alia, include: murder, homicide, rape, drinking liquor, adultery, fornication, the false accusation of fornication, armed banditry, apostasy, and blasphemy. As for the courts of justice, by virtue of the later passage of the law of criminal procedure in 1912 and the criminal code in 1304sh/1925, the French model was adopted and the crimes were categorized as petty offenses, misdemeanors, and felonies. While the crimes were defined in the criminal code, the determination of their categories was left to the courts of justice; these determinations were mostly made based on the degree and harshness of the punishments, varying from small fines to life imprisonment.[218] Despite a failure to enumerate the crimes in the Courts for Major Crimes, the additional articles suggested by Mudarris to the law of civil procedure clarified the civil cases that would establish the original jurisdiction of the Shari'ah Courts. According to article 145 of the said law, the courts of justice had to refer the following cases to the Shari'ah courts:

> (1) Where the conflict was based on lack of knowledge as to Shari'ah issues, (2) Marriage and divorce cases, (3) Verdicts issued *in absentia* on Shari'ah-related matters, (4) Disputes for resolution of which a verdict on the following would become necessary: *iflās* (insolvency), limitation of the insolvent in interference with his properties, confiscation of property of the refraining party from payment of his judicially sentenced debts or when a *taqās* (requital payment) should be made, (5) Disputes in which resolution is limited to *bayyina* (a technical juristic term signifying testimony of two witnesses in certain disputes) or taking oath, (6) Disputes raised by the ambiguity and vagueness or antithetical phrases of fatwas which the disputants have invoked in their defense, (7) Cases of dispute as to the authenticity of endowments or wills, and executorial duties of endowed or testamentary properties, (8) Cases where it becomes necessary to assign an executor or supervisor for endowed properties, or a guardian [for an interdicted] or executor [for a will].[219]

It was also mentioned (in article 148) that if disputant parties would originally consent that their disputes, other than in the aforementioned cases, be tried in courts of justice, the said court will proceed. If not, the Shari'ah courts will assume jurisdiction and the case should be referred to them.[220] Despite the enumeration, the issue of distinction between Shari'ah-based disputes and *'urfī* (literally meaning custom-based) ones was still unresolved. There was an ambiguity as to what the non-Shari'ah cases were. In an administrative directive issued before the passage of law on judicial organization, Mushīr al-Dawlah had enumerated the *'urfī* matters as follows:

> (1) Administrative cases regarding wages and compensation, (2) Taxation and the assignment of administrative dues and all the relevant matters that should comply with enacted laws and regulations, (3) All the matters related to state-owned properties and lands for which the ministry of finances would affirm the state's ownership, (4) All the other *'urfī* matters that are governed by the specific order of laws and regulations and customary practices which have usually been under the state's rule, and (5) Commercial matters that are under the jurisdiction of commercial courts.[221]

In order to further clarify the non-Shari'ah disputes, following the passage of the law of civil procedure in 1911, the Majlis passed the following amendment to the law of judicial organization:

> The *'urfī* disputes resolution of which the courts of justice have original jurisdiction include those matters that are enforced in all or parts of the

> country according to *qawā'id-i ma'mūlah* (practiced norms) or the statutory laws of the nation on politics or economics or the social order as in the following detailed cases: disputes raised by the journals [i.e., press crimes], judicial proceedings, and the execution of verdicts; allegations of violations against norms and laws; all the disputes concerning governmental privileges and obligations whether they be between individuals, or individuals and the government; disputes on *asnād-i rasmī* (notarized or official documents that were written and registered in notaries) and whatever else had been registered in governmental agencies or those registered in the [Organization for the Registration of Documents]; and allegations of forgery including the falsification of such writings and documents.[222]

As can be perceived, the constitutionally ordained duality of the courts and consequent issue of each court's jurisdiction was an indisputable presumption for every piece of legislation in the judicial system. It can also be perceived that in the enacted laws, as long as Mudarris was in the Majlis and Article Two of the Constitution was being followed, the distinctions between Shari'ah and non-Shari'ah issues were observed. It is also clear that there was no disagreement on the non-Shari'ah-based affairs, and that the laws later enacted by the Majlis provided a broad base for *'urfī* matters; they included all of the political, economic, and social laws. The absence of any objection from Mudarris regarding such broad inclusion provides further evidence that the constitutionalist jurists believed that the members of the Majlis have the final say on those issues, and that their determinations are supported by the premises of religious validity. The selected jurists did not assume authority in reviewing the comprising elements of what the majority of members had opined and passed, either. Another basis for drawing this conclusion is the common grounds upon which a mutually productive interaction took place. The incredible role of Mudarris in passing the law of criminal procedure, in which to a substantial degree the rights to fair trial for the accused were secured, is of undeniably special importance. The combination of two sets of prescriptive and proscriptive standards provided the grounds for the passage of judicial laws in Iran. The prevailing *Uṣūlī* approach to the traditional procedures of Shari'ah court proceedings provided a prescriptive model that found strong support in Shī'ī jurisprudence. The proscriptive element belonged to the long-standing absolute violation of any imaginable right to fair trial in the state's practice of arrest, detention, interrogation, and legal assistance. To the extent that Mudarris himself was the initiator and supporter of the legality of some of the rights, such a combination proves the fact that the open-mindedness and deep juristic knowledge of Mudarris played a huge role in establishing the jurisprudential validity of limitation on the state's power in such areas.

Second: these fruitful interactions amounted to the passage of other important laws that were not judicial but were similarly important. One of these involved the enactment of a democratic election law[223] in the Second Majlis. Due to the guild-orientation of elections, and according to article two of the first election law passed in September 1906, the electors had to own landed properties of certain value or own equally valued businesses. Article four of the law also provided that those who are famous for "*fasād-i ʿaqīdah*" (having notoriously evil doctrines) or "*tajāhur bi fisq*" (explicit acts of commission of sins), or had been accused of theft and homicide or similar crimes whose innocence had not been declared by Shari'ah standards, were barred from being elected. The Second Majlis reduced the value in the requirement of ownership of properties or businesses to a very low amount so that the great majority of people could participate as electors, and changed the subjective measure of having notoriously evil doctrines to the objective proof of "*khurūj az dīn*" (a desertion of religious faith) in the presence of a competent, qualified jurist-judge. As to the ambiguities ascribed to Shari'ah standards of a declaration of innocence—an ascription that, for some members of the Majlis, could take an indefinite period—Mudarris said, "God forgives everyone. One repents and God forgives. The circle [of absence of forgiveness] is very small [i.e., God rarely and exceptionally denies forgiving a repentant] and is limited to very clear cases. Punishment is limited in Islam. Anyone who knows even a little bit about it knows how it works [i.e. to say, the principle of a presumption of innocence is all-inclusive and wide]."[224] Following Mudarris's position, the Second Majlis finally took the view that only those who were convicted of such crimes should be barred from being elected. On the protection of non-Muslim religious groups, the Second Majlis also approved that an elected member from each faith should represent Zoroastrians, Jews, and Gregorian Christians in the Majlis.[225]

The passage of the election law is yet another manifestation of the congruity between what the Religious Leaders and the constitutionalist jurists had in mind and recommended to the Majlis,[226] on the one hand, and the opinions held by the members of the Majlis, despite their affiliation with apparently non-Islamic political parties, on the other.[227] Successful experiences in the passage of judicial and election laws resulted in the emergence of a spirit of cooperation and mutual understanding between the jurists and the leaders of the Majlis as manifest in the later passage of the groundbreaking Civil Code (in three stages: 1307sh/1928, 1313sh/1934, and 1314sh/1935), which led to the further codification of Shari'ah rules in their proper context.[228]

One last important point is that a six-year (1299sh–1305/1920–1926) process of deceitful reinstatement of despotism through the installment of

Reza Khan and the Pahlavi monarchy by British colonialism, and a long period then after, culminated in a total disregard for not only Article Two, but also the whole Constitution itself. The extent of damages that these violations inflicted is insurmountable. The gradual elimination of jurists' supervision of judicial drafts and enactments, and the practical abolition of the Shari'ah Courts began right after Reza Khan established his iron hand over the political life of the nation through explicit and recurrent manipulation of elections in the Sixth Majlis (i.e., 1926–1928). The results of these actions were not limited to the elimination of Shari'ah courts, whose jurisdiction on criminal and civil cases represented the legal tradition of Shīʿī Law and every element of the dynamism that was embedded in it. Further violations of the right to a fair trial in the courts of justice were also at stake. On the one hand, the deprivation of jurists from their constitutionally sanctioned and statutorily vested authority of adjudication, coupled with policies that deteriorated religious intellectual centers in Iran, caused a rift between the jurists and the legislative or political processes in Iran. It all amounted to the seclusion and detachment of a majority of jurists from politics, which manifested in their return to and reliance on quietism as well as their adoption of traditional and traditionist approaches to Shīʿī jurisprudence. This is something for whose failure the jurists must assume their own share of responsibility. It was tantamount to drying out the source and fountainhead of the legal tradition, emptying the judiciary from those who represented the legal tradition, and replacing them with judges and judicial authorities who had recently graduated from foreign law schools but were incapable of making real connections with the juristic component of the Iranian legal system. On the other hand, it is especially important to note that throughout the fifty-seven-year rule of the Pahlavi Kings, both Reza Khan (1305sh–1320sh/1926–1941) and Muhammad Reza Shah (1320sh–1357sh/1941–1979) never allowed the implementation of constitutional guarantees of judicial proceedings over political and press crimes, that is, jury proceeding. All the individuals with political causes, including many of the students, professors, jurists, journalists, writers, artists, and politicians with as high a status as Muhammad Mussadeq, were indicted by security charges and tried in military tribunals that were more oppressive than other courts and presided over by army generals appointed by the Pahlavi king.

Notes

Introduction

1. Rosenfeld, *Constitutionalism*, 3.
2. Sartori, "Constitutionalism."
3. The idea of differentiating between substantial—in terms of "belief and idea that government should be restrained"—and relational—in terms of "methods and techniques of restraining power"—components of constitutionalism belongs to Carl. J. Friedrich as seen in his books *Constitutional Government and Politics*, 101; and *Constitutional Government and Democracy*, 126, respectively. For a more recent treatment of such distinction, see Sajó, *Limiting Government*, 9–10, 69–103.
4. Tushnet, "Comparative Constitutional Law," 1230.
5. Franklin and Baun, *Political Culture*, 4–6.
6. Ferejohn, *Constitutional Culture*, 10.
7. Thomas Paine, *Rights of Man*, 302–303, cited in McIlwain, *Constitutionalism*, 4, 8; emphasis added.
8. McIlwain has found it as inherent incorporation of the constituent power of people, sanctioned by the binding effect of the constitution (ibid.).
9. On the usage of "precommitment," mostly in the discussion of a democratic context, e.g., see Holmes, "Precommitment and the Paradox of Democracy"; Waldron, *Law and Disagreement*, 255–282. "Metaconstitutional" and "preconstitutional" have been offered by Larry Alexander in critique of the concept of precommitment. See his *Constitutionalism*, 13; and "Constitutionalism," 248–258. These two terms are suggested as a collection of agreed-upon symbols instead of precommitment.
10. By a normal society, I mean a society that is free from unwanted crises imposed by external disruptions. Colonialism and imperialism in contemporary history have been heavily involved in—and responsible for—such disruptions in Muslim societies. "Post-conflict" is the latest adjective that has been coined to exemplify a crisis-ridden society. For an analysis of the constitutional protection of habeas corpus in Latin American states after democratization in the form of return to historically embedded constitutional norms, see Brewer-Carias, *Constitutional Protection*.
11. Loughlin and Walker, *Paradox of Constitutionalism*.

12. Rest assured, I completely agree with East European constitutional lawyers on both the inevitability and the extreme difficulty of constitutional borrowing. See Osiatynski, "Paradoxes of Constitutional Borrowing." Moreover, I do concur with Robert Goodin in avoiding any suggestion of militating against getting ideas from elsewhere (ibid., 244, fn.2). However, as Osiatynski has argued, an unavoidable clash has developed in the East European examples between the interests that promote and those that bar such borrowings on the part of "important cultural factors that create resistance to, distortion of, or change in constitutional ideas and institutions" (ibid., 245).
13. Kautz, *Supreme Court.*
14. In a more technical comparative setting, e.g., the notion of transparency of the American model of judicial review is contrasted with other methods of judicial deliberations. On this issue, see Lasser, *Judicial Deliberations*; Huls, *Legitimacy of Highest Courts.*
15. The concept of "legal tradition" is by no means a stranger to the literature. Borrowing in part from Alasdair MacIntyre's definition of tradition and Patrick Glenn's reference to the legal tradition, I should make it clear that by "legal tradition" I mean a philosophical phenomenon in which the normative authority of formal sources of law, as an historically extended, socially embodied concept or argument, has been maintained and continues to remain so. Constitutionalism well represents one of those concepts and arguments in any legal tradition. See MacIntyre, *After Virtue*, 207; Glenn, *Legal Traditions of the World*, xxiv; Glendon et al., *Comparative Legal Traditions*, 17.
16. For a seminal treatment of the role of religious teachings in the formation of the idea of constitutionalism, see Friedrich, *Transcendent Justice.* In his historical survey of American constitutionalism, Friedrich claims: "If one reviews the overall course of American thought as embodied in the Declaration of Independence, the Articles of Confederation and the Constitution, one is bound to conclude that the ideas are not new. Whether one considers constitutionalism as such, or the related notions of a separation of powers, rationally based on human rights derived from natural law, of federalism, and of democracy, they are part and parcel of the great heritage of Christian Europe" (see his *Declaration of Independence*, xxvii).
17. Mottahedeh, "Afterword," 178.
18. For an excellent juridical approach to Islamic constitutionalism, see Abou El Fadl, "Constitutionalism"; for a skillful analysis of the relation between classical juristic texts and the concept of rule of law, see Mallat, *Islam and Public Law*, 1–15.
19. Mallat, *Introduction*, 156.
20. For some of the cases and opinions, see Sherif, "Rule of Law in Egypt," 1–34.
21. Cromartie, *Constitutionalist Revolution*, 8.
22. Ibid., 3.

1 *UṢŪLĪ* JURISPRUDENCE AND REASON

1. Primarily relying on the Qur'an itself, jurists developed a prominent line of legal thought that later came to be known as *Āyāt al-Aḥkām* (verses of rules), the deductive method of analysis of the legal implications of those Qur'anic verses in which a general or specific legal rule is ordained. It is believed, by different estimates, that there are 500–600 verses of this kind in the Qur'an, which make up around 10 percent of all verses. From early on, the genre of *Āyāt al-Aḥkām* literature developed in the history of Islamic law. While there is disagreement on who wrote the first book, legal historians have mentioned two books with the title of "*Kitāb Aḥkām al-Qur'an,*" written by Muhammad ibn Sā'ib Kalbī (d. 146/768) and Muhammad ibn Idrīs Shāfi'ī (d. 204/819), Mudīr-Shānachī, *Āyāt al-Aḥkām*, 2–3. The limited number of this kind of verses in the Qur'an suggests that it is not a Book of Law per se. In fact, there are more verses on rules of ethics than rules of law. By reference to the concept of *Āyāt al-Aḥkām*, Uṣūlī jurists did not intend to suggest that for discovering the law, jurists are to only consider verses of rules and disregard rules of ethics. For a systematic analysis of the relation between the rules of law and rules of ethics in Islamic law, see Khaled Abou El Fadl, "The Place of Ethical Obligations."
2. In Shī'ī sources, see, e.g., al-Murtaḍā, *al-Dhakhīra*, 186–198; al-'Allama, *Kashf al-Murād*, 106–117; *Nahj al-Ḥaqq*, 72–79. In Sunni sources, see, e.g., Makdisi, *Ibn 'Aqīl*, 93–94, 122, 134, 166, 171, 200, 205, 232, 260; Ibn Rushd, *Manāhij al-Adilla*, 115–119; Ibn Qayyim al-Jawzīyya, *I'lām al-Muwaqqi'īn*, III: 3, 8 (last citation is from al-'Ajam, *Mawsū'at*, 825).
3. Qur'an, 2:282, 3:18, 4:57 and 126, 5:8, 6:114 and 152, 7:29, 16:90, 21:47, 30:30, 42:15, 45:22, 46:19, 49:9, 55:6 and 8–9, 57:25. Of all the traditions attributed to the Prophet, the most striking is the one where he has said: "*Bi l'-'adlu qāmat al-samāwāti wa al-arḍ* (Earth and the skies are founded upon justice)" (Muṭahharī, *'Adl-i Ilāhī*, 36).
4. By no means an exhaustive treatment, the estimate is that there are 300 verses in the Qur'an on the concept of "reason," including 40 referring directly to *'aql* (reason), 4 referring to *al-'uqalā'* (the reasonable individuals), and 5 referring to *ta'qqul* (to reason and to rationalize). The list can go on with Qur'anic synonyms and specific terms equivalent to the previous terms: *'ilm* (knowledge, and its derivatives, 902 verses), *tafakkur* (thinking, 18 verses), *ḥikma* (wisdom, and its derivatives, 203 verses), *al-'ulamā'* (the knowledgeable, 6 verses), *al-rāsikhūn fi al-'ilm* (the determined in obtaining knowledge, 3 verses), *'ulu 'l-albāb* (the wise, 16 verses), *'ulu 'l-nuhā* (the well-versed, 2 verses), *ahl al-dhikr* (the researchers of Divine Books, 2 verses), *yaqīn* (certitude, and its derivatives, 28 verses), and *fiqh* and *tafaqquh* (apprehension and discernment, 19 verses).
5. Shī'ī rationalist jurists are also known as *'Adlīyya* (adherents to Divine Justice). Mainly oriented toward theological doctrines, the term *'Adlīyya* refers to the epistemology of those rationalist Muslim jurists who held the Divine's justice as the core of religion/jurisprudence, and shares common grounds with theodicy

and the role of justice in philosophy of law. In general, Shī'ī jurists share similar doctrines with Mu'tazila, the famous theological school in Sunni rationalism. This similarity can also be verified by the fact that when in Shī'ī sources the term is used, it largely bears the implications of rationalism in Islamic law. With this in mind, the Shī'ī jurisprudence is also known as *'Adlīyya*. For centuries, the main intellectual conflict in Islamic theology and law was between the *Ash'arī* discourse, on the one hand, and *Mu'tazilī* theologians and Shī'ī rationalist jurists, on the other. For further study of *'Adlīyya* and sources, see Ja'farī Langrūdī, *Maktab-hāye Ḥuqūqī*, 111-133. The most vigorous counterarguments against *Ash'arīyya* in the Shī'ī law and theology belong to 'Allāma, especially his *Nahj al-Ḥaqq*. Also, for the *Uṣūlī* perception of Divine as the most reasonable, see Bojnūrdī, *'Ilm Uṣūl*, pp. 325–328, 329, 330.

6. Sulaym ibn Qays al-Hilālī (d. 76/698), one of the first Shī'ī transmitters of *ḥadīth*, in his *Kitāb* reports that Ali, the fourth Rightly Guided caliph and the first Shī'ī Imam, has said: "What people say about the Prophet is comprised of true and vain, truth and falsehood, abrogating and abrogated, particular and general, sustained and overruled, and well preserved and delusive. Even during the life of the Prophet, they attributed falsehood to him to the point that the Prophet said: 'O people, attribution of false statements against me has risen up. Whoever intentionally attributes them to me, should prepare his place in the fire'" (Ansārī, *Asrār-i 'Āl-i Muhammad,* 268). In another place, Ali described four categories of people who attributed statements to the Prophet: the lying hypocrites, those who are mistaken, those who are ignorant, and those who memorize truthfully. He clarified that only the last group consists of true relaters of traditions (*Nahjul Balagha*, Sermon 209, 423).
7. Juristic treatment of the concept of *ikhtilāf* and its categorization amounted to yet another prominent line of rational thought in an originally textualist legal tradition. This was a discursive, precise, and essentially combined conceptual and methodological discourse among the jurists that produced important multivoluminous compendiums of well-discussed and well-documented scholarly debates, especially in the area of disagreements on the deduction of Law. For the sources and a brief and informative history, see Pakatchi, "Ikhtilāf al-ḥadīth," 168–173.
8. Al-Marwazī, *Ikhtilāf al-Fuqahā'*, 9.
9. Abdullah Dārimī, *Sunan*, I:151, quoting 'Awn ibn Abd Allah, a Kūfan intellectual and poet (d. 115/737) to that effect (citation is from Pakatchi, "Ikhtilāf al-ḥadīth," 171).
10. On Prophet Muhammad's reaction, in addition to supra note 6, Shahābi cites Qādi Abu Yusuf's *Kitāb al-Radd 'alā Siyar al-'Awzā'ī*, according to which the Prophet is known to have said: "Only those *ḥadīth*s, attributed to me, that agree with the Qur'an are mine and the ones which contradict it are not" (*Adwār-i Fiqh*, I: 406–407). On the collection of the traditions during the life of Muhammad, Shiites believe that the Prophet dictated his rules to Ali, which later came to be known as the Book of Ali, and was handed down by the existing Imam to the succeeding Imam at each given time. On the Book of Ali and its content, see Shahabi, in ibid., 407–409; Modarressi, *Tradition and Survival*, 4–12; Jafari Langrudi, "Kitāb-i Ali," 261–267.

11. By criticizing rationalist jurists for their reliance on reason, Astarābādī, an important figure of the *Akhbārī* School in Shīʿī law, believed that whatever is necessary in *fiqh* has already been clearly stated in the words of Imams (*Al-Fawā'id al-Madanīyya*, 37–179, esp. 39–40).
12. For narrative reports in Sunni sources on the existence of other Prophetic traditions in which prohibition on recording or transmission could be inferred, and of the reluctance of the second Rightly Guided Caliph, ʿUmar ibn al-Khaṭṭāb, in compilation of the traditions during his caliphate (13–23/635–675), see, e.g., Suyūṭī, *Tanwīr al-ḥawālik fī Sharḥ Mu'aṭṭā al-Imām Mālik*; and Qāḍī Abū Yūsuf, *Kitāb al-Radd 'alā Sīyar al-'Awzā'ī*, both cited in Shahabi, *Adwār*, I: 410–411.
13. Abd al-Majīd Maḥmūd, a prominent legal historian, cites several sources from Muslim jurists and lexicographers on different applications of the term "*sunnah*" in Arabic—literally meaning "method, nature, and norm"—and contrasts them with its legal applications. Defining Sunnah as "binding sayings and doings of the Prophet which is regarded as the highest example of behavior in all temporal and spiritual affairs," and relying on classical jurists, Maḥmūd raises the question of how and when one can draw an equation between "*qawl*" or *Ḥadīth* and Sunnah. Finally, he concludes that in the relationship between the Sunnah and the *Ḥadīth*, general consideration can be made for the application of *Ḥadīth* to theoretical issues, and the application of Sunnah to practical ones—something he finds the cause for *ijtihād* in legal argument. Maḥmūd, *Al-Madrasat al-Fiqhiyya*, 3–7.
14. Numerous Muslim jurists believe in the instances of absence of the Text. For example, in Shīʿī law, see al-Subḥānī, *Uṣūl al-Fiqh al-Muqāran fimā lā Naṣṣa fīh*; and in Sunni law, see Khallāf, *Maṣādir al-Tashrīʿ al-Islāmī fī mā lā Naṣṣa fīh*.
15. On the history and major sources of the development of *'Ilm al-Rijāl* in Shīʿī jurisprudence, see Al-Subḥānī, *Kullīyāt fī 'Ilm al-Rijāl*, 57–105.
16. Application of the balancing and preferring techniques was not limited to the content of the *ḥadīth* itself and included formal factors such as inconsistencies in the body of the traditions or existence of conflicting traditions as well as the credibility of transmitters. For technical treatment of *ʿilm al-jarḥ wa al-ta'dīl'* in Shīʿī jurisprudence, see Al-Subḥānī, *Uṣūl al-Ḥadīth*, 153–192; for an analytical treatment, mainly from a jurisprudential-hermeneutical perspective, see Abou El Fadl, *Speaking*, 96–133.
17. Abou El Fadl, *Speaking*, 41; al-Subḥānī, *Uṣūl al-Ḥadīth*, 23, 39–40; Ṣubḥī Ṣāliḥ, *'Ulūm al- Ḥadīth*, 111–113. It should be mentioned here that my arguments about the categories of reports are a simplified version of the juristic treatment, and thus, do not reflect its technicalities.
18. Al-Bihbahānī, *Al-Fawā'id al-Ḥā'irīyyah*, 101–103; al-Anṣārī, *Al-Ḥāshīya 'alā Istiṣḥāb al-Qawānīn*, 153–154; al-Muẓaffar, *Uṣūl al-Fiqh*, II: 26.
19. Al-Astarābādī, *Al-Fawā'id al-Madanīyya*, 75, 98, 104, 277. As mentioned earlier, in note 11, al-Astarābādī believed the Qur'an should be interpreted solely in the light of the traditions of the infallible Imams.
20. Al-Astarābādī, *Dānishnāma*, 5; *Al-Fawā'id al-Madanīyya*, 120–123.

21. Al-Astarābādī made at-length arguments in defense of all the collected reports. See *Al-Fawā'id al-Madanīyya*, 120–178, 268; *Dānishnāma*, 6.
22. Al-Astarābādī, *Al-Fawā'id al-Madanīyya*, 256–258, 260.
23. Ibid.; almost all over the book, esp. 180–195, 259, 261, 262, 264, 265.
24. Modarressi, *Introduction*, 42, 45, 46.
25. See the following arguments.
26. On the theological origins of the phrase and its importance in Shīʿī theology, see Modarressi, *Crisis*, 127–131.
27. Pakatchi, "uṣūl-i fiqh," 299.
28. Al-Murtada, *Intiṣār*, 6 (citation is from ibid.).
29. A Prophetic tradition that reports: *Al-'aqlu asāsu dīnī.*
30. A tradition attributed to Imam Ali that says: *Al-'aqlu rasūl al-ḥaqq.*
31. A tradition attributed to Imam Mūsā Kāzim, the seventh Shīʿī Imam. Rationalist jurists such as al-Bihbahānī, the great founder of the *Uṣūlī* School in Shīʿī Law, have invoked the aforementioned traditions in proof of the probative value of reason as a source of jurisprudence by explaining them as "proof based on many similar traditions" (*al-Fawā'id al-Ḥā'irīyya*, 96).
32. Al-Mufīd, *Al-Tadhkiratu bi Uṣūl al-Fiqh*, 28.
33. Ibid., 44–45.
34. On al-Ṣadūq, see Modarressi, *Introduction*, 4, 33, 40–41, 62; Pakatchi has called him a staunch *Akhbārī* ("Ibn Bābiwayh," 64); Gurjī, *Tārīkh*, 134–140.
35. Al-Mufīd, *Taṣḥīḥ al-I'tiqād*, 34–35.
36. Ibid., 125.
37. Al-Murtaḍā argued on the Shīʿī standards of '*ḥadd al-mustawfā li sharā'iṭ irtifā'al-kidhb 'an khabarihim*' (the conditions sufficient for lifting the falsehood from traditions) (*Al-Dhakhīrah*, 341–355). He was a staunch opponent of such unreliable traditions and wrote extensively against their validity and applicability. For more on his arguments, see "Jawābāt al-Masā'il al-Tabbānīyyāt," in his *Rasā'il*, I:18–99.
38. Al-Murtaḍā, *Al-Dharī'ah ilā Uṣūl al-Sharī'ah*, II:519–530.
39. As an important source about this concept with reliable English translation, see al-'Allāma, *Al-Bābu 'l-Hādī 'Ashar*, 50–53; in Mu'tazilite literature, one of the main sources is al-Asad Ābādī, *Al-Mughnī*, XIII; Gimaret, "Muʿtazila," 789a–791a.
40. A*l-Dhakhīrah*, 323–324.
41. Ibid., 326. Other jurists also upheld this opinion. Centuries later, the Iranian philosopher-jurist Mīr Dāmād put this idea in yet another brilliant context and said: "Revelations are God's gifts to reason" (*Jadhawāt wa Mawāqīt*, 85). This note is originally taken from the philosophical discussions made on the notion of *lutf* by Professor Ebrāhīmī Dīnānī, *Mājarāy-e Fikr-e Falsafī*, II:58–73, esp. 69. The exact sentence from Mīr Dāmād is: "*Sam'īyyāt alṭāf-i ilāhī ast dar 'aqlīyyāt.*"
42. Muhammad ibn Yaʿqūb ibn Isḥāq al-Kulaynī al-Rāzī (d. 329/940) is the author of *Kitāb al-Kāfī*, one of the major four books or *Kutub al-Arba'ah* on Shīʿī sources of traditions. On al-Kulaynī, see Gurjī, *Tārīkh*, 131–134.

43. Jawābāt Masā'il al-Ṭarāblusīyyāt al-Thālitha,' Mas'alat 13, *Rasā'il*, I: 410. As Modarressi has mentioned, both Kulaynī and Shaykh al-Ṣadūq have acknowledged the authenticity of what they have transmitted in their books (*Introduction*, 33). Gurjī, by citing al-Murtaḍā's other books, has also mentioned that al-Murtaḍā explicitly recommended "mandatory caution" against Kulaynī's transmitted traditions (*Tārīkh*, 165). Rationalist critique of compilers was of utmost importance in the avoidance of Shī'ī jurists' complete reliance on compiled traditions.
44. Ibid.
45. Gurjī, *Tārīkh*, 177.
46. Qur'an, 4:165, 20:134, 17:15, and some other verses.
47. Al-Murtaḍā, *Al-Dharī'a*, II:809, 836–837; *Al-Intiṣār*, 75; Al-Nāṣiriyyāt, 254; al-Ṭūsī, *Al-Udda*, II:741–742; *Al-Khilāf*, I:71, 73; al-Muḥaqqiq al-Ḥillī, *Ma'ārij al-Uṣūl*, 212; *Al-Mu'tabar*, 6; al-'Allāma, *Mabādī al-Wuṣūl*, 242–243; al-Shahīd al-Awwal, *Al-Dhikrā*, I:52; al-Shahīd al-Thānī, *Tamhīd al-Qawā'id*, 271; al-'Āmilī, *Zubdat al-Uṣūl*, 244; al-Bihbahānī, *Al-Fawā'id al-Ḥā'irīyyah*, 239–261; *Al-Rasā'il al-Uṣūlīyya*, 350; al-Anṣārī, *Farā'id al-Uṣūl*, I:448–452; Ākhūnd, *Kifāya*, 338–344; Nā'īnī, *Fawā'id al-Uṣūl*, II:22–23, 50, 56, III:365–366; *Ajwad al-Taqrīrāt*, II:186; al-'Arāqī, *Maqālāt al-Uṣūl*, II:149–178, 201–220; al-Īravānī, *Al-Uṣūl fī 'Ilm al-Uṣūl*, 293–314; al-Khu'ī, *Miṣbāḥ al-Uṣūl*, II:256, 284–288; al-Ḥakīm, *Al-Uṣūl al-'Āmma*, 479–492, 511–518; cf. al-Ṣadr, *Durūs*, II:321–324; Khomeini, *Al-Istiṣḥāb*, 241–242. Also in Sunni Law, see al-'Ajam, *Mawsū'at*, I:492 and the sources cited.
48. Divine's final intention as manifested in the *khiṭāb*, e.g., if it is commanding or prohibiting, proscriptive or prescriptive, and so on.
49. The scope of *khiṭāb* and whether it includes all or specific group of people, a general or specific act, and so on.
50. It means the way in which a jurist can prove that the pronouncement has been made by God or not.
51. *Al-Mu'tabar*, 5–6; al-Muẓaffar, *Uṣūl*, II:110; Pakatchi, "Uṣūl," 301.
52. Al-Muẓaffar, *Uṣūl*, II:111, Pakatchi, "Uṣūl," 301–302.
53. Qur'an, 4:53.
54. The rules found in the Qur'an, 24:6–9, and 33:4, 58:1–4, limited the legality of two pre-Islamic types of divorce and sanctioned remedial measures for breach of those restrictions. 'Allāma meant that only the Prophet or Imams are able to obtain conclusive knowledge about the exact nature of those divorces or the Qur'anic sanctions.
55. Al-'Allāma, *Mabādī al-Wuṣūl*, 240–241.
56. Bahā' al-Dīn al-'Āmilī, *Zubdat al-Uṣūl*, 15–16; al-Bihbahānī, "Jawāz al-'Amal bi al-Ẓann wa 'adami Jawāzihi," in his *Al-Fawā'id al-Ḥā'irīyya*, 117–125.
57. As an important part of the Islamic logic, it relates to the conceptualized or assentable definition and realization of the concepts. In line with Aristotelian Formal Logic, 'Allāma believed that *'ilm* (knowledge) is established in the form of *taṣawwur* (conceptualization) or *taṣdīq* (assent) (*Al-Jawhar al-Naḍīd*, 271–320). Generally, "*taṣawwur* is defined as the mental grasping of an object apart from any assertion as to whether or not the object corresponds to the

external reality it is supposed to represent... *Taṣdīq* is also the mental grasping of an object, but with the assertion that the relation of correspondence between this object and the external reality it represents is true. This does not mean that assent is always true but only that it is an assertion of truth" (Inati, "Logic," 806–807). ʿAllāma believed that intellectual visualization accompanied by assent could be acquired either by *iktisāb* (acquisition) or by *ḍarūra* (necessity). A *ḥadd*, or something similar to it, establishes our acquisition of conceptualization, and a *burhān,* or something similar to it, establishes our assent. An acquired or necessitated knowledge is obtained when we have a conceptualization or assent as to the falsity or truth of the objects' factual existence. For further discussion of the terms, see al-ʿAllāma, *Taslīk al-Nafs*, 23–24; Ḥā'irī Yazdī, *Kāvush-hā*, 227–228. On the usage and definition of the terms in Shīʿī *Uṣūl al-Fiqh* in English, see al-Ṣadr, *Lessons*, 174, 175.

58. This paragraph is heavily based on al-ʿAllama, *Mabādī al-Wuṣūl*, 242–244.
59. There is an extensive literature on the life and work of Abū Jaʿfar Muhammad ibn Ḥassan ibn Ali Ṭūsī (d. 460/1067), known as Shaykh al-Ṭā'ifah. In addition to Modarressi, *Introduction*, 44–45, for the most comprehensive study of Ṭūsī, see Kungrah, *Yādnāmah*, esp. I:167–213, II:1–9, 489–559, 701–721, and III:365–489; also see Charles J. Adams, 'The Role of Shaykh al-Ṭūsī in the Evolution of a Formal Science of Jurisprudence among the Shīʿah,' *Islamic Studies*, 10:173–180.
60. For centuries Shīʿī jurists had rebutted the notion of *ijtihād* as inherently resembling two Sunni methods of derivation of law, i.e., *qīyās* (analogy) and *istiḥsān* (discretionary opinion).
61. Pakatchi, "Islām: Andīshahhā," 453.
62. For a complete list of all 117 titles, see al-Tustarī, *Iḥqāq al-Ḥaqq*, I:51–59; for an incomplete list of 25 titles in an English source, see Schmidtke, *Theology of al-ʿAllāma*, 267–269.
63. A mentor of ʿAllāma and a great Iranian philosopher, Ṭūsī has been credited as one of the main commentators of Ibn Sīnā. On his life and works, see Mudarress Raḍawī, *Aḥwāl wa Āthār*; in English, see Dabashi, "Khwājah Naṣīr al-Dīn al-Ṭūsī."
64. ʿAllāma discussed *al-maḥsūsāt* (things perceptible through senses) as the foundation of belief and faith, and *idrāk* (perception) as the rational reflection of *maḥsūsāt* in mind, and declared both concepts as the sources of knowledge, and finally found *al-ʿulūm al-ḍarūrīyya al-kullīyya* (necessary knowledge in general) as a branch of things perceptible by senses (*Nahj*, 39–52; *Al-Asrār al-Khafiyyah*, 25–31). Ebrāhīmī Dīnānī, a professor of philosophy, correctly expresses his surprise about how ʿAllāma laid out the methods of acquiring knowledge by considering *al-maḥsūsāt* as its foundation. He also rejects any intellectual coincidence between Western philosophical school of sensationalism and ʿAllāma's approach to the senses, based on the simple fact that ʿAllāma's argument preceded sensationalism (*Mājarā*, II:275–282).
65. Al-ʿAllāma, *Nahj*, in most pages; on Ash'arite discourse on predestination and free will, see Wolfson, *Philosophy of Kalam*, 663–710.

66. Qur'an, 9:122.
67. Al-ʿAllāma, *Taḥrīr al-Aḥkām*, I:31–32.
68. Similar arguments in Christianity have been made under the theories of infralapsarianism and supralapsarianism.
69. I will discuss this issue in further detail later.
70. Al-Murtaḍā, *Al-Dharīʿa*, II:808.
71. Al-Mufīd, *Taṣḥīḥ*, 143.
72. Ibid.; al-Murtaḍā, *Al-Dharīʿa*, II:808; al-Ṭūsī, *ʿUdda*, II:750.
73. As al-Ṣadr has argued, contemporary Shīʿī jurists have taken two different approaches to the issue: (1) The large majority of them have adopted adherence to the theological origins of prohibition of undeclared punishments. Among them, Nā'īnī is the most notable. (2) A minority has adopted the theory of "*ḥaqq al-ṭāʿah*" or the divine's right to be abided in any occasion (*Durūs*, II:321–324). The latter group holds that there is no unstated rule and the Law, in its entirety, has been ordained—and probably conveyed—by God. Therefore, in his effort to examine the existence of *al-maṣlaḥat al-mulzima* (required interest) in the rules of Shari'ah, the jurist must take that divine right into serious consideration. As a matter of *taʿabbud* (submission) to God, the latter group argues, it is our duty to (1) preserve God's right to our obedience, and (2) when in doubt as to what Divine has ordained, choose to primarily take the charge of duty (*ishtighāl*) rather than exempting it. Al-Ṣadr himself also belongs to the minority. On al-Ṣadr's thoughts, see *Durūs*, II:323 and *Ghāyat al-Fikr*; for Nā'īnī's views, see his *Al-Fawā'id al-Uṣūl*, III:74–76, 365–380, and esp. 389–390.
74. Al-Bihbahānī, *Al-Fawā'id*, 239–261; *Al-Rasā'il*, 349–420, esp. 351–353; al-Anṣārī, *Farā'id*, II:135–142; Ākhūnd, *Kifāya*, 339; Nā'īnī, *Al-Fawā'id al-Uṣūl*, III:74–76, 365–380, and 389–390; al-Ḥakīm, *Al-Uṣūl*, 481–484; Shams al-Dīn, *Al-Ijtihād*, 373–376.
75. "God does not burden a soul beyond what He has given him. God will bring ease after hardship" (Qur'an, 65:7).
76. Famously called *ḥadīth al-rafʿ* (the tradition of removal), it is known that the Prophet has said: "[Actual liabilities deriving from] nine things have been removed from my ummah. They will not be charged for what they have done by mistake; by lapse of memory; under coercion; by not knowing; by not being able to bear; in emergency; by being envious; by being agitated; and by allured thoughts against the people without speaking about it." Shīʿī jurists believe this tradition only lifts the punishment, and does not legitimize the acts mentioned therein. For further discussions, see Ākhūnd, *Kifāya*, 339; Nā'īnī, *Fawā'id*, III:348; Muḥaqqiq Dāmād, *Qawāʿid*, IV:99–101. Bihbahānī invokes sixteen more authenticated traditions in support of non-liability when the rule is unknown to the individual (*Al-Rasā'il*, 354–357).
77. Al-Bihbahānī, *Al-Fawā'id al-Ḥā'irīyya*, 239–240.
78. The general line of the discussion is based on al-Muẓaffar's arguments in his *Uṣūl*, II:29–33.
79. Therefore, a general knowledge of the rule and its existence will suffice to make the rule applicable and effective.

80. Anṣārī has said: "The extent of investigation is where the conscience is assured as to inexistence of rule. In our time, when the jurist suspects whether or not there is a rule for a duty, he searches in the four [Shīʿī] books [of traditions] and other reliable books of traditions which are easily available to people, to the extent that makes him believe in the inexistence of such indicator. Such investigation will be sufficient for application of the presumption of non-liability" (*Farā'id*, II:157–158). Interestingly, Anṣārī continued to admonish excessive scrupling because it amounts to the jurist's unnecessary caution, ignorance as to other duties, and distressful situation for the laity. It is obvious that referring to the books of tradition, in Anṣārī's opinion, had to be made with technical considerations of validity.
81. *Akhbārī*s had held that acquiring a dispositive knowledge that establishes certitude is the sole source of knowing the Shari'ah rules, and only the reports attributed to the infallible persons—i.e., the Prophet and the Imams—provide that disposition and certitude. Hence, other methods or means of acquisition of knowledge are invalid (Al-Astarābādī, *Al-Fawā'id al-Madanīyya*, 180, 185). They also condemned suppositional finding because it amounted to disagreement among the jurists, irresolvable conflicts, and difficulty in establishing certitude in religious matters (ibid., 190).
82. Al-Bihbahānī, *Risālat al-Ijtihād*, 16.
83. Ibid., 21.
84. Al-Bihbahānī, *Al-Fawā'id al-Ḥā'irīyya*, 117–125.
85. This is a very complicated set of arguments, and what follows is a brief and simplified presentation.
86. Al-Bihbahānī, *Risālat al-Ijtihād wa al-Akhbār*, 6; al-Anṣārī, *Farā'id*, I:254, 256; Ākhūnd, *Kifāya*, 311, 312.
87. Al-Bihbahānī, *Risālat al-Ijtihād wa al-Akhbār*, 8; al-Anṣārī, ibid; Ākhūnd, ibid.
88. Al-Bihbahānī, *Risālat al-Ijtihād wa al-Akhbār*, 16; al-Anṣārī, *Farā'id*, I:255–256; Ākhūnd, ibid.
89. Al-Bihbahānī, *Risālat al-Ijtihād wa al-Akhbār*, 8; al-Anṣārī, *Farā'id*, I:256–257; Ākhūnd, *Kifāya*, 311, 312–313.
90. *Uṣūl al-ʿamalīyya* (procedural principles) is an equivalent of legal presumptions in Common Law or Civil Law traditions. The underpinning wisdom of procedural principles in Shīʿī law is heavily based on logical propositions that can be called the theory of dialectical relation between the situations and the duties. According to Anṣārī, who brilliantly argued in the most detailed fashion for refinement of those principles, a duty-bound individual will be engaged in three occasions of knowledge as to the determinative rules of the status of duty. First occasion is when we have conclusive knowledge about the existence of the rule, technically called *qatʿ bi al-ḥukm*. On this occasion, the duty is incumbent on the individual and he/she is obligated with its performance because such rule is inherently valid and there is no need to establish its validity. The second occasion is when our knowledge is limited to

the suppositional existence of rule for the duty, known as *ẓann bi al-ḥukm*. In this situation, the presumption is that the individual has made utmost efforts to discover the rule and by preponderance of evidence has come to believe that the rule exists. Such supposition can be established by prima facie appearance of the Text, less than reliable reports, and rational arguments. On this occasion, it is possible to assume validity for such suppositional knowledge, but there is no certitude in assured existence of the rule. This is where, by application of the procedural rules, we examine whether the duty is incumbent upon the individual or not. The third occasion is when our knowledge does not rise beyond doubtful existence of the rule, or *shakk bi al-ḥukm*. On this occasion, after implementation of utmost effort, the individual is unable to determine whether there is any rule or not. Since a doubtful knowledge cannot establish a reliable connection with the sources of law, thus, according to the principle of ugliness of punishment without prior statement of rule, there is no duty incumbent on the individual. It should be noticed that application of procedural rules establishes functional validity of a rule only, and not more. In other words, by applying them, we only presume the existence or inexistence of a duty, and we still do not know the final truth about the existence or inexistence of the rule or our duty. For an extensive treatment of procedural rules in Shīʿī law, see al-Anṣārī, *Farā'id*, I:27–73 (on first occasion), 74–419 (on second occasion), and 420–452 (on third occasion).

91. *Istiṣḥāb* or continuity of what has previously been established "holds that a previously known state of affairs or ruling is presumed to continue" (al-Ṣadr, *Lessons*, 186).
92. *Iḥtīyāṭ* or precaution of what can cause detriment to the duty-bound individual "consists in going out of one's way to make sure one complies with possible as well as with certainly known divine injunction. Ishtighāl or engagement is synonymous" (ibid).
93. *Takhyīr* or choice is given to the duty-bound for adopting either performance of or refusal of performance of a duty where the precaution is not applicable.
94. Al-Anṣārī, *Farā'id*, I:254, 267–272; Ākhūnd, *Kifāya*, 311, 313–315.
95. Al-Anṣārī, *Farā'id*, 289; Ākhūnd, *Kifāya*, 311.
96. Al-Bihbahānī, *Al-Fawā'id al-Ḥā'irīyya*, 136–140; al-Anṣārī, *Farā'id*, I:355–359.
97. Al-Bihbahānī, *Al-Fawā'id al-Ḥā'irīyya*, 487–488; *Risālat al-Ijtihād*, 343–345; al-Anṣārī, *Farā'id*, I:205–228.
98. Al-Bihbahānī, *Risālat al-Ijtihād*, 345–346; *Al-Fawā'id al-Ḥā'irīyya*, 488–491; al-Anṣārī, *Farā'id*, I:116–119; Ākhūnd, *Kifāya*, 293–307.
99. Al-Bihbahānī, ibid; al-Anṣārī, *Farā'id*, I:143; Ākhūnd, *Kifāya*, 328.
100. On these arguments and qualifications, Bihbahānī is not alone. Other Shīʿī *Uṣūlī* jurists, prior to and after him, had also made similar arguments.
101. Al-Bihbahānī, *Al-Fawā'id al-Ḥā'irīyya*, 127–128.

102. Qur'an, 10:36.
103. Al-Bihbahānī, *Risālat al-Ijtihād*, 16.
104. Al-Bihbahānī, *Al-Fawā'id al-Ḥā'irīyya*, 128–129.
105. Here, Bihbahānī makes an example: "any word that does not mean *khamr* (wine) by itself does not conceptualize its rule (permissibility of drinking) or what the source of disagreement is. It is because of the locus at which the word has been posited in a specific rule for a specific issue that we can render its drinking permissible. Not because it is possible to render permissible drinking everything which is not wine" (ibid., 129).
106. Ibid., 135–140.
107. Al-Astarābādī, *Al-Fawā'id al-Madanīyya*, 555.
108. Al-Bihbahānī, *Al-Fawā'id al-Ḥā'irīyya*, 129–130.
109. Ibid., 101–103.
110. Ibid., 140.
111. Al-Bihbahānī, *Risālat al-Ijtihād*, 19.
112. A comprehensive analysis of the *Uṣūlī* doctrine of reason, by itself, can be the subject of an important book that is yet to be written. What follows is a brief and general introduction of the topic. Apparently, *Uṣūlī* jurists have made many sophisticated arguments on every aspect of the grand methodology of *uṣūl al-fiqh*, which after Bihbahānī went well beyond theology and logic and extensively took philosophical orientation. According to. Ḥā'irī, Nā'īnī was the first contemporary *Uṣūlī* jurist who employed highly technical philosophical concepts in his arguments (*Kāvush-hā*, 254). Thus, introducing all the details is practically impossible unless one would translate, at least, the multivoluminous works of Nā'īnī. My report of the doctrine, to the best of my understanding, is also more of a narration than developing new ideas. Therefore, in cases of inconsistencies, I should be held accountable, not the authors.
113. Mīrzā Abu al-Qāsim Qummī, author of *Qawānīn al-Uṣūl*, is one of the most famous *Uṣūlīs* whose book, for a long time, was taught in Shī'ī intellectual centers, and still is considered one of the most authoritative hornbooks of *uṣūl al-fiqh*. He was, perhaps, the most prominent disciple of Bihbahānī.
114. Feyz, *Mabādī*, 66; for more of valid reports on reason in Shī'ī School, see Gharawī, *Maṣādir*, 183–185.
115. Al-Khu'ī, *Ajwad al-Taqrīrāt*, III:73.
116. Bojnūrdī, *'Ilm Uṣūl*, 318–319.
117. Al-'Allāma, *Nahj*, 52.
118. Ibid.
119. This is based on a report that says, "God has provided people with two proofs: one that is apparent [external] and the other one, which is hidden [internal]. The apparent proof is His Messengers and the Imams, and the hidden one is reason" (Kulaynī, *Uṣūl al-Kāfī*, I:19).
120. Gharawī cites a source from al-Baḥrānī, in which this *Akhbārī* jurist rejected the credibility and validity of the intuition-based knowledge as a source (*Maṣādir*, 215–216).
121. Qur'an, 1:5.

122. Muslim philosophers, with different philosophical orientations, have elaborated on this point. Ibn Ṭufayl (d. 581/1185), an Aristotelian, in his famous book entitled "*Risāla Ḥayy ibn Yaqḍān*" has brilliantly argued, in the form of narrating a story, that a thoughtful human being by rational application of his pristine constitution can reach the same laws that are revealed through Messengers of God. Prior to him, Ibn Sina (d. 428/1037), a precursor Aristotelian philosopher in Islamic philosophy, though with different objective in mind, had narrated a similar story. Sohravardī (d. 587/1191), an Illuminationist philosopher, has also written an additional ending to Ibn Tufayl's story. The idea of intuitional knowledge derived from *fiṭrah* is different from what pure intuitionists claim.
123. Bojnūrdī, *'Ilm Uṣūl*, 320.
124. Al-Muẓaffar, *Uṣūl*, I:202; Nā'īnī, *Fawā'id al-Uṣūl*, III:59; al-Khu'ī, *Ajwad al-Taqrīrāt*, II:21–24.
125. Al-Ḥuṣarī, *Naẓarīyyat al-Ḥukm*, 22.
126. *Akhbārīs* have also denied the ability of reason to recognize the beauty or ugliness of an act and to relate it to mandate or prohibition of its rule. See Gharawī, *Maṣādir*, 213.
127. Al-Ḥuṣarī, *Naẓarīyyat*, 22, 23, 26.
128. Al-Kalāntarī, *Maṭāriḥ al-Anẓār*, II:372. For more on Shī'ī theological rejection of predestination, see al-'Allāma, *Kashf al-Murād*, 62–64; Sha'rānī, *Kashf al-Murād*, 423–438.
129. Al-Muẓaffar, *Uṣūl*, I:199.
130. Ibid., 200.
131. Ibid., 201.
132. Ibid., 202.
133. Many Muslim jurists and theologians have written on *al-Ḥikma* (the wisdom) and found it a fertile ground for enriching their knowledge of Divine Law. Among the Shī'ī ones who collected the words of wisdom from their Iranian, Indian, and previous Messengers' sources, the most famous one was Ibn Miskawayh (d. 421/1030), *Tarjumah-i Jāvīdān Kherad Mushkwayh Rāzī*. Among those who wrote extensively on the subject was Naṣīr al-Dīn Ṭūsī, the author of *Akhlāq-i Muḥtashamī* and *Akhlāq-e Nāṣerī*. Another collection of words of wisdom, heavily based on Ibn Miskawayh's book, which is edited and added with the Roman wisdom, is from a contemporary, brilliant Sunni Muslim philosopher 'Abd al-Raḥmān Badawī, the author of *Ḥikmat al-Khālida*. On why Muslim jurists tended toward words of wisdom, one of the editors wrote: "In their minds, learned Muslims always had two main approaches when they remembered the past utterances and articulations of knowledge: (1) Priority of importance is to be given to what has been said over who has said. It is attributed to Imam Ali, the first Imam of the Shiites, to have said: 'Do not look who has said, look what has been said,' and (2) they perceived the wisdom as their lost beloved and wherever they could find it, they would grasp and then apply it. Prophet Muhammad has said: 'Getting to know *al-kalimat al-ḥikma* (the word of wisdom) is the faithful man's long cherished goal.' And the Seventh Imam, after repeating and emphasizing the

Prophet's saying at the beginning of his statement, has said: 'Then it is upon you to know the word of wisdom before it is gone [out of your reach], put an end to its absence from your world, and make it appear'" (Dānishpazhūh, "Introduction," *Tarjumah-i Jāvīdān Khirad*, 2). Bearing in mind that *Ḥikma* traditions are also common in Sunni sources, for further elaboration and the list of Muslim books, precise and meticulous bibliography and chronology of the arguments in both Shīʿī and Sunni sources, see Dānishpazhūh's and Badawī's introductions to their editions of Ibn Miskawayh.

134. Al-Muẓaffar, *Uṣūl*, I:205.
135. Qur'an, 2:233, which in pertinent part reads: "no soul should be compelled beyond capacity."
136. Bojnūrdī, *'Ilm Uṣūl*, 325–328.
137. Modarressi, *Introduction*, 4.
138. Al-Kalāntarī, *Maṭāriḥ al-Anẓār*, II:335; Feyz, *Mabādī*, 68.
139. There is a controversy as to correctness and applicability of this principle among *Uṣūlī*s, on the one hand, and *Akhbārī*s and conservative mujtahids who claim adherence to *Uṣūlī* doctrines, on the other. Some believe in the correctness of the latter part of the principle where it states: "whatever is ordered by religion is also ordered by reason." Some believe in the reason's ability of apprehending beauty and ugliness, but deny correlation. Some others believe in correlation but doubt as to applicability of the rational findings, and thus, prioritize on following the rules of religion, and so on. Anṣārī, in response to one of the opponents of the correlation, namely al-Fāḍil al-Tūnī (d. 1071/1660), has said: "I swear to my life, how a reasonable man, based on such weak arguments, can question the truth of what all the *'Adlīyya* have consensually agreed on it?" (al-Kalāntarī, *Maṭāriḥ al-Anẓār*, 341; Feyz, *Maṣādir*, 68–69).
140. Qummī has said: "In the discussion of rational evidence, mere realization of the ugliness is sufficient to judge his doer blameworthy. Based on that judgment, it is rationally proven that the act or object in question is also *qabīḥ sharʿī wa ḥarām sharʿī* (found ugly and prohibited by religion)" (Feyz, *Mabādī*, 66). Feyz makes an interesting point that Qummī has not mentioned any juristic objection against the rule of correlation, because such objection would have required Qummī to respond and make counterarguments. Feyz concludes that by the time of Qummī, the idea of correlation was widely accepted.
141. Al-Sabzawārī, *Muhadhdhab*, VIII:166; al-Bujnūrdī, *Al-Qawāʿid al-Fiqhīyya*, I:173; al-Muḥaqqiq al-Dāmād, *Kitāb al-Ḥajj*, III:588; al-Sīstānī, *Qāʿidat lā Ḍarar*, 61.
142. Shahabi, *Advār*, I:61–64; Kātūzīyān, *Falsafah-i Ḥuqūq*, II:427.
143. Despite lexicographic differences between "order" and "rule" in Arabic, the juristic impart of the definitions is similar.
144. Mishkīnī, *Iṣṭilāḥāt al-Uṣūl*, 74–75.
145. Ibid., 75.
146. Ibid., 75–76.
147. Feyz, *Mabādī*, 199–200.
148. Ibid.

149. *Akhbārī*s believe in the inapplicability of reason in the scope of *shari'ah al-tawqīfiyya* (laws that are exclusively limited to Divine's jurisdiction of legislation), which connotes implications and juristic results similar to sovereignty orders. The issues restricted to Divine Jurisdictional Laws are yet to be clarified. It can be inferred from the *Akhbārī* discourse that there is nothing but Divine Jurisdiction and all the Laws are revealed by the Imams' reports! Thus, there is no room for application of reason. Conservative '*Uṣūlī*' jurists who render *iḥtīyātī* (precautionary) opinions in the majority of issues are also more inclined to adhere to those reports than reason. Hence, there is not much practical difference between them and *Akhbārī*s. For some of the *Akhbārī* sources on this, see Gharawī, *Maṣādir*, 221.
150. See al-Kalāntarī, *Maṭāriḥ al-Anẓār*, II:420–427; al-Hamadānī, *Miṣbāḥ*, X:282; Nā'īnī, *Kitāb al-Ṣalāṭ*, II:71–72; *Al-Makāsib*, I:181–182; al-Khu'ī, *Mawsū'at*, XVII:407–408; Shahābī, *Adwār*, I:21–23.
151. Qur'an, 4:59.
152. Notice that Shī'ī commentators of the Qur'an have concluded that only Shī'ī Imams truly represent God and the Prophet.
153. Mishkīnī, *Iṣṭilāḥāt*, 75; al-Muẓaffar, *Uṣūl*, I:217–218; Feyz, *Mabādī*, 200; Bojnūrdī, *'Ilm Uṣūl*, 330; Ayāzī, *Fiqh Pazhūhī*, 259–260.
154. Al-Muẓaffar, *Uṣūl*, I:217.
155. Nā'īnī has offered the authoritative theory of *tatmīm kashf* (complementing the discovery) on validity of reference to the primary impart of the text, and said: "*Alfāẓ* (terms in their prima facie appearance) do not amount to *kashf tāmm* (complete discovery). They establish probability. In the realm of *'ālam i'tibār al-tashrī'ī* (notional legislation), however, God considers such incomplete discovery as complete" (Bojnūrdī, *'Ilm Uṣūl*, 334).
156. Bojnūrdī, *'Ilm Uṣūl*, 335.

2 Authority: Theories, Models, Discords

1. Obviously, there is a huge body of literature in the primary and secondary sources on Imāmah written by Shī'ī or non-Shī'ī scholars, which makes it virtually impossible to introduce all of them in an endnote. However, for primary sources, some of the major books written by Shī'ī jurists and theologians are: al- Mufīd, *Kitāb al-Awā'il al-Muqaddamāt*; and *Al-Irshād*; al-Murtaḍā, *Al-Shāfi fi al-Imāmah*; and *Al-Dhakhīrah*; al-'Allāma, *Nahj al-Ḥaqq wa Kashf al-Ṣidq*; and *Kitāb al-Alfayn*; al-Tustarī, *Iḥqāq al-Ḥaqq wa Izhāq al-Bāṭil*. For non-Shī'ī primary sources, see al-Qāḍī 'Abd al-Jabbār, *Al-Mughnī: XX, Fī al-Imāmah*; and al-Māwardī, *Al-Aḥkām al-Sulṭānīyya*. For English sources, see Madelung, "Imāma" in *Encyclopedia of Islam, Second*, III:1163b–1169a; Lambton, *State and Government*, 219–241.
2. This is the most important point of conflict between the Shī'ī and Sunni Muslims that from early on jurists and theologians of each *Madhhab* have been engaged in. Each camp invoked different historical facts and traditions attributed to the Prophet that related to the issue and sometimes went

to extreme details. On the historical event and explanation of the views in English, see Madelung, *The Succession to Muhammad.* For an analytical argument of the duties incumbent upon the Prophet's successor, a view held for the most part by both Shīʿī and Sunni jurists, see Abou El Fadl, *Rebellion,* 27–28.

3. For historical discussions on deviations from the Prophetic model, see Crone and Hinds, *God's Caliph,* 24–42, 59–80; Lambton, *State and Government,* 171–173.
4. Al-Mufīd, *Awā'il al-Maqālāt,* 74.
5. On the theological concept of *lutf* in Shīʿa as "anything for proving that God will and does only that which is good, so it brings the human beings close to His obedience and keeps them far from disobedience," see Chapter 1 notes 39 and 41.
6. Al-Murtaḍā, *Al-Dhakhīrah,* 415–416; al-ʿAllāma, *Kashf al-Murād,* 181–183; al-Miqdād, *Sharḥ Bāb,* 59–61, 149–151; for the English translation of al-ʿAllāma's *Bāb al-Ḥādī 'Ashar,* see Miller, *Al-Bābu 'l-Ḥādī 'Ashar,* 62–64.
7. Al-Miqdād, *Sharḥ Bāb,* 59, quoting al-ʿAllāma's *Bāb*; al-ʿAllāma explains the Imam as "the one who protects the Laws and guards them from excess and decrease" (*Kashf al-Murād,* 183).
8. Miller, *Al-Bāb,* 62; Modarressi describes the Imam as "the head of the Muslim community, the successor to the Prophet, and the guardian of all Muslim religious and social affairs" (*Crisis,* 6); *Kharāj,* 155; Abou El Fadl, *Rebellion,* 27; for additional Shīʿī sources, see Modarressi, *Kharāj,* 155, fn.5.
9. Ṭabāṭabā'ī, *Shī'a dar Eslām,* 189–197; *Shi'ite Islam,* 184–189.
10. Al-Murtaḍā, *Al-Shāfī,* I:36; al-ʿAllāma, *Kashf al-Murād,* 184–187; al-Miqdād, *Sharḥ Bāb,* 61–63; Miller, *Al-Bāb,* 64–68; on the explanation of the term in English, see Madelung and Tyan, "iṣma," in *Encyclopedia of Islam, Second,* IV:182b–183b.
11. Al-Murtaḍā, *Al-Shāfī,* II:5–12; Modarressi, *Crisis,* 5.
12. Al-ʿAllāma, *Kashf al-Murād,* 184–185; *Nahj,* 164, 170–171. Al-Miqdād in commenting to al-ʿAllāma has also added: "the required ability of prohibiting the oppressor from committing oppression, and, defending the oppressed against the oppressor" (*Sharḥ Bāb,* 61); for extensive polemical discussions with Mu'tazilah and *Ghulāt* (extremists in Shīʿa who ascribed metaphysical capacities to the Imams), see al-Murtaḍā, *Al-Shāfī* , I:36–102; another extensive polemical discussion with *Ash'arīyya* was made by al-ʿAllāma, *Nahj,* 172–374.
13. Ṭabāṭabā'ī, *Shī'a,* 189–191; *Shi'ite,* 184–186.
14. Al-Muẓaffar, *'Ilm al-Imām,* 57–58.
15. Ibid., 58; Ṭabāṭabā'ī, *Shī'a,* 189–191; and *Shi'ite,* 184–186. One should notice that the characteristics of the Imams' knowledge are not antithetical to the general source of their knowledge, i.e., receiving it from the Prophet. It is completely possible to be subject to Divine Benevolence by being the full recipient of the Prophet's knowledge, and thus, become a treasurer of knowledge, and so on. On the human based source of the Imams' knowledge, see exegetics of the Qur'an such as al-Ṭabrisī, *Majmaʿ al-Bayān,*

III:261, IV:205; Muhammad ibn Shahrāshūb, *Mutashābih al-Qur'an*, I:211; Ṭabāṭabā'ī , *Al-Mīzān*, commentaries on the verse 26 of the Chapter 72 where the Qur'an reads: "He is the knower of the Unknown, and He does not divulge His secret to anyone."

16. Al-Muẓaffar, *'Ilm al-Imām*, 58.
17. Ibid., 59–60.
18. Ibid., 60.
19. Ibid., 62.
20. Modarressi, heavily relying on original sources, explains how the concept of Imāmah transformed from a claim to rule to the spiritual leadership that to the most part was conditioned to such mastery and skill in discovering the legal rules of religion (*Crisis*, 53–105). For that matter, the leading Shī'ī theologians used to examine the legal knowledge of those candidates for such leadership whose appointment by testament was under question (ibid., 59, fn. 25).
21. Ibid., almost everywhere in book, esp. 6–10.
22. Modarressi, *Kharāj*, 214.
23. Madelung, "Authority in Twelver Shiism," 163–173, esp. 170.
24. *Kharāj*, 158–159.
25. Ibid., 159, fn.1.
26. Ibid., 159.
27. Ibid., 160. For further discussion on historical events, see Lambton, *State*, 264–287.
28. Qur'an, 4:59.
29. There was a virtual flux of quasi-jurisprudential treatises in justification of the so-called *salṭanat mashrū'a* or legitimate sultanate during this period. Most of the authors of these treatises were members of the kings' court or recipients of their gifts. For example, Ibn Naṣr Allah Damāvandī, the author of "Risāla Tuḥfat al-Nāṣirīyya fī Ma'rifat al-Ilāhīyya," written in 1264/1847, did not hesitate to employ a mystical interpretation of the universe colored with "philosophical" arguments on the crucial impact of "the three levels of Divine Uniqueness, *aḥadīyyat al-dhāt*, *aḥadīyyat al-ṣifāt*, and *aḥadīyyat al-af'āl* (Divine Inherent Uniqueness, uniqueness of Divine Attributes, and uniqueness of Divine Acts) in creation of beings [that is, humans and angels] and *ittiḥād al-thiqlayn* (the unity of their specific weight), which was aimed at culminating the purpose of creation, that is, *al-insān al-kāmil* (the perfect human)" to justify the rule of king. According to the author, such "perfect humans could be found in two categories of the human beings: the Messengers of God and the just kings who had intended to support the religion and were God's Shadows on Earth!" Not surprisingly, the conclusion was that the despots like Qājār kings were among the latter category. Obviously, these treatises do not occupy any meaningful place in this book. On *Sūfī* (pseudo-mystical) origins of such treatises, see Modarressi, *Crisis*, 48–49; the complete text of Damāvandī's treatise can be found in Zargarīnejād, *Rasā'il-i Sīyāsī*, II:7–50; for more description of the genre, see Zargarīnejād, *Rasā'il-i Mashrūṭīyyat*, 58–61.

30. Modarressi, *Kharāj*, 215. Modarressi continues that one of the said jurists "was excommunicated by the *'ulamā'* (the learned jurists)." In support of Modarressi's discussion, I find it useful to translate an excerpt from al-Qummī, famous as Ṣāḥib al-Qawānīn: "On the story of [the Qājār king's] being *ulu 'l-amr*, that is certainly void... the Shī'a by unanimity has held that the *ulu 'l-amr* mentioned in the Qur'an means the Imams, may peace be upon all of them, and the transmitted traditions and reports to this effect are numerous [and replete with such designation], so [interpretation of a] Divine Command on the imperativeness of absolute obedience to sultan, who is likely to be an oppressor and ignorant to Divine Rules, is *qabīḥ* (ugly). Therefore, the reason and the reports support each other on concluding that the one whose obedience is ruled to be mandatory by God is someone who is infallible and well versed on all the knowledge, except in the state of emergency and impossibility of rendering service to the Infallible [that is, the Hidden Imam]. In that case, it would be imperative for instance to follow a just mujtahid. If the necessity of defending against the enemies of religion is exclusively restricted to the [act of] the Shiites' sultan, whoever he may be, it is sometimes mandatory for the duty-bound individual to assist him, not out of obedience but because of imperative duty of defense and assistance against the enemies' dominance" (Al-Qummī, "Naqd-e Malfūfah-e Mīrzā 'Abd al-Wahhāb," cited in Kadīvar, *Taḥawwul*, 190). (Phrases in the brackets and parentheses are mine).
31. Modarressi, *Kharāj*, 160; Lambton, *State*, 242–263; Cf. Madelung, "A Treatise of the Sharīf al-Murtaḍā," 30; for a counterargument against Madelung, see Calder, "Legitimacy and Accommodation in Safavid Iran."
32. Abd al-Ali al-Karakī was a prominent jurist. Because of his undoubting juristic authority, in the last year of life (1533), the then Safavid king issued a decree by which al-Karakī was in charge of holding the "religious authority" of the whole empire's territory. It is reported that the king has said: "You deserve the authority to rule more than me, because you are the deputy of the Imam and I am one of your agents who implements your orders" (Ṣifatgul, *Sākhtār*, 156); on his distinguished role in the development of Shī'ī jurisprudence, see Modarressi, *Introduction*, 50–51; for an English translation of the decree, see Amir Arjomand, *Authority*, 252–256.
33. Quoted from *Aḥsan al-Tawārīkh*, a famous historical source of the Safavid era, and cited in Ṣifatgul, *Sākhtār*, 155.
34. Ṣifatgul, *Sākhtār*, 153. One of the main issues, the land tax or kharāj, was subject to hot debates among all Muslim jurists. Al-Karakī articulated the Shī'ī doctrine of land tax and provided the Safavid kings with the right to demand and collect it. For a comprehensive and authoritative analysis of the issue in Islamic law, see Hossein Modarressi's *Kharāj in Islamic Law*.
35. Although al-Karakī made no specific juristic discussion on this division, my conclusion is based on his practical model of cooperation with the Safavid kings. For a historical narrative of interactions between the king and al-Karakī, see Ja'fariyān, *Khāndān-e Karakī*, 173–195.
36. Al-Karakī is among the first jurists who have specifically utilized a report, famously known as "*maqbūlah 'Umar ibn Ḥanẓala*" for proving the competent

jurists' status as "deputies of Imam." Before him, only Shahīd al-Awwal had mentioned the report in the introduction to his *Dhikrā al-Shī'a*, and a short reference in his *Ghāyat al-Murād*, I:164. Al-Karakī's discourse later became the stronghold of juristic discussion of *wilāyat al-faqīh* by jurists such as Ahmad Narāqī and Khomeini. Shī'ī jurists have extensively discussed the legal implications of the said, and similar, report. On this, see, e.g., an English translation of Anṣārī's arguments in Sachedina, *The Just Ruler*, 119–172.

37. For a brilliant discussion of the issue in the History of Islam, see George Makdisi, "Authority in the Islamic Community," 117–126.
38. According to Shī'ī law, it is permissible for an individual to work for an unjust ruler. As will be discussed in chapter 3, Shī'ī jurists allowed it when performance of commanding right and prohibiting wrong became mandatory. Thus, al-Karakī could have justified his cooperation with Safavid King on that basis.
39. For authoritative description of the juristic debates, see al-'Allāma, *Mukhtalaf al-Shī'ah*, III:250–253; al-Najafī, *Jawāhir*, IV:312–342.
40. Al-Karakī, Risāla 113, 115, also quoted in al-Najafī, *Jawāhir*, IV:314.
41. Al-Karakī, Risāla, 113.
42. The Arabic phrase *al-sulṭān al-'ādil* in this context has been generally used as an equivalent and clear reference to the Imam in juristic arguments, and not just sultan/just king. For further clarification, see al-'Allāma, *Nihāyat al-Iḥkām*, II:14; Modarressi, *Kharāj*, 158; and explanation and references cited by Calder in his "Legitimacy and Accommodation," 104, fn, 22.
43. Deputies of Imam are held to be divided into two major categories: "deputy in general" who is assumed to be the jurists, and "specified deputy" who is directly appointed by the Imam to be his deputy. I will discuss later that al-Karakī was one of the leading authorities to theorize the extended scope of the first category deputies' authority.
44. Al-Karakī, Risāla, 113; *Jāmi' al-Maqāṣid*, quoted in: Al-Najafī, *Jawāhir*, IV:315.
45. Al-Karakī, Risāla, 128–130, in which he enumerated and explained thirteen qualifications of such jurist, very similar to the qualifications that jurists like al-'Allāma had set before. On this, see discussions relevant to ijtihād in chapter 1.
46. These three points are my inferences from al-Karakī's sophisticated opinion. In his introductory discussions, al-Karakī raised two relevant issues: (A) if the mandate of a rule is lifted, is performance of the act in question permissible? His answer was negative. By nullification of the mandate of performing an act, e.g., Friday Prayer in the time of occultation, he argued, the permission to act, that is, performance of the Prayer, will only apply to the nature of the necessarily obligatory/mandate or recommendation of the act. In addition, where a mandate is lifted, the rule cannot automatically transform to recommendation. Therefore, if the jurist wishes to allow performance of the Friday Prayer, he ought to prove its necessitated obligatory nature. (B) if the Imam is not available to render the rule or appoint the leader of Prayer or . . . , then, who should fill in his position? Al-Karakī believed that the

competent jurist is the Imam's deputy. In consequence, al-Karakī followed the prior jurists' opinion on permissibility of the performance of the Prayers, but did not submit to concluding its individually mandatory nature. Because he believed that in the absence of the Imam, permissibility in terms of giving religious priority to performing an act is limited to the mandate or recommendation. Now, since the indicators do prove the mandate, such conclusion is to be optional, not individually binding. The reason is that by occultation of the Imam, the jurists have considered the society without Imam to be on the brink of sedition and mischief (*mathār al-sharr wa al-fasād*), and it is not to the benefit of society to render it absolutely mandatory.

47. Al-Karakī, Risāla, 117. As will be discussed in chapter 3, this view did not amount to consensus among the Shīʿī jurists of next generations.
48. Similar phrase is used by al-ʿAllāma: "*li anna l'-ijtimāʿ maẓannt al-tanāzuʿ wa al-ḥikma taqtaḍī ʿadamih, wa innamā yaḥṣilu bi l'-sulṭān* (because the society is suspicious [of being in] to contention, and wisdom requires its absence, and such [absence] is acquired by [the presence of the Imam") (*Nihāyat al-Iḥkām*, II:14).
49. Al-Karakī, Risāla, 117. I have to provide the reader with an additional piece of information here: Friday Prayer is to be performed at noon, which coincides with the noon prayer. There are debates as to whether the individual should perform the noon prayer consequent to Friday Prayer or prior to that, and other issues. According to the jurists, performance of the noon prayer is a conclusively mandated individual duty, but as is clear, performance of Friday Prayer is not. In order to rebut the claim of certainty as to the Friday Prayer's mandatory rule, al-Karakī invokes the previous jurists' opinions on the absence of certainty (al-ʿAllāma, in: *Mukhtalaf*, III:253), and that the absence renders performance of Friday Prayer subject to application of the presumption of non-obligation, otherwise, it would be an unbearable duty.
50. Al-Karakī, Risāla, 113; al-Najafī, *Jawāhir*, IV:333. Optionally mandatory means the performance of the act is left to the duty bound Muslims to opt for either of the following: (1) performing the Friday Prayer by providing the prerequisites: following the leader of prayer appointed by the deputy of Imam, and assemble with the intention of performing the Friday Prayer. It is held that the sufficient number of such individuals is five or seven. (2) Attending the congregation of the Friday Prayers, and choosing to perform the noon prayer instead of the Friday Prayer.
51. Majlisī mentions a tradition attributed to the Prophet to have said: "there are two classes in my *ummah* (community) such that if they are righteous and worthy, my community will also be righteous, and if they are corrupt, my community will also be corrupt...they are jurists and kings" (Muhammad Bāqir Majlisī, *ʿAyn al-Ḥayāt*, 487, citation and translation from Lambton, *State*, p. 283); another translation can also be found in Amir Arjomand, *Authority*, 286.
52. In the throne ceremony of the last Safavid king, Majlisī in his inaugural speech said: "After the occultation of the last Imam, Divine, by furthering His Grace upon the remainder of this community, entrusted the just, competent, and wise kings with *maqālīd-e farmānravāyī* (the reins of power), so the

masses of subjects and all the notables would rest under their covering shadow of security and would become free from the oppression of the oppressive masters, because as has been said, 'when the Divine wills a group of people's benefit and good and welfare and security, He will throne a king whose intention is to provide the faithful with their welfare and good" (Ṣifatgul, *Sākhtār*, 503–504).

53. In support of his position, Majlisī cited a report attributed to the seventh Shīʿī Imam, where according to Majlisī, the Imam has said: "You the Shiites do not bend your necks by disobeying your king, if he is just, ask God to maintain his stay in power, and if he is oppressor, appeal to God to guide him. Because your benefit is in the benefit of your king and the king is like a kind father. Do wish for him like you wish for yourself, and do not want for him what you do not want for yourself" (*Ḥilyat al-Muttaqīn*, 174).
54. Majlisī wrote a book called "Rajʿat" on the traditions related to the return/reappearance of the Hidden Imam and made comparable parallels between the supposed signs of the Imam's return and the Safavid kings. At the time, Majlisī was explicitly and impliedly criticized by his contemporary colleagues for misinterpreting those traditions and ascribing them to the kings for the sake of mundane riches and power. On this, see Ṣifatgul, *Sākhtār*, 503–506, 507–510; on general invalidity of Majlisī's attributions to the Imams through collection of invalid and suspicious reports/traditions, including the issue of the last Imam's return/reappearance, see Modarressi, *Crisis*, 48–49, esp. fn 162.
55. Majlisī's father, who was also heavily decreed with religious authority by the king, wrote a surprisingly tough-worded book of "law" on the religious minorities' duties. In the book, he ordered them to obey and carry out the rules on how to wear clothes or behave in the presence of a Shiite, or other degrading social duties. On this, see Ṣifatgul, *Sākhtār*, 556–566, 588–589, in which the author, by quoting and citing reliable sources, reproduces the official reports of transmission of such rules to state ordinances and how they were implemented. Ṣifatgul mentions a wrong title of the book, that is, "*Aḥkām-i Ahl-i Dhimma*." At best, it must have been a part of Majlisī the father's famous book, that is, *Ṣawāʿiq-i Ṣāḥibqarāniyya*. I am grateful to Professor Modarressi for this clarification.

3 The 1905 Constitutional Revolution: Shi'i Jurisprudence and Constitutionalism

1. There is a vast literature on the 1905 Constitutional Revolution in English, let alone in Persian. For partial translation of one of the most important Persian sources into English, see Kasravi, *Constitutional Revolution*; for another important source in English, see Browne, *Persian Revolution*.
2. The title "shadow of God" was a stranger to the Uṣūlī jurists, and undoubtedly, the kings' entitlement for utilizing its religious-political implications was heavily qualified by the limits that a juristic analysis could put forward. For Qummī, an *Uṣūlī* jurist who scrutinized that title, "shadow of God" purported one of the three meanings. First, a just and caring king's shadow under

which the weakened oppressed people could resort to and seek justice and security, heal their wounds, and find remedy through fair proceedings against the oppressors. Second, a sham valueless shadow that does not provide meaningful shelter, which is embodied in the kings who are supposed to reflect the Divine's Grace to the people but immerse themselves in the pursuit of mundane hubris pleasures and interests instead, and ignore the duty of treating their constituencies justly and protect them from injustice and oppression. The third meaning refers to a king who mirror images of the Divine so everyone who looks at him can also believe in the existence of an All Forgiving and All Merciful God who is the creator of the skies, the earth, and the human being. It was obvious that for Qummī the then ruling Qājār kings represented the second type. On his thoughts, see his "*Irshād Nāmah-i Mīrzā-yi Qummī*," 370–371, as cited in Kadīvar, *Taḥavvol*, 199. For the type of discourse that pro-kings "jurists" developed for the proof of kings' legitimacy and entitlement of attributions like shadow of God, see Chapter 2, n 29.

3. At the time, taking sanctuary in the foreign embassies was a sociopolitical practice of peaceful opposition against the despotic monarchy. Primarily, it used to be exercised in high-ranking jurists' houses, but was banned during the early Qājār rule. Taking refuge in the British Embassy by no means suggests that the British diplomats off-handedly supported the people's demands. They neither made efforts to lay political stress against the king, nor did they offer support to the people because of that.
4. Browne, *Persian Revolution*, 353.
5. On the formation of Anglo-Russian Treaty in English, see Mirfendereski, *Diplomatic History*, Chapter 21, 85–94; for the official text of the treaty, see Parry, *Consolidated Treaty Series*, Vol. 205, 404–408; for official documents in Iran's Ministry of Foreign Affairs, see Hassannia and Tatari, *Gharārdād-e 1907.*
6. Azimi, *Quest for Democracy*, 42–43; cf. Katouzian, *State and Society*, 55–68.
7. For more of the chronology of events, see Afary, *Iranian Revolution*, xvii–xxi.
8. In order to get a sense of how the Russian Tsarist army literally slaughtered the constitutionalists and demolished the constitutional revolution's achievements in the northern parts of Iran, see Browne, *Letters from Tabriz*. The British invasion of the southern parts of Iran was not without brutality either. For official documents on the atrocities of the two Empires' invasions in Iran's Ministry of Foreign Affairs, see Torkamān, *Hujūm-e Inglīs va Rūs*.
9. A complete documentation of the minutes of these deliberations has neither been collected at the time nor fully published. However, there are very important historical documents remaining in exclusive possession of the Iranian parliament access to which has always been heavily restricted before and after the 1979 Revolution. For a reliable collection of all the deliberations as were published in the journals at the time, see Mīrzā Ṣāleḥ, *Modhākirāt*, 49, 51, 56, 58, 59, 60, 64, 65, 66, 70, 72, 75–77, 79–85; and Arāqī, *Ḥuqūq-i Asāsī*, 57–82.
10. For a complete account of the excuses and reactions of the Royal Court, see Kasravi, *Constitutional Revolution*, 228–257, and Browne, *Persian Revolution*, 133–146.

11. Senate was established in 1964, i.e., almost half a century after the decree on the Fundamental Laws was issued!
12. For a reliable English translation of the Fundamental Law, see Browne, *Persian Revolution*, 362–371.
13. For a reliable English translation of the Supplementary Fundamental Laws, see ibid., 372–384.
14. Translation is mostly based on ibid., 373, to which I have made some minor modifications. This article later became famous as "*Aṣl-e Ṭarāz*" or Balancing Article. I will discuss juristic implications and technicalities of this article in chapter 4.
15. Article 2 (the Balancing Article) was directly proposed by Shaykh Faḍl Allah Nūrī (d. 1327/1909), who at the time was one of the supporters of the new system and a jurist member of First Majlis. For more on Nūrī, see Chapter 4, fn. 4, cf. Martin, "Shaykh Faḍl Allah Nūrī," in *Encyclopedi of Islam, Second*, VIII:140a–140b.
16. *Marājiʿ al-Taqlīd*, plural form of *Marjaʿ al-Taqlīd* (literally meaning source of emulation), is the highest religious rank in Shīʿī hierarchy of authority that belongs to the most learned jurists whose vast knowledge and mastery of jurisprudence are recognized, not only by other jurists but also by the common people. The term "emulation" purports to every individual's recognition of the most learned jurist, and his/her pledge to follow such a jurist's opinions. My translation of the term as "religious leader" is intended to include such jurist's both mastery and leadership. For more, see Stewart, "Islamic Juridical Hierarchies and the Office of Marjaʿ al-Taqlīd," in Clarke, *Shīʿite Heritage*, 137–157.
17. Mullā Muhammad Kāẓim Khurāsānī, famous as Ākhūnd, was unquestionably a brilliant *Uṣūlī* mind and the most prominent Shīʿī leader during the Constitutional Revolution. He was one of the best disciples of Anṣārī and his successor Muhammad Hassan Shīrāzī (d. 1312/1894), famous as Mīrzā-ye Buzurg and the leader of a major national resistance against Nāṣir al-Dīn Shah—the Qājār king in 1890. Ākhūnd was a multidisciplined *Uṣūlī* jurist with vast scholarship on jurisprudence and philosophy, and mentored at least 120 competent jurists who represented the next generation of Shīʿī religious leaders. It is a well-established historical fact that between 1200 and 2200 students used to attend his lectures every day. He is the author of *Al-Kifāyat al-Uṣūl*, one of the best books on Shīʿī *Uṣūl al-Fiqh*, which is the main advanced coursebook on Uṣūl in Shīʿī seminaries since 1903. Ākhūnd's famous disciples as well as other prominent jurists have heavily commented on this book. After the death of Shīrāzī, Ākhūnd was recognized by consensus of the jurists as the next Shīʿī religious leader. In addition to his religious credentials, he was also the most influential leader of the 1905 Constitutional Revolution. His letters, telegraphs, and edicts on different occasions were the most powerful source of legitimacy of the national demands for a constitution and a parliament. He was very active in reinstatement of constitutionalism in Iran and dethroning the deviant despot king Muhammad Ali Shah, who bombarded the Majlis and declared the Constitution abrogated in 1908. As a Shīʿī leader cognizant of colonial politics,

Ākhūnd declared holy war against Italian invasion of Libya in 1911. He also declared holy war against the two Empires' armies after Russia and the Great Britain allied to divide Iran in 1910–1911. He decided to travel to Iran and lead the national resistance against the 1907 treaty and the occupation of northern cities of Iran by Tsarist army, but passed away on the day that he had planned to leave Najaf. The cause of his sudden death is still unknown, but there is a serious suspicion that the secret agents of an Anglo-Russian conspiracy poisoned him. Ākhūnd wrote at least twenty books and treatises, mostly about *uṣūl al-fiqh*, and two commentaries on philosophical works of Mullā Ṣadrā and Sabzawārī. For a full account of his life in Persian, see Kifāyī, *Margī dar Nūr*, esp. 278–294, on his death; for a complete bibliography and major vectors of his thoughts, see Ākhūnd, *Sīyāsat Nāmeh*, 7–31; for an English biography, see Hairi, "Khurāsānī," *Encyclopedia of Islam, Second*, V:61a–62a; on the importance of incentives and the competition among the leading professors of seminaries to augment their patronage at the time and the prominent status of Ākhūnd, see Litvak, *Shi'i Scholars*, 21–44, 90–95.

18. Ākhūnd, *Sīyāsat Nāmeh*, 167, 169, 172, 174, 177, 182, 189, 190, 213, 215, 217, 241, 246, and especially 247.
19. There is a huge literature in Persian produced by prominent Iranian historians. For an English acknowledgment, see Lambton, "The Persian ʿUlamā and the Constitutional Reform."
20. Ādamīyyat, *Fikr-i Āzādī*.
21. As an incontrovertible historical proof for the importance of the jurists' opinion, one should analyze the fatwa issued in 1307/1890 by Grand Ayatullah Hassan Shīrāzī (d.1312/1894) against the then king's grant of tobacco trade known as regie. On this, see Ādamīyyat, *Imtiyāz-namah-i Rizhī*, and Lambton, "The Tobacco Regie: a Prelude to Revolution."
22. Abdullah ibn Muhammad Naṣīr Najafi, famous as Māzandarānī, was one of the disciples of al-Anṣārī and Mīrzā Ḥabībullah Rashtī (one of the most famous disciples of Anṣārī, d. 1312/1894), and a very prominent jurist whose signature was next to Ākhūnd's in the letters, fatwas, and telegraphs sent from Najaf.
23. Husayn ibn Khalīl Tihrānī was one of the disciples of Anṣārī and Ṣāḥib al-Jawāhir (d. 1266/1849, a very famous Shīʿī jurist), and a prominent *Uṣūlī* jurist and religious leader. He was recognized to enjoy the same religious status as that of Ākhūnd, and used to sign the letters, fatwas, and telegraphs as "Najl al-Marḥūm Mīrzā Khalīl" next to Ākhūnd's and Māzandarānī's. These three were known as "*Marāji'i Thalātha*" or Trite Religious Leaders of the Revolution.
24. On the life of Muhammad Hussein Gharawī Nā'īnī, see Hairi, *Shi'ism and Constitutionalism*, 109–51.
25. For a compilation of at least six treatises of this kind, see Zargarīnezhād, *Rasā'il-i Mashrūṭiyyat*, 399–668.
26. While admonishing the despot king to revive the constitutional order, in one of his letters Ākhūnd wrote, "Although the benefits and merits of constitutionalism were briefly clear to us at the time, we scrutinized its characteristics to

find out whether or not the notion of constitutionalism includes any jurisprudential inhibitions or conflicts with an important priority [in religious rules]. By an in depth and extensive examination, we concluded that the foundations and the essential principles of constitutionalism derive from '*sharʿ-i qawīm-i Islam*' (the upright Islamic Shari'ah). By comparing the Articles of the Laws that relate to Shari'ah as well as the inclusion of a number of jurist-members for *taṣḥīḥ va tanqīḥ* (correction and review), as provided in Article 2, we found them unmistakably correct and legitimate. Not only does the Constitution close the gates of oppression and aggression that were not restricted to any limits during the despotic rule. It also includes all the important objectives and necessary reforms that we had always had in mind and longed for years to protect and free the religion and the government from the enemies' clutch [i.e., the colonial governments]. For us, National Consultative Assembly [Majlis] is the institution that we wished so the government and the people unite together. Majlis is also the key for the enlightenments and achievements that other [constitutionalist] nations have accomplished from which we [i.e., Iranians, Muslims] had deprived ourselves" (*Sīyāsat Nāmeh*, 204). In another important letter, Ākhūnd, Māzandarānī, and Mīrzā Khalīl wrote about their similar in-depth study of despotism (ibid., 212).

27. For the historical events that amounted to the 1905 Constitutional Revolution in English, see Kasravi, *Constitutional Revolution*, 7–152; Browne, *Persian Revolution*, 31–97; Afary, *Iranian Revolution*, 17–36.
28. By popular sovereignty, I am referring to the general definition of the term that "encompasses an array of variations on the theme that the legitimacy of government depends on the consent of the people." O. Potter, *Federalist Vision*, 15; cf. Van Caenegen, *Historical Introduction*, 90 (presenting the idea as that the government exists for the people and not the other way round).
29. By contractarian or contractualist approach in Shīʿī doctrine, I am generally referring to the commonly known paradigm of exchange of the mutual rights, which was introduced to the philosophy of politics as "social contract" and developed by thinkers such as Hobbes, Locke, Rousseau, and Kant. While in a religious context rights are considered to emerge either by the Divine Order or His Approval, main source of rights in the social contract discourse is perceived to be the nature, and thus, "free" from Divine intervention. If the concept of "natural law" can be interpreted as human being's rational attempt in finding the laws that govern the objects in their natural setting, then, it can also be said that drawing either of equation or distinction between Divine law and natural law in the Shīʿī doctrine is subject to negotiation between the methodological requirements of discovering the laws from their Divine or independent rational origins and the revelation. In other words, even if we do not submit to the idea of social contract in the Shīʿī doctrine, the role of independent reason in juristic design of the individual's rightful relationship with others—be it individuals, the society, or the ruler—and the legal analysis of the choice between compromising or safeguarding individual rights is undeniably evident. I will later introduce the First Shīʿī Imam's delineation of a right-oriented relation between the ruler and the ruled, which is more

consonant with bargaining or contractarian approach than other explanations. For a brilliant analysis of the relation between the law of reason and the Enlightenment, which for all its philosophical underpinning was a moral, ultimately religious breakthrough to a new attitude to life, in the context of reformulation of a social philosophy manifested in a jurisprudence that was to produce a vast change in public thought and enormous reforms in public life, see Wieacker, *History of Private Law*, 249–256. On the contractarian paradigm, see Rosenfeld, "Contract and Justice"; Vallentyne, "Contractualist Philosophy of Law," 159–161; and Medina, "Social Contract," 808–810. For a brief discussion on the origins of contractarian doctrine in U.S. constitutionalism, see Ferejohn, *Constitutional Culture*, 20–22 (discussing Originalist theories for interpreting the Constitution as distribution of bargaining power among social entities). For a debatable interpretation of the social contract theory in Shīʿī jurisprudence, see Akhavi, "Shiite Theories of Social Contract," 137–155; cf. Aziz, "Popular Sovereignty," 181–198.

30. In addition to theological and juristic discussions against tyranny in Islamic law, another prominent line of anti-despotic discourse was originally reflected in political philosophy of Fārābī (d. most probably 339/950). More resembling Plato and Socrates than Aristotle, Fārābī made a typology of political regimes in the hypothetical city-states within which madīnat al-taghallubiyya (the regime of tyranny or domination) was categorized as the worst alternative to madīnat al-fāḍila (the virtuous city ruled by, borrowing from Plato, a philosopher-king). Philosopher-jurist Abu al-Hassan ʿĀmirī (d. 381/991) also argued against "Madīnat al-Shaqiyya" (the brutal-city) in which tyranny is the rule of the day. Given that succeeding generations of philosopher-jurists modeled their political arguments after these typologies, especially Fārābī's, it would, therefore, be irrelevant to discuss whether Fārābī and ʿĀmirī were Sunni or Shiite. Among them was Naṣīr al-Dīn Ṭūsī (d. 672/1274), a Shīʿī philosopher-jurist, who, based on his powerful discourse on philosophy of ethics, strongly condemned the tyrannical regime. With the demise of philosophical orientation in Islamic thought, it was the jurists who took it upon themselves to write against the oppressor rulers in their juristic arguments. This should not suggest that Muslim jurists had completely ignored the philosophical aspects of the argument. Shaykh al-Ṭā'ifa, in his *Al-Mabsūṭ*, I:204 and II:8, referred to tyrants as "al-mutaghallib ʿalā amr al-muslimīn" (dominant over the Muslims' affairs) and "a'immat al-jawr" (leaders by oppression). Interpreting the Qur'anic verse 2:124, Shaykh al-Ṭā'ifa, in his *Al-Tibyān*, I:499, found no legitimacy for an oppressor ruler. Main jurists of Ḥilla School followed the course. Muḥaqqiq (676/1277) in his *Sharāyiʿ al-Islam*, Fāḍil Miqdād (826/1422) in his *Al-Nāfiʿ Yawm al-Ḥashr fī Sharḥ Bāb al-Ḥādī ʿAshar* and *Al-Lawāmiʿ al-Ilāhiyya fi al-Mabāḥith al-Kalāmiyya*, and others argued extensively on the legal aspects of an oppressive rule. It was, again, a philosopher, Mullā Ṣadrā (d. 1050/1640), who revived the political philosophy of anti-despotism, whose sophisticated philosophical theory of the relation between the soul and the being amounted to yet another refutation of tyranny and despotism. On Fārābī and his political philosophy in English,

see Abu Nasr Farabi, *On the Perfect State*; and Mahdi, "ALFARABI." On ʿĀmirī, see Rowson, "Al-ʿĀmirī," 216–221; on Mullā Ṣadrā's political philosophy, especially, see Khamene'i, *Falsafah-i Siyāsī*.

31. Very few Iranian scholars have attempted to analyze the juristic roots of constitutionalist jurists' political leadership and ratification of the 1907 Constitution. Muḥsin Kadīvar, "Andīsha-hi Siyāsī-ye Ākhūnd Khurāsānī," in Group of scholars, *Mabānī-ye Mashrūṭīyyat-i Iran*, 219–264; and Dāwūd Fīraḥī, "Mabānī-ye Fiqhī-ye Mashrūṭah-Khwāhī" (ibid., 195–218); Enayat, *Modern Islamic Political Thought*, 164–175.
32. Nā'īnī complained that previous jurists had failed to discuss the issues related to government properly. *Tanbīh al-Ummah*, 59–60.
33. This issue does not exclusively belong to Islamic theories of sovereignty. As Potter reports, by late sixteenth century–early seventeenth century the main understanding of sovereignty was limited to the general formula of God→king transfer of power. Citing Donald S. Lutz, she continues that early manifestations of popular sovereignty appeared in the works of premodern European thinkers such as Jean Bodin; Philippe du Plessis-Monray, Suarez, and Bellarmine, *Federalist Vision*, 15–17. However, interestingly, she continues: "The expression 'popular sovereignty' does not appear in *The Federalist* or in the seventeenth and eighteenth century treatises of the natural rights theories who explore the notion in detail" (ibid.).
34. Imam Ali ibn Abū Ṭālib, *Nahj al-Balāgha*, Sermon 216 (partial translation is from Sayed Ali Reza, *Peak of Eloquence: Nahjul Balagha*, 432–433; modifications, additions and bolded texts are mine). This important sermon was addressed to a crowd of more than fifty thousand Muslims in the Ṣiffīn Battle with Muʿāwīya, the first Umayyad contender to the Caliphate, which is a very important point in the history of Islam. For some of the historical aspects of this war and a vigorous analysis of its legal implications on the relation between the ruler and the ruled in Islamic law, see Abou El Fadl, *Rebellion*, esp. 40, 44, 46; "Constitutionalism," 75–76.
35. Arguing for the Divine rules on the mutual rights and duties of the ruler and the ruled requires an extensive treatment. For a comprehensive Shīʿī study, see Montaẓerī, *Dirāsāt*, in general, and especially I:29–74, where the author enumerates fifteen duties for an Islamic ruler.
36. The notion of "*naṣīḥat al-a'immat al-muslimūn*" (advising the rulers) was not new in the Caliphate doctrine of political governance either. Merits of the people's right to express their objections against the unjust rulers were already established by valid traditions. In one of them, the Prophet had praised expression of the truth before an oppressive ruler as the most favorable jihad in God's judgment, Al-Musnad al-Ahmad, Section on "Kalimat Ḥaqq li Imām Jā'ir," 5/125, and in the other, he equated the religion with counseling and advising the ruler, Ṣaḥīḥ al-Muslim, Kitāb al-Īmān, Section 23, tradition 55. (Traditions are quoted and cited in Montaẓerī, *Mabānī*, II:388–389.)
37. Imam Ali, *Nahj al-Balāgha*, Sermon 216, translation is from Reza, *Peak of Eloquence*, 434–435, with my modifications in translation.

38. On the importance of *shūrā* (consultation), Nā'īnī says that the Prophet considered it as one of the rights of the ruled. Moreover, his strife to maintain its implementation, as the most applied measure in making his political decisions, was intended to establish and protect the inherent liberty of the individuals and the equality of all with the ruler in an Islamic state. *Tanbīh al-Ummah*, 55. I will return to this point in chapter 4.
39. Khaled Abou El Fadl's reference in his "Constitutionalism," 75, to a conception of Shari'ah that is solely based on aḥkām, and ignoring of the methodology and principles, can be directly applied in analyzing the position taken by the proponents of just sultanate.
40. Nūrī, "Risālah-i Ḥurmat," 153–154, 163–164; *Rasā'il,* I:265–266; Tabrīzī, "Kashf al-Murād," 128, 134–136, 138–140.
41. In this chapter, I will only discuss the views of those jurists who are considered contemporary to the 1905 Revolution. On Qummī, see Chapter 1, endnote 113. The following excerpts and quotations are translated from his, *Jāmi' al-Shatāt*, I:385–386.
42. Ibid., II:125, 129.
43. Ibid., I:385.
44. Ibid., I:386–387; II:66, 125, and 130.
45. Ibid., I:385, 386; II:66, 129, and 130.
46. Qummī cited a report that said, "If our Imam rises [that is, decides to end his occultation], your share of the revenues will be more than what is now," and concluded: "It can be inferred from this report that the reason of permissibility [of the collection and distribution of such revenues in a non-Shiite sultanate] is that they [i.e., the Shiites] have received their due" (ibid., II:129). For more references on this issue, see Modarressi, *Kharāj*, 163, fns 2 and 3.
47. On this, see Baḥr al-'Ulūm, *Bulghat al-Faqīh*, I:37–38, III:211.
48. See chapter 2. I will discuss this point further in chapter 4.
49. Ākhūnd, *Sīyāsat Nāmeh*, 213.
50. Although, as mentioned before, the title of "shadow of God" for the king had taken its coinage from the pseudo-philosophical and mystical interpretations of the being and the creation, there were jurists who did not hesitate to call the Qājār King "*sultan-i Islam*" (the king of Islam) or "*sultan-i Islam-panāh*" (1, a king who seeks shelter under Islam, 2, king the protector of Islam) and "*shāhanshāh-i muslimīn*" (the king of kings of Muslims)! On this, in addition to sources introduced in note 2, see Nūrī, "Tadhkirat al-Ghāfil," 185, 186. Similar or exact titles were mentioned in Nūrī's letters to the despot king who ordered the bombardment of the Majlis and invoked these references to justify the "Shari'ah based legitimacy" of his tyranny.
51. Ākhūnd, *Sīyāsat Nāmeh*, 292.
52. Ibid., 240.
53. This is a reference to those anti-constitutionalist jurists who had written several treatises against liberty and equality as inscribed in the Constitution, which enjoyed the Religious Leaders' support. For them, liberty was equal to chaos, right to education for all citizens—including the women—was tantamount to the women's corruption, and freedom of expression was a means to

vilify the religion because censuring the books and journals was disallowed in the Article 20 of the Constitution. This was an obvious misrepresentation of the Constitution and Majlis. Not only had Article 20 banned publication of books and journals that vilified the religion, but also the First Majlis, in Articles 4, 17, and 33 of the Press Law enacted in 1326/1907, had provided that publication of any religious book should receive the approval of the Bureau of Religious Sciences, established in the Ministry of Sciences, and publication of immoral antireligious remarks in the journals was declared a criminal offense. It is obvious that the anti-constitutionalist propaganda was based on populist and low-key propaganda intended to abuse and to provoke the people's religious emotions by degrading the constitutional rights with semi-juristic reasoning. For example, see Nūrī, *Rasā'il,* I:150, 262, 263, 265–266, 287–288; "Risālah-i Ḥurmat," 158, 162.

54. "Al-La'ālī," 521.
55. *Tanbīh al-Ummah*, 18–27. Nā'īnī made it clear that his analysis was heavily based on Imam Ali's interpretation (*Nahj al-Balāgha*, Sermon 192) of those Qur'anic verses in which references were made to the children of Israel, more specifically in 20:47.
56. Ibid., 27–28.
57. Ibid., 28. Original translation of this excerpt only is by Mahmoud Sadri in Kurzman, *Modernist Islam*, 122–123. (Translating only the first chapter of the book, the translator has been generally successful in conveying the meaning of this very sophisticated book and its author's style, which is replete with highly technical juristic terms and arguments. A note, however, is in order here. Notwithstanding their non-Arabic mother language, Arabic has been the main and standard language in which Muslim jurists, including the Shī'ī constitutionalist jurists, have written their books. Therefore, writing for an Iranian audience, highly sophisticated *Uṣūlī*s such as Nā'īnī usually thought in Arabic and wrote in Persian. This has led to either the miscomprehension of Nā'īnī's book or the inability to match its bilingual nature. The translator, in some instances, has been unable to manage this problem. Thus, mainly relying on the translator, here I have made some modifications and adjustments that I found necessary).
58. Ibid., 28–34.
59. The editor of Nā'īnī's book, Ayatullah Mahmoud Ṭāliqānī, narrates the story as follows: "Before the Prophet's appointment to Messengership, Muhammad and his wife, Khadījah, had agreed to marry their daughter, Zaynab, to Abi al-'Āṣ, Khadījah's nephew. After public announcement of Prophecy of Muhammad, the Quraysh tribe decided to put the Prophet in family problems by inducing Abi al-'Āṣ to divorce Zaynab, which he denied. Abi al-'Āṣ, however, did not deny attending the war against Muslims and was arrested as a prisoner in the War of Badr. At the time, the rule for an infidel war prisoner was one of execution or payment for freedom. The majority of Muslims chose to accept the payment. Zaynab sent a necklace for her husband's freedom, which was originally part of the dowry that the Prophet and Khadījah had given her. While being emotional at the sight of the necklace, the Prophet left the

decision on accepting or rejecting the payment to all Muslims and said, 'This necklace is part of my daughter's dowry. It is up to you to accept it or resend it back and release Abi al-ʿĀṣ.' Muslims decided to resend the necklace and to free their war prisoner. Then, the Prophet asked Abi al-ʿĀṣ to allow Zaynab, who was coerced to stay in Mecca, to join the Prophet in Medina. Abi al-ʿĀṣ agreed and arranged for Zaynab's return to Muhammad. Quraysh members attacked Zaynab's carriage and caused abortion of her child. However, Zaynab succeeded to join the Prophet. At a later time, Muslims attacked a Meccan trade caravan and seized its merchandise. Abi al-ʿĀṣ as the trustee of Meccan traders decided to travel to Medina and ask for the return of the goods. Now in his father's camp, Zaynab provided refuge for her husband, unbeknownst to the Prophet. Providing refuge for non-Muslims or enemy combatants was an individual right of Muslims so they could secure temporary protection and full consideration of legal circumstances for refugees of interest. Originally, this was a custormry right of tribesmen that provided tribal protection for a fellow tribesman in cases of unjust punishments. Zaynab announced her protection of Abi al-ʿĀṣ. The Prophet announced his unawareness of Zaynab's decision too and, once again, left it to the Muslims to choose between keeping the merchandise for themselves and returning them to Abi al-ʿĀṣ. The right to own the enemy's seized goods was, retrospectively, a competing customary right for anyone. Muslims decided to let Abi al-ʿĀṣ retain possession of all the seized merchandise and return them to Meccan traders" (ibid., 29–30). For historical sources, see Muhammad ibn Jarīr al-Ṭabarī (d. 310/922), *Ta'rīkh* (Beirut: Mu'assasat al-Aʿlamī li 'l-Maṭbūʿāt, n.d.) II:164 [citation is from Sayyid Javād Varaʿī, editor of another edition of *Tanbīh al-Ummah*, 60–61].

60. Ibid., 30; also see Ibn Athīr (d. 630/1232), *Al-Kāmil* (Beirut: Mu'assasat al-Turāth al-ʿArabī, 1414/1993), I:534–537 (last citation is from Varaʿī, supra note 60).
61. Ibid., 31–32. The story is narrated by Muhammad Bāqir al-Majlisī, *Biḥār al-Anwār* (Beirut: Dār Iḥyā' al- Turāth al-ʿArabī, first edition, 1408/1987), XXII:508. The report on the Prophet's statement on prohibition of discrimination in punishments can be found in Muslim ibn al-Ḥajjāj al-Nīshābūrī (d. 261/874), *Ṣaḥīḥ Muslim ma'a Sharḥ al-Nawawī* (Beirut: Dār al-Kutub al-ʿIlmiyya, n.d.), VI:155 (citations are from Varaʿī, supra note 60, mentioning that the tradition attributed to the Prophet was not reported in Shīʿī collections).
62. Ibid., 16 (the second Caliph), 33, 36 (Imam Ali).
63. Later, I will discuss the opinions of Ākhūnd, and other *Uṣūlī* jurists, on the jurisdictional scope of the infallibles' competence and his argument that the Prophet as well as Imams did never declare any religious rule that was in conflict with the individuals' established rights. For Ākhūnd and many other *Uṣūlī* jurists, including the constitutionalist jurists, the Qur'anic statement of the Prophet's guardianship over the Muslims' lives (Qur'an, 33:6) did not accrue to legal guardianship, as an element of the infallible persons' rule.
64. At the core of Nā'īnī's arguments on the causes of transformation of the Prophetic model of rule to the Umayyad despotism was the ignorance of

Shari'ah-based limitations (*kamā ja'alah al-Shāri'*) on the rule and the ruler, *Tanbīh al-Ummah*, 16–17, and especially 55. In fact, by giving the examples, he rendered his opinion on the limited guardianship of the infallible persons. I will return to this issue later.

65. This conclusion is supported by the *Uṣūlī* doctrine of correlation between the rational findings of practical reason and rules of Shari'ah, which provided genuine unity between what the rational people find mandatory and the Shari'ah rules. Another relevant argument, as discussed in chapter 1, is the theory of dividing Shari'ah rules to two categories of ratifying rules (*aḥkām imḍā'ī*) and constituting rules (*aḥkām ta'sīsī*) and the fact that there were many custom-based societal regulations that Shari'ah ratified as binding and regulatory.
66. For a complete collection of these letters, see Hamidullah, *Majmū'at al-Wathā'iq*; al-Aḥmadī, *Makātīb al-Rasūl*, which contains more historical accounts and explanations; and Mahdavī Dāmghānī, *Wathā'iq*; for a fairly comprehensive analysis of "*Wathīqat al-Madīna*" and the legal construction of the tribal-interreligious relationship among the Medinese groups, see Lecker, *Constitution of Medina*.
67. These orders and recommendations are replete in almost all the letters. For the one famous as "Covenant with 'Amr ibn Ḥazm," which is a long letter and contains all the details, see Hamidullah, *Majmū'at*, 104–108; Dāmghānī, *Wathā'iq*, 160–169; a comprehensive analysis of the letter is provided in al-Aḥmadī, *Makātīb*, 197–219.
68. Treatment of this issue requires an extensive study of the history of Islamic Law in its early stages. Although Orientalists have made an important contribution to this issue, a genuinely fair treatment is yet to be made.
69. Nā'īnī, *Tanbīh al-Ummah*, 66, 76.
70. Ibid., 4–5, 27, 36–38, 60–63, 66, 73–76
71. Arjomand, "Islam and Constitutionalism," in his *Constitutional Politics*, 35.
72. The phrase "*ḍarūrīyyāt-i dīn*" (necessities of the religion) in its juristic sense mainly refers to major religious issues such as the prayers and belief in the uniqueness of God. As a recurrent phrase in the writings of the constitutionalist jurists, in either of singular or plural forms, it is easy to see how equating establishment and protection of a constitutionalist system as well as institutions such as Majlis with necessities of religion can reveal the degree of *Uṣūlīs*' belief in the juristic validity of constitutionalism.
73. These two phrases refer to anti-constitutionalist jurists who adduced juristic validity to their opinions.
74. "Non-infallible" is intentionally worded to include everyone except the person of the Hidden Imam.
75. Ākhūnd, *Sīyāsat Nāmeh*, 204, 207.
76. All the constitutionalist jurists who issued fatwas or wrote in support of constitutionalism considered universally rational findings of reason as valid basis for analyzing constitutionalism. Furthermore, they believed that all such findings had been previously recognized by the Qur'an and Prophetic Sunnah. For example, see especially Ākhūnd and Māzandarānī, "Lāyaḥa-yi

Hay'at-i ʿUlamā," in Ākhūnd, *Sīyāsat Nāmeh*, 246–247, in which they analyzed the underpinning philosophy of constitutionalism of "world's free and constitutionalist states" and discussed the Iranian model's on its basis; Nāʾīnī, *Tanbīh al-Ummah*, 1–3, where after mentioning the West's "progress and perseverance in translation, interpretation, and application" of the Qur'anic teachings on civilization in the aftermath of the Crusades, from one hand, and "the concomitant regression of the people of Islam and their subjugation at the hands of unbelievers resulted in such a state that Muslims gradually forgot the principles of their own historical origins...and thought that the commandments of Islam are contrary to civilization, reason, and justice—the fountainhead of progress" (translation is from Sadri, Kurzman, *Modernist Islam*, 116). For similar views on the religious origins of constitutionalism in West, see especially Friedrich, *Transcendent Justice*; on the European countries' acquisition of Arabic books during and after the Crusades, see Jones, "Piracy, War, and the Acquisition"; on the translation of Islamic texts as a prelude for Renaissance, see d'Alverny, "Translations and Translators," 439–444.

77. The issue in this fatwa was whether it was permissible to force the government officials to seek the jurists' approval for their activities, or attempt to reduce the aggression and ask for enacting regulations that require indiscrminatory implementation, when the despotic government's officials have aggressively and regularly oppressed the people over taxes and customs tariffs. For the complete text of the question and fatwa, see Ākhūnd, *Sīyāsat Nāmeh*, 164–166.
78. In one of his fatwas, Ākhūnd clearly stated that "the *Uṣūlī* rational and jurisprudential prohibition of oppression and beauty of justice is the basis upon which constitutionalism, and the enactment of Constitution and the establishment of parliament, is founded" (*Sīyāsat Nāmeh*, 219).
79. As an extremely important concept, there are 288 verses in the Qur'an where the term *ẓulm* (oppression) and its philological derivatives have been mentioned with absolute condemnation. The depth of rejection, condemnation, and prohibition of the term will be further revealed when literally equivalent terms such as *ta'addī* (to engage in aggression; 107 Qur'anic verses) or Qur'anic equivalents of oppression such as *kufr* (blasphemy; 528 verses) would be added. Other relevant terms, though not an exhaustive list, would be *ʿiṣyān* (insidious defiance against God), *shirk* (polytheism), *jabbārīyya* (tyranny), *jawr* (oppression), *istiḍʿāf* (forced application of oppression against the human beings), and *awlīyā' min dūn Allah* (rulers inferior to God); all should also be reviewed in their Qur'anic context. For simple word-checking of the aforementioned terms in Qur'anic verses, see, in general, books on *Kashf al-Āyāt* such as ʿAbd al-Bāqī, *Al-Muʿjam*, 207, 533–534, 551–556, 568–569, 588, 725–732, 876; and Fānī, *Al-Fihris*, 124, 162, 260–261, 268, 273, 315–316.
80. Ākhūnd, *Sīyāsat Nāmeh*, 203, referring to devastating wars with Russia. "Under Fath Ali Shah (reigned 1797–1834), Iran went to war against Russia, which was expanding from the north into the Caucasus Mountains, an area of historic Iranian interest and influence. Iran suffered major

military defeats during the war. Under the terms of the Treaty of Golestan in 1813, Iran recognized Russia's annexation of Georgia and ceded to Russia most of the north Caucasus region. A second war with Russia in the 1820s ended even more disastrously for Iran, which in 1828 was forced to sign the Treaty of Turkamanchai acknowledging Russian sovereignty over the entire area north of the Aras River (territory comprising present-day Armenia and Republic of Azerbaijan)." http://www.iranchamber.com/history/qajar/qajar.php.

81. Ibid, 204–205. Ākhūnd was referring to the impacts of borrowing money from Russia and the Great Britain for traveling to Europe, and undertaking devastating conditions for their high rates of usury repayment by mortgaging the income of Northern and Southern Customs Offices. To Ākhūnd, this was tantamount to "*istiqrāḍ az kuffār* (borrowing from the infidels) and *tarhīn-i mamlakat-i Shī'a* (mortgaging the Shiite country) to them, coupled with *yaghmā-yi amvāl-i Muslimīn* (embezzling the Muslims' properties) without spending it on building the country and closing the gates of the nation's need" (ibid., 203), making it clear that the king does not have any proprietary right on the national sources of wealth and treasury, because they belong to Muslims.
82. Al-Qummī, *Jāmi' al-Shatāt*, I:376–377.
83. Cf. Jalālī, *Dīdgāh-hāyi Mīlānī*, 334–335, defining the term as "Muslim population."
84. Ākhūnd, *Sīyāsat Nāmeh*, 219, 229.
85. Ibid., 213.
86. The first category is *al-jihad al-ibtidā'ī* (offensive holy war), which according to long-standing strong consensus of the jurists is no longer a duty for Muslims to perform. On general introduction and some juristic examples of the application of the term in Shī'ī jurisprudence, see Anṣārī, *Al-Mawsū'at*, VII:151–155.
87. Ākhūnd, *Sīyāsat Nāmeh*, 167, 169, 172, 177, 182, 184, 189, 190, 194, 213, 219, and 246.
88. Jurist Leaders wrote, "Today, the world's reasonable people unanimously agree that the necessities of this century are completely different from those of previous centuries. Any state and nation that does not acquire new methods and sciences on building new roads and factories that produce wealth, and fails to foster new sciences and industries, cannot become independent or safeguard its dignity. Maintaining the old methods will result to nothing but decadence and extinction. Thus, reaching these goals is tantamount to protecting '*Bayḍah-e Islam*' and all the efforts made in this regard are parts of the duties that relate to a defensive holy war, which is mandatorily and necessarily incumbent on Muslims. There is nothing more important than this [protecting '*Bayḍah-e Islam*'] in Shari'ah and everyone knows that the infidel states [a reference to colonialist states] have progressed by doing that, and extending their plundering and dominating hand to the sacred Islamic lands" (ibid., 213).

89. Later military aggressions of the colonialist states to invade Iran's territory proved the truth of such apprehensions.
90. Ākhūnd, *Sīyāsat Nāmeh*, 168.
91. Ibid., 197.
92. Ibid., 202–204 (prohibition of illegitimate hold of power by disregarding the people's consent).
93. Ibid., 208 (referring to civil war after demolishing of Majlis and abrogating the constitutional order).
94. Ibid. (inferring that the despot king had the duty to submit to the nation's legitimate demands for reinstatement of Majlis and restoration of the Constitution).
95. Ibid., 204.
96. Ibid., 214.
97. More relying on Anṣārī than other jurists, an *Uṣūlī* jurist has defined the phrase as follows: "the prima facie impart of the agency is the acceptance of an office from the unjust rulers. This means [as a subjective matter] registration of one's name in the unjust ruler's administration, to the effect that, because of this [subjective] registration, the registrant represents and employs the ruler's power in his acts. The representation is forbidden by its essence, thus, accepting office [in the impermissible acts] is prohibited, so is employment of that power" (Al-Iravānī al-Gharavī, *Ḥāshiyat Kitāb al-Makāsib*, I:251).
98. Al-Anṣārī, *Kitāb al-Makāsib*, II:69–71. One of the most cited traditions/reports provides that "prohibited agency from the oppressive ruler is tantamount to assisting him, and thus, committing a capital sin. The sin is capital because under an unjust rule, the right wears off and the wrong revives, oppression and corruption and aggression take hold and God's Books and Verses become nullified, the Prophets are murdered and the mosques are destroyed, and Divine Traditions and Laws change. Therefore, working and assisting and having business with unjust rulers are prohibited with the exception of necessity, like when eating a dead animal's meat becomes permissible under the necessity of survival." This tradition is from the Sixth Imam, Ja'far al-Ṣādiq, first reported in Al-Ḥarrānī (d. fourth century/tenth century), *Tuḥaf al-'Uqūl*, 242.
99. Al-Anṣārī, *Kitāb al-Makāsib*, 70.
100. Ibid., 85–100. Ṣāḥib al-Jawāhir in his *Jawāhir al-Kalām*, VIII:86, claims *ijmā'* (consensus) of the jurists' holdings on the issue.
101. Ṣāḥib al-Jawāhir ascribes this position to Muhammad Mahdī ibn Murtaḍā al-Ṭabāṭabā'ī (d. 1212/1797) to have taken in his *Maṣābīḥ al-Aḥkām* (*Jawāhir al-Kalām*, VIII:83). For the traditions with an all-encompassing prohibition, see Al-Ḥarrānī, *Tuḥaf*, 242; Al-Ḥurr al-'Āmilī, *Waṣā'il al-Shī'a*, XVII:83–86, 177–183, 188–189, 194, some of the earlier jurists' writings on this issue are also introduced in Modarressi, *Kharāj*, 159–160, fns 6, 8, 9, and 10.
102. Ṣāḥib al-Jawāhir, *Jawāhir al-Kalām*, 83.
103. Al-Anṣārī, *Kitāb al-Makāsib*, II:72–84.

104. Anṣārī attributes this opinion to some of jurists, but does not specify them (ibid., 72). The editors of the book have introduced the following two sources where the opinion at issue can be found: Ibn al-Barrāj (d. 481/1088), *Al-Muhadhdhab* (Qum, Iran: Mu'assasat al-Nashr al-Islāmī, 1406/1985), I: 346; and Mahdī al-Narāqī (d. 1244/1828), *Mustanad al-Shī'a fi al-Aḥkām al-Shari'ah* (Qum, Iran: Maktabat Ayatullah Al-Marʿshī, 1405/1984), II:350. Similar reference is made by Ṣāḥib al-Jawāhir, in his *Jawāhir al-Kalām*, VIII:83, to a commentary on al-Ṭabāṭabā'ī's *Maṣābīḥ* written by one of his disciples.
105. Quṭb al-Dīn al-Rāvandī (d. 573/1177), *Fiqh al-Qur'an* (Qum, Iran: Maktabat Ayatullah Marʿashī, 1405/1984), II:24 (referring to the Qur'anic verse 12:55; this citation is from the editors of *Kitāb al-Makāsib*).
106. Al-Anṣārī, *Kitāb al-Makāsib*, II:72.
107. Anṣārī explains that the term "agency" mentioned in the traditions of Imams, by its connotation at the time, meant agency from an unjust ruler (ibid., 73).
108. On the discussion of the legitimacy of land tax during the time of Imam's absence, Modarressi writes: "Those jurists who do not support the faqīh's total succession to the Imam should therefore recognize a kind of legitimacy for just Shīʿī ruler who appeared in the time of the occultation of the Imam." Then, he proposes three interrelated approaches developed in Shīʿī Law for resolving this dilemma. "First, transferability of the Imam's vested right of collecting the land tax revenues to other rulers who have the same function as the Imam. In this specific case, to protect the Shiites from suffering great financial damages, if the unjust ruler did in fact undertake the most important interest of the community. Second, the nature of kharāj is such that it is immaterial who collects it, because the state lands are deposited with the holder of the land and not owned by him. Third, matters such as kharāj fall within the functions of the practical system by which in practice the community is ruled, even if it is unjust and the ruler is a usurper" *(Kharāj*, 161–163). Although I will further analyze the juristic-political implications of Anṣārī's discourse shortly, one can suggest that Anṣārī shows tendencies to different extent to all three approaches in Modarressi's categorization and utilizes them to prove his theory of independent sphere of individual's scope of self-determination.
109. Anṣārī invoked some tradition/reports that are attributed to the Prophet for the correctness of his approach. These reports announce that in Reckoning Day, God will free the rulers who have governed the people by adherence to the Divine Orders, and if governed by aggression, God will punish them by sending them to the hell (al-Ḥurr al-ʿĀmilī, *Wasā'il al-Shī'a*, XVII:189–190). In other reports, attributed to the Imams, good governance is described as "being just to the people, providing people with easy access to the ruler for expressing their needs and grievances, and looking into and accommodating their needs, for all of which God will reward such rulers with the heaven" (ibid., 193).

110. Al-Iravānī, *Ḥāshiyat Kitāb al-Makāsib*, I:252. The latter part of the text, as translated earlier, reads, "*bal yakūn bi nafsihi khārijan min al-adillat takhaṣṣuṣan.*" The author concluded that Anṣārī's claim of consensus and textual validity of the duty and rational proof should be upheld and no counterargument would be acceptable. It is also noticeable that due to general exclusion of common interests from the prohibited acts, next generations of jurists did not discuss the issue in their juridical treatment of "*makāsib al-muḥarrama*" (prohibited gains), i.e., where Anṣārī made his original arguments.
111. Ibid.
112. Al-Anṣārī, *Kitāb al-Makāsib*, II:72–75.
113. Ibid., 75.
114. Ibid., 76–77. Anṣārī cites at length those reports that praise individuals, with similar intention by being God's agents in the aggressive rulers' courts, who educate rulers with sound reasoning and arguments and direct the rulers' policies toward Muslims' interests.
115. Modarressi, *Introduction*, 4.
116. Al-Anṣārī, *Kitāb al-Makāsib*, II:77–84.
117. These results are based on my analysis of, and heavy reliance on, Anṣārī's lengthy arguments.
118. This notion has been established by Shaykh al-Ṭūsī and supported by other *Uṣūlī* jurists, such as Ibn Idrīs and al-Muḥaqqiq, to whom Anṣārī made direct references and quotations (ibid., 77–78).
119. Ibid., 83.
120. Ibid., 79, 80, 81, 82, where Anṣārī referred to the opinions proposed by Shahīd al-Thānī (d. 966/1559), Sabzawārī (1090/1679), and al-Najafī (d. 1266/1850), which were different—in extent and technical context—from, but relevant to, Anṣārī's arguments.
121. Ibid., 83–84.
122. Ibid., 84.
123. Ibid., 80
124. Anṣārī mentioned that determination of the mandate of commanding right is independently proven by the reason "as has been discussed at its place." It is not clear that by mentioning "its place," Anṣārī is referring to the jurisprudential analysis of reason-based proof of the issue in previous jurists' books, or his own writings (ibid., 82). On the "previous jurists' opinions" in Shīʿī law, see Cook, *Commanding Right*, 270–272.
125. Al-Anṣārī, *Kitāb al-Makāsib*, 84.
126. Similar independence can be inferred from the *Uṣūlī* jurists' arguments on the requirement of the Imam's permission for performance of forbidding wrong when it involves violence or levels of violence. Jurists such as al-Murtaḍā, Ibn Idrīs, and ʿAllāma argued that there is no such requirement. Michael Cook reports that ʿAllāma believed when the duty is found to be mandatory by "the good order of the world (*li-maṣāliḥ al-ʿālam*), and so like other goods, is not dependent on any condition" (*Commanding Right*, 268, fn. 105). Thus the fact that it is obligatory for us as was obligatory for the Prophet and the Imams.

127. In chapter 4, I will discuss that such quintessential congruity amounts to the Shiite postulation of the key characteristic of the political power, i.e., "*amānah*" (utmost duty of care based on trusteeship), which is supported by the concept of "*shūrā*" (the duty of consultation with the people) as ordained in the Qur'an and practiced by the Prophet.
128. Al-Anṣārī, *Kitāb al-Makāsib*, II:77–78 (mentioning al-Ṭūsī, *Al-Nihāya*, 356, and Ibn Idrīs, *Al-Sarā'ir*, II:202, citations are from the editors of *Kitāb al-Makāsib*). For more citations on the issue of legitimacy of land-tax collected by an unjust ruler, see Modarressi, *Kharāj*, 160, fn. 9.
129. In fact, Anṣārī had taken a quietist position in the political issues of his time.
130. I will discuss his opinion later.
131. On the importance of the duty of commanding right and forbidding wrong, in addition to Michael Cook, *Commanding Right*, 253–260 (introducing some of the traditions/reports based on which the early Shīʿī jurists developed their theory of the duty), see Muhammad Mahdī al-Narāqī (d. 1209/1794), *Jāmiʿ al-Saʿādāt*, II:44–46 (citing and quoting those traditions that consider the duty as equal to "*al-qiyām bi al-qisṭ*" [rising up for the establishment of justice]). I have to point out that Narāqī (different from his son, Ahmad [d. 1245/1829]), was not an activist jurist. A contrast between these two sources reveals the fact that although Cook was aware of al-Narāqī's book (in fact Cook cites the book at 296–297, fn. 298), he shows a tendency to rebuff the idea that the Shīʿī jurists had a high regard at and invoked activist traditions/reports (ibid., fn. 304, and other places). It is noticeable that this is not the only highly debatable opinion that Cook has rendered in his book. He fails to discuss the ideas of Anṣārī and the constitutionalist jurists, and thus, leaves a huge intellectual gap in his survey. Then, he leaps to the ideas of Ayatullah Khomeini and some unimportant Iranian writers' works published after the 1979 Revolution! Thus, it is not surprising that after finally recognizing the important role of the discourse of commanding right and forbidding wrong in the contemporary Muslims' views on issues such as human rights—and I now can add, constitutionalism—he renders the discourse to be as a "device used to defend Islam against the charge of deficiency" (*Commanding Right*, 532)!?
132. Although my conclusion can be inferred from the constitutionalist jurists' approach to the issue, and not directly from Anṣārī, it is my understanding that it should be perceived as originally derived from Anṣārī. When he argued that the duty is "*wājib kifāyī*," as discussed before, Anṣārī could well be referring to individual rights. This note will be clarified in my later discussion on *ḥisba*.
133. In general, *ḥisbiyya* and *ḥisba* are juristic terms of art that refer to the duty of undertaking legitimate efforts to act on behalf of the third party or public interests where fulfillment of an expedient issue is left unattended.
134. *ʿUrfī* (customary) issues should be viewed in contrast with Shari'ah-based issues. At the time, the division of issues into customary and Shari'ah-related categories was an established linguistic reference to nonreligious and religious issues where every nonreligious one was considered *ʿurfī* or customary.

It was obvious that legal resolution of *shar'ī* or Shari'ah-based issues was, and continues to be, left to the learned jurists. Similar division was employed in Article 71 of the 1907 Constitution, which had required the Shari'ah-related disputes (*umūr-i shar'ī*) to be decided by competent jurists and all other ones (*umūr-i 'urfī*) by nonjurist judges. I will return to this concept in chapter 4.

135. Ākhūnd, *Sīyāsat Nāmeh*, 215. The constitutionalist jurists represented one of the most brilliant legal thoughts in Shī'ī jurisprudence. Calling people to strive for constitutionalism and reinstatement of a fallen parliament and equating it with jihad in a religious fatwa is undoubtedly unprecedented, and serves as an exemplary evidence of the *Uṣūlī* jurist's creativity, dynamism, and comprehensiveness in approaching purely juristic concepts.
136. Because of its relevance to administrative law, and given the longer history of governance in Sunni world, Sunni jurists have dealt with *ḥisba* matters more than Shī'ī jurists. The original text in which *ḥisba*, as a legal-juristic concept, has been used is Māwardī's famous book of *Al-Aḥkām al-Sulṭāniyya*, where he discussed it at a very highly technical level as an equivalent of the duty of commanding right and forbidding wrong, its manifestation in the society, and how it needs to be dealt with by the government (ibid., 299–322). For additional sources as "manuals for the market supervisor" in Sunni Law, see Cook, *Commanding Right*, 154, 315, 331, 368–373. The earliest Shī'ī source in which the term has been introduced as an equivalent of the duty of commanding right seems to be Shahīd al-Awwal (d. 786/1384), *Al-Durūs*, II:45–48. For additional sources in Shī'ī law, see Cook, *Commanding Right*, 296–297, fn. 298. For an historical treatment of the term in Islamic governments, see Talbi et al., "Ḥisba."
137. Al-Qāḍī Abū Ya'lā (d. 458/1065), a famous Ḥanafī jurist also known as Ibn Farrā', has defined the term as "The *Ḥisba* is commanding the right when its omission has appeared and prohibiting the wrong when its commission has appeared" (Al-'Ajam, *Muṣṭalaḥāt*, I:566).
138. In addition to the sources in supra note 137, see Ibn Ikhwah (or Ibn Ukhuwwa; d. 729/1328), a famous Shāfi'ī jurist, *Ma'ālim al-Qurba fī Aḥkām al-Ḥisba*. The whole book includes the author's extensive discussions on the legal and practical duties of muḥtasib (official authority in charge of undertaking the duty, censor, the market inspector); a Persian translation of the book is Ja'far Shu'ār, trans., *Ā'īn-i Shahrdārī dar Qarn-i Haftum* (Tehran: Bungāh-i Tarjuma va Nashr-i Kitāb, 1347sh/1968; the citation is from Muntazirī, *Mabānī*, III:794–795]; in Shāfi'ī Law, see Buckley, trans., *The Book of the Islamic Market Inspector: Niḥāyat al-Rutbah fī Ṭalab al-Ḥisba*.
139. Abu Ḥāmid Muhammad Ghazzālī (d. 505/1111), *Iḥyā' 'Ulūm al-Dīn*, II:701–707. On the importance of Ghazzālī's theory of commanding right in Islamic law, see Cook, *Commanding Right*, 427–468, especially 450–59, where Cook claims Ghazzālī's influence, inter alia, on Ibn Ukhuwwa (ibid., 453), and on Shī'ī jurists (ibid., 455, fn. 192).
140. Ibn Ukhuwwa, *Ma'ālim al-Qurba*, 7–14.
141. Al-Māwardī, *Al-Aḥkām al-Sulṭāniyya*, 300; Ibn Ukhuwwa, *Ma'ālim al-Qurba* (English translation is from the editor). Translation of qaḍā to the

courts of law and maẓālim to the courts of wrongs is from Wafaa H. Wahba, *The Ordinances*, 261.

142. Al-Māwardī, *Al-Aḥkām al-Sulṭāniyya*, 303–308; Ibn Ukhuwwa, *Ma'ālim al-Qurba*, 22–27. Ibn Qayyim Al-Jawziyya distinguished the rights of God and the individuals by three possibilities of compromise, exchange, and forfeiture of rights. If the individual has the legal capacity to subject his right to any of these possibilities, the right is not God's (al-ʿAjam, *Muṣṭalaḥāt*, I:578, citing *I'lām al-Muwaqqi'īn*, I:16, 108). Thus, it is by the sole authority of the individual that a right can be subjected to any of the three possibilities, not the government or others. For an English source on categories of rights, see Vesy-Fitzgerald, "Nature and Sources of the Sharīʿa," 100–112.

143. Al-Māwardī, *Al-Aḥkām al-Sulṭāniyya*, 308–322; Ibn Ukhuwwa, *Ma'ālim al-Qurba*, 27–32. Obviously, the examples given in the text are by no means conclusive, and each category/subcategory in classic or premodern juristic books has been treated extensively with detailed analysis and many more examples.

144. Classic jurists used to discuss the concept of right within different theological and philosophical themes, which they deemed to be intertwined with right. A long list of authorities and sources could be mentioned here. For a comparative analysis of possibility of individual rights in Sunni law with extensive references to different authoritative sources, see Abou El Fadl, "Constitutionalism," 86–92; al-Dirīnī, heavily based on al-Shāṭibī (d. 790/1388) and his doctrine of "*maqāṣid al-Shari'ah*" (objectives of Shari'ah), examines six different sets in which a dialectical relationship between the notion of ijtihād and two concepts of *ḥaqq* (the right) and *'adl* (justice) is established (*Al-Manāhij al-Uṣūliyya*, 20–22).

145. Ibn Ukhuwwa at the opening of his first chapter mentioned, "The *ḥisba* is one of the foundations of the religious affairs, which was implemented from the early period [of the Islamic state] by the persons of the leaders [including the Prophet himself]. With the intention of seeking religious rewards and for the interest of all, through which, when necessary, they commanded the right and prohibited the wrong in order to establish peace and order among the people" (ibid., 7).

146. In their analytical jurisprudence of the concept of *ḥisba*, jurists did not hesitate to consider it as one of God's rights, i.e., a public duty in which an element of worshipping God is embedded. For example, Abī al-Walīd Ibrāhīm, known as Ibn al-Shiḥnah al-Ḥanafī (d.882/1477), discussed on different categories of legal actions where the judge, as a result of his public duty, was required to decide on behalf of an absentee's rights or protect the potential rights of an heir when the number and relationship of the heirs to a deceased were not clear. He found these and many cases of similar nature to include God's rights; see his *Lisān al-Ḥukkām*, 226–231.

147. The processes in which the office of *muḥtasab* demised are yet to be studied in detail. I believe the context of such study should include two distinctive facts: first, the authority to hold the office was vested in caliphs and kings to

nonclerical officials. These appointments were not devoid of political interests of the ruler, and second, popular objections to the way that the duty was performed. Willem Floor offers the negative social status of the *Muḥtasib* in the public's eye because of corruption that had plagued the office as a source of people's rebellion against the office; see his "The Office of Muhtasib in Iran," 61–63. In addition to Talbi et al., "Ḥisba," for more on the sociopolitical history of the office, see Buckley, trans., *Niḥāyat al-Rutbah*, 1–11.

148. Shahīd al-Awwal assigned the title of "Kitāb al-Ḥisba" for the pertinent section of discussions on the duty of commanding right and prohibiting wrong (*Al-Durūs*, II:45–48); Al-Karakī defined it as "a mandatory rising for countering the wrong and supporting the right" (*Jāmi' al-Maqāṣid*, V:373); al-Kāshānī, *Mafātiḥ al-Sharāyi'*; 'Kitāb Mafātīḥ al-Ḥisba wa al-Ḥudūd, II:47–65; al-Qummī, *Jāmi' al-Shatāt*, II:465–466; Gulpāyigānī, *Majma' al-Masā'il*, I: 514–515; cf. Al-Baḥrānī, *Ajwabat al-Masā'il al-Bihbahāniyya*, 66–76 (in a brief discussion intended to prove the jurist's guardianship of the issues related to *ḥisba*, mainly on the basis of similarities between adjudication of legal disputes and the *ḥisba* issues).

149. Historically, the position of "*muḥtasib*" was established in Safavid Dynasty with the title of *Muḥtasib al-Mamālik* (Market Inspector of the Provinces), mostly in charge of regulating the prices of goods, punishment of the violators, and referring the cases to judicial authorities. On this, see Floor and Faghfoory, *Dastur al-Moluk*, 71. Here, my point is that this office was not directly governed by religious authorities. The exact relationship between the office and the religious authority in Qājār Dynasty is not clear, Mansur Sefatgol, "From Dār al-Salṭana," 71–83, but the primary separation of the office from religious authorities seems to hold true in its latter period. Note that one of the causes for the guilds to join the 1905 Revolution was that the governor of Tehran had ordered, without any judicial verdict, public performance of flogging a well-known businessman for seemingly violating market pricing rules.

150. For nonlitigious examples, see al-Qummī, *Jāmi' al-Shatāt*, II:467–468, IV:499–506, 561–565.

151. Ja'farī Langarūdī, *Mabsūṭ*, III:1659–1660; al-Shahrakānī, *Mu'jam al-Muṣṭalaḥāt*, 30–31.

152. A prominent contemporary jurist, with an admonishing tone has said: "To determine a *ḥisba* issue is really difficult and seriously problematic. It is recommended to be cautious and avoid discussing it unless there is a compelling necessity" (Gulpāyigānī, "Al-Hidāya," 793).

153. Khomeini, *Kitāb al-Bay'*, II:459.

154. One of those genius minds is Mīr 'Abd al-Fattāḥ Marāghī (d. 1250/1834), a prominent *Uṣūlī* jurist famous as Mīr Fattāḥ. He enumerated at least thirty-three occasions in which the duty could realize, mostly with litigious nature (*Al-'Anāwīn al-Fiqhiyya*, II:561–562). Previous jurists had claimed an authority for the jurist, as the general deputy of Imam in all those occasions. Mīr Fattāḥ made sophisticated juristic arguments in refutation of such general authority for the jurists in favor of the rational individuals and the most trustworthy of the faithful among Muslims.

155. Mīr Fattāḥ, *Al-'Anāwīn al-Fiqhiyya*, II:562–563.
156. Baḥr al-ʿUlūm, *Bulghat*, III:290; al-Sayyid Riḍā al-Ṣadr, *Al-Ijtihād wa al-Taqlīd*, 403.
157. Al-Ṣadr, *Al-Ijtihād wa al-Taqlīd*; Shams al-Dīn, *Al-Ijtihād wa al-Taqlīd*, 307. Notice the stark similarities between the Shīʿī jurists' definition and the ones suggested by Sunni jurists.
158. Al-Shahrakānī, *Muʿjam al-Muṣṭalaḥāt*, 31; Jaʿfarī Langarūdī, *'Ulūm-i Islāmī*, I:316–325; cf. al-Narāqī, *Jāmiʿ al-Sa'ādāt*, II:47, 49, 50, 51, 53, and 54, using the term generally as the legitimate reaction of a duty-bound Muslim who has sufficient knowledge of the qualifications of wrong acts, and chooses to react and positively impact the wrongdoing individuals so they would not repeat it. The duty-bound individual's act may include admonishment, explicit or hidden expression of repulsion. The author mentions that it is not permissible for a beneficiary of the reaction as well as those who do not have sufficient knowledge to undertake the duty of forbidding wrong.
159. The exact original reads: "*wa hiya al-qurbat al-maqṣūd minhā al-taqarrub ila Allah ta'ālā, wa mawriduhā kullin ma'rūf 'alima irādat nafsi wujūdihi fi al-khārij shar'an min ghayri naẓarin min al-Shāriʿ ila min yūjid dhālik al-ma'rūf*" (*Al-Ijtihād*, 403).
160. Before analyzing the opinions, two caveats are in order: first, the following analysis is based on the Shīʿī School of jurisprudence. Obviously, similar analyses can be developed in Sunni Schools. Second, a much more articulated analysis should entail the philosophical arguments relevant to the broader concept of justice, the role of reason, and jurisprudential debates on the relation between the right and the rule. It is not possible to make such comprehensive analysis for each case at this point.
161. Al-ʿAllāma, *Qawā'id al-Aḥkām*, II:165.
162. Ibid., III:563.
163. Al-Miqdād, *Al-Tanqīḥ*, I:433; similar opinion is held by the majority of jurists such as Al-Najafī, *Jawāhir al-Kalām*, XVII:403.
164. Al-Miqdād, *Al-Tanqīḥ*, II:386.
165. Al-Miqdād, *Al-Tanqīḥ*, II:393–394, ascribing this opinion to Al-Ṣadūq; similar opinion has been held by numerous jurists on legally binding decisions made by *ʿudūl al-mu'minīn* (the most just of the faithful). Notice the similarity with the phrase used by the constitutionalist jurists, i.e., *'uqalā'-i Muslimīn va thiqāt-i mu'minīn* (the reasonable of Muslims and the trustworthy of the faithful people); Baḥr al-ʿUlūm, *Bulghat*, IV:73.
166. Al-Miqdād, *Al-Tanqīḥ*, III:258, ascribing this opinion to Al-Muḥaqqiq.
167. *Ḥudūd* are crimes for which the punishment has been predetermined, and include major offences such as murder, theft, adultery and fornication, rebellion, insult against one's honor, sodomy, and apostasy.
168. Al-Karakī, *Jāmiʿ al-Maqāṣid*, VIII:214; this opinion was rendered in response to some Sunni jurists' opinions on prohibition of representation in *ḥudūd* crimes.
169. Āl ʿUṣfūr, *Al-Anwār*, XIII:10–11.

170. Ibid., 16, 133–135; similar opinion is held by many other jurists, as recent as Sayyid Ahmad Khwānsārī, *Jāmi' al-Madārik*, III:434–435.
171. Ibid., XIV:214; similar opinion has been held by a majority of jurists, such as Baḥr al-'Ulūm, *Bulghat*, I:322, in the case of receiving a gift from the sultan that later is known to be other individual's property. This requires the duty of *ri'āyat maṣlaḥat al-mālik* (observing the owner's exigent proprietary rights) in preventing harm and damage to the owner's property, and calls the possessor *qābiḍ ḥisba* (*ḥisba* holder).
172. Baḥr al-'Ulūm, *Bulghat*, I:346–347.
173. *Mahr* is a mutually agreed amount of money or property that should be paid to the wife at her will before, during, or even after when the marriage is dissolved.
174. Al-Najafī, *Jawāhir al-Kalām*, XXI:304.
175. According to Shari'ah, the wife has a right to receive *nafaqa* (alimony) from her husband as long as she is married and for a specified period after the husband's death or the dissolution of the marriage. In the latter period, the heirs and the executor should honor the wife's right and consider the amount of unpaid alimony as the husband's debt.
176. Al-Najafī, XXXI:388.
177. Ibid., XXXII:291.
178. Ibid., XXI:304.
179. Al-Karakī, *Jāmi' al-Maqāṣid*, VIII:214; "Risāla Ṣalāt al-Jum'a" in *Rasā'il*, I:142, discussed it with reference to "*mā li 'l-nīyāba fihi madkhal*" (what is derivable from and relevant to deputation) and "*mā yakūnu qābilan li 'l-nīyāba*" (what could be subject to deputation); also see Al-Najafī, *Jawāhir al-Kalām*, XVI:155, 173.
180. I will discuss this important issue later in chapter 4.
181. Apparently, there are also theological analyses that are not presented here.
182. Al-Anṣārī, *Kitāb al-Makāsib*, II:125–154.
183. Ibid., 126, 131, 132, 133, 135, and 136.
184. Ibid., 137.
185. Ibid.
186. Ibid., 137–143.
187. Ibid., 140.
188. For example, Qur'an, 3: 104.
189. Shaykh al-Ṭā'ifa Al-Ṭūsī, *Al-Iqtiṣād*, 147; al-'Allāma, *Qawā'id al-Aḥkām*, I:524; al-Shahīd al-Awwal, *Al-Lum'a al-Dimashqiyya*, 84; al-Shahīd al-Thānī, *Rawḍat al-Bahiyya*, II:409; al-Miqdād, *Kanz al-'Irfān*, 210.
190. Al-Qā'inī, "Yanābī' al-Wilāya," 373, 375–376.
191. In Sunni law, see, e.g., al-'Ālim, *Al-Maqāṣid al-'Āmma*; for an English explanation of these five objectives, see Raysuni, *Imam al-Shatibi*, 137–147, and references cited there, both sources are heavily based on Al-Shāṭibī's classic work, *Al-Muwāfaqāt*; in Shī'ī law, see Muntaẓirī, *Risāla-yi Ḥuqūq*; Mūsawī Gharawī, *Mabāni-ye Ḥuqūq dar Islām*.
192. According to Islamic law of wills, it is a mandatory duty of an individual, whose appointment as the executor has been made public in the testament,

to undertake the duty of execution. It is so assumed that the deceased has a continuing right over his properties— only over one-third—that should be honored after death. Two notes are in order. First, Anṣārī argues that although it is individually mandatory for the appointed executor to undertake the duty—thus, according to his theory, all the individually mandated duties are stripped from two characteristics of agency and compensation—it is permissible to compensate such services by the rule discovered from textual and consensual indicators. Second, it is also clear that the institution of executor in Islamic Law, like other legal systems, is related to public order. In other words, a testament has to be honored as an element of public order within which the suborder of an individual's properties is devised by its owner.

193. "A ruling which imposes an obligation directly upon an individual...that is characterized as one of mandatory; encouraged, permissible, discouraged and forbidden" (al-Ṣadr, *Lessons*, 182).
194. According to Islamic law, in addition to a mother's mandatory duty to preserve her newborn baby's life by breast-feeding, she has a corresponding right to be compensated for the act of breast-feeding. The right was originally introduced in Qur'an, 65:6, as one of women's financial rights that should be honored, especially in a divorce case. Anṣārī made it clear that not only is the mother's duty mandatory because of the child's right to life, but it is also one of the necessities of social order (*Kitāb al-Makāsib*, 140).
195. "A ruling which does not impose an individual obligation directly but rather sets up an institution (such as marriage or private property) from which a variety of individual obligations subsequently flow...There is no declaratory ruling which does not involve one or more injunctive rulings" (al-Ṣadr, *Lessons*, 176–177).
196. Al-Anṣārī, *Kitāb al-Makāsib*, 141–142.
197. Baḥr al-ʿUlūm, *Bulghat*, III:290; Al-Shahrakānī, *Muʿjam*, 31; Jaʿfarī Langarūdī, *ʿUlūm-i Islāmī*, I:316–325.
198. Al-Ḥakīm, *Minhāj al-Ṣāliḥīn*, I:489.
199. For more on this, see Abou El Fadl, "A Distinctly Islamic View of Human Rights."
200. In the absence of a constitutionally instituted legislative power it was normal to the premodern jurists to view the issue in a noncodified context. It is noticeable that the following two laws, both related to *ḥisba*, were among the legislatve out-product of Majlis after the reestablishment of order in Iranian society: (1) '*Qānūn-i Taṣdīq-i Inḥiṣār-i Wirāthat*' (Law on Verification of Exclusive Heirs), passed in 1309sh/1930, and (2) '*Qānūn-i Umūr-i Ḥisbī*' (Law on Ḥisba Matters), passed in 1319sh/1940. The latter law mostly included the rules of guardianship of the insane and the minors, the rights and duties of testators, distribution of the deceased's assets among heirs, protection of the deceased's assets before distribution, liquidation of the assets, and some other minor issues. Some of the jurists who had the constitutional authority of overseeing the enactments approved these laws.

201. A traditional custom based on which a fugitive could take refuge in a sacred place or in a powerful person's house until a fair trial was guaranteed.
202. Although sometimes functioning as a useful instrument in the interest of justice, this double-natured practice could easily be abused by criminals and protectors both. On the history and practice of bast-nishīnī during the Qājār period, see ʿAbbās Khāliṣī, *Tārīkhchah-i Bast-Nishīnī*. It is interesting to notice that reform-minded chancellors in nineteenth-century Iran sought to disassociate the legal benefits of the practice from its sociocultural implications when they attempted to establish a structured court system.
203. Among those who have argued against the widespread deputyship in the twentieth century, Ayatullah Abū al-Qāsim al-Khu'ī (d. 1413/1992) is undoubtedly the most important jurist. On his views, see *Al-Ijtihād wa al-Taqlīd*, 256–264; *Mawsū'at*, I:360–363; *Miṣbāḥ al-Fiqāha*, V:53–76. On the other hand, Ayatullah Khomeini's views are perceived as the most prominent, best introduced in *Kitāb al-Bayʿ*, II:615–669.
204. Al-Narāqī, *'Awā'id al-Ayyām*, 536, 581; al-Qā'inī, "Yanābīʿ al-Wilāya," 381–385, very cautiously suggests that in absolute exigent circumstances where the society is on the verge of total disorder, the jurist, as the holder of *ḥisba* authority, should undertake the duty of guardianship of the kings and their ministers; Khomeini, *Kitāb al-Bayʿ*, II:465–466, argues for the jurist's guardianship in general; as a *ḥisba* duty, Gulpāyigānī makes the provision that "it is not improbable if one would say that protection of the properties of those incapacitated individuals who do not have guardians—and the duty of rising up for their interests, which is one of the public duties related to the politics of society and order of the Ummah and preservation of the community, is of certain authorities of the jurists, and it is mandatory to refer these issues to them" ("Al-Hidāyat," 818–819); Hussein Ali Muntaẓerī, *Dirāsāt*, I:572 (this is his previous position, which he repudiated later).
205. Baḥr al-ʿUlūm, *Bulghat*, I:13.
206. Ibid.
207. Ibid., III:211.
208. Ibid., 210.
209. Al-Anṣārī, *Kitābal-Makāsib*, III:559–560; Gulpāyigānī, "Al-Hidāyat," 818.
210. Al-Anṣārī, ibid; Gulpāyigānī, ibid.
211. Al-Anṣārī, *Kitābal-Makāsib*, III:546–548. In this context, the principal right-holder is God who has vested in the infallible persons the authority to protect what is His and how His Law should be implemented.
212. Qur'an, 33:6, which in the pertinent part reads: "The prophet is closer to the faithful than they are themselves."
213. Baḥr al-ʿUlūm, *Bulghat*, III:217–218.
214. Kāshif al-Ghiṭā', *Kashf al-Ghiṭā'*, 394, 395 (he is famously known to have set the principle); al-Narāqī, *'Awā'id al-Ayyām*, 529; Mīr Fattāḥ, *Al-'Anāwīn*, II:561; Ṣāḥib al-Jawāhir, *Jawāhir al-Kalām*, (CD-ROM version) VIII:82; Al-Anṣārī, *Kitābal-Makāsib*, III:546; Baḥr al-ʿUlūm, *Bulghat*, III:214.

215. This maxim as usually referenced in juristic books includes only "*amwālihim*" (belongings). However, as Muḥaqqiq Dāmād reports, jurists are convinced that inexistence of "*anfusihim*" (lives) is due to the jurists' habitual reference to the combination of "*amwālihim wa anfusihim*" in their arguments, and not because they did not believe in the inclusion of "lives" in the original texts (*Qawā'id-i Fiqh*, I:233–234); also see Muhammad Kāẓim Al-Ṭabāṭabā'ī Al-Yazdī, *Ḥāshiya 'alā al-Makāsib*; and Muḥsin Al-Ṭabāṭabā'ī Al-Ḥakīm, *Mustamsik Al-'Urwat al-Wuthqā*, X:17 (citations are from Muḥaqqiq Dāmād).
216. Being based on many Qur'anic verses such as 2:279, 4:5, 6:152, 17:34, 36:71, 57:7, and 70:24, the authors of major books on "*Qawā'id al-Fiqhiyya*" have analyzed this heavily supported maxim. For example, see Āl Kāshif al-Ghiṭā', *Taḥrīr al-Majalla*, I:90; al-Shīrāzī, *Kitāb al-Qawā'id al-Fiqhiyya*, 135; al-Narāqī, *'Awā'id al-Ayyām*, 57; al-Makārim al-Shīrāzī, *Al-Qawā'id al-Fiqhiyya*, II:17; Al-Īrawānī, *Durūs Tamhīdiyya fī al-Qawā'id al-Fiqhiyya* (Beirut: Dār al-Maḥāsin, 1426/2005), 93–113; Shafā'ī, *Majmū'ah-i Qawā'id-i Fiqh*, 120; Muḥaqqiq Dāmād, *Qawā'id-i Fiqh: Bakhsh-i Madanī* (Tehran: SAMT, fifth edition, 1381sh/2002), I:227–234, II:112–131; and many other sources. The text of the maxim can be found in Al-Majlisī, *Biḥār al-Anwār*, II:273; Al-Bayhaqī, *Al-Sunan al-Kubrā*, VI:100; Al-Aḥsā'ī, *'Awālī al-La'ālī*, I:222. (All the citations, except the ones for which I have provided the details here, are from Pazhūhishkadah-i Fiqh va Ḥuqūq, *Ma'khadh-shināsī*, 240). The maxim has also been famous as *qā'idat al-salṭana*.
217. For example, in Shī'ī law the father has a right to preapprove and permit his virgin daughter's marriage. It is legally presumed that father can make a better decision about the interests of his daughter than the daughter can. Accordingly, in cases of disapproval, if the daughter believes that her father's refrain is based on ill premises, she can initiate judicial proceeding and ask for permission from the court.
218. The rule has been cited in two main versions in jurists' writings: "*Al-ḥākimu [or al-sulṭānu] walīyyun man lā walīyyu lah*" (the judge [or the ruler] is the guardian of all for whom no guardian has been appointed). Examples of citation of "*al-ḥākim*" are: Mīr Fattāḥ, *al-'Anāwīn*, II:562, 563; Ṣāḥib al-Riyāḍ, *Riyāḍ al-Masā'il*, VI:404–405. The examples of record by "al-sultan" are: Al-Qā'inī, "Yanābī' al-Wilāyat," 313–386; al-Narāqī, *'Awā'id al-Ayyām*, 534; al-Anṣārī, *Kitāb al-Makāsib*, III:558–559.
219. First version is the one that I have mentioned in the text. In the second version "*al-ḥākim*" and in the third "*al-Imam*" have been registered instead of "*al-sulṭān*."
220. Ṣāḥib al-Riyāḍ, *Riyāḍ al-Masā'il*, VI:405–406, III: 265, defining *al-ḥākim* as "the Just Imam when is available or someone appointed to represent him." In the time of occultation of Imam, the author believes, in general or in specific matters, "a jurist with all the qualifications for issuing fatwa is the Imam's representative."
221. Al-Anṣārī, *Kitāb al-Makāsib*, III:558–559.

222. Al-Narāqī, *'Awā'id al-Ayyām*, 536, 581; Khomeini, *Kitāb al-Bay'*, II:465–466, arguing for the jurist's guardianship in general; Muntazerī, *Dirāsāt*, I:572.
223. Al-Karakī, *Jāmi' al-Maqāṣid*, XI:266; *Rasā'il*, I:142–143; before al-Karakī, Shahīd al-Awwal had mentioned, perhaps for the first time, the concept of general deputyship (*Al-Durūs*, I:246, 262; *Ghāyat al-Murād*, I:164, and other places).
224. Al-Kāshānī, *Mafātīḥ al-Sharāyi'*, II:81, 106, III:179, 186, requires a permission from the infallible Imam for taking the position of judge (III:247), i.e., a specific text for every judicial task that would provide such authority to be vested in a jurist.
225. Ṣāḥib al-Riyāḍ qualifies the status of jurist's deputyship of Imam by "*adillat al-niyāba*" (evidences of agency) in each case. *Riyāḍ al-Masā'il*, VI:405.
226. I will introduce some of them in the following notes.
227. All the sources will be introduced in notes. Ṣāḥib al-Riyāḍ insists that the title of "*faqīh*" belongs to a "*mujtahid*" who has mastered the knowledge of Shari'ah rules. He will be titled as "*mufti*" when he issues a fatwa, which is based on that knowledge. *Riyāḍ al-Masā'il*, IX:235.
228. Al-Ardabīlī makes a compelling case that the jurist's authority is based on the rational faculty required for determination of "*maṣāliḥ al-'āmma*" (best interests of the community) where employing the discretionary authority becomes necessary in preservation of the order of adjudication and society. *Majma' al-Fā'ida*, XII:19.
229. Kāshif al-Ghiṭā' heavily employed the phrase "*ri'āyat maṣlaḥat al-Muslimīn*" (observance of the Muslims' best interest). *Kāshf al-Ghiṭā'*, 343, 357, 394, 398, 399, and 415. Prevalence of references of this nature renders him to have qualified the jurist's authority in adjudication to be applied on the basis of *ḥisba*.
230. Al-'Āmilī, *Miftāḥ al-Karāma*, X:3.
231. In this and the following notes, only general opinions are introduced. Obviously, these jurists held different opinions on the details of each issue, which will be introduced to the best possible extent. There is a consensus among the jurists on the issue of adjudication: Al-Shahīd al-Thānī, *Masālik al-Afhām*, II:384; al-Ardabīlī, *Majma' al-Fā'ida*, VII:546; al-Sabzawārī, *Kifāyat al-Aḥkām*, "Kitāb al-Qaḍā"; al-Kāshānī, *Mafātīḥ al-Sharāyi'*, II:50, III:247; al-Hindī, *Kashf al-Lithām*, II: "Kitāb al- Qaḍā'; Ṣāḥib al-Ḥadā'iq holds, "to the extent that Shari'ah has vested the authority of issuing judicial verdicts" (*Ḥadā'iq al-Nāḍira*, XIII:258, XXIV:411); 'Āmilī holds, "authority of the jurist is to adjudicate only because the jurist is a narrator of the Sunnah." He strictly held that the jurist's complete authority derives from his *ḥisba* discretions on "determination of the parties' interests" (*Miftāḥ al-Karāma*, VI:126, 132); Kāshif al-Ghiṭā' held, "if the execution of punishments was derived from the duty of commanding right and prohibiting wrong, then a non-jurist is also allowed to hold the office of judge" (*Kāshf al-Ghiṭā'*, 408, 420); Ṣāḥib al-Riyāḍ, *Riyāḍ al-Masā'il*, IX:247, 251; Qummī held, "it is a mandatory public duty that

is to be performed by jurist because of his mastery on science and piety" (*Ghanā'im al-Ayyām*, 604).

232. Ibid.
233. The authority of guardianship is limited to those who are unable, to the most part, to practice their proprietary rights, i.e., the interdicted and the absent individuals. In this context, the authority is more or less similar to the ones that a surrogate court judge has. To this extent, the following jurists held opinions that are generally close to each other: Al-Shahīd al-Thānī, *Al-Rawḍat al-Bahiyya*, I:361; al-Ardabīlī considers this to be among the authorities of those jurists who hold the office of judge (*Majma' al-Fā'ida*, IX:230); Sabzawārī held that the acting judge is charged with the duty of providing shelter and care for a lost child who has been found and there is no information about his/her parents (*Kifāyat al-Aḥkām*, "Al-Luqaṭa"); Ṣāḥib al-Ḥadā'iq did not permit the jurist to decide on a minor girl's marriage and considered it to be among the exclusive rights of the Imam (*Ḥadā'iq al-Nāḍira*, XXIII:235); al-'Āmilī held that the authority is not absolute, like the authority that an owner has over his property, it is "*manūṭ bi 'l-ḥāja wa al-maṣlaḥa fa taqaddara bi qadrihā*" (qualified by the existence of need and expedience to the extent that has been allowed; *Miftāḥ al-Karāma*, V:164); Kāshif al-Ghiṭā' limited the authority to those jurists who hold the office of judge (*Kashf al-Ghiṭā'*, 142, 371, 399).
234. Shahīd al-Thānī briefly accepted that such authority can be vested (*Masālik al-Afhām*, I:54; and *Al-Rawḍat al-Bahiyya*, I:182); Ardabīlī allowed authority only on the Imam's share (*Majma' al-Fā'ida*, IV:358); al-Sabzawārī, *Kifāyat*, "Kitāb al-Khums: Al-Maqṣad al-Khāmis"; Ṣāḥib al-Ḥadā'iq considered it as one of the Imam's reserved rights, so he did not agree on the jurist's authority (*Ḥadā'iq al-Nāḍira*, XII:447); Kāshif al-Ghiṭā' only mentioned the rules, not the jurist's authority (*Kashf al-Ghiṭā'*, 339, 342, 343); Ṣāḥib al-Riyāḍ, *Riyāḍ al-Masā'il*, III:320; al-Qummī, *Ghanā'im al-Ayyām*, 384.
235. Shahīd al-Thānī found it recommendatory, not mandatory, to pay the tax to the jurist (*Masālik al-Afhām*, I:48); Ardabīlī found it acceptable only in receiving "*fiṭra*" (a specific alms payable to the people in need at the end of fasting month; *Majma' al-Fā'ida*, IV:285); Ṣāḥib al-Madārik, *Madārik al-Aḥkām*, IV:262; Sabzawārī believed in caution, i.e., limited authority (*Kifāyat*, "Kitāb al-Zakāt: Al-Maqṣad al-Rābi"); Ṣāḥib al-Riyāḍ allowed it only if the tax-payer voluntarily pays to the jurist, and held there is no authority for the jurist to ask for payment (*Riyāḍ al-Masā'il*, III:256, 257); al-Qummī, *Ghanā'im al-Ayyām*, 341.
236. Al-Shahīd al-Thānī, *Al-Rawḍat al-Bahiyya*, I:88; al-Sabzawārī, *Kifāyat*, "Kitāb al-Ṣalāt: Al-Maqṣad al-Thānī"; Hindī considered it as one of the Imam's reserved rights, so he did not agree on the jurist's authority (*Kashf al-Lithām*, I: Mabḥath Ṣalāt al-Jum'a); Ṣāḥib al-Riyāḍ considered it as one of Imam's reserved rights (*Riyāḍ al-Masā'il*, II:431).
237. Shahīd al-Thānī believed in possibility of execution (*Al-Rawḍat al-Bahiyya*, I:225); Ardabīlī believed it is one of the discretionary authorities, so, basically he found it possible to execute the punishments but left it to the jurist

to make the proper decision according to the parties' or the public's interests (*Majma' al-Fā'ida*, VII:546); Sabzawārī did not believe in the possibility of execution, and considered it as one of the Imam's reserved rights (*Kifāyat*, "Kitāb al-Qaḍā"; Al-Faṣl al-Thālith: fi al-tawaṣṣul ila al-ḥaqq'); Hindī believed in the possibility as such, but mentioned that if the punishment is executed in the process of performing the duty of commanding right and forbidding wrong, then it is also permissible for non-mujtahids to execute it (*Kashf al-Lithām*, II: "Kiṭāb al-Ḥudūd"; Kāshif al-Ghiṭā', *Kashf al-Ghiṭā'*, 420); Qummī did not believe in the possibility, and considered it as one of the Imam's reserved rights (*Jāmi' al-Shatāt*, old edition, 764).

238. Almost all of the jurists believed that their authority did not extend to public property such as seas, mines, jungles, and so on, except for "*mīrāth man lā wāritha lah*" (heirless legacy) on which different opinions were rendered. Shahīd al-Thānī on public property: one of the Imam's reserved rights (*Al-Rawḍat al-Bahiyya*, I:139, II:331), unclaimed legacy must be used as the incomes from public properties are expended (*Masālik al-Afhām*, I:54); Ṣāḥib al-Madārik on public property: one of the Imam's reserved rights (*Madārik al-Aḥkām*, V:412–413, 419); al-Sabzawārī on public property: one of the Imam's reserved rights (*Kifāyat*, "Kitāb al-Khums, Tatimmat"), the authority for the jurist over unclaimed legacy derives only from his authority in adjudication ("Kitāb al-Mīrāth, Al-Faṣl al-Rābi"); Ṣāḥib al-Ḥadā'iq, *Ḥadā'iq*, XII:470–480 (one of Imam's reserved rights); Ṣāḥib al-Riyāḍ on public property: one of the Imam's reserved rights (*Riyāḍ al-Masā'il*, III:306–313); Qummī on public property: one of the Imam's reserved rights (*Jāmi' al-Shatāt*, I:208), found authority of mujtahid on unclaimed legacy (*Ghanā'im*, 380).

239. Al-Narāqī, *'Awā'id al-Ayyām*, 529–582.

240. *Al-Kāfī*, I:2, 32; *Biḥār al-Anwār*, II:21, 92; *Wasā'il*, XVIII:53. All citations of endnotes 242–258 on the reports/traditions are from Ali Awasaṭ Nāṭiqī, editor of Narāqī's book.

241. *Al-Kāfī*, I:5, 33.

242. *Al-Faqīh*, IV:302, 905; *Wasā'il*, XVIII:18, 100.

243. *Al-Kāfī*, I:3, 38; *Wasā'il*, II:924.

244. *Al-Kāfī*, I:5, 46.

245. Al-Sha'īrī, *Jāmi' al-Akhbār*, 38.

246. *Fiqh al-Riḍā*, 338.

247. *Al-Iḥtijāj*, II:264.

248. Al-Ṭabrisī, *Majma' al-Bayān*, IX:253; al-Shahīd al-Thānī, *Munyat al-Murīd*, 121.

249. *Kanz al-Fawā'id*, II:33.

250. *Al-Iḥtijāj*, II:283; *Wasā'il*, XVIII:101.

251. *Biḥār al-Anwār*, II:2–3.

252. *Al-Faqīh*, III:1–2; *Al-Kāfī*, VII:4, 412; *Wasā'il*, XVIII:4.

253. *Al-Faqīh*, III:5, 18; *Al-Kāfī*, I:10, 67; *Wasā'il*, XVIII:98.

254. *Tuḥaf al-'Uqūl*, 338.

255. *Al-Faqīh*, III:5, 18; *Al-Kāfī*, I:10, 67; *Wasā'il*, XVIII:98.

256. Al-Ṣadūq, *'Ilal al-Sharāyi'*, 252–254.
257. Al-Narāqī, *'Awā'id al-Ayyām*, 538.
258. Ibid., 539–582.
259. Ibid., 536.
260. Ibid., 537.
261. Narāqī is referring to the content of some of the traditions/reports.
262. Al-Narāqī, *'Awā'id al-Ayyām*, 538–539.
263. Ibid., 582.
264. Ibid., 539. Narāqī wrote: "Now, keep these two general reasoning close to your arguments, and apply them to every sub-issue or on every detail—something that all the jurists have discussed on 'personal issues'—and there is no [further] need to discuss all the types and categories of that kind after you mastered these two reasoning." Narāqī's reference to *"al-masā'il al-shakhṣiyya"* (personal issues) can be translated in two, though very different, ways: (1) if it is translated to "personal issues," then it means the details that every jurist has personally found relevant to the flow of discussion. This is not unusual, but definitely not common, either. (2) The closest term to the phrase is *"al-aḥwāl al-shakhṣiyya,"* which is a well-known technical term for "personal status." This could be a good choice, especially when we note that the majority of areas of authority, except the ones that require consensus, are all related to the personal status of the interdicted individuals. If the latter translation were true, then we should conclude that by the phrase "all social affairs," Narāqī meant the affairs related to the people in need of guardianship and nothing else, something that accords to the jurists' general perception of social affairs, at the time.
265. On Narāqī's close relationship with the royal court, see Hā'irī, *Nakhostīn*, 332–333, 338, 342.
266. In one instance, Narāqī, fed up with the injustices on the people by one of the king's governors, ordered the governor to be dismissed from Kāshān, the city of his residence. The king summoned Narāqī to his court and impeached him angrily. In reaction to the king's anger, Narāqī lifted his hands to the sky and prayed: "Oh God, this oppressor King has appointed yet another oppressor governor, I removed the oppressor governor but now this oppressor King is angry at me." Historians have reported that at this point he attempted to curse the king in his prayers. When the king realized what Narāqī was about to do, he apologetically ran to him, pulled his hands down, and then agreed to appoint a new governor. On the historical report, see Tunukābunī, *Qiṣaṣ al-'Ulamā*, 165. Hā'irī mentions that events of this nature were exceptional in the relation between him and the king, and thus, it is not possible to consider Narāqī as a dissident (*Nakhostīn*, 342).
267. In addition to being a jurist, Narāqī was a poet. By using a demagoguery language that in some occasions gets very close to the colloquial and obscene, he criticizes the corrupt behaviors that people were engaged in in his poems. Although his poems do not have real literary value, it should be counted as yet another aspect of his character. For more on this, see his *Mi'rāj al-Sa'āda*. It is noticeable that Narāqī presented this book to the then Qājār king.

268. Al-Narāqī, *Mi'rāj al-Sa'āda*, 8–10.
269. Narāqī quoted and cited an invalid report from the seventh Imam in which he has said: "You the Shiites, do not bend your necks by disobeying your king, if he is just ask God to maintain his stay in power, and if he is oppressor, appeal to God to guide him, because your benefit is in the benefit of your king, and the king is like a kind father. Wish for him what you wish for yourselves, and do not want for him what you do not want for yourselves" (ibid., 479–480). The same report was also cited by Majlisī, see Chapter 2, note 53.
270. Īzad panāhī, *Ahmad Narāqī*, 68–71. This idea has found good amount of support in Iran after the 1979 Revolution.
271. The original arguments against the jurist's *wilāyah*, on whether or not they have an independent authority to allow individuals in specific circumstances to employ dispositional authority over others' rights or properties, belong to Anṣārī and his strong refutation of Narāqī's discourse on the all-inclusive *wilāyah* of jurist. On this, in general, see al-Anṣārī, *Kitāb al-Makāsib*, III:545–560. Following Anṣārī, Ākhūnd in his *Ḥāshiyat al-Makāsib* (92–96), Nā'īnī in his *Al-Makāsib wa al-Bay'* (II:332–339) and his *Munyat al-Ṭālib* (I:325–329), and Baḥr al-'Ulūm in his *Bulghat* (I:251–252 and other places) discussed the relation between a jurist's *wilāyah* and the notion of possibility of Imam's valid permission during the time of occultation. This line of thought was continued by 'Arāqī in his *Sharḥ Tabṣara* (V:40–41) and others. The citation for 'Arāqī is from Kadīvar, "Andīsha-ye Siyāsī-ye Ākhūnd Khurāsānī," 261.
272. These jurists' arguments are replete with highly technical discussions of the substantive and prima facie impart of the traditions/reports that Narāqī put forward to prove his controversial theory. For the most part, it is based on those technical arguments that Anṣārī and Ākhūnd drew their conclusions from. I am not convinced that without introducing such arguments, it is ever possible to present their opinions properly. The main lines of arguments are adopted from Dāwūd Fīraḥī, "Mabānī-ye Fiqhī-ye Mashrūṭah-Khwāhī az Dīdgāh-i Ākhūnd Khurāsānī." However, all the substantive arguments as well as the citations are mine. A reliable translation of the arguments made by Anṣārī can be found in Abdulaziz Sachedina, *Just Ruler*, 215–229.
273. Al-Anṣārī, *Kitāb al-Makāsib*, III:545–546.
274. Ibid., 548, 551.
275. Anṣārī argued that only the Imam, or anyone who is customarily considered as the holder of political rule, has the authority to render permissions as to specified public affairs. However, he did not find necessary the Imam's, or for that matter the customary ruler's, permission for the majority of public affairs (ibid., 548–551). In other words, he held that only in specified—i.e., where previous jurists have consensus or there is incontrovertible evidence as to its existence—issues such permissions are to be given.
276. Ibid., 553.
277. Ibid., 553–554.

278. This paragraph heavily relies on Fīraḥī, "Mabānī," 200–203.
279. Ākhūnd, *Ḥāshiyat al-Makāsib*, 92.
280. Ibid., 92–93.
281. Ibid.
282. See endnote 253.
283. Ākhūnd discussed the content of the tradition and rejected its inclusiveness, heavily rebutted the idea, and invited his students to deeply analyze this issue. Ibid., 94–95.
284. Ibid., 95
285. On the presumption of nonobligation, see chapter 1.
286. It is necessary to explain this technical juristic concept in further detail: in many judicial cases, a judge or jurist is always in doubt as to whether or not a specific rule is applicable. Every doubt, apparently, has different levels. A judge/jurist may resolve his doubt by reaching some levels of certainty on one or more subissue/s involved in the broader issue at hand. However, he may be unable to establish similar resolution of doubt as to other subissue/s. A limited certainty, obviously, does not provide the necessary level of certainty that would convince the judge/jurist to apply the rule, partially or wholly, to all parts of the issue. In other words, the limited certainty does not extend to other unresolved subissues. Such limited certainty is defined as "*qadr al-mutayaqqin*." Technically, Muslim jurists use this term with the intention of restricting the scope of the rule that they are discussing about, not expanding it. For more elaboration, see Jaʿfarī Langarūdī, *Dānish-nāmah*, V:48–51; *Mabsūṭ*, IV:2882. He cites, inter alia, Ibn Ḥazm, *Al-Iḥkām fī Uṣūl al-Aḥkām*, II:3630, where Ibn Ḥazm has defined the term as "*aqalli mā qīl*" (the least of what can be said; *Dānish-nāmah*, V:51).
287. Ākhūnd, *Ḥāshiyat al-Makāsib*, 95.

4 CONSTITUTIONALIST JURISPRUDENCE

1. "Lāyiḥa-yi Mashrūṭiyyat," Ākhūnd, *Sīyāsat Nāmeh*, 246; Zargarīnezhād, *Rasā'il*, 485–486.
2. The reference to Shari'ah in anti-constitutionalist jurists' opposition to constitutionalism should be viewed as a "legitimate" shield behind which they vehemently attacked every development in establishment of constitutionalism in Iran.
3. Nūrī, "Risālah-i Ḥurmat," 163, 165. Nūrī was undoubtedly the most controversial leader of anti-constitutionalist jurists. At the beginning of the Revolution, he was a prominent jurist figure in the constitutionalist camp but converted to anti-constitutionalist after a power fight with other leaders. Once being a member of First Majlis, he actively pushed for the jurists' oversight over the Majlis's enactments and successfully drafted the famous Article Two of the 1907 Supplement. As long as he continued to sit in Majlis, he enjoyed high respect of all other members even during his several long

leaves to take refuge in one of holy shrines near Tehran in protest against what he claimed to be "deviation from the religious goals of the Revolution." In the early stages of Nūrī's activities, i.e., 1325/1907, Ākhūnd recommended due degree of tolerance and respect to Nūrī (*Sīyāsat Nāmeh*, 176). Kadīvar, the editor of Ākhūnd *Sīyāsat Nāmeh*, refers to a letter of Ākhūnd's in which he has mentioned about a personal friendly letter to Nūrī (ibid.). After Nūrī disregarded all that tolerance and respect and continued his opposition by issuing provocative fatwas and several attempts to trailing people behind his cause, Trite Religious Leaders found him responsible for stirring the social order, firmly banned him from further engagement in Majlis (ibid., 177) and every other social activity (ibid., 178), and issued a fatwa on his exile to the Eastern part of Iran (ibid., 180–181). If what he has written in his "Risālah-i Ḥurmat" is true, Nūrī must have decided to repudiate membership of Majlis after he was told that the term "equality," as incorporated in Article Eight of the 1907 Supplement, was intended to provide equality among all citizens. Apparently, he must have found equality outrageously in conflict with Islamic teachings. Nūrī had always been very close to the king and the royal court, and after abrogation of constitutionalism and bombarding Majlis, praised the despot king for taking the right actions in "protection of Islam." Then, he openly and aggressively fought for reinforcement of the king's power, which he thought was weakened before and during the civil war. He wrote and disseminated declarations and daily journals in support of the king and against the constitutionalists. After the victory of constitutionalists in the civil war, he led several demonstrations against the reestablishment of Majlis and restoration of constitutionalism, which amounted to his accusation regarding criminal charges of betrayal and stirring the social order. Surprisingly, the revolutionary council, sitting as a court, sentenced him to death. He was executed in 1909. The death sentence and execution were certainly extreme reactions that the Najaf Leaders would have never approved of. At the time, there was a rumor about his close ties to the Russian Embassy in Tehran, which was never proven. He was a staunch supporter of wilāyat al-faqīh (jurist's guardianship) and his opinions found a belated but extensive support among some leading jurists of the clerical establishment in the Islamic Republic.

4. Nūrī, Tadhkirat al-Ghāfil, 175.
5. Tabrīzī argued that fear of God is more important than equality (Kashf al-Murād, 137); Nūrī, Tadhkirat al-Ghāfil, 161–162.
6. Nūrī, Risālah-i Ḥurmat, 159–161; Tadhkirat al-Ghāfil, 177, 178, 182.
7. Tabrīzī, Kashf al-Murād, 128. I will explain the anti-constitutionalist jurists' opinions on the concept of equality later in this chapter.
8. Nūrī, Risālah-i Ḥurmat, 154, 166; Tadhkirat al-Ghāfil, 175, 182, 188; Tabrīzī believed that "because of Shari'ah, there is no need to refer to reason" (Kashf al-Murād, 125, 131, 132, 136, and 138).
9. Tabrīzī wrote: "There are unknown treasures of knowledge in Shari'ah that everyone would be surprised" (Kashf al-Murād, 123, 138). "Christian nations do not have such a Scripture that would guide them in the details of civil and political problems, thus, they cling on their reasonable individuals and form

parliament. We [the Shiites] do not need to rely on our disabled reason... and establish Majlis" (ibid., 132), "the foreign laws are laws of pagans" (ibid., 142); Nūrī also wrote: "the idea of constitutionalism derives from secularism and other new isms" (Risālah-i Ḥurmat, 153). "Constitutionalism is tantamount to obedience to Satan" (ibid., 158).

10. Tabrīzī, Kashf al-Murād, 146; Nūrī, Risālah-i Ḥurmat, 158, 166; Tadhkirat al-Ghāfil, 179, 180, 186.
11. Tabrīzī, Kashf al-Murād, 131–132, 136, 138–139, and 143–146; Nūrī, Risālah-i Ḥurmat, 154; Tadhkirat al-Ghāfil, 175–176.
12. Tabrīzī, Kashf al-Murād, 126, 132, 141; Nūrī, Risālah-i Ḥurmat, 158, 166; Tadhkirat al-Ghāfil, 177–178.
13. Tabrīzī, Kashf al-Murād, 134, 136; Nūrī, Risālah-i Ḥurmat, 158, 159, 161, 162, 166; Tadhkirat al-Ghāfil, all the pages, esp. 175, 177–178, 179, 180, 182, 184, and 186. Tabrīzī, however, came close to the idea of a senate-like assembly whose members were from "noble families and jurists" and appointed by the king, which would, with complete compliance with Shari'ah, oversee all the people's and administrators' acts and prevent commission of prohibited ones. Such an assembly's oversight was qualified by two major conditions: full cooperation with the king and following jurists' lead in determination of wrong and right (ibid., 138–139).
14. Tabrīzī wrote: "Since the amount of corruption created by the constitutionalist rule is larger than the despotic rule, thus, by the rule of reason, the despotic rule is more acceptable" (Kashf al-Murād, 121, 127, 140). He also reasoned against the legitimacy of Majlis and the necessity of referring all the legal questions to the jurists by invoking the general rational proposition that an uneducated ignorant should refer to a learned, suggesting that the members of Majlis were either ignorant or uneducated (ibid., 143); Nūrī invoked the religious and rational proof for the duty of seeking justice, discussed that the issue is how one would reach justice, and concluded: by adhering to two bases of "bearing with the religious rules" and "power and might of a king" (Risālah-i Ḥurmat, 163); in another context, he invoked the rationality of belief in the prophecy of Muhammad and impossibility of change in Shari'ah rules because of the time and place concerns, then concluded that Majlis is instituted to change Prophetic rules (Tadhkirat al-Ghāfil, 175). He argued that reason is one of the four sources of law, but rejected the function of reason that is established by the majority of opinions or by determination of the core of Law (ibid., 177).
15. At least, at two occasions, Nā'īnī accused them of using lines of reasoning similar to that of *Akhbārīs*, *Tanbīh al-Ummah*, 74, 76.
16. Nūrī, Risālah-i Ḥurmat, 163–164.
17. Tabrīzī argued that "establishment of Majlis was the cause for weakening the king of Islam" (Kashf al-Murād, 141); Nūrī prayed for the despot king's long and eternal life and throne (Risālah-i Ḥurmat, 167); praised the king's patience in enduring all the assaults against him with unprecedented calmness (Tadhkirat al-Ghāfil, 185); called Majlis "the house of debauchery and infidelity" and "house of infidels" (ibid., 179, 186 and many other places);

objected against the constitutionalists' weakening of the king and praising his bravery for demolishing Majlis (ibid., 185–186); praised the king for destroying the foundation of constitutionalism and explaining it as God's Punishment (ibid.,187); and demanded people to pray and show their gratitude for the termination of constitutionalism and its corruptions (ibid., 188).

18. Article one of The Royal Law of September 9, 1906, on Regulations for the Election to the National Assembly provided: "The electors of the nation in the well-protected realms of Persia in the Provinces and Departments shall be of the following classes: (i) Princes and the Qājār tribe, (ii) Doctors of Divinity and Students, (iii) Nobles and Notables, (iv) Merchants, (v) Landed proprietors and peasants, (vi) Trade-guilds" (Browne, *Persian Revolution*, 355).
19. Tabrīzī argued that "the only valid consensus is the one which is established by jurists, not the consensus of bookseller and greengrocer and grocer and corn chandler and blacksmith" (Kashf al-Murād, 132); Nūrī demeaned the members of parliament and said: "a valid wilāyah, in the time of Imam's occultation is vested only in the jurists, not in grocers and tailors" (Risālah-i Ḥurmat, 154).
20. Nūrī had mentioned that the king has the authority to issue executive orders and proclaim regulations in the administration of public duties (Tadhkirat al-Ghāfil, 176–177).
21. Nā'īnī, *Tanbīh al-Ummah*, 9. The term "*salṭanat*" literally means domination, which in Iranian political literature has always been an equivalent of monarchy. However, Nā'īnī was referring to its general meaning. He suggested more synonyms to possessive/despotic rule that are equally important: *isti'bādiyya*, *i'tisāfiyya*, and *taḥakkumiyya*, meaning, respectively, subjugating, coercive, and authoritarian (ibid.). All of the translations, in this and in subsequent notes, bold and italics as well as phrases in parentheses are mine, unless otherwise stated. As mentioned before, for several reasons, the text is archaic and complicated, and has caused numerous misunderstandings. Such level of sophistication is embedded in the text as its characteristic, to which I had to maintain the loyalty of a translator. In order to represent both the authenticity of the author's style of writing and reasoning and his objectives in using the chosen words and style, I have limited my modifications to minor few ones. However, when necessary I have broken the lengthy sentences so that the text would be as accessible as possible.
22. Ibid., 12. Similar to previous type of rule, Nā'īnī suggested more meaningful synonyms: *muqayyada*, *'ādila*, *mas'ūla*, and *dastūriyya*, meaning, respectively, conditioned, just, accountable, and constitutional (ibid.).
23. Ibid., 10–11, 16.
24. Ibid., 7. Original translation—with minor modifications—is from Sadri in Kurzman, *Modernist Islam*, 118. Notice that "essential constitution of Islam" is offered to translate *bayḍat al-Islam*.
25. See following notes for "Constitution."
26. This is a reference to the general idea—developed in the doctrine of Imāmah—that every non-Imam who holds the power is a usurper of the Imam's exclusive right to rule. The importance of equation between a legitimate rule—i.e., the Imam's—and the usurped rule—i.e., a non-Imam's—is undeniable.

27. This is a reference to Article 32 of the 1907 Supplement Law (the amended Constitution) in which citizens were entitled to send their complaints against any malfunction of the executive, legislative, and judicial agencies to a specific commission in the Majlis, known as the Grievances Commission.
28. Nā'īnī is referring to the human nature's propensity to commit sins, and thus, the human community's loss of enjoyment an entitled, virtuous, rightful, and moral life.
29. Nā'īnī, *Tanbīh al-Ummah*, 11–13.
30. Ibid., 42–43, 51-53.
31. Ibid., 43.
32. Ibid., 43, 47.
33. On more discussions about Sunni doctrine of limitations, see Abou El Fadl, "Constitutionalism," 79–86.
34. Nā'īnī mentions that achieving full implementation of that limitation is secured only by the characteristic of infallibility of an Infallible Imam (*Tanbīh al-Ummah*, 45–46).
35. Ibid., 46.
36. On technicalities of *qadr al-mutayaqqin*, see chapter 3, note 286.
37. Nā'īnī, *Tanbīh al-Ummah*, 46. This paragraph in Nā'īnī's book has caused an understandable confusion among many of his legal and nonlegal interpreters about his final opinion on *wilāyat al-faqīh*. It is unfortunate that many of those who have concluded Nā'īnī is a proponent of jurist's guardianship have failed to notice that in his much more technical arguments on the theory of jurist's guardianship he has denied all-inclusive authority of jurists. It is noticeable that at the end of the paragraph he merely opines on the issue of undertaking the duties, and not exclusive assignment of charge to the jurists. On the one hand, he does not reject the idea of other rational individuals' engagement with the charge and its undertaking. They have also failed to follow his methodology of argument in this text, i.e., technicality embedded in the concept of *qadr al-mutayaqqin*, and the fact that he had viewed both sides' arguments in order to support his opinion by common grounds held between opponents and proponents of jurist's general deputyship. On the other hand, it is an undeniable fact that he decided to write this book with the objective of providing juristic validity for constitutionalism, as manifested in a Constitution where a selected group of unspecified jurists were assigned the duty of balancing Majlis's enactments with Shari'ah in limited constitutional occasions. It is also of utmost importance to notice undeniable facts surrounding his opinion on jurists' duty to employ *wilāyah* on the issues of disorder in society. In a time that Majlis was demolished by the despot king, a civil war was at place to restore it, and prominent constitutionalist jurists such as Ākhūnd had undertaken the charge of leadership duties, it was not unusual for an *Uṣūlī* jurist to invoke the broadest grounds for consensus. Hundreds of inquiries were directed at Ākhūnd, and different layers of the population were seeking after his solutions for the right action to be carried out in the restoration of constitutional order in society. The prevailing presumption, by people and high-ranking members of the fallen Majlis, was that Ākhūnd—due to his

remarkable juristic status at the time—was the sole religious authority who would select those jurists in charge of constitutional balancing duty. I will discuss the occasions of the aforementioned constitutional balance in further detail later in this chapter.

38. Maḥallātī argues that the source of the ruler's *wilāyah*, including that of Imam's, is exactly similar to the *mutawallī* (the executor) of the endowed property (Al-La'ālī, 498). It is important to notice the obvious legal fact that an executor is not the owner of the endowed property. According to Maḥallātī's opinion, Imam also is in charge of protecting the rights of the people, which in turn means that Imam is not the owner of the power to rule. In other words, people are the owner of power.
39. Nā'īnī, *Tanbīh al-Ummah*, 47.
40. In order to elaborate on his opinion on the absence of usurpation of the Imam's exclusive authority in a limited rule, Nā'īnī employed a technical and comparable juristic argument on possibility of *taṭhīr* (purging from impurity, cleanness) of an object that we know is *mutanajjis bi 'l-'araḍ* (sullied by external factors such as an accident). In Nā'īnī's clear words, establishment of jurists' general deputyship from Imam is only possible with regards to technical limitations of "the least certainty." According to juristic rules of physical purity, as long as the stain or dirt is with the object, it is impure unless the stain or dirt is removed. When in doubt as to complete removal of stain, depending on the levels of doubt, the jurist is allowed to issue a fatwa on presumption of either purity or impurity of the object. Nā'īnī used this example to argue that the executor's usurpation of the beneficiaries' rights is a possessive disposition, similar to the impurity of the object. Requiring the executor to abide by the rules that govern the endowed property, prohibiting him from abuse and waste of its profits, and controlling his actions are like removing the source of impurity from the object. Although Nā'īnī did not directly argue the notion of political rule, using similar logic one can infer that usurpation of the Imam's exclusive right to rule is like the impurity with the object, and to impose controlling measures in a limited rule—so it would not transmute to a possessive rule—is like removing the impurity. On the notion of authority in these three cases, Nā'īnī holds that it is the jurist who renders the rule of presumptive purity of the impure object, it is also the beneficiaries, by the verdict of a judge—again the jurist—who constitute the controlling organ over the executor, and based on the jurist's presumptive general deputyship from Imam, he has the power to control over the limited rule. The most important point in the third case is that the Constitution had already established the controlling body. Therefore, by implementation of the balancing oversight of the selected jurists on some of the Majlis's enactments, the notion of usurpation of the Imam's exclusive right was presumed to be removed from the rule. The scope of jurists' authority will certainly depend on the scope of oversight and balance that was proposed in the Constitution.
41. Ibid., 47–49.
42. Ibid., 49–50.
43. Qur'an, 3:159, 42:38.

44. Nā'īnī argued: "The address of the pronoun in this verse is all the ummah, not specific individuals. Its particularization to the rational individuals and members of *ahl al-ḥall wa al-'aqd* is due to *munāsibat ḥukmiyya* (affinity by impart of the injunction) and *qarīna maqāmiyya* (conjunction by the status of the addressee), and not because of *ṣarāḥat lafẓiyya* (definitiveness of the utterance)" (*Tanbīh al-Ummah*, 53).
45. Qur'an, 3:159.
46. Nā'īnī, *Tanbīh al-Ummah*, 53.
47. Ibid., 98–99.
48. Ibid., 53.
49. The Prophet resorted to consultation with his companions or all Muslims, at least in twenty-two occasions that all have been validly recorded in history books. On this, see Abd al-Ali Bāzargān, *Shūrā va Bay'at*, 169–172, and sources cited there. Nā'īnī mentioned one of the most famous one, i.e., the *Uḥud* war, in which the Prophet consulted with Muslim warriors and despite his personal opinion accepted the majority's opinion (Ṭabarī, *Tārīkh*, III:1016; citation from Bāzargān, ibid.).
50. Imam Ali ibn Abū Ṭālib, *Nahj al-Balāgha*, Sermon 216. For details, see the discussions on rights-based doctrine in Shī'ī law, chapter 3.
51. Ibid.
52. Maḥallātī, Al-La'ālī, 498.
53. Supra, chapter 3, discussions of *wilāyah*.
54. The maxim provides, "*Mā lā yudrika kulluh, lā yutrik kulluh*" (if you cannot attain the whole, do not leave the whole). Nā'īnī, *Tanbīh al-Ummah*, 36.
55. In the aftermath of demolishing Majlis and in the midst of the civil war, the despot king was wary about the constitutionalist jurists' leading role in restoration of Majlis and asked for anti-constitutionalist jurists' collective fatwa about constitutionalism. Obviously, they all opined on the illegitimacy and issued a fatwa to that effect. Then, the king wrote a letter to the Trite Religious Leaders and invoked the fatwa for legitimacy of his acts. Ākhūnd rejected the religious validity of the anti-constitutionalist jurists' fatwa and called their reasoning "*ukdhūba-hāyi Ṣiffīnī va ughlūṭa-hāyi jadīd*" (lies similar to those spread during the *Ṣiffīn* Battle in Imam Ali's reign and new captious questions) (Ākhūnd, *Sīyāsat Nāmeh*, 192 [king's letter], 213 [Ākhūnd's response]).
56. Ibid., 212.
57. Ibid., 214–215.
58. Using a reverse address in yet another rejection of just-sultanate discourse, Nā'īnī admonished the anti-constitutionalist jurists—who had condemned Majlis as anti-Islamic. He wrote, "It is regretful that we the worshipers of oppressor rulers of the age and conveyors of the despotism's religious branch have been so ignorant about the proofs in the Qur'an, Sunnah, Shari'ah rules, and the conduct of our Prophet and Imam! Instead of saying that this Consultative Assembly is *hādhā biḍā'atunā raddat ilaynā* (that is all what we have in our disposal to pass [or offer]), we rule it out as anti-Islam. It is as if we have not even read the all-apparent verse in Qur'an, which was just mentioned

[3:159], or have not understood its content, or because of its conflict with our own desires and tyranny, we have revived the story told in Qur'an [2:101]" (*Tanbīh al-Ummah*, 56, 83). The said verse reads, "When a messenger was sent to them by God affirming the Books they had already received, some of them put [His message] behind their backs as if they had no knowledge of it."

59. Ibid.
60. Ibid., 59–60, 83; Ākhūnd, *Sīyāsat Nāmeh*, 214–215.
61. In his book, Nā'īnī extensively engaged with "abhorred tyranny's sources of power" and the ways of controlling and eradicating them. According to him, those sources were: public ignorance, religious despotism, royalism and devotion to kings, division of nation, persecution and torture of freedom fighters, the rich and powerful class's innate propensity to condemned cause of despotism and normalization of oppression and tyranny, and using police power to suppress the nation. In retrospect, the ways of curing people's failures and rooting out despotism were tolerance for their ignorance by providing them with the means of incremental progress toward awareness and enlightenment, education and practice of commanding right and forbidding wrong, and establishment of political parties with the objective of national unity and practice of constitutional rights to freedom of expression and press (ibid., 105–137).
62. By typical positivist approach, I mean applying a juristic methodology that exclusively seeks a textual evidence for the proof of validity, like the type of approach that *ahl al-ḥadīth* or *Akhbārī*s had taken.
63. As discussed before, in chapter 1, the *Uṣūlī* doctrine on reason was based on the correlation between the religious rules and law of reason, on one hand, and the retrospective relation between speculative intelligence and practical reason, on the other. All the arguments made there are relevant to the constitutionalist jurists' conception of "substitution of infallibility."
64. Maḥallātī wrote: "There has been a divinely ordained set of rights—for the collective community of Muslims in Islamic nations—for which a variety of benefits and detriments have been devised. Imam is *naẓẓām-i kull wa jāmi'-i shatāt* (general organizer of the order of things and point of reference in conflicts) and has absolute *wilāyah* to determine those rights in an Islamic state, to relay them to the whole community of people, and to implement them properly" (Al-La'ālī, 498–499). Therefore, the rights were embedded in Shari'ah and Imams were originally assigned to protect, and not to limit, them.
65. Maḥallātī wrote: "Now that it has become clear that all the general aspects of civilization and the interests of the nation belong to people, and one should refer to them for proof or rejection of those aspects and national interests, then it is imperative that people elect their trustees. The elected trustees are point of reference to determine the interests and detriments of society, and to relegate their enactments—for implementation—to the ruler. Therefore, the elected people are the rational determining power—similar to speculative intelligence—of the community, and the executive branch is its practical reason and practical power" (ibid., 497).
66. For the references, see chapter 3, Rights-Based Doctrine.

67. It should be noticed here that the entire constitutionalist jurists' writings in defense of constitutionalism were written after the Constitution had been adopted. So, they did not attempt to suggest a platform for or a draft of constitution. In fact, they not only considered the 1907 Constitution as sufficiently fulfilling and promising, but also avidly defended its legitimacy against the anti-constitutionalist jurists' attacks and declarations on its illegitimacy and opposition to religion. Therefore, their writings should be perceived as tools for interpreting the 1907 Constitution.
68. In his short time of reign, Imam Ali encountered different kinds of opposition raised by the so-called companions who undermined legitimacy of his egalitarian rule and demanded special political privileges and economic advantages. Not acquiescing to such demands, Ali had to face numerous civil wars between him and different groups of them. In the last war, Ali had to fight with Umayyad leaders who had seized the governorship of Syria and attempted to take the office of caliphate. During the war, when the Umayyad army found itself on the verge of defeat, they used tricks and asked for arbitration where a binding Qur'anic solution could be determined. At first, Ali did not agree to such arbitration but was coerced to accept it after the majority of the Muslim soldiers pressed for the arbitration. *Khawārij* were a group of ultra-extremist Muslims in Imam Ali's army who first pushed for arbitration, but after the Umayyad arbitrator cheated, turned against Ali and claimed that the rule of Qur'an cannot be subject to arbitration! For more on the dynamics of discussion between Ali and *Khawārij*, see Abou El Fadl, "Constitutionalism," 75–76.
69. *Tanbīh al-Ummah*, 74, 76.
70. Ibid., 74–75.
71. Also see Enayat, *Modern Islamic Political Thought*, 170.
72. Ākhūnd and Māzandarānī, two of the Trite Religious Leaders wrote letters of approval, in a very strong fashion, of all the content and conclusions made in both *Tanbīh al-Ummah* and Al-La'ālī, which were published along with the books in 1327/1909. Tihrānī, the third of the Leaders, had passed away at the time.
73. *Tanbīh al-Ummah*, 64, 75.
74. Ibid., 14, 57–58.
75. Ibid., 70–71. I will discuss later that in the constitutionalist jurists' mind, all the legislature's enactments were supposed to be measured by the standard of "absence of conflict with Shari'ah" and not by "accordance or compatibility" with it.
76. Ibid., 69. This is not the only place where Nā'īnī approved that all the citizens, regardless of any religious affiliation, have the right to enjoy equality in rights. He later mentioned that the right to participate in consultation is universal and includes "non-Islamic groups" too, and every religious minority should have their representative in Majlis (ibid., 89).
77. Maḥallātī, Al-La'ālī, 511.
78. *Tanbīh al-Ummah*, 12, 15, 16, 56, 58, and 59. I will discuss later that by Shari'ah rules, Nā'īnī and other constitutionalist jurists meant the general

immutable rules, and not the laws that deal with everyday activities and needs.

79. While Nā'īnī did not enumerate the rules to be incorporated in the text of Constitution, he mentioned them throughout his book. Therefore, the following are my version of those rules.
80. *Tanbīh al-Ummah*, 12, 15, 59. Undoubtedly, Nā'īnī is the first Iranian jurist who has made general references to something that in modern theory is known as vertical control.
81. Maḥallātī, Al-La'ālī, 502–513. It is noticeable that Maḥallātī first discussed them as general duties of the state—that have been subject to the absolute power of Qājār despot kings' abuse for a long time. In a constitutionalist state those duties, he argued and concluded, should be incorporated in the text of Constitution along with the legislative authority of Majlis to enact relevant detailed laws.
82. Translation is from Browne, *Persian Revolution*, 374. The phrase "*qawānīn dawlatī*" (state laws) was incorrectly translated by Brown to "laws."
83. The anti-constitutionalist jurists did not categorize their analyses. The following five hypotheses are based on my reading of their opinions. I have already discussed the theological roots of their opinions. On the hypotheses, see Tabrīzī, Kashf al-Murād, 133, 136; Nūrī, Risālah-i Ḥurmat, 154, 158, 160–162, 166; Tadhkirat al-Ghāfil, 176–178.
84. Nūrī wrote: "Our law is Islam, which thanks to God has been preserved and categorized, generation after generation, by *ruwāt akhbār* (the narrators of reports), *muḥaddithīn* (collectors of Traditions), and *Mujtahidīn* (jurists), and is being preserved now by many of its *ḥafaẓa* (can be translated as protectors or those who memorize)" (Risālah-i Ḥurmat, 152).
85. Nūrī, Tadhkirat al-Ghāfil, 175, 176; for similar language in Akhbārī sources, see Al-Astarābādī, *Al-Fawā'id al-Madanīyya*, 75, 98, 104, 277.
86. Tabrīzī , Kashf al-Murād, 136.
87. Nā'īnī called the anti-constitutionalists' discussions "*ṣūrat-i qabīḥa*" (ugly face) and "*mughāliṭa mughriḍāna*" (malevolent sophistry), and their opposition to equality, which was based on those traditional rules of Shari'ah "*khud namāyī*" (show off) (*Tanbīh al-Ummah*, 70, 71). He referred to Tabrīzī's arguments as "*hafawāt ḥimliyya az jahala wa mutanassikīn-i Tabriz*" (loaded with mistakes from the illiterate and pretenders to piety of the city of Tabriz) (ibid., 77).
88. On the constitutionalist jurists' defense of equality and its direct relevance to the concept of rule of law, see Nā'īnī, ibid., 68–71; Maḥallātī, Al-La'ālī, 518–519. For a similar conflict between "abstract principles of certain unalienable rights" and "legal traditions in British Common law" where commitment to equality of rights was subject to serious constitutional challenges in favor of traditional rules in the nineteenth century America, see Sullivan, *Constitutional Context: Women and Rights Discourse in Nineteenth Century America*.
89. At the time, only Ākhūnd was universally recognized to have such high religious rank and caliber. Also see later discussions on compliance to Shari'ah.

90. *Tanbīh al-Ummah*, 87–89.
91. Ibid., 89.
92. Ibid., 70–71.
93. Reference to geographical regions is a habitual statement of jurists when they discuss the Imam's open-handedness. It usually connotes "as far as the Imam's power is extended" or "wherever the open-handedness is available."
94. *Tanbīh al-Ummah*, 98.
95. The issue of finality or nonfinality of jurists' opinions is an important topic in Islamic law, which mainly revolves around presumption of validity of a juristic finding.
96. My argument includes a part of the debates between the two groups, which mostly revolved around the impact of the deceased jurists' opinions on the broader issue of *ijmāʿ* (consensus) among the jurists. Al-Astarabādī, the so-called founder of the new *Akhbārī* School, had originally rejected the division of individuals into *Mujtahid*s and *Muqallid*s (followers), but later generations of *Akhbārī*s repudiated this overall rejection and accepted the institution of *Mujtahid*. They, later, rejected the impermissibility of following a deceased *Mujtahid*. On the main arguments and reasoning of both sides, see al-Amīn, *Dā'irat al-Maʿārif*, II:218–220; for the *Uṣūlī*s' arguments, see Anṣārī's opinions in al-Kalāntarī, *Maṭāriḥ al-Anẓār*, II:431–454; Ākhūnd, *Kifāya*, 476–480; for *Akhbārī*s' arguments, see al-Astarabādī, *Al-Fawā'id al-Madanīyyah*, 149, 263; al-Jazā'irī, *Manbaʿ al-Ḥayāt fi Ḥujjīyyati Qawl al-Mujtahidīn min al-Amwāt*, in Ṣifatgul, *Sākhtār*, 576.
97. See chapter 3, note 187 and the accompanying text.
98. Al-Shahīd Al-Thānī, *Ḥāshiyat*, 304; *Masālik al-Afhām*, III:9.
99. Due to historical and political reasons, such open-handedness did not materialize in the Shiite history except in Imam Ali's caliphate. Consequently, in order to maintain physical existence of the Shiites, many of the succeeding Imams adopted *taqīyya* (dissimulation) in their political reactions to the Umayyad and Abbasid rulers. There is an extensive body of literature on the details of dissimulation, as an undoubtedly important subject in Shīʿī history and jurisprudence. For example, see al-Bihbahānī, *Maṣābīḥ al-Ẓalām*, III:353; al-Khu'ī, *Miṣbāḥ al-Fiqāha*, I:449, 453.
100. Depending on the jurists' analysis of the concept, they have rendered opinions as to a variety of issues. For example, some argued that in the time of absence of Imam and when in doubt as to the possibility of issuing permission, it is impermissible to undertake implementation of all duties that are specifically devised for Imam (Baḥr al-ʿUlūm, *Bulghat*, I:226); Narāqī mentioned the opinion of those jurists who believed performance of Friday Prayer was not mandatory in the absence of an Imam who has the power of administration (*Mustanad al-Shīʿa*, VI:13); ʿArāqī strongly considered "*basṭ al-yad*" as a conclusive condition for the validity of permission rendered in favor of jurist and the claim of any deputyship from the Imam (*Sharḥ Tabṣarat*, IV:325); Hamadānī opined that in the absence of the power of administration for a jurist to spend the land-tax on its religiously required expenses, he does not have authority for collecting those taxes (*Ḥāshiyat*, 323); Qummī held that

due to absence of "*basṭ al-yad*," a jurist is neither allowed to execute predetermined punishments, nor render judgments to that effect (*Jāmiʿ al-Shatāt*, 764); for similar reasons, Ṣāḥib al-Riyāḍ held that it is permissible for a jurist to receive alms paid voluntarily by alms-payer, otherwise the jurist has no genuine authority to demand payment (*Riyāḍ al-Masāʾil*, III:256, 257); for more relevant arguments on this with regard to why al-Karakī did not agree with individually mandatory duty of performance of Friday Prayer and held it optionally mandatory, see chapter 2.

101. In numerous instances, Ākhūnd invoked such original authority. He wrote: "Since the public have united around the cause of constitutionalism and establishment of Majlis, it is mandatory for the king to concede and to support their demand" (*Sīyāsat Nāmeh*, 167); "in the time of occultation of the Hidden Imam, political power belongs to the public of Muslims" (ibid., 204); "in the time of occultation, undertaking of all the customary and *ḥisba* issues is vested in the reasonable and reliable individuals among Muslims" (ibid., 215); "all the national wealth belongs to the people" (ibid., 216); "people have an original right to elect their representatives" (ibid., 247); "in any constitutionalist nation, the ownership of authority in all affairs belongs to people '*bi al-aṣāla wa bi al-istiḥqāq*'(as both principals and by entitlement; ibid., 288); "the essence and truth of electing representatives of House of Consultation [Majlis], is in the placement of authority—owned by being the principal holder or by rightful acquisition—of people to the representatives for the limited time of their tenure (ibid.); "the honor and purity of the religion and the motherland is in reliance in and protection of the people's human national and religious rights" (ibid., 292).
102. In a letter, dated January 11, 1909, to the International Court of Justice at The Hague (on rejecting the validity of the despot king's agreement with the Russian Empire to loan a huge amount of money with devastating usury interest in absence of Majlis's constitutional approval), Ākhūnd and Māzandarānī wrote: "There has been a long history of Iranians' crusade for restitution of their natural and God-Given liberty from the despot rulers... they succeeded to win their natural rights from the monarch in the last year of Muẓaffar al-Dīn Shah's rule, and established a constitutional order instead of the previous despotic one... now that the present despot king has voided all the national sensitivities to the degree of extinction... we as the religious leaders of the nation find it necessary to let the civilized world know that since the people have been coerced by deprivation from their parliament and abrogation of their Constitution, the king's agreement is not approved by Iranians and they will not accept its legality" (ibid., 197).
103. *Tanbīh al-Ummah*, 98.
104. Ibid.
105. Ibid., 101.
106. Ibid.
107. Ibid.
108. Ibid., 98; emphasis added.

109. On text-based rules and the process by which they were combined and perceived with *dalā'il 'aqlī* (rational arguments or proofs), see chapter 1.
110. According to Ṭabāṭabā'ī, the most notable contemporary Shī'ī commentator of the Qur'an, the Qur'anic rules are generally about the protection of human's life, such as necessity of progeny and marriage, shelter, food, and so on, and obedience to God. For him, all those rules are based on and in complete harmony with the creation of human being, and thus, there is no conflict between them and the human being's natural appeals to God. *Islam wa Insān-i Mu'āṣir*, 36–46.
111. For example, recommending marriage with slaves at 4:25, or inviting Jews and Christians to refer their legal disputes to Muslim judges who are required to decide justly at 5:42–43.
112. For example, on prohibition of infanticide because of poverty or the infant's gender at 81:8-9, 16: 59, 17:31, 6:151, or intercalating at 9:37, or requiring the spouses to choose their arbitrators when in marital disputes instead of arbitrary divorce at 4:35.
113. For example, the question of remarriage of the Prophet's wives after his death at 33:52–53, or prohibiting men from calling their wives "mother," which was a demeaning behavior of men against women at 58:2.
114. For example, in cases of illness or unavailability of water or being in travel, the individual is allowed to perform ablution with sand, instead of water at 5:6.
115. For example, verse 22:78 says: "He has chosen you and laid no hardship on you in the way of faith," or verse 5:6 declares, "God does not wish to impose any hardship on you," and verse 2:185 sets out that "God wishes ease and not hardship for you."
116. Verse 2:286 reads: "God does not burden a soul beyond capacity. Each will enjoy what good he earns, as indeed will suffer from the wrong he does," which has been invoked extensively by Muslim jurists for the validity of presumption of nonobligation; see chapter 1.
117. See chapter 1.
118. For example, the mandate of veil for women was an after-the-fact issue that was revealed in 5/626, making it questionable whether the rule of Qur'an, 14:31, is one of the rules that were originally mandatory, or subject to historical contingencies, or subject to gradual development of Islamic society.
119. *Tanbīh al-Ummah*, 98–99, 53.
120. Mishkīnī, *Iṣṭilāḥāt al-Uṣūl*, 232–233.
121. Ibid.
122. There are other arguments that a jurist should make to render a valid opinion on the nature and implications of the text. For a list of typical arguments that are made in a book of *Uṣūl al-Fiqh*, see al-Ṣadr, *Lessons*, 54–119, 137–144; on the balancing and preferring factors, see Abou El Fadl, *Speaking*, 40–47.
123. On the differences between sovereignty and guidance commands, see chapter 1.
124. See arguments in chapter 1.
125. *Tanbīh al-Ummah*, 98.

126. Ākhūnd, *Sīyāsat Nāmeh*, 217.
127. It should be reminded that *Uṣūlī*s believe the great majority of what has been attributed to the Prophet and Imams lack a valid chain of transmission and, thus, have limited scope of applicability.
128. See chapter 1.
129. This is one of the most complicated and technical arguments in Islamic law. Therefore, I will only introduce some of the main lines of arguments as proposed by Shīʿī jurists in a simplified fashion. For a general argument in Shīʿī jurisprudence, see Mishkīnī, *Iṣṭilāḥāt al-Uṣūl*, 98–101; for an authoritative Shīʿī opinion, see Ākhūnd, *Kifāyat al-Uṣūl*, 468–470; for commentary on Ākhūnd's holdings, see al-Fīrūzābādī, *'Ināyat al-Uṣūl*, VI:193–199; and al-Shīrāzī, *Al-Wuṣūl ilā Kifāyat al-Uṣūl*, V:410–416; for a more technical argument in English, see Abou El Fadl, *Speaking*, 145–161.
130. *Fawā'id al-Uṣūl*, III:150.
131. Other examples are fasting, special taxes, or prohibitions on consuming wine, usury, insult, and backbiting.
132. Like the text of the Qur'an or *akhbār mutawātir* (the traditions/reports that are transmitted by a reliable chain of transmitters whose veracity and trustworthiness are admitted and approved by the jurists, and reach their source of utterance, i.e., the Prophet or the infallible Imam).
133. Other examples are: *bayyina* (testimony of two just witnesses) as evidence in proof of legal issues such as marriage or ownership or crimes, *'amāra taṣarruf aw yad* (the fact of one's possession of an object), *sūq al-Muslimīn* (the customs of Muslims' market) like *'amāra tadhkiyya* (presumption of cleanliness of the merchandise), and so on.
134. On procedural principles, see chapter 1, note 91.
135. Al-Muẓaffar, *Uṣūl*, II:38–41.
136. Ibid.
137. Ibid., 33–36.
138. Ibid.
139. See chapter 1, note 55.
140. *Tanbīh al-Ummah*, 79.
141. As introduced before, Ākhūnd, as the "jurist who had the dispositive authority in determination of rules of Shari'ah" had already made comparative analysis between the ways constitutionalism was perceived in the other nations and its characteristics with Iranian case. See supra note 1.
142. Nā'īnī, *Tanbīh al-Ummah*, 7.
143. Ibid., 59.
144. Muḥsin Kadīvar, a well-known Iranian prominent scholar, has suggested that by making reference to "characteristic of *wilāyah* aspect" of constitutionalism in Iran and the permission of a jurist with dispositive authority, Nā'īnī intended to facile the establishment and legitimacy of the legislative authority of Majlis through general permission of such jurist. In other words, rather than pushing for a systematic supervision of the special committee on the enactments, Kadīvar continues, Nā'īnī insisted on the jurist's dispositive authority whose general permission to Majlis on enacting laws would

accommodate the requirement of *wilāyah*. On this, see Muḥsin Kadīvar, "Sharʿ-i Shurāye Nigahbān dar muqābil-i Majlis," in http://www.kadivar.com/Index.asp?DocId=410&AC=1&AF=1&ASB=1&AGM=1&AL=1&DT=dtv (last visited November 15, 2008). In my opinion, this opinion gains its strength from two sets of facts. First, at the time, Ākhūnd was the highest ranking jurist with dispositive authority, had already heavily supported Majlis, and Nā'īnī would certainly have considered this fact in his opinions. Second, the validity of the dual juristic resolutions that Nā'īnī offered for meeting the requirements of constitutionalism.

145. Maḥallātī, Al-Laʿālī, 542.
146. Ibid., 542–543.
147. Ākhūnd, *Sīyāsat Nāmeh*, 247, 248, 259.
148. In one of their letters, Ākhūnd and Māzandarānī declared that defending the homeland was Muslims' "*waẓīfah musallam qānūnī* (unfailing legal duty)" (ibid., 294). It should be noticed that Religious Leaders, based on the religious nature of the act of defense of *bayḍah-i Islām* (homeland of Islam), had previously issued fatwas and mandated such defense as a religious duty. Reference to "legal" instead of "religious" mandate of the duty is a clear evidence of the Religious Leaders' belief in legitimacy of laws enacted by Majlis, to the extent of their equal validity with religious rules.
149. In addition to Article 2, see Articles 4, 72, 85, 96, 112, and 165 of both the 1979 and the 1989 Constitutions of the Islamic Republic of Iran.
150. For that matter, the Shīʿī jurists have used the following terms: *talaqqī* (acquisition [with radiant clarity] by revelation, which has exclusively been used for the Prophet Muhammad); *akhdh bi taʿlīm al-Rasūl aw bi ilhām min Allah* (reception by the Prophet's teachings or by inspiration from God, exclusively been used for the infallible Imams), and *istinbāṭ al-aḥkām min al-ʿumūmāt* (discovery of rules from general sources [i.e., the Qur'an and Sunnah], which has been used only for mujtahids/jurists), Al-ʿAllāma, *Mabādi al-Wuṣūl*, 240–241. According to Shīʿī doctrine of *ijtihād*, neither the Prophet nor the infallible Imams practiced *ijtihād*. In the context of my discussion, it is the last term, i.e., *istinbāṭ* (discovery), that bears the technicality, not *tashkhīṣ* (determination). For the preservation of these distinctions in the Shīʿī juristic tradition, see, e.g., al-Bihbahānī, "Risālat al-Ijtihād wa al-'Akhbār" in *Al-Rasā'il*, 15–16; Ākhūnd, *Kifāya*, 463; Muhammad Bāqir Al-Ṣadr, *Al-Fatāwā al-Wāḍiḥa*, 103; *Al-Maʿālim*, 28–35.
151. The proscription in the second qualification is laid on the subject of a condition, which is inherently prohibited by Shari'ah, e.g., purchase or sale of alcoholic beverages. In the fourth one, however, the discussion revolves around the subjects that are not inherently prohibited but their conditionality or validity as a contractual condition is against the Shari'ah, e.g., conditioning a tenant's "absolute responsibility" for the damages, including the defective premises repairing of which is within the landlord's obligations.
152. Al-Anṣārī, *Kitāb al-Makāsib*, VI:25; emphasis added.

153. Generally being part of an important Prophetic tradition, which states that "the faithful are obligated to their [mutually agreed] conditions," this report is from Imam Ali who said: "Thus, Muslims are obligated to their conditions except the ones that permit what is forbidden or forbid what is permitted" (ibid., VI:12, 22–23).
154. The second tradition cited by Anṣārī (ibid., 26) is from Ibn Zahra according to which the Prophet has said: "As long as the Qur'an or Sunnah has not prevented a condition, its conditioning among Muslims is permissible" (*Ghunyat al-Nuzū'*, II:215).
155. Al-Anṣārī, *Kitāb al-Makāsib*, VI:26.
156. Ibid., 26-27. The titles of the rules are mine.
157. These are two major titles, recognized by the Text itself, which transform the main injunctions imparted from the general rules to one that can even completely oppose them. Like the rule for performance of daily prayers, which is mandatory, but if the individual is sick or under duress or necessity or other mitigating circumstances, the rule may transform to delay or even forbiddance. The first general rules are known as "*Aḥkām Awwalīyya*" (Primary Injunctions) and the second ones are "*Aḥkām Thānawīyya*" (Secondary Injunctions). Both prominent Shī'ī and Sunni jurists have extensively studied the issue of categorization of rules in Islamic law mostly in *Uṣūl al-fiqh* works. For a Shī'ī terminological definition, see al-Shahrakānī, *Mu'jam*, 30; on the importance of the issue in the concept of *ijtihād* in a contemporary Shī'ī context, see Shams al-Dīn, *al-Ijtihād wa al-Taqlīd*, 156–157, 171; in Sunni context, see generally al-Shāṭibī, *Al-Muwāfaqāt*, III:138–141.
158. Al-Anṣārī, *al-Makāsib*, VI:29, 31.
159. Ibid., 32. The apparent impart of the utterance will prevent coming to existence of doubt and subsequent reference to the procedural or practical principles.
160. Ibid., 31.
161. Ibid. It should be noticed that such presumption, like any other practical principles, does not necessarily get the jurist to the true rule.
162. Ibid., 35.
163. Ibid. Notice that there are specific recognized circumstances in Shari'ah during which, in a restricted scope, such transition of permitted acts to forbiddance is allowed. Those circumstances are father's command, binding oaths, and solemn pledges, which are all legally capable of forbidding a permitted act temporarily. For example, one can take an oath to limit eating meat to once in a week or ban it for a limited period of time. However, he is not allowed to ban it forever, because no one can change the nature of what God has originally rendered permitted.
164. Anṣārī mentioned specific traditions as such external indicators (Ibid., 36).
165. Ibid., 37.
166. It should be mentioned that there certainly were some disagreements on the details of the arguments that Anṣārī introduced to the field. However, his general ideas were mostly accepted. What I have introduced in my presentation of the theory are those general lines of thought and methodological

conclusions. The following four are among the most famous commentaries on Anṣārī's *Kitāb al-Makāsib* in which the methodology of Anṣārī has been widely accepted: Ākhūnd, *Ḥāshiya 'alā al-Makāsi*, 237–241; Nā'īnī, *Munyat al-Ṭālib*, II:103–111; al-Īrawānī, *Ḥāshiya Kitāb al-Makāsib*, III:272–284; al-Kumpānī (d. 1361/1942), *Ḥāshiya Kitāb al-Makāsib*, V:125–153.

167. Al-Ḥakīm, *Minhāj al-Ṣāliḥīn*, II:59-60; al-Tabrīzī, *Ḥidāyat al-Ṭālib*, V:86–116; Khomeini, *Kitāb al-Bay'*, V:153, 157–158; al-Khu'ī, *Al-Shurūṭ*, I:103–113. It is also noticeable that the Islamic Republic's Constitution has adopted the methodology of absence of conflict (Articles 72, 91, and 96), but it is debatable whether or not the Guardian Council has correctly applied it in all occasions.
168. This was especially important because the mid-Qājār rule's strong tendency to mysticism and Sufism had plagued the relationship between the kings and jurists, and to that effect, the kings and the people.
169. The historical facts are mostly introduced in Muhammad Turkamān, "Hay'at-i Mujtahidīn: Dawrah-i Duwwum"; "Hay'at-i Mujtahidīn: Duwwum tā Shishum."
170. See Articles 43, 45, 46 of the Fundamental Law, 1906.
171. Turkamān, "Hay'at-i Mujtahidīn: Dawrah-i Duwwum," II:17–18; Ākhūnd, *Sīyāsat Nāmeh*, 248–249.
172. Turkamān, "Hay'at-i Mujtahidīn: Dawrah-i Duwwum," II:19–20.
173. Ibid., II:22–23; Ākhūnd, *Sīyāsat Nāmeh*, 259–261. Majlis heavily, and to some extent unduly, procrastinated selection of the jurists, which caused irreparable damages to the normal process of implementation of Article Two. Bihbahānī, as one of the most famous jurist leaders of the 1905 Revolution in Tehran, topped the list and his selection by consensus was one certainly expected result. However, an anarchist, whose affiliation to the Democrat Party was strongly rumored, assassinated him on June 16, 1910. The Democrat Party was one of the main political parties with a strong faction in Majlis.
174. Turkamān, "Hay'at-i Mujtahidīn: Dawrah-i Duwwum," II:33–34.
175. According to Article 27 Majlis was the interpreter of Constitution.
176. Turkamān, "Hay'at-i Mujtahidīn: Dawrah-i Duwwum , II:33. Ākhūnd and Māzandarānī believed "majority of the votes or drawing lot" were two different methods, and the term "consensus" was to be interpreted as "majority of votes" (ibid., II:20–21; Ākhūnd, *Sīyāsat Nāmeh*, 249). This was a wise advice that if taken would prevent resorting to lot for such an important decision.
177. Majlis finally selected the jurists on August 13, 1910 (Turkamān, "Hay'at-i Mujtahidīn: Dawrah-i Duwwum," II:27-39). Interestingly, Maḥallātī had slightly less than the majority of the votes in three of four ballots, but he was not among the ones chosen by lot.
178. From five selected jurists, one was already a member of Majlis, three of them had to join Majlis from which one passed away shortly (January 1, 1911), and remaining two regretted and sent their letters of resignation to Majlis (September 1 and November 8, 1910). Three substitute jurists were selected (on September 3 and November 11, 1910, and January 25, 1911) from which

two informed Majlis of their delay due to personal concerns (September 21, 1910, February 14, 1911), and the third regretted (January 16, 1911). The recurrent selection of the substitute jurists raised the issue of whether or not a list with less than twenty names met the constitutional thresholds. After hot debates, Majlis opined on the constitutionality and selected the substitute jurists (ibid., II:39–48). It should be noticed that the tenure of Majlis was due to end on December 20, 1911, but it was closed down one month earlier than this date.

179. Although resolving historical questions of fact is not what I have attempted to undertake here, the issue of mutual failure of the selected jurists who did not call for the duty, and a Majlis that did not vigorously demand their cooperation cannot be explained without careful attention to the following facts: (A) Jurists, (1) the atmosphere of terror and execution against jurists in Tehran: in an unfair trial without hearing, Nūrī was sentenced to death and executed on July 31, 1909; Bihbahānī was assassinated on June 16, 1910; jurists were heavily insulted in daily journals and government, formed mainly from previous regime's authorities, intentionally disregarded its duty to control them. Not only jurists as high ranking as Nā'īnī were subject to the journalistic attacks, but also Ṭabāṭabā'ī, one of the two jurist-leaders of the Revolution in Tehran, resigned from further involvement and refrained from running for Majlis in protest against such abuse of freedom of press. A very upset Ākhūnd sent a letter to the prime minister and strongly complained about the government's actions on opening gamble houses and bars, and inaction against publication of anti-Islamic articles in newspapers (*Sīyāsat Nāmeh*, 254); (2) absence of a structured organization by which the authority of leading jurists, i.e., Ākhūnd and Māzandarānī, could be employed; (3) independence of jurists in acceptance or rejection of their selection. (B) Majlis, (1) British and Russian Empires unduly issued political ultimatums and military threats (October 1910–November 1911); (2) a failed coup by a former king, which was heavily supported by the Russian Empire (July–August 1911); (3) prime minister, backed by the Russian military might and British Empire's political support, carried out a successful coup (December 1911) through which most important northern cities of Iran were bombarded and occupied by Russian troops; (4) some members of Majlis, especially Taqīzādeh, then controversial leader of the Democrat Party, led terrorist operations against the officials and did not hesitate to make every effort to delay or postpone or even ban formation of the special committee and other constitutional duties of Majlis. Ākhūnd and Māzandarānī wrote a letter to Majlis to the effect that their efforts to admonish Taqīzādeh so he would change his course of actions had been futile, and declared his disqualification of being a member of Majlis (ibid., 257–259). Taqīzādeh was later expelled from Majlis, and left the country immediately. According to Mīrzā Ṣāliḥ, election of Taqīzādeh, as the representative of Tabriz, was tainted and suspicious of fraud at the first place (*Buḥrān-i Dimukrāsī*, 15–18).

180. On the rise of Reza Khan to power in Iran, see, e.g., Katouzian, *State and Society in Iran*, especially 214–342.

181. Turkamān, "Hay'at-i Mujtahidīn: Dawrah-i Duwwum," II:57–58; Zerang, *Taḥawwul*, I:218.
182. According to the 1907 Constitution, this issue was in original jurisdiction of members of Majlis.
183. Letter dated March 6, 1910; Ākhūnd, *Sīyāsat Nāmeh*, 260–261.
184. In a letter to Majlis published on April 4, 1911, religious leaders made a clear reference to the two (ibid., 282–283).
185. For a descriptive report of the justice system and long-standing failures of judicial reform in Iran in the time period of my discussion, though with some minor discrepancies with the facts, see Floor, "Change and Development."
186. Letter to Majlis published on April 4, 1911 ; Ākhūnd, *Sīyāsat Nāmeh*, 282.
187. Dealing with this issue requires an in-depth historical analysis of the jurists' role in adjudication. In general, it is an undisputed fact that jurists, to different degree, have been called to take on judicial offices throughout Islamic history, either by the caliphs/rulers or by the people. As discussed in chapter 2, however, an efficient judicial structure was obviously dependent on the state and on whether or not it was capable of providing and maintaining an orderly system and organization of justice. There was also a nonstate judgeship in place in Iran during the Qājār rule in which jurists were subject to the disputant parties' reference and call for judgment at a local level. Although only high-ranking jurists with established authority in knowledge were subject to the individuals' trust and payment of religious taxes and dues, referring to local jurists for adjudication was mostly out of need for resolution of disputes in a type of social order that did not accommodate that legitimate demand. High-status jurists, mostly involved in education, were located in religious intellectual centers—the most famous of which were in cities such as Najaf, Samarra, and Karbala in the Iraq of today. The students after graduation, mostly in the form of obtaining *ijāza* (permission) from their professors, would usually go back to their hometowns and begin to educate the faithful. Depending on the local jurists' piety and knowledge, and the degree of their favorable reception in small societies—itself being subject to personal contacts with people and the big names from whom they had obtained their credentials and for whom they were commissioned to collect religious taxes—their popularity and number of trusting followers varied. Such a faith-based cycle in a disordered system of justice where the people would not find reliable source of fairness and rule of law functioned relatively well in resolving the disputes, with different verdicts from one jurist to the other. However, there were two major problems in this process: distance in knowledge between the local jurists and the followers, and, potentiality of the adjudicating jurist's abuse of trust and the resulting power. As long as the jurist's piety and knowledge was a reflection of the followers' legitimate need to rule-based fair judgments, the trust element was maintained. To the most part, the jurist was in charge of a sustained trust by a high level of moral care and faithful adherence to rationality and justice embedded in the Qur'an and Sunnah. At a practical level, however, the high-ranking jurists had no power to control the local jurist-judges, especially if the latter were

able to find a way to attach to the state power. For more on the role of jurists in adjudication, see Kazemi, *Religious Authority*; Litvak, *Shi'i Scholars*.

188. This seems to be the regular course of action conventionally adopted by Majlis. According to one report, after discussion in the pertinent commissions the drafts were sent to the selected jurists for review, and then proposed to floor debates. The report is about the position of "*mudda'ī al-'umūm*" (prosecutor), which was suggested and added to the draft after the selected jurists' review (Turkamān, "Hay'at-i Mujtahidīn: Dawrah-i Duwwum," II:48–49).
189. Turkamān reports that one of the members referred to the objection of Mīrzā Zayn al-'Ābidīn Qummī (one of the three attending selected jurists who died shortly after his selection) to an issue during the floor debates, which resulted in consequent accommodative enactment of the law (ibid., II:48).
190. Mudarris, a disciple of Ākhūnd and Muhammad Kāẓim Yazdī (d.1337/1919), was a prominent jurist. After the dissolution of Qājār (1925)—itself being a controversial event in Iranian history—Mudarris heavily opposed Reza Shah, the new king and eponym of Pahlavi monarchy, who was installed and strongly supported by the British government from his early days of rise to power as an army general. After stabilizing his power, Reza Shah ordered the exile of Mudarris in 1928 to one of the least developed cities of Iran, and then his assassination in 1937.
191. Zerang, *Taḥawwul*, I:184–186, 188, 204, 217, 218, 219, and 367.
192. Kasravi, *Constitutional History*, especially 86-97. It is equally important to know that the social discontent against the justice system was also in part due to the corruption of jurist-judges, with different ranks, who practiced in either state-sponsored courts or independent ones.
193. On this see Floor, "The Secular Judicial System," 9–60.
194. On this important fact in any analysis of the long-standing duality of court system in Iran, see Ādamīyyat, *Amir Kabir*, especially 307–317; *Andīshe-ye Taraqqī*, especially 170–189.
195. Ādamīyyat and Nāṭiq, *Afkār-i Ijtimā'ī*, 375–376; Ettehadied (Nezam Mafi), "The Council for the Investigation of Grievances."
196. Ādamīyyat and Nāṭiq, *Afkār-i Ijtimā'ī*, 395, 406.
197. Ibid., 375–377, 396.
198. Ibid., 392.
199. Ādamīyyat and Nāṭiq have reported some of those margins where the king had cursed the grieving individuals because they suggested reform. The authors have also published excerpts of the letters where they mention of the local authorities' total disregard to king's orders, to the extent that even the king himself complained about those recalcitrant authorities (ibid., 378, 385, 411–413).
200. Arbitrary taxing, coercive collection of overtaxed dues, making farmers leave their lands and houses for indefinite time, murder, bribing the king's inspectors by arranging for debauched parties, threatening people from complaining, and so on. Ibid: 378–379, 380–381, 382, 383, 384, 387, 389, 391, and 396–399.

201. Disregarding the people's objections against overtaxing, depriving people from their traditional occupations and making the arrangements for their own relatives to take the jobs (ibid., 382–383); overtaxing, objection against taxing based on false reports (ibid., 385); violation of the farmers' rights (ibid., 383); (overtaxing and assault against women, asking for payment of the census expenses from people, asking for the soldiers' expenses (ibid., 386, 380, 383); overtaxing, robbery and assault against farmers (ibid., 387); undue authorization of unauthorized individuals to collect taxes (ibid., 388); overtaxing, destruction and plundering the farmers' harvest in their absence (ibid., 389); overtaxing and chaining farmers' representatives (ibid., 390); requiring people to pay same taxes for several times, coercing them to pay illegal fines (ibid., 398); constant intrusion to farmers' houses in the state of drunkenness, coercing the female residents to dance, sending old women to citizens' parties to spy on beautiful women and then kidnapping them by police and raping them (ibid., 408–409); and so on.
202. Ibid., 381–382, 398; requesting exemption because of reduction in the harvest (ibid., 382–384); requesting exemption because of famine (ibid., 391).
203. Sending fake telegraphs about the citizens' satisfaction of the local authorities to the central government (ibid., 390); the telegraph center's chief sent several false reports in order to obtain the proper order from the central government, such as unduly heavy taxes levied against the specific individuals whose wealth or properties were subject to his greed (ibid., 391); the chief of telegraph center demanded and collected undue fines (ibid., 395); the chief of the telegraph center refraining from sending people's messages and complaining telegraphs to the central government (ibid., 395–396); objection to the authorities' decisions on water rights (ibid., 397–398); police chiefs' abuse of power in collection of extra taxes (ibid., 399–400).
204. Ibid., 406.
205. Complaint about the abusive manner of the Russian authority as the director of the Costumes Office in North of Iran, which its income was mortgaged to repay the loan borrowed from Russia for the King's expenses in his travels to Europe (ibid., 402); abuse of power of British authority as the director of Costumes Office in South of Iran, which was similarly mortgaged for repayment of loans borrowed to pay the damages of nullification of concessions made to British traders (ibid., 403).
206. Ibid., 404–405.
207. Foreigners' ownership of lands in Iran has always been illegal. The complaint was about Russian subjects' possession of the lands that were registered in their names, which was in conflict with the Iranian owners' established title on the same land (ibid., 384–385).
208. Ibid., 399–400.
209. A graphic report of destruction and change of the once populated regions of Semnān and Dāmaghān (two cities in the south of Tehran) into uninhabitable places when the citizens emigrated and left their houses and belongings behind because of the governors' oppression can be found at ibid., 388–389. Another report about the plundering of farmers' and businessmen's

properties and merchandise by local authorities, the police's inability to secure the social order, and the post office's delays or inactions in delivering the central government's orders to local authorities, and so on can also be found at ibid., 391–392.

210. The first draft of the law on judicial organization did not mention the Shari'ah courts as if they were not supposed to be established. Mudarris strongly rejected the draft in floor. The draft was about to fail completely until some members of both Majlis and the ministry of justice tried to save the draft's life and reconcile Mudarris and Mushīr al-Dawlah, who finally compromised on eight articles—for the establishment of Shari'ah courts—proposed by Mudarris. On this, see the quotation cited from Justice Muḥsin Ṣadr, in Zerang, *Taḥawwul*, I:205.
211. This law, originally named "Temporary Law of Criminal Procedure" including 556 articles, was among the laws whose ratification process took place after the Second Majlis was closed down in November 1911. Since the legislative process of this law had only been completed in the first review of its draft in Majlis and was stopped at article 171 in the second review, the ministry of justice, due to importance of the law, approved that a semi-legislative commission continue the process. Mudarris was appointed as one of the members of that commission. Third Majlis later in July 1915 ratified the law.
212. See Floor, "The Secular Judicial System," 9–60; Schneider, "Religious and State Jurisdiction"; cf. Mohammadi, *Judicial Reform and Reorganization*, 43–54.
213. Many of the famous jurists have written about the concept of adjudication in one way or another. Thus, it is virtually impossible to cite all of them in an endnote. For an authoritative *Uṣūlī* example, see al-Anṣārī, *Al-Qaḍā' wa al-Shahādāt.*
214. Zerang, *Taḥawwul*, I:265. Author correctly believes that the problem of lack of precedent in jurists' adjudication was minor. Historians, in general, agree that jurists' practice of adjudication was rule-based, legitimate, and much more systematic than the state-sponsored "justice system" (Ādamīyyat, *Amir Kabir*, 358-359; *Andīshe-ye Taraqqī*, 189–190).
215. A reliable and critical analysis of the clerical adjudication is yet to be made. For some cases of local jurists' abuse, see Ādamīyyat and Nāṭiq, *Afkār*, 410, 411; Ādamīyyat, *Amir Kabir*, 358-359; *Andīshe-ye Taraqqī*, 189–190; Floor, "Change and Development," especially 131–133, and sources mentioned there.
216. Articles 417, 421, 425, referenced in Zerang, *Taḥawwul*, I:169–170.
217. Article 421, quoted in Zerang, ibid., 209.
218. Zerang cites a book of collected criminal students dated 1931 but fails to provide further explanation (ibid., 209). However, the crimes were categorized by their punishments in the following way: small fines and up to six months of imprisonment for petty offences; imprisonment for six months up to two years for misdemeanors; any punishment higher than two years of imprisonment for felonies.
219. Persian text is from ibid., 206.

220. Ibid.
221. This directive was issued on December 15, 1909. It should be mentioned that commercial courts had already been established prior to the 1905 Revolution. Persian text is from ibid., 204.
222. The amendment was passed in June 1923. Persian text is from ibid., 207–208.
223. This is another subject of research for which a thorough legal-juristic analysis is yet to be made. For some historical facts and social analysis, see Ettehadieh (Nezam Mafi), *Majlis va Intikhābāt.*
224. Persian text is quoted in ibid., 152.
225. Ibid., 152–153.
226. While putting emphasis on the essential importance of correct selection of representatives for Majlis, Ākhūnd and Māzandarānī heavily recommended people to elect those who are competently trustworthy, and prohibited any failure because of the lack of due diligence by electing "individuals accused of evil thoughts and those who were mindless about religion" (Ākhūnd, *Sīyāsat Nāmeh*, 288). In a separate letter, Ākhūnd mentioned that careful election of right-minded individuals with right tendencies to and capable of protecting the religion and nation is more important than selecting leaders of prayer in Islam and following a nonsuitable one. He also reminded people about their responsibility towards choosing the right members, for which no one else would be held accountable. Ibid., 289–290.
227. The law was passed in October 1911; Ettehadieh, *Majlis va Intikhābāt*, 152.
228. The committee on drafting the Civil Code appointed eight well-known jurists of Tehran—as members—to participate in the arguments and for drafting the articles of the first volume, which included more than two-thirds of the Code. Zerang, *Taḥawwul*, I:383–386.

Bibliography

Arabic and Persian Sources

ʿAbd al-Bāqī, Muhammad Fu'ād, *Al-Muʿjam al-Mufahras li Alfāẓ al-Qur'ān al-Karīm bi Ḥāshiyat al-Muṣḥaf al-Sharīf* (Qum, Iran: Intishārāt Islāmiyya, 6th edition, 1384sh/2005)

Abī al-Walīd, Ibrāhīm, known as Ibn al-Shiḥnah al-Ḥanafī (d. 882/1477), *Lisān al-Ḥukkām fī Maʿrifat al-Aḥkām*, published together with Ali Ibn Khalīl al-Ṭarābulusī (d. 843/1440), *Muʿīn al- Ḥukkām fīmā Yataraddadu bayn al-Khaṣmayn min al-Aḥkām* (Cairo: Muṣṭafā al-Bābī al-Ḥalabī, 1973)

Ādamīyyat, Fereydūn (d. 1387sh/2008), *Amīr Kabīr va Iran* (Tehran: Khwārazmī, 8th edition, 1378sh/1999)

———, *Andīshah-i Taraqqī va Ḥukūmat-i Qānūn:ʿAṣr-i Sipahsālār* (Tehran: Khwārazmī, 3rd edition, 1385sh/2006)

———, *Fikr-i Āzādī va Muqaddamah-i Nahḍat-i Mashrūṭīyyat* (Tehran: Intishārāt Sukhan, 1340sh/1961)

———, *Shūrish bar Imtiyāz-nāmah-i Rizhī: Taḥlīlī Siyāsī* (Tehran: Payām, 1360sh/1981)

Ādamīyyat, Fereydūn (d. 1387sh/2008) and Homā Nāṭiq, *Afkār-i Ijtimāʿī va Siyāsī va Iqtiṣādī dar Āthār-i Muntashir-nashudah-i Dawrān-i Qājār* (Tehran: Intisharat-i Agah, originally published in 1345sh/1975, renewed edition by Nima Books in Germany, n.p., n.d.)

Āl ʿUṣfūr (d. 1216/1801), *Al-Anwār al-Lawāmiʿ fī Sharḥ Mafātīḥ al-Sharāyiʿ* (in *Jāmiʿ Fiqh Ahl al-Bayt*, Qum, Iran: Computer Research Center of Islamic Sciences, CD-ROM version, 2005)

al-Aḥmadī, Ali ibn Hussain Ali, *Makātīb al-Rasūl* (Beirut: Dār al-Muhājir, n.d.)

al-ʿAjam, Rafīq, *Mawsūʿat Muṣṭalaḥāt Uṣūl al-Fiqh ʿind al-Muslimīn* (Beirut: Maktabat Lubnān Nāshirūn, 1998)

al-ʿĀlim, Yūsuf Ḥāmid, *Al-Maqāṣid al-ʿĀmma li ʻl-Shariʻah al-Islāmiyya* (Brentwood, MD: The International Institute of Islamic Thought, 1412/1991)

al-ʿĀmilī, Bahā' al-Dīn, *Zubdat al-Uṣūl maʿa Ḥawāshī al-Muṣannif ʿalayhā*, edited by Ali Jabbār Golbāghī Māsūlah (Qum, Iran: Intishārāt Dār al-Bashar, 1383sh/2005)

al-ʿĀmilī, Jawād (d. 1226/1811), *Miftāḥ al-Karāma*, (in *Jāmiʿ Fiqh Ahl al-Bayt*, Qum, Iran: Computer Research Center of Islamic Sciences, CD-ROM version, 2005)

al-ʿĀmilī, Muhammad ibn Ḥasan al-Ḥurr, *Tafṣīlu Wasāʾil al-Shīʿa ilā Taḥṣīl al-Shariʿah*, edited by Jawād al-Shahrastānī (Beirut: Muʾassasat Āl al-Bayt li Iḥyāʾ al-Turāth, 1424/2003, 2nd edition)
al-Amīn, Hassan, *Dāʾirat al-Maʿārif al-Islāmiyyat al-Shīʿa* (Beirut: Dār al-Taʿāruf li ʿl-Maṭbūʿāt, 1415/1995)
al-Anṣārī, Sheikh al-Murtaḍā (d. 1281/1864), *Al-Ḥāshīya ʿalā Istiṣḥāb al-Qawānīn*, edited by a group of researchers (Qum, Iran: Bāqirī, 1415h/1994)
———, *Al-Qaḍāʾ wa al-Shahādāt* (Qum, Iran: Majmaʿ al-Fikr al-Islāmī, 1426/2005)
———, *Farāʾid al-Uṣūl* (Beirut: Muʾassasat al-Aʿlamī li al-Maṭbūʿāt, 1411/1991)
———, *Kitāb al-Makāsib*, edited by a group of scholars (Qum, Iran: Majmaʿ al-Fikr al-Islāmī, 1420/1999)
al-ʿArāqī, Ḍiyāʾ al-Dīn (d. 1361/1942), *Maqālāt al-Uṣūl* (Qum, Iran: Majmaʿ al-Fikr al-Islāmī, 1423/2003)
———, *Sharḥ Tabṣarat al-Mutaʿallimīn* (in *Jāmiʿ Fiqh Ahl al-Bayt*, Qum, Iran: Computer Research Center of Islamic Sciences, CD-ROM version, 2005)
al-Ardabīlī, al-Muqaddas (d. 993/1585), *Majmaʿ al-Fāʾida wa al-Burhān* (in *Jāmiʿ Fiqh Ahl al-Bayt*, Qum, Iran: Computer Research Center of Islamic Sciences, CD-ROM version, 2005)
al-Asad Ābādī, Al-Qāḍī Abi al-Hassan ʿAbd al-Jabbār, *Al-Mughnī fi Abwāb al-Tawḥīd wa al-ʿAdl* (originally published by a group of scholars in Cairo, Egypt, 1963; reprint in Lebanon, n.d.)
al-Astarābādī, Muhammad Amīn , *Al-Fawāʾid al-Madanīyya,* edited by Raḥmat Allah Raḥmatī Arākī (Qum, Iran: Muʾassasat al-Nashr al-Islāmī, 1426/2005)
al-Baḥrānī, al-Muḥaddith (d. 1186/1772), *Ajwabat al-Masāʾil al-Bihbahāniyya*, (in *Jāmiʿ Fiqh Ahl al-Bayt*, Qum, Iran: Computer Research Center of Islamic Sciences, CD-ROM version, 2005)
al-Bihbahānī, al-Waḥīd (d. 1205/1791), *Al-Fawāʾid al-Ḥāʾirīyyah* (Qum, Iran: Majmaʿ al-Fikr al-Islāmī, 1424h/2003)
———, *Al-Rasāʾil al-Uṣūlīyya*, edited by Muhammad Yathribī al-Kāshānī (Qum, Iran: Muʾassasat al-Bihbahānī, 1416/1995)
———, *Maṣābīḥ al-Ẓalām*, (in *Jāmiʿ Fiqh Ahl al-Bayt*, Qum, Iran: Computer Research Center of Islamic Sciences, CD-ROM version, 2005)
al-Bujnūrdī, Hassan (d. 1395/1975), *Al-Qawāʿid al-Fiqhiyya* (in *Jāmiʿ Fiqh Ahl al-Bayt*, Qum, Iran: Computer Research Center of Islamic Sciences, CD-ROM version, 2005)
al-Dirīnī, Fatḥī, *Al-Manāhij al-Uṣūliyya fi al-Ijtihād bi al-Raʾy fi al-Tashrīʿ al-Islāmī* (Damascus: Dār al-Rashīd, 1396/1976, 1st edition)
al-Fīrūzābādī (d. 1410/1989), *ʿInāyat al-Uṣūl fi Sharḥ Kifāyat al-Uṣūl* (in *Jāmiʿ Fiqh Ahl al-Bayt*, Qum, Iran: Computer Research Center of Islamic Sciences, CD-ROM version, 2005)
al-Gharāwī, Muhammad ʿAbd al-Ḥusayn Muḥsin, *Maṣādir al-Istinbāṭ bayn al-Uṣūliyyīn wa al-Akhbāriyyīn* (Qum, Iran: Markaz al-Nashr-Maktab al-Aʿlām al-Islāmī, 1413/1992)

al-Ghazālī, Abu Ḥāmid Muhammad (d. 505/1111), *Iḥyā' 'Ulūm al-Dīn*, translated to Persian by Mu'ayyid al-Dīn Muhammad Khwārazmī in 620/1223, edited by Hussein Khadīv Jam (Tehran: Intishārāt 'Ilmī va Farhangī, 4th edition, 1376sh/1997)
al-Ḥakīm, Muhammad Taqī, *Al-Uṣūl al-'Āmma li al-Fiqh al-Muqāran: Madkhalun ilā Dirāsat al-Fiqh al-Muqāran* (Beirut: al-Mu'assasat al-Duwalīyyah, 2001, 4th edition, reprinted by Baik Fadak, n.p, 2005)
al-Ḥakīm, Muḥsin al-Ṭabāṭabā'ī (d. 1390/1970), *Minhāj al-Ṣāliḥīn: bi hāmishahu wa al-ta'līq 'alayh Muhammad Bāqir al-Ṣadr* (Beirut: Dār al-Ta'āruf li 'l-Maṭbū'āt, 1410/1990)
al-Ḥalabī, Ibn Zahra (d. 585/1189), *Ghunyat al-Nuzū'* (Qum, Iran: Mu'assasat al-Imām al-Ṣādiq, 1417/1996)
al-Hamadānī, Riḍā bin Muhammad Ḥādī (d. 1322/1904), *Ḥāshiyat Kitāb al-Makāsib* (in *Jāmi' Fiqh Ahl al-Bayt*, Qum, Iran: Computer Research Center of Islamic Sciences, CD-ROM version, 2005)
———, *Miṣbāḥ al-Faqīh* (in *Jāmi' Fiqh Ahl al-Bayt*, Qum, Iran: Computer Research Center of Islamic Sciences, CD-ROM version, 2005)
al-Ḥarrānī, Ibn Shu'ba (d. 4th century/10th century), *Tuḥaf al-'Uqūl 'an Āl al-Rasūl*, edited by Hussain al-A'lamī (Najaf, Iraq: n.p., sixth edition, 1417/1996)
al-Ḥillī, Ḥasan ibn Yūsuf ibn al-Muṭahhar, famous as al-'Allama (d. 726/1325), *Al-Bābu 'l-Hādī 'Ashar: A Treatise on the Principles of Shī'ite Theology*, translated by William McElwee Miller (London, UK: The Royal Asiatic Society of Great Britain and Ireland, 1958)
———, *Al-Jawhar al-Naḍīd fī Sharḥ Manṭiq al-Tajrīd*, translated with comments by Manūchihr Ṣāni'ī Darrahbīdī (Tehran: Ḥikmat, 1385sh/2006)
———, *Al-Asrār al-Khafiyyah fi al-'Ulūm al-'Aqliyya: al-Ṭabī'īyyāt*, edited with comments by Ḥisām Muḥyuddīn al-Ālūsī and Ṣāliḥ Mahdī al-Hāshim (Beirut: Mu'assasat al-A'lamī lil Maṭbū'āt, 1426/2005)
———, *Kashf al-Murād fi Sharḥ Tajrīd al-I'tiqād* (Beirut: Dār al-Amira, 1427/2006)
———, *Mabādī al-Wuṣūl ilā 'Ilm al-Uṣūl* (Tehran: al-Maṭba'at al-'Ilmīyya, 1404/1984)
———, *Mukhtalaf al-Shī'a fi Aḥkām al-Shari'ah* (Qum, Iran: Būstān-i Kitāb, 1423/2002)
———, *Nahj al-Ḥaqq wa Kashf al-Ṣidq* (Beirut: Dār al-Kutub al-Lubnānī, 1982)
———, *Nihāyat al-Iḥkām fi Ma'rifat al-Aḥkām* (Beirut: Dār al-Aḍwā', 1406/1986)
———, *Qawā'id al-Aḥkām*, (in *Jāmi' Fiqh Ahl al-Bayt*, Qum, Iran: Computer Research Center of Islamic Sciences, CD-ROM version, 2005)
———, *Taḥrīr al-Aḥkām al-Shari'ah 'alā Madhhab al-Imāmiyya*, edited by Ibrāhīm al-Bahādurī (Qum, Iran: Mu'assasat al-Imām al-Ṣādiq, 1420/1999)
———, *Taslīk al-Nafs ilā Ḥaẓīrat al-Quds*, edited by Fāṭima Ramaḍānī (Qum, Iran: Mu'assasat al-Imām al-Ṣādiq, 1426/2007)

al-Hindī, al-Fāḍil (d. 1135 or 1137/1722 or 1724), *Kashf al-Lithām* (in *Jāmi' Fiqh Ahl al-Bayt*, Qum, Iran: Computer Research Center of Islamic Sciences, CD-ROM version, 2005)

al-Ḥuṣarī, Ahmad, *Naẓarīyyat al-Ḥukm wa Maṣādir al-Tashrī' fī Uṣūl al-Fiqh al-Islāmī* (Beirut: Dār al-Kitāb al-'Arabī, 1407/1986)

Ali ibn Abu Talib, Imam, *Nahjul Balagha; Peak of Eloquence: Sermons, Letters and Sayings*, translated by Ali Reza (New York, NY: Tahrike Tarsile Qur'an Inc., 2002)

al-Iravānī al-Gharavī, Mīrzā Ali (d. 1354/1935), *Al-Uṣūl fī 'Ilm al-Uṣūl* (Qum, Iran: Iḥyā' al-Turāth al-Islāmī, 1422/2001)

———, *Ḥāshiyat Kitāb al-Makāsib* (Qum, Iran: Dār Dhaw il-Qurbā, 1421/2000)

al-Iravānī, Bāqir, *Durūs Tamhīdiyya fī al-Qawā'id al-Fiqhiyya* (Beirut: Dār al-Maḥāsin, 1426/2005)

al-Kalāntarī (d. 1292/1875), *Maṭāriḥ al-Anẓār: Taqrīrāt al-Anṣārī* (Qum, Iran: Majma' al-Fikr al-Islāmī, 1428/2007)

al-Karakī, *Jāmi' al-Maqāṣid* (in *Jāmi' Fiqh Ahl al-Bayt*, Qum, Iran: Computer Research Center of Islamic Sciences, CD-ROM version, 2005)

———, "Risāla fī Ṣalāt al-Jum'a," in Rasūl Ja'farīyān, ed., *Davāzdah Risālah-i Fiqhī dar bārah-i Namāz-i Jom'ah az Rūzgār-i Safavī* (Qum, Iran: Anṣāriyān, 1382sh/2003)

al-Kāshānī, Muḥsin Fayḍ (d. 1091/1680), *Mafātīḥ al-Sharāyi'* (in *Jāmi' Fiqh Ahl al-Bayt*, Qum, Iran: Computer Research Center of Islamic Sciences, CD-ROM version, 2005)

al-Khu'ī, Abu al-Qāsim (d. 1413/1992), *Ajwad al-Taqrīrāt: Taqrīr al-Abḥāth li Muḥaqqiq al-Nā'īnī* (Qum, Iran: Mu'assasat Ṣāḥib al-Amr, 1420/1999)

———, *Al-Ijtihād wa al-Taqlīd* (in *Jāmi' Fiqh Ahl al-Bayt*, Qum, Iran: Computer Research Center of Islamic Sciences, CD-ROM version, 2005)

———, *Mawsū'at al-Imam al-Khu'ī* (in *Jāmi' Fiqh Ahl al-Bayt*, Qum, Iran: Computer Research Center of Islamic Sciences, CD-ROM version, 2005)

———, *Miṣbāḥ al-Fiqāha* (in *Jāmi' Fiqh Ahl al-Bayt*, Qum, Iran: Computer Research Center of Islamic Sciences, CD-ROM version, 2005)

———, *Miṣbāḥ al-Uṣūl* (in *Jāmi' Fiqh Ahl al-Bayt*, Qum, Iran: Computer Research Center of Islamic Sciences, CD-ROM version, 2005)

al-Khu'ī, Muhammad Taqī, *Al-Shurūṭ aw al-Iltizāmāt al-Taba'īyya fī al-'Uqūd* (Beirut: Dār al-Muwarrikh al-'Arabī, 1414/1993)

al-Khurāsānī, Muhammad Kāḍim, famous as Ākhūnd (d. 1329/ 1911), *Ḥāshiyat al-Makāsib* (in *Jāmi' Fiqh Ahl al-Bayt*, Qum, Iran: Computer Research Center of Islamic Sciences, CD-ROM version, 2005)

———, *Kifāyat al-Uṣūl* (Beirut: Mu'assasat Āl al-Bayt li Iḥyā' al-Turāth, 1412/1991)

———, *Sīyāsat Nāmah-i Khurāsānī*, edited by Muḥsin Kadīvar (Tehran: Intishārāt Kavīr, 1385sh/2006)

al-Kulaynī, Muhammad ibn Ya'qūb (d. 329/941), *Uṣūl al-Kāfī*, translated to Persian with comments by Jawād Muṣṭafawī (Tehran: Intishārāt Vafā, 1382sh/2004)

al-Kumpānī, Muhammad Hussain al-Iṣfahānī (d. 1361/1942), *Ḥāshiya Kitāb al-Makāsib* (Qum, Iran: Dār al-Iḥyā' al-Turāth, 1418/1997)
al-Majlisī, Muhammad Bāqir, *'Ayn al-Ḥayāt* (in *Jāmi' Fiqh Ahl al-Bayt*, Qum, Iran: Computer Research Center of Islamic Sciences, CD-ROM version, 2005)
———, *Ḥilyat al-Muttaqīn* (in *Jāmi' Fiqh Ahl al-Bayt*, Qum, Iran: Computer Research Center of Islamic Sciences, CD-ROM version, 2005)
al-Marāghī, Mīr 'Abd al-Fattāḥ ibn Ali al-Husaynī (d. 1250/1834), famous as Mīr Fattāḥ, *Al-'Anāwīn al-Fiqhiyya* (Qum, Iran: Mu'assasat al-Nashr al-Islāmī, 1417/1996)
al-Marwazī, Al-Imām Abī 'Abd Allah Muhammad ibn Naṣr (d. 294h/906), *Ikhtilāf al-Fuqahā'*, edited with comments by Muhammad Ṭāhir Ḥakīm (Riyadh: Maktabat Aḍwā' al-Salaf, 1420/2000)
al-Māwardī, Abū al-Ḥasan (d. 450/1058), *Al-Aḥkām al-Sulṭāniyya wa al-Wilāyat al-Dīniyya* (Beirut: Dar Al-Kotob Al-Ilmiyah, 1427/2006)
al-Miqdād, al-Fādil (d. 826/1422), *Al-Tanqīḥ al-Rāyi' li Mukhtaṣar al-Sharāyi'* (in *Jāmi' Fiqh Ahl al-Bayt*, Qum, Iran: Computer Research Center of Islamic Sciences, CD-ROM version, 2005)
———, *Kanz al-'Irfān* (in *Jāmi' Fiqh Ahl al-Bayt*, Qum, Iran: Computer Research Center of Islamic Sciences, CD-ROM version, 2005)
———, *Sharḥ Bāb al-Ḥādī 'Ashar from Al-'Allāma*, translated to Persian and edited by Ali Aṣghar Ḥalabī (Tehran: Intishārāt Asāṭīr, 4th edition, 1383sh/2004)
al-Mufīd, Muhammad ibn Nu'mān (d. 413/1022), *Al-Tadhkiratu bi Uṣūl al-Fiqh* (Beirut: Dār al-Mufīd, 1414/1993)
———, *Awā'il al-Maqālāt*, edited by Ibrāhīm Anṣārī (Qum, Iran: Kungrah-i Hizārah-i Sheikh Mufīd, 1413/1992)
———, *Taṣḥīḥ al-I'tiqād* (Beirut: Dār al-Mufīd, 1414/1993)
Al-Muḥaqqiq al-Ḥillī, Najm al-Dīn Ja'far (d. 676/1278), *Al-Mu'tabar fī Sharḥ al-Mukhtaṣar* (Qum, Iran: Mu'assisat Sayyid al-Shuhadā, 1407/1987)
———, *Ma'ārij al-Uṣūl* (Qum, Iran: Mu'assisat Āl al-Bayt, 1403/1983)
al-Muḥaqqiq Dāmād, Muhammad (d. 1388/1968), *Kitāb al-Ḥajj* (in *Jāmi' Fiqh Ahl al-Bayt*, Qum, Iran: Computer Research Center of Islamic Sciences, CD-ROM version, 2005)
al-Murtaḍā, al-Sharīf (d. 436/1044), *Al-Dhakhīra fī 'Ilm al-Kalām* (Qum, Iran: Mu'assasat al-Nashr al-Islāmī, 1419/1998)
———, *Al-Dharī'ah ilā Uṣūl al-Sharī'ah*, edited by Abu al-Qāsim Gurjī (Tehran: Tehran University Press, 1346sh/1968)
———, *Al-Intiṣār fī Infirādāt al-Imāmiyya* (Qum, Iran: Mu'assasat al-Nashr al-Islāmī, 1415/1995)
———, *Al-Masā'il al-Nāṣiriyyāt* (Tehran: Markaz al-Thaqāfat wa al-'Alāqāt al-Islāmiyya, 1417/1996)
———, *Al-Shāfī fī al-Imāma*, edited by 'Abd al-Zahrā al-Ḥusaynī al-Khaṭīb (Tehran: Mu'assasat al-Ṣādiq li l-Ṭibā'at wa al-Nashr, 1426/2006)
———, *Rasā'il al-Sharīf al-Murtaḍā* (Beirut: Mu'assasat al-Nūr li al-Maṭbū'āt, probably 1405/1984)
al-Muẓaffar, Muhammad Riḍā (d. 1383/1963), *Uṣūl al-Fiqh* (Beirut: Dār al-Ta'āruf li al-Maṭbū'āt, 1425h/2004)

al-Muẓaffar, Muhammad Ḥusayn, *'Ilm al-Imām*, translated to Persian with additional footnotes by Ali Shīrvānī Harandī (Tehran: Intishārāt al-Zahrā', n.d.)
al-Najafī, Muhammad Hassan (d. 1266/1850), *Jawāhir al-Kalām fī Sharḥ Sharāyi' al-Islām* (Beirut: Mu'assasat al-Murtaḍā al-'Ālamiyya, 1412/1992)
———, *Jawāhir al-Kalām fī Sharḥ Sharāyi' al-Islām* (in *Jāmi' Fiqh Ahl al-Bayt*, Qum, Iran: Computer Research Center of Islamic Sciences, CD-ROM version, 2005)
al-Narāqī, Ahmad (d. 1245/1829), *'Awā'id al-Ayyām* (Qum, Iran: Markaz al-Nashr, 1375sh/1996)
———, *Mi'rāj al-Sa'āda* (Tehran: Intishārāt Dihqān, 6th edition, 1385sh/2006)
———, *Mustanad al-Shī'a fī Aḥkām al-Shari'ah* (Mashhad, Iran: Mu'assasat Āl al-Bayt li Iḥyā' al-Turāth, 1415/1994)
al-Narāqī, Mahdī (1209/1794), *Jāmi' al-Sa'ādāt fī Mujibāt al-Najāt* (Qum, Iran: Ismā'īliān, 1386sh/2007)
al-Qā'inī, Abū Ṭālib al-Husseinī Al-Khurāsānī (d. 1293/1876), "Yanābī' al-Wilāya," in Raḥmān Sitāyesh and Mahrīzī, eds., *Rasā'il fī Wilāyat al-Faqīh* (Qum, Iran: Mu'assasat Būstān-i Kitāb-i Qum, 1384sh/2005), pp. 318–386
al-Qummī, al-Muḥaqqiq (d. 1231 or 1233/1815 or 1817), *Ghanā'im al-Ayyām* (in *Jāmi' Fiqh Ahl al-Bayt*, Qum, Iran: Computer Research Center of Islamic Sciences, CD-ROM version, 2005)
———, *Jāmi' al-Shatāt fī Ajwabat al-Su'ālāt* (in *Jāmi' Fiqh Ahl al-Bayt*, Qum, Iran: Computer Research Center of Islamic Sciences, CD-ROM version, 2005)
al-Sabzawārī (d. 1090/1679), *Kifāyat al-Aḥkām*, (in *Jāmi' Fiqh Ahl al-Bayt*, Qum, Iran: Computer Research Center of Islamic Sciences, CD-ROM version, 2005)
———, *Muhadhdhab al-Aḥkām* (in *Jāmi' Fiqh Ahl al-Bayt*, Qum, Iran: Computer Research Center of Islamic Sciences, CD-ROM version, 2005)
al-Ṣadr, al-Sayyid Riḍā (d. 1415/1994), *Al-Ijtihād wa al-Taqlīd* (Beirut: Dār al-Kitāb al-Lubnānī, 1395/1976)
———, "Nigāhī bi Āthār-i Fqihīye Shaykh-i Ṭūsī," in Kungrah, *Yādnāmah-i Shaykh al-Ṭā'ifah Abū Ja'far Muhammad ibn Ḥassan Ṭūsī* (Mashhad, Iran: Dānishgāh-i Mashhad, 1349–1354sh/1970–1976), III., pp. 264–317
al-Ṣadr, Muhammad Bāqir (d. 1980), *Al-Fatāwā al-Wāḍiḥa Wifqan li Madhhab 'Ahl al-Bayt* (Beirut: Dār al-Ta'āruf li al-Maṭbū'āt, 1401h/1981)
———, *Al-Ma'ālim al-Jadīdah li al-Uṣūl* (Beirut: Dār al-Ta'āruf al-Maṭbū'āt, 1410/1989)
———, *Durūs fī 'Ilm al-Uṣūl; al-Ḥalaqat al-Thālitha* (Beirut: Dār al-Ta'āruf lil Maṭbū'āt, 1410/1989)
———, *Ghāyat al-Fikr fī Uṣūl al-Fiqh: Mabāḥith al-Ishtighāl* (Beirut: Dār al-Ta'āruf lil Maṭbū'āt, 1408/1988)
al-Shahīd al-Awwal (d. 786/1384), *Al-Dhikrā fī Aḥkām al-Shari'ah* (in *Jāmi' Fiqh Ahl al-Bayt*, Qum, Iran: Computer Research Center of Islamic Sciences, CD-ROM version, 2005)
———, *Al-Durūs al-Shar'iyya* (Qum, Iran: Mu'assasat al-Nashr al-Islāmī, 1417/1996)

———, *Ghāyat al-Murād*, (in *Jāmiʿ Fiqh Ahl al-Bayt*, Qum, Iran: Computer Research Center of Islamic Sciences, CD-ROM version, 2005)

———, *Al-Lumʿa al-Dimashqiyya* (in *Jāmiʿ Fiqh Ahl al-Bayt*, Qum, Iran: Computer Research Center of Islamic Sciences, CD-ROM version, 2005)

al-Shahīd al-Thānī (d. 966/1559), *Ḥāshiyat Sharāyiʿ al-Islam* (in *Jāmiʿ Fiqh Ahl al-Bayt*, Qum, Iran: Computer Research Center of Islamic Sciences, CD-ROM version, 2005)

———, *Masālik al-Afhām* (in *Jāmiʿ Fiqh Ahl al-Bayt*, Qum, Iran: Computer Research Center of Islamic Sciences, CD-ROM version, 2005)

———, *Rawḍat al-Bahiyya* (in *Jāmiʿ Fiqh Ahl al-Bayt*, Qum, Iran: Computer Research Center of Islamic Sciences, CD-ROM version, 2005)

———, *Tamhīd al-Qawāʿid* (Qum, Iran: Markaz al-Nashr li Maktab al-Iʿlām al-Islāmī, n.d.)

al-Shahrakānī, Ibrāhīm Ismāʿīl, *Muʿjam al-Muṣṭalaḥāt al-Fiqhiyya* (Beirut: Mu'assasat al-Ḥidāya, 1423/2002)

al-Shāṭibī, Abi Isḥāq, *Al-Muwāfaqāt fī Uṣūl al-Shariʿah*, edited by Al-Shaykh Ibrāhīm Ramadhān (Beirut: Dār al-Maʿrifat, 6th edition, 1425/2004)

al-Shīrāzī, Muhammad al-Hussainī, *Al-Wuṣūl ilā Kifāyat al-Uṣūl* (Qum, Iran: Dār al-Ḥikma, 1377sh/1998)

al-Sīstānī, Ali al-Hussainī, *Qāʿidatu lā Ḍarar wa lā Ḍirār* (in *Jāmiʿ Fiqh Ahl al-Bayt*, Qum, Iran: Computer Research Center of Islamic Sciences, CD-ROM version, 2005)

al-Subḥānī, Jaʿfar, *Kullīyāt fī ʿIlm al-Rijāl* (Qum, Iran: Mu'assasat al-Imam Ṣādiq, 1385sh/2006)

———, *Uṣūl al-Fiqh al-Muqāran fīmā lā Naṣṣa fīh: Dirāsāt Mutawāḍiʿat li-Aḥkām al-Mawḍūʿāt allatī lam yurida fīhā Naṣṣ fī al-Kitāb wa al-Sunnah* (Beirut: Mu'ssasat al-Tārīkh al-Arabī, 2005)

———, *Uṣūl al-Ḥadīth wa Aḥkāmihi fī ʿIlm al-Dirāyah* (Qum, Iran: Mu'assasat al-Imam Ṣādiq, 1384sh/2005)

al-Tabrīzī, Mīrzā Fattāḥ al-Shahīdī (d. 1372/1952), *Ḥidāyat al-Ṭālib ilā Asrār al-Makāsib* (Qum, Iran: Dār al-Fiqh li 'l-Ṭibāʿa wa al-Nashr, 1385sh/2006)

al-Ṭūsī, Shaykh al-Ṭā'ifa (d. 460/1067), *Al-Iqtiṣād al-Hādī ilā Ṭarīq al-Rashād* (in *Jāmiʿ Fiqh Ahl al-Bayt*, Qum, Iran: Computer Research Center of Islamic Sciences, CD-ROM version, 2005)

———, *Al-Uddat fī Uṣūl al-Fiqh* (Qum, Iran: Setareh, 1417/1996)

———, *Kitāb al-Khilāf* (Qum, Iran: Mu'assisat al-Nashr al-Islāmī, 6th edition, 1425/2004)

al-Tustarī, Nūr Allah al-Ḥusaynī al-Marʿashī (d. 1019/1610), *Iḥqāq al-Ḥaqq wa Izhāq al-Bāṭil*, edited by Al-Sayyid Shihāb al-Dīn al-Marʿashī al-Najafī (Qum, Iran: Maktabat Ayatullah al-ʿUẓmā al-Marʿashī al-Najafī, n.d.)

Ansārī, Ismāʿīl, *Asrār-i Āl-i Muhammad*, a Persian translation of *Kitāb Sulaym ibn Qays al-Hilālī* (Qum, Iran: Dalili Mā, 1382sh/2003)

Anṣārī, Muhammad Ali, *Al-Mawsūʿat Al-Fiqhīyya al-Muyassara wa yalihā Al-Mulḥaq Al-Uṣūlī* (Qum, Iran: Majmaʿ al-Fikr al-Islāmī, 1427/2008)

ʿArāqī, Ahmad, *Ḥuqūq-i Asāsī-yi Iran* (Tehran: Shirkat Eqbāl, 1331sh/1952)

Ayāzī, Muhammad Ali, *Fiqh Pazhūhī-yi Qur'an: Darāmadī bar Mabānī-yi Naẓarī-yi Āyāt al-Aḥkām* (Qum, Iran: Bustān-i Kitāb, 1380sh/2001)

Badawī, 'Abd al-Raḥmān, *Ḥikmat al-Khālida* (Cairo: Maktabat al-Nahḍat al-Miṣrīyya, 1952)

Baḥr al-'Ulūm, Muhammad Taqī Āl (d. 1326/1908–1909), *Bulghat al-Faqīh* (Tehran: Maktabat al-Ṣādiq, 1403/1984)

Damāvandī, Ibn Naṣr Allah, "Risāla Tuḥfat al-Nāṣiriyya fī Ma'rifat al-Ilāhiyya" written in 1264/1847, in Gholām Hossein Zargarīnejād, *Sīyāsat-Nāmahā-yi Qājārī: Rasā'il-i Sīyāsī* (Tehran: Intishārāt Mu'assasa Taḥqīqāt va 'Ulūm Insaānī, 1386sh/2008), II., pp. 7–50

Davānī, Ali, "Sayrī dar Zindagī-yi Shaykh Ṭūsī," in Kungrah, *Yādnāmah-i Shaykh al-Ṭā'ifah Abū Ja'far Muhammad ibn Ḥassan Ṭūsī* (Mashhad, Iran: Dānishgāh-i Mashhad, 1349–1354sh/1970–1976), I., pp. 187–212

Ebrāhīmī Dīnānī, Ghulāmhossein, *Mājarā--yi Fikr-i Falsafī dar Jahān-i Islām* (Tehran: Tarh-e No, 1377/1998)

Ettehadied (Nezam Mafi), Mansoureh, *Majlis va Intikhābāt: az Mashrūṭa tā Pāyān-i Qājārīyyah* (Tehran: Nashr Tārīkh Iran, 1375sh/1996)

Fānī, Kāmrān, and Bahā'uddīn Khorramshāhī, *Al-Fihris al-Mawḍū'ī li 'l-Qur'ān al-Karīm* (Tehran: Farhang Mu'āṣer, 1364sh/1985)

Fātimī, Sayyid Aḥmad, "Shaykh Ṭūsī va Ibn Idrīs," in Kungrah, *Yādnāmah-i Shaykh al-Ṭā'ifah Abū Ja'far Muhammad ibn Ḥassan Ṭūsī* (Mashhad, Iran: Dānishgāh-i Mashhad, 1349–1354sh/1970–1976), III., pp. 461–488

Feyz, Alireza, *Mabādī-yi Fiqh va Uṣūl* (Tehran: Intishārāt-i Dānishgāh-i Tehran, 1384sh/2006, 17th edition)

Fīraḥī, Dāwūd, "Mabānī-yi Fiqhī-yi Mashrūṭah-Khwāhī az Dīdgāh-i Ākhūnd Khurāsānī," in Group of Scholars, *Bar-rasīyi Mabānī-yi Fikrī va Ijtimā'ī-yi Mashrūṭīyyat-i Iran: Buzurgdāsht-i Muhammad Kāẓim Khurāsānī* (Tehran: Mu'assisah-i Taḥqīqāt va Tawsa'ah-i 'Ulūm-i Insānī, 1384sh/2005), pp. 195–218

Group of Scholars, *Jāmi' Fiqh Ahl al-Bayt* [CD-ROM, Complete Library of the Jurisprudence of Members of the Prophet's House], (Qum, Iran: Computer Research Center of Islamic Sciences, 1384sh/2005)

Gulpāyigānī, Muhammad Riḍā (d. 1414/1993), "Al-Hidāyat ilā man lah al-wilāyat," in Muhammad Kāẓim Raḥmān Sitāyesh and Mahdī Mahrīzī, eds., *Rasā'il fī Wilāyat al-Faqīh: 12 Baḥthan Fiqhiyyan ḥawlan Wilāyat al-Faqīh* (Qum, Iran: Mu'assasat Būstān-i Kitāb-i Qum, 1384sh/2005), pp. 780–819

———, *Majma' al-Masā'il* (in *Jāmi' Fiqh Ahl al-Bayt*, Qum, Iran: Computer Research Center of Islamic Sciences, CD-ROM version, 2005)

Gurjī, Abu al-Qāsim, "Shaykh-i Ṭūsī va 'Uddat al-Uṣūl," in Kungrah, *Yādnāmah-i Shaykh al-Ṭā'ifah Abū Ja'far Muhammad ibn Ḥassan Ṭūsī* (Mashhad, Iran: Dānishgāh-i Mashhad, 1349–1354sh/1970–1976), III., pp. 365–460

———, *Tārīkh-i Fiqh va Fuqahā'* (Tehran: SAMT Publications, 17th edition, 1382sh/2004)

Ḥā'irī, Abd al- Ḥādī, *Nakhostīn Rūyārūyihā-yi Andīsha-garān-i Iran bā Do Ravīyyah-i Tamaddon-i Būrzhūāzī-yi Gharb* (Tehran: Amir Kabir, 1380sh/2001, 4th edition)

———, *Tashayyuʿ va Mashrūṭiyyat dar Irān va Naqsh-i Irāniyān-i Muqīm-i ʿArāq* (Tehran: Amir Kabir, third edition, 1381sh/2002)

Ḥāʾirī Yazdī, Mahdī, *Kāvush-hāyi ʿAql-i Naẓarī* (Tehran: Amir Kabir Publication, 1361sh/1982)

Hamidullah, Muhammad, *Majmūʿat al-Wathāʾiq al-Siyāsiyya fī al-ʿAhd al-Nabawī wa al-Khilāfat al-Rāshidah* (Cairo: Maṭbaʿat Lajnat al-Taʾlīf wa al-Tarjama wa al-Nashr, 1941)

Hassannia, Mohammad, and Ali Tatari, eds., *Qarārdād-i 1907* (Tehran: Khānah-i Kitāb, 1386sh/2007)

Ibn Ikhwah [or Ibn Ukhuwwa] (d. 729/1328), *Maʿālim al-Qurba fī Aḥkām al-Ḥisba*, edited by Reuben Levy (London: Luzac, 1938), E. J. W. Gibb Memorial Series, Vol. 12

Ibn Miskawayh (d. 421/1030), *Tarjumah-i Jāvīdān Khirad Mushkuwayh Rāzī*, edited by Muhammad Taqī Dānishpazhūh (Tehran: Intishārāt Dānishgāh Tehran, 1359sh/1980)

Ibn Rushd (d. 595/1198), *al-Kashf ʿan Manāhij al-Adilla fī ʿAqāʾid al-Millah* (Beirut: Dār al-Kutub al-ʿIlmīyya, 1423/2002)

Īzad panāhī, Sajjād, *Andīshah-i Siyāsī-yi Mullā Ahmad Narāqī* (Tehran: Būstān Kitāb, 1384sh/2005)

Jaʿfarī Langrūdī, Mohammad Jaʿfar, *Dāʾirat al-Maʿārif-i ʿUlūm-i Islāmī* (Tehran: Ganj-i Dānish, 1363sh/1984)

———, *Dānish-nāmah-i Ḥuqūqī* (Tehran: Amir Kabir, 2nd edition, 1372sh/1993)

———, "Kitāb-i Ali," in his *Tārīkh-i Muʿtazila: Falsafah-i Farhang-i Islām* (Tehran: Ganj-i Dānish, 1368sh/1989)

———, *Mabsūṭ dar Termīnolozhī-yi Huqūq* (Tehran: Ganj-i Dānish, 1999)

———, *Maktab-hāyi Ḥuqūqī dar Ḥuqūq-i Islām* (Tehran: Ibn Sīnā, 1353sh/1974)

Jaʿfariyān, Rasūl, *Naqsh-i Khāndān-i Karakī dar Taʾsīs va Tadāvum-i Dawlat-i Safavī* (Tehran: Nashr-i ʿIlm, 1387sh/2008)

Jalālī, Ghulām Rezā, ed., *Dīdgāh-hāyi ʿIlmīyi Ayatullah al-ʿUẓmā Sayyid Muhammad Hussain Mīlānī* (Mashhad, Iran: Bunyād Pazhūhish-hāyi Islāmī, 1386/2007)

Kadīvar, Jamīlah, *Taḥawwul-i Guftimān-i Sīyāsī-yi Shiʿa dar Iran* (Tehran: Ṭarḥ-i Nō, 1379sh/2000)

Kadīvar, Muḥsin, "Andīshah-i Siyāsī-yi Ākhūnd Khurāsānī," in Group of Scholars, *Bar-rasīye Mabānī-ye Fikrī va Ijtimāʿī-ye Mashrūṭīyyat-i Iran: Buzurgdāsht-i Muhammad Kāẓim Khurāsānī* (Tehran: Muʾassisah-i Taḥqīqāt va Tawsaʿih-i ʿUlūm-i Insānī, 1384sh/2005), pp. 219–264

Kāshif al-Ghiṭāʾ, Sheikh Jaʿfar (d. 1228/1813), *Kashf al-Ghiṭāʾ* (in *Jāmiʿ Fiqh Ahl al-Bayt*, Qum, Iran: Computer Research Center of Islamic Sciences, CD-ROM version, 2005)

Kātūzīyān, Nāṣir, *Falsafah-i Ḥuqūq* (Tehran: Intishār, 3rd edition, 1385sh/2006)

Khāliṣī, ʿAbbās, *Tārīkhchah-i Bast va Bast-Nishīnī dar Iran* (Tehran: Intishārāt ʿIlmī, 1366sh/1988)

Khallāf, Abd al-Wahhāb, *Maṣādir al-Tashrī' al-Islāmī fi mā lā Naṣṣa fīh* (Kuwait: Dār al-Qalam, 1392/1972)

Khamene'i, Muhammad, ed., *Falsafah-i Siyāsī dar Ḥikmat-i Mullā Ṣadrā* (Tehran: Bonyād Ḥikmat Mullā Ṣadrā, 1386sh/2007)

Khomeini, Rūḥ Allah (d. 1368sh/1989), *Al-Istiṣḥāb* (Tehran: Mu'assasat al-'Urūj, 1417/1997)

———, *Kitāb al-Bay'* (in *Jāmi' Fiqh Ahl al-Bayt*, Qum, Iran: Computer Research Center of Islamic Sciences, CD-ROM version, 2005)

Khorramshāhī, Bahā'uddīn, trans., *Qur'ān-i Karīm* (Tehran: Jāmī & Nīlūfar Publications, 1997)

Khwānsārī, Sayyid Ahmad (d. 1405/1984), *Jāmi' al-Madārik fī Sharḥ Mukhtaṣar al-Nāfi'* (in *Jāmi' Fiqh Ahl al-Bayt*, Qum, Iran: Computer Research Center of Islamic Sciences, CD-ROM version, 2005)

Kifāyī, Abd al-Husayn, *Margī dar Nūr: Zindagāni-yi Ākhūnd Khorāsānī* (Tehran: Zavvār, 1359sh/1980)

Kungrah-i Hizarah-i Shaykh-i Ṭūsī, *Yādnāmah-i Shaykh al-Ṭā'ifah Abū Ja'far Muhammad ibn Ḥassan Ṭūsī* (Mashhad, Iran: Dānishgāh-i Mashhad, 1349–1354sh/1970–1976)

Maḥallātī, Muhammad Ismā'īl, "Al-La'ālī al-Marbūṭah fī Wujūb al-Mashrūṭah," in Zargarīnezhād, *Rasā'il-i Mashrūṭiyyat: 18 Risālah va Lāyiḥa dar bārah-i Mashrūṭiyyat* (Tehran: Intishārāt Kavīr, 1374sh/1995), pp. 495-549

Mahdavī Dāmghānī, Maḥmūd, *Wathā'iq: Nāma-hāyi Ḥaḍrat-i Khatmī Martabat va Khulafā-yi Rāshidīn* (Tehran: Chāp va Nashr Bunyād, 1365sh/1986)

Maḥmūd, Abd al-Majīd, *Al-Madrasat al-Fiqhiyyat li 'l-Muḥaddithīn: Madkhal li Dirāsat al-Ittijāḥāt al-Fiqhiyya 'inda Aṣḥāb al-Ḥadīth* (Cairo: Maktabat Al-Shabāb, 1972)

Mīr Dāmād, Muhammad Bāqir (1040/1630–1), *Jadhawāt wa Mawāqīt* (Tehran: Miras Maktoob, 1380sh/2001)

Mīrzā Ṣāleḥ, Gholāmhossein, *Mudhākirāt-i Majlis-i Awwal: Tawsa'ah-i Siyāsī-yi Iran dar Varṭeh-i Siyāsat-i Baynolmilal 1324–1326* (Tehran: Intishārāt Māziyār, 1384sh/2005)

———, *Buḥrān-i Dimukrāsī dar Majlis-i Awwal: Yāddāsht-hāyi Mīrzā Faḍlalī Āqā Tabrīzī* (Tehran: Negāhe Mo'āṣer, 1387sh/2008)

Mishkīnī, Ali Akbar, *Iṣṭilāḥāt al-Uṣūl* (Qum, Iran: Nashr al-Ḥādī, 7th edition, 1384sh/2005)

———, *Muṣṭalaḥāt al-Fiqh* (Qum, Iran: Nashr al-Hādī, 4th edition, 1384sh/2005)

Montaẓerī, Hossein Ali, *Dirāsāt fī Wilāyat al-Faqīh wa Fiqh al-Dawlat al-Islāmīyya* (Beirut: Al-Dār al-Islāmiyya, 1409/1988)

———, *Dirāsāt fī Wilāyat al-Faqīh wa Fiqh al-Dawlat al-Islāmīyya*, translated to Persian with the title "Mabānī-yi Fiqhī-yi Ḥukūmat-i Islāmī" by Mahmūd Ṣalavātī (Tehran: Intishārāt Kayhan, 1367sh/1988)

Mudīr-Shānahchi, Kazem, *Āyāt al-Aḥkām* (Tehran: SAMT Publication, 2004)

Muḥaqqiq Dāmād, Muṣṭafā, *Qawā'id-i Fiqh* (Tehran: Markaz-i Nashr-i 'Ulūm-i Islāmī, 1383sh/2005)

———, *Qawā'id-i Fiqh: Bakhsh-i Madanī* (Tehran: Markaz Nashr 'Ulūm Islāmī, 12th edition, 1384sh/2005)

Musavi Bojnourdi, Kazem, ed., *Dā'irat al-Ma'ārif-i Buzurg-i Islāmī* [Great Encyclopedia of Islam, abbreviated as GEI] (Tehran: Markaz Da'erat al-Ma'aref-e Bozorg-e Eslami, 1377sh/1998)

Mūsavī Bojnūrdī, Muhammad,*'Ilm Uṣūl* (Tehran: Mu'assasa Chāp va Nashr 'Orūj, 1379sh/2000)

Mūsawī Gharawī, Sayyid Muhammad Jawād (d. 1384sh/2004), *Mabāni-yi Ḥuqūq dar Islām* (Isfahān, Iran: Jahād-i Dānishgāhī, 1373sh/1994)

Muṭahharī, Murtaḍā (d. 1358sh/1979), *'Adl-i Ilāhī* (Tehran: Intishārāt Ṣadrā, 1385sh/2007)

Nā'īnī, Muhammad Hossein (d. 1355/1936), *Al-Fawā'id al-Uṣūl: min ifāḍāt al-Mīrzā Muhammad Hussayn al-Gharawī al-Nā'īnī* [collection of Nā'īnī's lectures compiled and edited by Muhammad Ali al-Kāzim al-Khurāsānī (d. 1365/1945), with comments by Ḍīyā' al-Dīn al-'Irāqī (d. 1361/1942)] (Qum, Iran: Mu'assasat al-Nashr al-Isāmī, 1424/2003, 8th edition)

———, *Al-Makāsib wa al-Bay'* (in *Jāmi' Fiqh Ahl al-Bayt*, Qum, Iran: Computer Research Center of Islamic Sciences, CD-ROM version, 2005)

———, *Kitāb al-Ṣalāṭ* (in *Jāmi' Fiqh Ahl al-Bayt*, Qum, Iran: Computer Research Center of Islamic Sciences, CD-ROM version, 2005)

———, *Munyat al-Ṭālib* (in *Jāmi' Fiqh Ahl al-Bayt*, Qum, Iran: Computer Research Center of Islamic Sciences, CD-ROM version, 2005)

———, *Tanbīh al-Ummah wa Tanzīh al-Millah*, edited by Maḥmūd Ṭāliqānī (d. 1358sh/1979), (Tehran: Firdawsī, 1334sh/1955)

———, *Tanbīh al-Ummah wa Tanzīh al-Millah*, edited by Sayyid Javād Vara'ī (Qum, Iran: Būstān-i Kitāb, 1382sh/2003)

Nūrī, Faḍl Allah (d. 1328/1908), *Rasā'il, I'lāmiyyah-hā, Maktūbāt va Rūznāmah*, edited by Muhammad Turkamān (Tehran: Rasā, 1362sh/1983)

———, "Risālah-i Ḥurmat-i Mashrūṭah," in Zargarīnezhād, *Rasā'il-i Mashrūṭiyyat: 18 Risālah va Lāyiḥa dar bārah-i Mashrūṭiyyat* (Tehran: Intishārāt Kavīr, 1374sh/1995), pp. 151–167

Pakatchi, Ahmad, "Aṣḥāb Ḥadīth," in Bojnourdi, GEI, IX, pp. 113–126

———, "Ibn Bābiwayh," in Bojnourdi, GEI, III., pp. 62–66

———, "Ikhtilāf al-ḥadīth," in Bojnourdi, GEI, VII., pp. 168–173

———, "Islām: Andīshahhā-yi Fiqhī dar Sadahhā-yi Muti'akhkhir," in Bojnourdi, GEI, VIII., pp. 453–456

———, "Uṣūl-i Fiqh," in Bojnourdi, GEI, IX, pp. 289–306

Pazhūhishkadah-i Fiqh va Ḥuqūq, *Ma'khadh-shināsī-yi Qawā'id-i Fiqhī* (Qum, Iran: Būstān-i Kitāb, 1379sh/2000)

Ṣāḥib al-Ḥadā'iq (d. 1186/1772), *Al-Ḥadā'iq al-Nāḍira*, (in *Jāmi' Fiqh Ahl al-Bayt*, Qum, Iran: Computer Research Center of Islamic Sciences, CD-ROM version, 2005)

Ṣāḥib al-Madārik (d. 1009/1600), *Madārik al-Aḥkām* (in *Jāmi' Fiqh Ahl al-Bayt*, Qum, Iran: Computer Research Center of Islamic Sciences, CD-ROM version, 2005)

Ṣāḥib al-Riyāḍ , *Riyāḍ al-Masā'il fī Taḥqīq al-Aḥkām bi al-Dalā'il* (Mashhad, Iran: Mu'assasat Āl al-Bayt li Iḥyā al-Turāth, 1376sh/1997)

Ṣāliḥ, Ṣubḥī, *'Ulūm al- Ḥadīth wa Muṣṭalaḥātihi*, translated to Persian by 'Ādil Nādir Ali (Tehran: Uswah, 1383sh/2005)

Shahābi, Mahmūd, *Adwār-i Fiqh* (Tehran: The Ministry of Islamic Culture and Guidance, 1366sh/1987)

Shams al-Dīn, Muhammad Mahdī, *Al-Ijtihād wa al-Taqlīd* (Beirut: Mu'assasat al-Duwalīyya, 1419/1998)

Sha'rānī, Abu al-Hasan, trans., commentator., *Kashf al-Murād: Sharḥ Tajrīd al-I'tiqād* (Tehran: Intishārāt Islāmiyya, 12th edition, 1388sh/2009)

Ṣifatgul, Manṣūr, *Sākhtār-i Nahād va Andīshah-i Dīnī dar Iran-i 'Aṣr-i Ṣafavī* (Tehran: Rasā, 1381sh/2003)

Ṭabāṭabā'ī, Muhammad Hussein (d. 1361sh/1982), *Islam va Insān-i Mu'āṣir* (Qum, Iran: Risālaṭ, 1397/1976)

———, *Shī'a dar Islām* (Qum: Daftar-i Intishārāt-i Islāmī, 16th edition, 1383sh/2004)

Tabrīzī, Muhammad Hussain, "Kashf al-Murād min al-Mashrūṭah wa al-Istibdād," in Zargarīnezhād, *Rasā'il-i Mashrūṭiyyat: 18 Risālah va Lāyiḥa dar bārah-i Mashrūṭiyyat* (Tehran: Intishārāt Kavīr, 1374sh/1995), pp. 113–146

Tahami, Gholamreza, *A'lām-i Tārīkh-i Islām* (Tehran: Intishār Publication, 1386sh/2007)

Tunukābunī, Muhammad ibn Sultan (d. 1302/1884), *Qiṣaṣ al-'Ulamā* (Tehran: 'Ilmī Farhangī, 1383sh/2004)

Turkamān, Muhammad, ed., *Asnādī dar-bārah-i Hujūm-i Englīs va Rūs bi Iran* (Tehran: Daftar-i Moṭāla'āt-i Siyāsī va Baynolmilalī, 1370sh/1992)

———, "Naẓārat-i Hay'at-i Mujtahidīn: Sayr-i Taṭawwur-i Aṣl-i Duwwum-i Qānūn Asāsī dar Dawrah-i Duwwum-i Taqnīnīyya," in Bunyād Mustaḍ'afān, *Tārīkh-i Mu'āṣir-i Iran* (Tehran: 1369sh/1990), II., pp. 15–57

———, "Naẓārat-i Hay'at-i Mujtahidīn bar Quwwah-i Qanūn-gudhārī: Sayr-i Taṭawwur-i Aṣl-i Duwwum-i Qānūn Asāsī az Pāyān-i Dawrah-i Duwwum tā Pāyān-i Dawrah-i Shishum-i Taqnīnīyya," in Bunyād Mustaḍ'afān, *Tārīkh-i Mu'āṣir-i Iran* (Tehran: 1370/1991), III., pp. 51–68

Ṭūsī, Khwāja Naṣīr al-Dīn, *Akhlāq-e Nāṣerī*, edited by Mujtabā Minovī and Ali Reza Ḥeydarī (Tehran: Intishārāt Khwārazmī, 5th edition, 1373sh/1994)

———, *Akhlāq-i Muḥtashamī*, edited by Muhammad Taqī Dānishpazhūh (Tehran: Intishārāt Dānishgāh Tehran, 1339sh/1960)

Zargarīnezhād, Ghulām Hussain, *Rasā'il-i Mashrūṭiyyat: 18 Risālah va Lāyiḥa dar bārah-i Mashrūṭiyyat* (Tehran: Intishārāt Kavīr, 1374sh/1995)

———, *Sīyāsat-Nāmahā-yi Qājārī: Rasā'il-i Sīyāsī* (Tehran: Intishārāt Mu'assasa Taḥqīqāt va 'Ulūm Insaānī, 1386sh/2008)

Zerang, Muhammad, *Taḥawwul-i Niẓām-i Qaḍā'ī-yi Iran* (Tehran: Intishārāt Markaz Asnād Inqilāb Islāmī, 1382sh/2003)

English Sources

Abou El Fadl, Khaled, *And God Knows the Soldiers: The Authoritative and Authoritarian in Islamic Discourse* (Lanham, MD: University Press of America, 1997)

———, "Constitutionalism and the Islamic Sunni Legacy" 1 UCLA J. Islamic & Near E.L. 67 (2001)

———, "A Distinctly Islamic View of Human Rights," in Shireen Hunter and Huma Malik, eds., *Islam and Human Rights: Advancing a U.S.-Muslim Dialogue* (Washington, DC: Center for Strategic and International Studies, 2005), pp. 27–42

———, "The Place of Ethical Obligations in Islamic Law" 4 UCLA J. Islamic & Near E.L. 1 (2004–2005)

———, *Rebellion and Violence in Islamic Law* (Cambridge, UK: Cambridge University Press, 2001)

———, *Speaking in God's Name: Islamic Law, Authority and Women* (Oxford, UK: Oneworld Publications, 2001)

Afary, Janet, *The Iranian Constitutional Revolution, 1906–1911: Grassroots Democracy, Social Democracy, and the Origins of Feminism* (New York: Columbia University Press, 1996)

Akhavi, Shahrough, "Shiite Theories of Social Contract," in Abbas Amanat and Frank Griffel, eds., *Shari'a: Islamic Law in the Contemporary Context* (Stanford: Stanford University Press, 2007), pp. 137–155

Alexander, Larry A., ed., "Constitutionalism," in William Edmundson and Martin Golding, eds., *Blackwell Guide to the Philosophy of Law and Legal Theory* (Oxford, UK: Blackwell Publishing Ltd., 2005), pp. 248–258

———, *Constitutionalism: Philosophical Foundations* (Cambridge, UK: Cambridge University Press, 1998, reprinted 2005)

al-Farabi, Abu Nasr, *On the Perfect State: Mabādī' ārā' ahl al-madīnat al-fāḍilah,* translated by Richard Walzer (New York: Oxford University Press, 1997)

Algar, Hamid, "Bihbihānī," in Encyclopedia of Islam (EI), 2nd edition, pp. 134b–135a

———, trans., *Constitution of the Islamic Republic of Iran* (Berkeley, CA: Mizan Press, 1980)

al-Raysuni, Ahmad, *Imam al-Shatibi's Theory of the Higher Objectives and Intents of Islamic Law* (London and Washington: The International Institute of Islamic Thought, 2005)

al-Ṣadr, Muhammad Bāqir, *Lessons in Islamic Jurisprudence*, translated by Roy Parviz Mottahedeh (Oxford, UK: Oneworld Publications, 2003)

Alverny, Marie-Thérèse de, "Translations and Translators," in Robert L. Benson et al., eds., *Renaissance and Renewal in the Twelfth Century* (Buffalo, NY: University of Toronto Press and the Medieval Academy of America, 1991), pp. 421–462

Arjomand, Said Amir, trans., "Two Decrees of Shāh Ṭahmāsp Concerning Statecracft and the Authority of Shaykh Ali al-Karakī," in Said Amir Arjomand ed., *Authority and Political Culture in Shi'ism* (Albany, NY: State University of New York, 1988), pp. 250–262

Azimi, Fakhreddin, *The Quest for Democracy in Iran: A Century of Struggle Against Authoritarian Rule* (Cambridge, MA and London: Harvard University Press, 2008)

Aziz, Talib M., "Popular Sovereignty in Contemporary Shīʿī Thought," in L. Clarke, ed., *Shīʿite Heritage: Essays on Classical and Modern Traditions* (Binghamton, NY: Global Publications, 2001), pp. 181–198

Brewer-Carias, Allan R., *Constitutional Protection of Human Rights in Latin America: A Comparative Study of Amparo Proceedings* (New York, NY: Cambridge University Press, 2009)

Browne, Edward G., *The Letters from Tabriz: The Russian Suppression of the Iranian Constitutional Movement* (Washington, DC: Mage Publishers, 2008)

———, *The Persian Revolution of 1905–1909* (London: Frank Cass & Co. Ltd, 1966)

Buckley, R. P., trans., *The Book of the Islamic Market Inspector: Niḥāyat al-Rutbah fī Ṭalab al-Ḥisba (The Utmost Authority in the Pursuit of Hisba) of Abd al-Rahman b. Nasr al-Shayrazi* (New York: Oxford University Press, 2000)

Calder, Norman, "Legitimacy and Accommodation in Safavid Iran: the Juristic Theory of Muḥammad Bāqir al-Sabzavārī (d. 1090/1679)," *Iran: Journal of British Institute of Persian Studies*, 25, London, 1987, pp. 91–105

Cook, Michael, *Commanding Right and Forbidding Wrong in Islamic Thought* (Cambridge, UK: Cambridge University Press, 2000)

Cromartie, Alan, *The Constitutionalist Revolution: An Essay on the History of England, 1450–1642* (New York: Cambridge University Press, 2006)

Crone, Patricia, and Martin Hinds, *God's Caliph: Religious Authority in the First Centuries of Islam* (Cambridge, UK: Cambridge University Press, originally published in1988, first paperback edition, 2003)

Dabashi, Hamid, "Khwājah Naṣīr al-Dīn al-Ṭūsī: The philosopher/Vizier and the Intellectual Climate of His Times," in Seyyed Hossein Nasr and Oliver Leaman, eds., *History of Islamic Philosophy* (Abingdon, UK: Routledge, originally published in 1996), pp. 527–584

Enayat, Hamid, "Iran: Khumayni's Concept of the 'Guardianship of the Jurisconsult'" in James P. Piscatori, ed., *Islam in the Political Process* (Cambridge, UK: Cambridge University Press, 1983), pp. 160–180

———, *Modern Islamic Political Thought*, foreword by Roy Mottahedeh (London: I.B. Tauris, 2004, originally published 1982)

Ettehadied (Nezam Mafi), Mansoureh, "The Council for the Investigation of Grievances: A Case Study of Nineteenth Century Iranian Social History," *Iranian Studies*, No. 1, Vol. XX, 1989, pp. 51–61

Ferejohn, John, et al., eds., *Constitutional Culture and Democratic Rule* (Cambridge, UK: Cambridge University Press, 2001)

Floor, Willem,., "Change and Development in the Judicial System of Qajar Iran (1800–1925)," in Charles E. Boseworth et al., eds., *Qajar Iran: Political, Social and Cultural Change* (Costa Mesa, CA: Mazda Publishers, 1992, originally published in1983), pp. 113–147

———, "The Office of Muhtasib in Iran," *Iranian Studies*, Vol. 18, No. 1, Winter 1985, pp. 53–74

———, "The Secular Judicial System in Safavid Persia," *Studia Iranica*, Vol. 29, No. 1, 2000, pp. 9–60

———, and Mohammad H. Faghfoory, trans., *Dastur al-Moluk: A Safavid State Manual Written by Mohammad Rafi' al-Dīn Ansāri Mostowfi al-Mamalek* (Costa Mesa, CA: Mazda Publishers, Inc., 2007)

Franklin, Daniel P. and Michael J. Baun, eds., *Political Culture and Constitutionalism: A Comparative Approach* (New York and London: M.E. Sharpe, Inc., 1995)

Friedrich, Carl J., *Constitutional Government and Democracy* (Boston, MA: Ginn and Company, 1950)

———, *Constitutional Government and Politics* (New York, NY: Harper and Row, 1937)

———, *Limited Government: A Comparison* (Englewood Cliffs, NJ: Prentice Hall, Inc., 1974)

———, *Transcendent Justice: The Religious Dimension of Constitutionalism* (Durham, NC: Duke University Press, 1964)

Friedrich, Carl J., and Robert G. McCloskey, eds., *From the Declaration of Independence to the Constitution: The Roots of American Constitutionalism* (Indianapolis and New York: The Bobbs-Merrill Company, Inc, 1954)

Gimaret, D., "Muʿtazila," in EI, 2nd edition, VII. 783a–793a

Glendon, Mary Ann, et al., *Comparative Legal Traditions: Text, Materials and Cases* (Saint Paul, MN: West Publishing Co, 2002)

Glenn, H. Patrick, *Legal Traditions of the World* (New York, NY: Oxford University Press, 2004)

Gordon, Scott, *Controlling the State: Constitutionalism from Ancient Athens to Today* (Cambridge, MA: Harvard University Press, 1999)

Hairi, Abdul-Hadi, "Khurāsānī," in EI, 2nd edition, V. 61a–62a

———, "Madjlisī," in Encyclopedia of Islam, 2nd edition, V. 1086b–1088b

———, *Shi'ism and Constitutionalism in Iran: A Study of the Role Played by the Persian Residents of Iraq in Iranian Politics* (Leiden, The Netherlands: Brill, 1977)

Holmes, Stephen, "Precommitment and the Paradox of Democracy," in Jon Elster and Rune Slagstad, eds., *Constitutionalism and Democracy* (Cambridge, UK: Cambridge University Press, 1988, reprinted 1997), pp. 195–240

Huls, Nick, et al., eds., *The Legitimacy of Highest Courts' Rulings: Judicial Deliberations and Beyond* (The Hague, Netherlands: T.M.C. Asser Press, 2009)

Inati, Shams, "Logic," in Nasr and Leaman, *History of Islamic Philosophy* , pp. 820–823

Jones, Robert, "Piracy, War, and the Acquisition of Arabic Manuscripts in Renaissance Europe," in *Manuscripts of the Middle East*, edited by Jan Just Witkam (Leiden: Tel Lugt Press, 1987), II., pp. 96–111

Kasravi, Ahmad, *History of the Iranian Constitutional Revolution*, translated by Evan Siegel (Costa Mesa, CA: Mazda Publishers, 2006)

Katouzian, Homa, *State and Society in Iran: The Eclipse of the Qajars and the Emergence of the Pahlavis* (London and New York: I.B. Tauris & Co. Ltd, 2000)

Kautz, Steven, et al., eds., *The Supreme Court and the Idea of Constitutionalism* (Philadelphia: University of Pennsylvania Press, 2009)

Kurzman, Charles, ed., *Modernist Islam 1840–1940: A Sourcebook* (New York: Oxford University Press, 2002)

Lambton, Ann K.S., "The Persian ʿUlamā and the Constitutional Reform," in Toufic Fahd and Robert Brunschvig, eds., *Le Shī'isme Imāmite* (Paris: Presses Universitaires de France, 1970), pp. 245–269

———, *State and Government in Medieval Islam* (New York: Oxford University Press, 1981, reprint 1991)

Lambton, Ann K.S., "The Tobacco Regie: A Prelude to Revolution," in her *Qājār Persia* (Austin: Texas University Press Edition, 1988), pp. 223–276 (the article was originally published in 1966)

Lasser, Mitchel De S.-O.I' E., *Judicial Deliberations: A Comparative Analysis of Judicial Transparency and Legitimacy* (New York: Oxford University Press, 2004)

Lecker, Michael, *The "Constitution of Medina": Muhammad's First Legal Document* (Princeton, NJ: The Darwin Press, Inc., 2004)

Litvak, Meir, *Shi'i Scholars of Nineteenth-Century Iraq: the "Ulama' of Najaf and Karbala"* (Cambridge, UK: Cambridge University Press, 1998)

Loughlin, Martin, and Neil Walker, eds., *The Paradox of Constitutionalism: Constituent Power and Constitutional Form* (New York: Oxford University Press, 2007)

MacIntyre, Alasdair, *After Virtue: A Study in Moral Theory* (Notre Dame, IN: University of Notre Dame Press, 2007, 3rd edition)

Madelung, Wilfred, "Akhbāriyya," in EI, 2nd edition, I. pp. 56b–57b

———, "Authority in Twelver Shiism in the Absence of the Imam," in George Makdisi and Dominque Sourdel, eds., *La Notion d'autorité au Moyen Age Islam, Byzance, Occident: Colloqués internationaux de la Napoule 1978* (Paris: Presses Universitaires de France, 1982), pp. 163–173

———, "Imāma," in EI, 2nd edition, III. 1163b–1169a

———, *The Succession to Muhammad: A Study of the Early Caliphate* (New York: Cambridge University Press, 1997)

———, "A Treatise of the Sharīf al-Murtaḍā on the legality of Working for the Government (*Mas'ala fi 'l-'amal ma'a 'l-sulṭān*)" in Bulletin of the School of Oriental and African Studies, XLIII. London, 1980, pp. 18–31

Mahdi, Muhsin, "ALFARABI," in Leo Strauss and Joseph Crospey, *History of Political Philosophy* (Chicago and London: The University of Chicago Press, 1963, 3rd edition, 1987), pp. 206–227

Makdisi, George, "Authority in the Islamic Community," in George Makdisi and Dominque Sourdel, eds., *La Notion d'autorité au Moyen Age Islam, Byzance, Occident: Colloqués internationaux de la Napoule 1978* (Paris: Presses Universitaires de France, 1982), pp. 117–126

———, *Ibn 'Aqīl: Religion and Culture in Classical Islam* (Edinburgh, UK: Edinburgh University Press, 1997)

Mallat, Chibli, ed., *Introduction to Middle Eastern Law* (New York: Oxford University Press, 2007)

———, *Islam and Public Law* (London, UK: Graham & Trotman Ltd, 1993)

Martin, Vanessa, "Shaykh Faḍl Allah Nūrī" in EI, 2nd edition, VIII. pp. 140a–140b

Mc Dermott, Martin, *The Theology of al-Shaikh al-Mufid* (Beirut: Dar al-Mashriq, 1978)

McIlwain, Charles Howard, *Constitutionalism: Ancient and Modern* (Ithaca, NY: Cornell University Press, 1940)

Medina, Vincent, "Social Contract," in Christopher Berry Gray, ed., *The Philosophy of Law: an Encyclopedia* (London & New York: Garland Publishing, Inc., 1999), Vol. II., pp. 808–810

Mirfendereski, Guive, *A Diplomatic History of the Caspian Sea: Treaties, Diaries, and Other Stories* (NY: Palgrave, 2001)

Modarressi Ṭabāṭabā'ī, Hossein, *Crisis and Consolidation in the Formative Period of Shi'ite Islam* (Princeton, NJ: Darwin Press, 1993)

———, *An Introduction to Shī'ī Law: a Bibliographical Study* (London, UK: Ithaca Press, 1984)

———, *Kharaj in Islamic Law* (London, UK: Anchor Press Ltd., 1983)

———, "Some Recent Analysis of the Concept of Majāz in Islamic Jurisprudence," *Journal of the American Oriental Society*, Vol. 106, No. 4, October–December 1986, pp. 787–791

———, *Tradition and Survival: A Bibliographical Survey of Early Shī'ite Literature* (Oxford, UK: Oneworld Publications, 2003)

Mohammadi, Majid, *Judicial Reform and Reorganization in 20th Century Iran: State-Building, Modernization and Islamicization* (London and New York: Routledge, 2008)

Mottahedeh, Roy Parviz, "Afterword," in Abbas Amanat and Frank Grieffel, eds., *Shari'a: Islamic Law in the Contemporary Context* (Stanford, CA: Stanford University Press, 2008), pp. 178–181

Moussavi Kazemi, Ahmad, *Religious Authority in Shi'ite Islam: From the Office of Mufti to the Institution of Marja'* (Malaysia: International Institute of Islamic Thought, 1996)

Muḥaqqiq Dāmād, Muṣṭafā, "The Role of Time and Social Welfare in the Modification of Legal Rulings," in L. Clarke, ed., *Shī'ite Heritage*, pp. 213–222

Osiatynski, Wiktor, "Paradoxes of Constitutional Borrowing," *International Journal of Constitutional Law*, 2, 2003, pp. 244–268

Parry, Clive, ed., *The Consolidated Treaty Series* (Dobbs Ferry, NY: Oceana Publications, Inc, 1968), Vol. 205

Potter, Kathleen O., *The Federalist Vision of Popular Sovereignty in the New American Republic* (New York: LBF Scholarly Publishing LLC, 2002)

Rosenfeld, Michel, ed., *Constitutionalism, Identity, Differences, and Legitimacy: Theoretical Perspectives* (Durham and London: Duke University Press, 1994)

———, "Contract and Justice: The Relation between Classical Contract Law and Social Contract Theory," 70 Iowa L. Rev. 769, 1985

Rowson, Everett K., "Al-'Āmirī," in Nasr and Leaman, *History of Islamic Philosophy* (Abingdon, UK: Routledge, originally published in1996) pp. 216–221

Sachedina, Abdulaziz, *The Just Ruler in Shi'ite Islam: The Comprehensive Authority of the Jurist in Imamite Jurisprudence* (Oxford and New York: Oxford University Press, 1988, reprinted in 1998)

Sajó, András, *Limiting Government: An Introduction to Constitutionalism* (Budapest, Hungary: Central European University Press, 1999

Sartori, Giovanni, "Constitutionalism: A Preliminary Discussion," *The American Political Science Review*, Vol. 56, No. 4, December 1962, pp. 853–864

Schmidtke, Sabine, *The Theology of al-'Allāma al-Ḥillī* (Berlin: Klaus Schwartz Verlag, 1991)

Schneider, Irene, "Religious and State Jurisdiction during Nāṣir al-Dīn Shah's Reign," in Robert Gleave, ed., *Religion and Society in Qajar Iran* (London and New York: RoutledgeCurzon, 2005), pp. 84–110

Sherif, Adel Omar, "The Rule of Law in Egypt from a Judicial Perspective: A Digest of Landmark Decisions of the Supreme Constitutional Court," in Eugene Cotran and Mai Yamami, eds., *The Rule of Law in the Middle East and the Islamic World: Human Rights and the Judicial Process* (London, UK: I. B. Tauris, 2002), pp. 1–34

Ṣifatgul, Manṣūr, "From Dār al-Salṭana-yi Iṣfahān to Dār al-Khilāfa-yi Ṭihrān: Continuity and Change in the Safavid Model of State-Religious Administration during the Qajars (1795–1895/1209–1313)," in Robert Gleave, ed., *Religion and Society in Qajar Iran* (London and New York: RoutledgeCurzon, 2005), pp. 71–83

Stewart, Devin J., "Islamic Juridical Hierarchies and the Office of Marjaʿ al-Taqlīd," in Clarke, *Shīʿite Heritage*, pp. 137–157

Sullivan, Kathleen S., *Constitutional Context: Women and Rights Discourse in Nineteenth Century America* (Baltimore, MD: Johns Hopkins University Press, 2007)

Ṭabāṭabā'ī, Muhammad Hussein, *Shiʿite Islam*, translation with introduction and notes by Seyyed Hossein Nasr (Albany, NY: SUNY, 1977, secnd? edition)

Talbi, Cahen M., et al, "Ḥisba," EI, 2nd edition, III. pp. 485b–490a

Tushnet, Mark, "Comparative Constitutional Law," in Mathias Reimann and Reinhard Zimmermann, eds., *The Oxford Handbook of Comparative Law* (New York, NY: Oxford University Press, 2006), pp. 1225–1257

Vallentyne, Peter, "Contractualist Philosophy of Law," in Christopher Berry Gray, ed., *The Philosophy of Law: An Encyclopedia* (New York and London: Garland Publishing, Inc., 1999), I., pp. 159–161

Van Caenegen, R.C., *An Historical Introduction to Western Constitutional Law* (New York: Cambridge University Press, 1995, reprinted edition, 2000)

Wahba, Wafaa H., *The Ordinances of Government* (Reading, UK: Garnet Publishing Ltd., 1996)

Waldron, Jeremy, *Law and Disagreement* (New York, NY: Oxford University Press, 1999)

Wieacker, Franz, *A History of Private Law in Europe*, translated by Tony Weir (New York: Clarendon Press and Oxford University Press, 1995, reprinted 2003)

Wolfson, Harry Austryn, *The Philosophy of Kalam* (Cambridge, MA: Harvard University Press, 1976)

Index